Dear Amana Radarange Oven Owner,

Welcome to the world of microwave cooking! We're sure you'll be pleased with your new Radarange Oven.

To be sure you get the full benefit from your Radarange Oven, please read the Use and Care Manual and the Introduction chapter of this cookbook thoroughly, even if you have owned a microwave oven before. This is not a typical introduction. Besides reviewing basic information, you will learn things that relate especially to your new, multi-feature Radarange Microwave Oven.

We recommend reading the Use and Care Manual carefully before you begin cooking. Be sure to keep your Use and Care Manual inside the front cover pocket of this cookbook so you can refer to it quickly.

As you learn to cook with microwaves, you'll find that you can prepare a wide variety of foods quickly and easily. On the front cover of this cookbook are some examples, such as Cranberry Squash (page 249), Strawberry-Rhubarb Pie (page 326), Ham (page 176), Corn-in-the-Husk (page 254), Quick Long Grain White and Wild Rice Mix (pages 108 and 109), Duckling (page 228) and defrosted Baked Bread (inside back cover).

With the versatility of the Radarange Oven, you can easily bake foods from scratch, or reheat purchased, ready-to-eat foods quickly.

We at the Ann MacGregor Test Kitchen know you will share our enthusiasm for microwave cooking.

Ann MacGregor

Ann MacGregor

All recipes contained in this book were created and tested by the staff of the Amana Refrigeration, Inc., Ann MacGregor Home Economics Department.

PRECAUTIONS TO AVOID POSSIBLE EXPOSURE TO EXCESSIVE MICROWAVE ENERGY

1) Do not attempt to operate this oven with the door open since open-door operation can result in harmful exposure to microwave energy. It is important not to defeat or tamper with the safety interlocks.

2) Do not place any object between the oven front face and the door or allow soil or cleaner residue to accumulate on sealing surfaces.

3) Do not operate the oven if it is damaged. It is particularly important that the oven door close properly and that there is no damage to the: (a) door (bent), (b) hinges and latches (broken or loosened), (c) door seals and sealing surfaces.

4) The oven should not be adjusted or repaired by anyone except properly qualified service personnel.

FOURTH EDITION

Contents

This chapter contains very valuable information. You should read the "Introduction" before you begin to cook in your Radarange Oven. There is no need to memorize all of the information. You can use this chapter as a handy reference anytime you have a cooking question.

General Cookbook Format

You will find that your **Amana Touchmatic II Radarange Microwave Oven Cookbook** is very easy to read and understand. It's also designed to lay completely flat so you won't "lose your recipe page" at an awkward time.

All of the recipes in this cookbook have been tested by a staff of trained home economists. The recipes have been selected on the basis of variety. You will find recipes that range from the gourmet type to the simple "good-home cookin' " type. Recipes from every food category are found, so you can use them as guides to adapt your own favorites.

Before reading individual recipes or beginning to cook, consult the first few pages of the particular chapter. Many hints and general instructions for preparing each food category are found at the beginning of each chapter. This information should help in answering all of your questions concerning specific types of foods. Also found at the beginning of each chapter are charts for convenience foods, frozen foods, and others. Always look for defrosting information at the beginning of each chapter.

Whenever you can't locate a particular food item in a chapter, consult the index. The item could be located in another area.

MICRO-TIPS are found in many of the recipes throughout the cookbook. These MICRO-TIPS are helpful hints which may give you garnish suggestions, serving tips, ingredient substitutions, or other information. Frequently, the MICRO-TIPS will suggest a particularly good use of a Radarange Oven feature for the particular recipe, such as the Automatic Temperature-Control or Temperature-Hold features. You will want to quickly scan recipes and make note of any MICRO-TIP information, before cooking.

Recipe-Reading Tips for Good Food Results

Always carefully follow the recipe.

Be certain to:

- **Use the exact utensil recommended.** The size, shape and material of the utensil are all important. Large size dishes are usually recommended to avoid boil-overs. Cooking a food in a differently-shaped dish than in the one recommended could cause the amount of cooking time to vary. Utensil materials can also cause a variation in cooking results. For example, glass lids retain moisture and decrease cooking time more than do paper towels, or no cover used at all. Be sure to use exactly what is recommended.

- **Use the exact cooking time recommended.** You will notice that most recipes give ranges of cooking time. A recipe may say, for example, "Cook in Radarange Oven on FULL POWER for 1 to 2 minutes, or until sauce is thickened". You can check the sauce after 1 minute, since it could be thickened adequately to serve. However, it may be necessary to allow the sauce to thicken for the extra minute. Notice that the words **"or until sauce is thickened"** are included. In each recipe, there will be stated a **visual** test, whereby you can determine whether the food has actually finished cooking by knowing what it should look like.

- **Use the same type of ingredients recommended and measure carefully.** When testing recipes for this cookbook, standard measuring utensils were used, as well as standard measuring methods. It is important in any type of cooking that measurements are accurate. Also, be careful in substituting ingredients. A general substitution chart is included on page 22 of this Introduction. MICRO-TIPS often recommend substitutions which will not alter cooking times or results. Do not make a substitution which is not recommended; food product results can vary tremendously. The only **exception** in substitutions is seasonings. Salt, pepper, and others can be easily added or deleted to suit personal tastes. In many recipes, you will notice in the preparation steps to "season as desired". Almost all spices can easily be substituted without affecting food results.

Increase the cooking time if you increase the size of a recipe. For example, 4 potatoes require longer cooking time than does 1 potato. 6 muffins will require a longer cooking time than 3 muffins. A general rule to follow when increasing the size of a recipe is: when doubling a recipe, increase the cooking time to **slightly less** than 2 times as long. (When tripling, increase the cooking time to **slightly less** than 3 times as long, etc.) Also, be certain to change the dish size accordingly.

Don't forget to decrease the cooking time, also, when **decreasing** the size of a recipe. A general rule to follow is: when cutting a recipe in half, decrease cooking time to **slightly more** than half. Again, be certain to change the dish size accordingly. See "Adapting Conventional Recipes", on page 18.

GLOSSARY OF MICROWAVE COOKING TERMS

Before actually reading recipes, you should familiarize yourself briefly with the following microwave cooking terms. You don't have to memorize! You can always quickly check this section if you see an unfamiliar term that you don't understand. The terms are in alphabetical order, so you can easily find a particular term.

ADAPTING CONVENTIONAL RECIPES: See section on page 18.

ARCING: A static discharge of electricity which causes a spark. This usually occurs between separated particles of metal, such as a metal twister for plastic bags, gold trim on a dish, or a metal utensil almost touching the side wall of cooking compartment causing a spark.

ARRANGING: Suggested placement of several items of the same food in the Radarange Oven to produce the most satisfactory cooking results for the particular food. Arrange foods as the recipe suggests. Example: Arrange potatoes in a circle, rather than in rows. When reheating plates of food, place dense foods near the outside of the dish where they will heat first.

AUTOMATIC TEMPERATURE CONTROL SYSTEM: See Session 5 of your Touchmatic II Use and Care Manual.

BROWNING: The change in outside food color which occurs in cooking. The degree of darkening relates to (1) the length of cooking time, (2) the type of food, (3) the surface temperature and (4) the weight and mass of the food. Noticeable color change begins in roasts and poultry as the food's surface temperature increases. For small, short-term cooking items, browning skillets or dishes are used to obtain a color change. Generally foods weighing more than 3 pounds will brown without using a browning skillet. See section on page 17.

BROWNING SKILLETS: Special microwave energy-absorbing dishes which, after preheating, produce heat for browning food by surface contact. See section on page 17.

BURSTING OR ERUPTING: The build-up of steam or pressure in the food product that causes the surface to split open. This may occur in foods such as apples, eggs, poultry and vegetables which are enclosed in a skin, shell or membrane. This could also occur with a plastic "membrane" such as a frozen vegetable plastic pouch. In order to prevent bursting, it is necessary to puncture or pierce the skin or membrane, or remove the shell.

CARRY-OVER COOKING TIME: Period of time during which some foods need to rest following their removal from the Radarange Oven. During this time, foods will finish cooking by themselves, without the need of extra microwave cooking time.

CONVERTING CONVENTIONAL RECIPES: See "Adapting Conventional Recipes" section on page 18.

COOK: To cause a temperature rise, physically changing food. Cooking changes a food from a raw to a cooked state. Also refers to a pad on the Radarange Oven which is used for programmed cooking. The "Cook" indicator light will be lit when cooking at FULL POWER, or when cooking on a lower Cookmatic Level.

COOKING GRILL: Special cooking dish which consists of a plastic or glass-ceramic rack insert that fits inside of a glass or glass-ceramic dish. Particularly used for meat cookery. See "Accessories", page 12.

COOKING TECHNIQUES: Methods to produce good cooking results. See section on page 13.

COOKING TIME: Time required to cook foods to a serving temperature in the Radarange Oven.

COOKMATIC LEVELS: Cookmatic Power Levels or settings. Each power level is particularly well suited for cooking different types of foods. The "Cookmatic Level" pad on the faceplate of your Radarange Oven is used for selecting one of the 10 Cookmatic Levels. For instructions on how to use, see Session 4 of your Touchmatic II Use and Care Manual.

COVERING OR WRAPPING: Placing a glass lid, plastic cover, paper towel or waxed paper over a dish, or around a food. Usually done to prevent spattering or to retain steam. Steam retention allows for a more even distribution of heat, more rapid cooking, and prevents dehydration of the food. Heavy-duty plastic wrap should be pierced to allow some steam to escape. Do not cover dishes unless stated in the recipe. Use the type of covering the recipe recommends. Paper towels or waxed paper covering don't retain steam to the same extent as plastic and glass. See "General Utensil Tips" No. 8, on page 13.

DEFROSTING (THAWING): Method of applying microwave energy to frozen foods with short intervals of power, during which time heat is distributed throughout the entire food and ice molecules are changed into water. Food should be completely defrosted before cooking begins. See "Defrosting" section on page 15.

DELICATE INGREDIENTS: Some ingredients such as eggs, cheese, seafood, milk and others are "special" or "delicate". These foods are best prepared on a lower Cookmatic Level or setting, rather than on FULL POWER.

DENSITY: Foods have different densities, and thus absorb microwaves in different ways. Porous foods, such as breads, allow microwaves to penetrate them instantly. Dense food items, such as meats, absorb microwaves on the exterior, while the center is heated by conduction. Thus, dense foods require a longer cooking or heating time. Foods of the same size, but having different densities, will cook at different speeds. For this reason, 2 or more foods in the raw state usually should not be cooked in the Radarange Oven at the same time, unless recommended in a recipe or menu. However, a plate containing all cooked foods can be easily reheated in the Radarange Oven. See "Reheating Cooked Foods" section on page 19. See "Meals All-At-Once", page 26.

ERUPTING: See "Bursting", page 5.

GLASS UTENSILS: See section on page 9.

HEATING: Warming a food to a desired temperature. Porous foods, such as breads, heat faster than foods which are dense, such as meats.

HIGH ALTITUDE COOKING: High altitude adjustments, necessary for conventional cooking, are usually not necessary for microwave cooking. The only change required may be to slightly increase the cooking time.

HOLDING TIME: Refers to the time required for a food to "rest" before beginning to cook. For example, foods must be allowed to stand or hold after defrosting before they begin cooking, so that the food is completely defrosted. A holding time can also be used between 2 different cooking periods. During a holding time, the food is allowed to equalize in temperature. A food should be covered during the holding time for best results.

METAL UTENSILS: See section on page 8.

OVERCOOKING: Occurs when a food has cooked too long and can cause drying out, toughening of foods, separating of sauces, and possible hard spots in some foods. Careful timing for short-term cooking items is necessary. Overcooking is not always visible. To avoid overcooking, be aware of carry-over cooking. See "Carry-Over Cooking Time," page 5.

PAPER UTENSILS: See section on page 9.

PIERCING: Breaking the skin or membrane of foods such as vegetables or eggs, which allows the steam to escape and prevents bursting. Either a knife, or the tines of a fork is used to make slits or holes, depending upon the type of food. Plastic wrap, or plastic cooking bags should also be pierced to allow steam to escape during cooking.

PLASTIC RACK: Insert which fits inside glass or glass-ceramic dish. Allows moisture and fat to drain off meat as it cooks. Can be used separately for heating breads, sandwiches, or other foods. See "Accessories", page 12.

PLASTIC UTENSILS: See section on page 10.

PREHEATING: Process of heating an empty browning skillet or grill, without lid or oil, inside the Radarange Oven for a specified length of time, depending upon the size of the skillet and type of food. The special coating on the skillet bottom will absorb microwaves, and become hot. This heat is used to brown small food items, such as small cuts of meat. See "Browning", page 17.

PROGRAMMING: See Session 6 of your Touchmatic II Use and Care Manual.

PUNCTURING: See "Piercing", page 7.

REARRANGING: See "Rearranging", page 14.

REHEATING: Bringing cooked foods to a serving temperature.

REHYDRATING: Replacing water or other liquid missing from freeze-dried foods.

RESTING: The amount of time suggested, either during or after cooking or defrosting, which will allow the heat in the foods to equalize or spread to the center of the foods. Sometimes referred to as carry-over cooking. See "Carry-Over Cooking Time", page 5.

ROASTING RACK: See "Plastic Rack", page 12.

ROTATING: See "Turning", page 8.

SETTINGS: There are 10 settings or Cookmatic Power Levels on your Radarange Oven. See Session 4 of your Touchmatic II Use and Care Manual.

SHIELDING: Covering parts of a large food item, such as a turkey, with thin strips of metal foil before cooking. This is done to prevent dehydration of exposed parts during cooking, such as legs or wing tips. The metal foil will "reflect" microwaves away from these areas. Metals should not be used in small food loads, such as for T.V. dinners. Use aluminum foil strips only when recommended in recipes.

"SPECIAL INGREDIENTS": See "Delicate Ingredients", page 6.

STANDING TIME: See "Holding Time", page 6.

STARTING TEMPERATURE: Temperature of foods when they are first placed inside the Radarange Oven for defrosting, heating, or cooking. Room temperature or warm foods heat more quickly than refrigerator temperature foods. For example, hot tap water will heat more quickly than cold.

START TIME: See Session 6 of Touchmatic II Use and Care Manual.

STEAMING: Cooking in covered utensil. Steaming allows for faster cooking.

STIRRING: Manual movement of foods within the cooking dish with a spoon or suitable utensil to distribute the heat generated by the microwaves. Soups, gravies and sauces are sometimes stirred during the cooking process. See "Stirring", page 14.

STRAW UTENSILS: See section on page 12.

TEMPERATURE PROBE: See Session 5 of your Touchmatic II Use and Care Manual.

THAWING: See "Defrosting", page 15.

THERMOMETERS: See "Thermometers", page 12.

TURNING: Includes two different types: 1) Inverting foods or **turning foods over** such as roasts, during the cooking cycle. 2) Rotating a dish in a clockwise manner. When using recipes in this book, turn or rotate a dish 180° or a half-turn, unless otherwise specified in the recipe. When using this Radarange Oven, little, if any, turning is required. See "Turning", page 14.

UNDERCOOKING: Cooking to a less-than-done degree, to allow for standing time or carry-over cooking time to complete the cooking. Some foods can be undercooked slightly so they won't overcook when reheated.

UTENSIL: Any dish or container that is used for Radarange Oven cooking.

VOLUME: The amount of food affects the amount of cooking time. A larger food volume requires a longer cooking time than does a smaller volume. See "Cooking Variables", page 13.

WOODEN UTENSILS: See "Wood, Straw", page 12.

UTENSILS AND ACCESSORIES

Your Radarange Oven will make it possible to use utensils that you have never used for cooking before. You will now be able to cook, as well as serve, on paper, glass or china plates.

There are only a few utensils, such as metal pots and pans, which should not be used in your Radarange Oven. Most utensils **can** be used. You will find that you already have many Radarange Oven-safe utensils in your kitchen.

Utensils Not to Use

There are some utensils which should not be used in a microwave oven. See the photograph for examples, on page 10.

- **Metal Utensils**
Metal utensils should not be used. This includes ceramic dishes with metal trim, foil pans, and aluminum foil (except when recommended in recipes). Metals reflect microwaves. Thus, metals will keep portions of food from cooking, by reflecting microwaves away from the food. The use of metal utensils can cause slower cooking, uneven cooking, and can even prevent cooking. The use of metal utensils also increases the amount of energy needed for microwave cooking and can damage the utensil or parts of any microwave oven.

The only time metal should ever be used in the Radarange Oven is when it is recommended in a recipe. For example, some recipes recommend using small strips of aluminum foil when cooking large meat and poultry items. Small strips of foil can be used to "reflect" microwaves away from exposed areas, such as poultry wing tips or legs, which tend to dehydrate or overcook.

But foil should be used only when cooking a large food item. Metal foil strips should not touch the oven door or sides.

T.V. dinners in foil trays contain too small a food load to heat using the metal tray. Simply remove your T.V. dinner from the metal tray, and place it on a ceramic or paper plate for defrosting and heating. Metal clamps or skewers should not be used. Use wooden skewers for shish kabobs, and tie roasting bags with string. Remove all metal pieces from poultry, if possible, before cooking. When defrosting, remove metal parts from poultry or meats as soon as possible.

- **Centura® Dinnerware and Corelle® Livingware Cups**
(closed-handle)
Do not use CENTURA Dinnerware by Corning in the Radarange Oven. This dinnerware contains a glaze which absorbs microwaves, causing the dishes to heat during cooking. The dishes can become hot enough to break. CORELLE Livingware closed-handled cups should not be used in a microwave oven, since they can also heat and break dur-

ing cooking. CORELLE Livingware cups having open handles may be safely used, as well as all other pieces of CORELLE Livingware.

• Melamine Dishes

Melamine dishes should not be used in a microwave oven because they contain metallic substances. They may crack during cooking.

• Lead Crystal

Do not use antique glassware that may contain metallic sub-stances, such as lead crystal. Such glass could break during cooking.

• Foil-Lined Paper

Foil-lined paper should not be used, due to the metallic content.

Utensils to Use

Many different utensils can be used in the Radarange Oven. See the photographs for examples, on page 11.

You may use most utensils made of non-metallic materials, and utensils that do not have metal trim or hardware (handles, etc.). Utensils are made of 4 basic materials:

1) Paper
2) Glass
3) Glass-Ceramic
4) Plastic

Utensils made from these four material types are generally safe for use in the Radarange Oven. However, there are some exceptions. Here are specific examples of utensils made from these four materials which **are** recommended for use in the Radarange Oven.

• Paper

Almost all paper products may be safely used. Paper plates, cups, towels, and napkins are several examples. Use plain white paper products rather than colored. Paper towels may be used to cover other cooking utensils during cooking, to help prevent the spattering of the Radarange Oven walls and interior. (Do not use paper towels which contain nylon or other synthetic fibers since the heated synthetic could cause the paper to ignite.) Paper towels or plates can also be used to absorb grease during the cooking of some foods, such as bacon. Paper products are particularly good for reheating foods. For example, breads should be wrapped in paper towels during reheating to keep them moist. Waxed paper, parchment paper, or flattened brown paper bags can be used to line the glass oven tray for cookie baking. Paper liners can be used to line plastic muffin trays. Vegetables can be heated in cardboard (paper) boxes, if the box is pierced or slit before cooking. When using any kind of paper in the microwave oven, follow the recipe timings carefully, and don't leave the paper in the microwave oven for an extended time, or it could ignite.

Newspapers should never be placed in a microwave oven. Some types of printers' ink can absorb microwave energy and could cause the paper to ignite.

• Glass

Most glassware can be safely used. Glass cake dishes, pie plates, measuring cups, custard cups, and sauce dishes can be safely used. Fire-King® glassware by Anchor Hocking, and Pyrex® by Corning are examples of Radarange Oven-safe glassware. Do not use antique glassware, or glassware having a metal trim. Be careful when using delicate glassware, because heat from the food could cause it to crack.

• Glass-Ceramic

Most glass-ceramic utensils can also be used in the Radarange Oven. Tableware such as plates, cups, or saucers made of most glass-ceramic materials can be used. Ceramic mugs, tube cake dishes, vegetable platters, or other serving dishes may be used. Some specific examples of glass-ceramics which can be safely used in the Radarange Oven are as follows: CORELLE Livingware by Corning (do not use Corelle closed-handled cups), CORNING WARE® by Corning, Cookmates® by Corning, French Chef cookware by Marsh Industries, and Temperware® by Lenox. Stoneware and china can generally be used, but it should be tested to determine whether it is Radarange Oven-safe. Some glazes used by manufacturers contain metallic substances and should not be used in a microwave oven. One example of a glass-ceramic that has a glaze not suitable for microwave oven use is CENTURA® by Corning. Many manufacturers will label packaging or the dishes themselves as being "microwave oven-safe". If you're not certain whether a dish is "microwave oven-safe" you can test your own glass-ceramic utensils by performing the utensil test. Dishes having a metal trim or metal parts should never be used in the Radarange Oven.

Utensil Test: Use this test to determine when a glass-ceramic utensil is safe to use in the Radarange Oven.

Place a glass measuring cup of water next to the empty dish to be tested in the Radarange Oven. Heat on FULL POWER for 1 minute, 15 seconds. At the end of this time, check the temperature of the tested dish. If the dish is cool and the water is very warm, the dish is safe for use. If the dish is slightly warm, it should be used for short-term cooking only. If the dish is hot and the water is cool, DO NOT USE THE DISH. (The dish will remain cool if it is not absorbing microwaves, and the microwaves are then absorbed by the water. The dish will become hot if it **is** absorbing microwaves, and the water will remain cool.)

• Plastic
Plastic utensils (except for melamine dinnerware) are generally safe for use in the Radarange Oven. (See No. 1 under "General Utensil Tips," on page 13.) Examples include plastic measuring cups, plastic bowls, plastic muffin trays and other plastic containers. Heavy-duty plastic wrap, such as Saran Wrap,™ may be used to cover other utensils to prevent spattering. Some types of plastic wrap should not remain in the Radarange Oven too long because they may become sticky or shrink. Pierce a hole in plastic wrap before cooking, to allow for steam to escape during cooking. Plastic wrap having foil edges should not be used. Styrofoam® cups and Styrofoam® dishes can be used in the Radarange Oven. They are especially good for reheating coffee and other foods. Plastic freezer containers can be used for defrosting and heating foods, but remember to first remove the plastic lids. Plastic baby bottles can be placed in the Radarange Oven for quick warm-ups, but remove restrictive lids. Plastic pouches, such as "boil-in-the-bag pouches", are good to use in the Radarange Oven. Simply pierce, or cut a small opening in the pouch to allow for steam to escape during cooking. Some packaged frozen vegetables-in-pouches even contain microwave cooking instructions on the packages. Plastic bags which are used with heat sealer units can also be used for cooking in the Radarange Oven. Just remember to pierce the bags before defrosting or cooking.

‹ **Don't use these utensils in a microwave oven:**

metal skillets
metal baking pans
metal TV dinner trays
metal twists
dishes with metal trim
Centura dinnerware
(upper left)

Use these utensils in a microwave oven

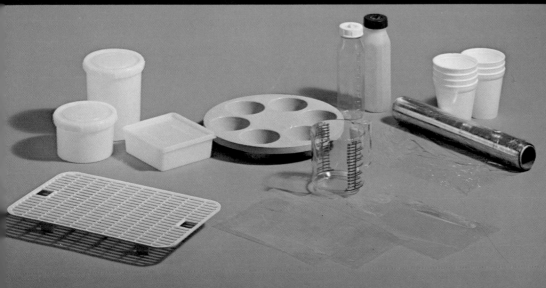

Use heat-set plastics, or plastics that are labeled "dishwasher-safe". Avoid cooking foods having a high fat content in plastic utensils, since fat gets very hot during cooking and may melt the plastic. If any food gets hot enough during cooking, the food itself, and not the microwaves, can melt plastics. Try to use plastic dishes for heating foods only to a serving temperature, or for short-term cooking. During long-term cooking, the food can become hot enough to melt some plastics.

Other Utensils to Use

- **Wood, Straw**

Wooden spoons, straw baskets, and other utensils made from these materials, can be used for quick re-heating periods, but are generally not recommended for long-term cooking. During long periods of cooking, these items may become too dry and can crack.

- **Shells**

Seafood shells, such as clam shells, or escargot (snail) shells, can be used as "utensils" in the Radarange Oven for heating seafood.

Natural Fiber Cloths

Cotton or linen cloths, such as dishcloths or napkins, may be used as coverings for utensils in the Radarange Oven. Avoid using cloths made from synthetic fabrics, such as nylon. Some synthetic fabrics can melt in the microwave oven.

ACCESSORIES

There are some special accessories you may wish to use in your Radarange Oven. They are briefly described here. These accessories can be ordered from your local Amana dealer.

Radarange Oven Glass Tray

This is one utensil that is included with your Radarange Oven. It should **always** be inside your Radarange Oven when it's in operation. However, this tray has some special benefits. You can remove the tray from the Radarange Oven, line it with waxed paper, and use it as a cookie sheet. The tray can also be used as a "platter" for cooking. The fluted edge will catch any spill-overs, and the tray is easily removed for cleaning. The Radarange Oven glass tray is dishwasher-safe.

Browning Skillets or Grills

Browning skillets or grills are ceramic utensils which con-

tain a special coating on the bottom that helps them to brown small foods items. Browning skillets are available in several different sizes. See "Browning," page 17.

Cooking Grill: Dish & Rack

The cooking grill consists of a glass or glass-ceramic dish which is fitted with a plastic or glass-ceramic rack insert. The rack can be used separately, or inside the dish. The cooking grill, or the two parts used together, is good for "grilling" meats, heating appetizers, and other uses. Calorie-watchers like the cooking grill, since fats can drip off the rack, away from meats. The dish captures all juices, which can be saved for gravy, and can even help in saving bacon grease for cooking. The rack can be used separately for heating sandwiches, breads and other foods.

Thermometers

No thermometer should be used **inside** the Radarange Oven while it's in operation, except the Automatic Temperature Control of your Touchmatic II Radarange Oven, or a specially designed microwave oven thermometer which has an all-plastic head.

General Utensil Tips

1. **All foods in this cookbook were tested using glass utensils.** If plastic utensils are used, the cooking time will need to be shortened to avoid overcooking, since foods generally cook faster in plastic utensils. If ceramic utensils are used, the cooking time will probably have to be lengthened, since most foods take longer to cook in ceramic utensils.
2. Be certain your dishes are suitable for microwave oven use.
3. Consult the recipe for the proper size utensil.
4. If you don't have the size of dish the recipe recommends, substitute a larger one. This will help to prevent "boil-overs". The amount of cooking time may be slightly less, due to the larger dish size. A larger dish will expose a greater surface area of the food to the microwaves.
5. Always select a utensil large enough to hold the food. Select a dish which has room for the food to expand during cooking. By using large dishes, you can avoid boil-overs.

6. Use round dishes whenever possible. Ring-molds are good utensils to use for baked goods. (You can invert a custard cup in an 8 or 9 x 2-inch round cake dish to create your own ring mold for breads or cakes.) See "Breads" chapter, page 79.

7. Utensils generally remain cool to the touch. However, during long-term cooking, the food may heat the dish. You may wish to keep hot pads handy to aid in removing foods which have cooked for long periods of time.

8. Always use the type of utensil **covering** recommended in the recipe. Waxed paper and paper towels don't retain moisture to the extent that heavy-duty plastic wrap and glass lids do. If a dish doesn't have a glass lid and the recipe says "cook, covered," substitute heavy-duty plastic wrap. Plastic wrap should be pierced, by making a 1-inch slit with a knife, when it's used as a covering. Paper towels or linen napkins are recommended for covering or even wrapping breads and cakes during reheating. A damp cotton cloth, such as a dishcloth, is recommended as a covering for rising breads. If a recipe does not state, "Cook in Radarange Oven, covered," then **don't** cover the food. Coverings, or lack of them, can greatly influence the amount of cooking time required.

9. Always be certain that a utensil contains food when in a microwave oven. Browning skillets or browning grills which are to be preheated are the only utensils which should be used empty in a microwave oven. See "Browning Skillets," page 17.

RADARANGE OVEN COOKING TECHNIQUES

Radarange Oven cooking **is** slightly different from conventional cooking. Although you can apply most of your conventional cooking knowledge to microwave cooking, you should be aware of special "cooking techniques" which are unique to microwave cooking.

Cooking Variables

Microwave cooking can be directly affected by different food variables.

The **shape** of foods can greatly affect the amount of cooking time. Foods that are flat and thin heat faster than foods which are chunky. For example, a casserole will cook faster in a flat dish, rather than if heaped in a small dish. Foods cut into small pieces will cook faster than large-shaped foods. Pieces should be of a uniform size and shape for more uniform cooking, or the smaller pieces will cook faster. The greatest amount of heating takes place within 3/4 of an inch of the food's surface. The interior of large food items, or dense foods, is heated by the heat conducted from the outer food layer. For best results, cook foods together which have similar sizes and shapes.

The **quantity or volume** of a food can affect the amount of cooking time. As the volume of the food is increased, the time required to cook or heat the item increases almost proportionately. If twice the amount of food is placed in the oven, it will take almost twice as long to cook. For example, if 1 potato cooks in 4 minutes, then 2 potatoes will require about 7 to 7-1/2 minutes of cooking time, or not quite 8 minutes. Increase the amount of cooking time when you increase the amount of food to be cooked.

The **density** of foods can greatly affect the amount of cooking time. Porous foods, such as breads, cakes or pastries, will heat much more quickly than dense meats of the same size. Porous foods absorb microwaves quickly throughout. Meats absorb microwaves mostly at the exterior surface, and the interior is heated by conduction, increasing the cooking time. Meats can be cooked in a sauce, if desired. Due to the moisture content, a sauce will heat rapidly. The heat will transfer to the meat, so the meat will heat faster due to heat by conduction as well as by microwaves.

The **starting temperature** of foods affects the amount of cooking time. Each temperature degree that the food item is to raise must be supplied with a definite amount of energy. Lower initial starting temperatures require more energy and more time to cook. Therefore, refrigerator temperature foods require a longer cooking time than do room temperature foods. Foods already slightly warm will heat very quickly in the Radarange Oven.

The **moisture content** of foods affects the amount of cooking time. The higher the moisture content is in a food the longer the amount of cooking time.

The **fat and sugar content** of foods affects the amount of cooking time. Foods containing high fat and sugar levels heat very quickly and may reach much higher temperatures than foods having low fat and sugar levels. Foods having lower fat and sugar levels require longer cooking times.

The **arrangement of food** within a microwave oven cavity affects the way in which the food cooks. Arrange foods as the recipe suggests. For example, arrange foods such as baked potatoes or cupcakes in a circle. When only one food item is being cooked, place it in the center of the Radarange Oven glass shelf for cooking.

Manipulation of Foods

You will find that your new Radarange Oven will require virtually no turning or rotating of cooking dishes. Some foods, such as large meats and poultry will need to be turned over halfway through the cooking time. Some foods, such as sauces, gravies, soups, stews, and beverages, will need to be **stirred** occasionally or halfway through cooking time because the **food** requires stirring for good results. If you prepared these foods conventionally, more constant stirring would be required.

With other foods, such as scrambled eggs, you may want to stir for a fluffier product. Some casseroles and other foods will need to be stirred halfway through the cooking time for maximum blending of food flavors.

In general, food will require little or no stirring or turning during cooking, in your new Radarange Oven.

If some recipes do suggest manipulating or moving food during cooking, you should be familiar with the several forms of manipulation:

- **Stirring**

Stirring is required less often in microwave cooking than in conventional cooking. In conventional cooking, you use a spoon to move food up from the bottom of a pan to evenly distribute the heat. In microwave cooking, you still stir to redistribute the heat within some foods, but you need to stir from the outside of a dish toward the inside or center. For the recipes in this cookbook, stir only as needed. If a recipe states to stir once or twice during cooking, stir at approximately even intervals. For example, in a 12-minute cooking period, if a recipe states to stir twice, stir after 4 minutes of cooking and again, after 8 minutes of cooking. However, it is not necessary to be precise. Stir only when necessary. When using lower Cookmatic Levels or settings, less stirring is required. Some examples of foods which may require stirring are puddings, some casseroles, some sauces, some soups, and some egg dishes. Some foods can't be stirred. These foods are rearranged or turned.

- **Rearranging**

A few foods which can't be stirred should be repositioned or rearranged during cooking. One example is baked custards. Rearranging allows for the most even cooking of foods. Foods which are cooked, covered, or which are cooked using lower Cookmatic Levels, usually require very little rearranging.

- **Turning**

There are actually two types of turning. Turning is done when foods cannot be stirred. Foods which are cooked, covered, or which are cooked at lower Cookmatic Levels usually require very little turning.

Turning foods over: Turning foods over is done to redistribute heat. Meat and poultry are two types of foods which are sometimes "turned over." Examples include large roasts, turkeys and whole chickens. Small meat items or poultry pieces may need to be turned over when in casseroles, or when in a browning skillet.

Rotating or turning dishes: There are a few foods which cannot be stirred, rearranged or turned over. Therefore, the actual cooking dish is turned or rotated. For the recipes in this cookbook, turn a dish one-half-turn or 180° unless otherwise stated. A half-turn means to grasp the dish and turn the portion of the dish that faces the Radarange Oven door around, until it faces the back of the oven. Examples of foods which are sometimes turned or rotated in a cooking dish include quiches and soufflés.

Cookmatic Power Levels

Many foods cook very well at full microwave power. However, just as some foods cook better conventionally at lower rather than higher oven temperatures, some foods cook better at lower rather than higher microwave power levels. Your

Amana Radarange® Microwave Oven has ten power levels to choose from. Each power level is particularly well suited for cooking different types of foods. Each recipe in this cookbook specifies the Cookmatic Level to be used for cooking. To learn how to use the Cookmatic Power Levels see Session 4 of the Touchmatic II Use and Care Manual.

Cooking Programs

Your Amana Touchmatic II Radarange® Microwave Oven's control allows it to remember up to four cooking programs. This means you can cook foods using the best techniques to optimize flavor and tenderness — yet all you need to do is program the instructions and start the oven.

Programmed recipes in this cookbook all have simple Touchmatic charts similar to the one illustrated below.

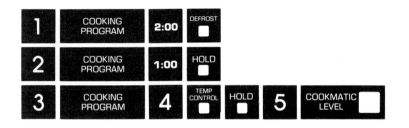

These charts tell you exactly which Touchmatic pads to touch and in what order. You read the chart from left to right, just like you read a sentence.

To learn to use the cooking programs, see Session 6 of your Touchmatic II Use and Care Manual.

Automatic Temperature Control System

Your Amana Touchmatic II Radarange Oven has an Automatic Temperature Control System which allows you to cook food to the precise temperature desired and hold the food at that temperature. You'll find this feature particularly helpful for cooking meats to the exact temperature you want. You can also use it to reheat leftovers, to warm soups and beverages and for many other cooking tasks. **The temperature probe is not intended for use as a candy thermometer.**

To learn to use the Automatic Temperature Control System see Session 5 of your Touchmatic II Use and Care Manual.

Automatic Start Time

The Automatic Start Time feature allows you to prepare a food and put it in the Radarange Oven up to 12 hours before you want it to start cooking. Automatic Start Time instructions in this cookbook are designed for preparing the food either four hours or nine to eleven hours before you want it to start cooking.

Oven designs and recipe instructions have been thoroughly tested to provide excellent results with the utmost in safety. However, there are a few common-sense rules you **must** follow when using the Automatic Start Time feature. To learn the "rules" and how to use the Automatic Start Time, see Session 6 of your Touchmatic II Use and Care Manual.

Defrosting

The ability to defrost foods quickly is a major benefit of your Radarange Oven. Microwaves defrost the outer-portion of the food, and the heat is carried to the center.

It's very important that most foods, especially meats, be totally defrosted, before they begin to cook. If they **aren't** totally defrosted before cooking, then the cooking will be uneven.

Most defrosting in this cookbook is accomplished by using the DEFROST pad, although defrosting can be accomplished by using lower Cookmatic Levels or settings. To learn how to program the oven for defrosting, see Session 4 of your Touchmatic II Use and Care Manual.

Follow the defrosting instructions for each specific food type in the individual chapters of this cookbook. Defrost charts are found toward the beginning of each chapter, if applicable. (For example, there is no Defrost Chart in the "Eggs and Cheese" chapter.)

- **General Hints for Defrosting Foods**
  1. Defrosting times can vary, depending upon the sizes, shapes, weights, and densities of the foods. If a food is not completely defrosted in the recommended amount

of time, allow it to stand for a few minutes at room temperature to complete defrosting.

2. The amount of defrosting time can vary, due to how solidly the food is frozen. (For example, a freezer in a combination refrigerator-freezer may not freeze foods as solidly as an individual freezer.)

3. Foods can be defrosted in their original wrappings. Loosen boxes or lids, and pierce plastic bags. Remove all metal parts. Metal clamps holding turkey legs should be removed during defrosting as soon as possible. Remove foods from metal containers before defrosting. See the "Metal Utensils" section on page 8.

4. Pierce the skins of foods such as frozen frankfurters before defrosting and heating.

5. Some larger foods may need to be turned over during defrosting, for the best results.

6. For faster defrosting, separate foods frozen in pieces as they thaw. For example, meat patties frozen together can be separated. Hamburger can be broken apart with a fork and stirred. Thawed hamburger should be removed as it defrosts, so it will not start to cook.

7. To determine whether foods such as meats are totally defrosted, insert a sharp knife in the center of the food to check for remaining ice crystals.

8. Do not completely defrost frozen fruits. Fruits taste "freshest" when served with some remaining ice crystals.

9. For best results, always bake frozen pie crusts in the Radarange Oven before adding the filling.

10. When defrosting cream pies or cakes which have frosting, turn them once or twice during the defrosting time. To avoid melting the frosting, do not completely thaw large cakes or cream pies.

11. When thawing frozen bread dough, do not allow it to cook. Frozen bread dough does not bake with good results in a microwave oven.

• Heating Defrosted Foods

1. To avoid dehydration, don't heat porous foods such as breads or cakes after defrosting them, unless you plan to eat them immediately.

2. Frozen fried foods can be cooked, but will not be crisp when prepared in a microwave oven. Examples: fish sticks, French fries, and onion rings.

3. Place uncooked cake or quick breads batter from commercial TV dinners in a 6 oz. custard cup. Cook the batter, separately, after the rest of the dinner. Also, heat any baked breads included in TV dinners, separately, after the rest of the dinner.

4. When cooking frozen pizza, use a preheated browning skillet or grill for the best results. A plastic rack, paper plate, or paper towel can be used. Do not use a glass or glass-ceramic plate, in order to prevent sogginess. Most pizzas fit best in a large browning skillet or grill. Larger pizzas may be cut into pieces to fit the skillet. See "Appetizers and Snacks" chapter, on page 41.

Freezer to Radarange Oven

1. When freezing homemade foods, freeze them in the same dish in which they will be defrosted and heated. Use containers which can be placed directly in the Radarange Oven. If you don't wish to use a dish for freezer storage, line the dish with foil. Arrange the food in the container and freeze. Once frozen, lift the food from the dish, using the foil extensions. Wrap the food tightly, and return it to the freezer. When ready to use, just remove it from the foil and return it to the baking dish or casserole. When you want to store food in the serving dish, just wrap the total dish in foil or place it in a heavy plastic bag.

2. Sectional-shaped paper plates work well for freezing your own homemade TV dinners.

3. Foods can be frozen in single portions, so that a single family member can later defrost and heat them quickly.

4. Freeze your own garden vegetables after first blanching them in the Radarange Oven. Frozen vegetables can be defrosted and heated within minutes in the Radarange Oven.

5. To save food preparation time, cook extra food in the Radarange Oven, or "planned-overs". Freeze these foods in Radarange-Oven-safe packaging. In the future, your food will be ready to eat in minutes, after it is quickly defrosted and heated. Pre-cooked foods should be used within 2 to 3 months.

Browning

When preparing food in the Radarange Oven, you will find that some foods will not brown the same as they do in a conventional oven. This is particularly true for baked goods, such as breads and cakes. But the lack of browning can be easily "disguised."

When baking a cake, for example, the frosting or a topping will cover the cake, and the lack of browning is not noticed. Also, dark-colored ingredients can be used in bread dough to simulate browning. Some examples are whole wheat flour, rye flour, raisins, dark brown sugar, or dark spices, such as cinnamon.

Browning is also easily achieved with meats. Meats which weigh 3 pounds or more will brown by themselves "naturally" in the Radarange Oven. This is because the exteriors of meats of this size become very hot during cooking. Many meats of this size have a high fat content, and fats also become very hot during cooking. This heat, plus the longer cooking times, are required for browning. Therefore, larger cuts of meats and poultry will brown by themselves.

For additional browning, a bottled browning sauce or soy sauce may also be used with meats. For poultry, a paste of shortening and paprika will give a golden-brown color.

Smaller cuts of meat do not require a very long cooking time. The exterior of smaller cuts will not become as hot as larger cuts during cooking, due to their short cooking time. Therefore, they will not brown to the same extent as they do when conventionally cooked. When preparing smaller cuts of meat in your Radarange Oven, a browning skillet or grill should be used in order to achieve maximum browning.

Browning Skillets

Browning skillets or grills are recommended for some foods used in this cookbook.

A browning skillet or grill has a special tin oxide coating on the bottom exterior which has the ability to absorb microwaves when the skillet is preheated empty in a microwave oven. As the tin oxide coating absorbs microwaves, the skillet bottom heats.

Browning skillets or grills can be used to brown many different foods. By preheating the skillet for different amounts of time, the amount of heat for browning will vary. The type of food you wish to brown will determine the amount of preheat time. Toasted cheese sandwiches or fried eggs don't require as much heat for browning as do small meats. Therefore, preheat times for eggs or bread items are shorter than preheat times for meats. For exact times, follow the manufacturer's instructions.

For more information concerning the use and care of browning skillets or grills, consult the use and care manual packaged with the browning skillet, or see the manufacturer's instructions.

Adapting Conventional Recipes

Most of your favorite conventional recipes can be easily prepared in the Radarange Oven. Since most foods cook 3 to 4 times faster in the Radarange Oven than in a conventional oven, reduce the amount of conventional cooking time to one-fourth or one-third for the Radarange Oven. For example, if a conventional recipe requires 1 hour of cooking time, reduce the cooking time to about 15 to 20 minutes for FULL POWER cooking in the Radarange Oven. Cook for about 15 minutes first. If necessary, add the additional few minutes. There are a few guidelines that need to be followed for converting. **Read the following tips before converting your own recipes.**

1. Use other recipes in this cookbook as guides. In this cookbook, the general hints for cooking various foods found at the beginning of each chapter will tell you how

to convert your own favorite recipes. (You may wish to reduce seasonings in your conventional recipes, since almost none of their flavor will be lost during microwave cooking.) For a particular type of food, read the specific information given in the chapter. Then find a similar recipe in that chapter in terms of actual ingredients and food type. For example, if you have a favorite meat ball recipe, one of the several meat ball recipes in this cookbook can be used as a guide. You should choose the meat ball recipe that most nearly matches your own. Then:

a. Use the same dish and covering recommended.

b. Use approximately the same cooking time.

c. Use the same Cookmatic Level or setting.

d. Test the food 1 to 2 minutes before it's supposed to be finished cooking. Your recipe could vary slightly, and may not require quite as much cooking time. You can cook for the extra 2 minutes, if necessary. Your recipe might even require a slightly **longer** cooking time than the "guide" recipe.

e. **Remember:** It's always best to slightly undercook a food, and then add a few seconds or minutes to finish the cooking, if necessary. Once a food is overcooked, you can't reverse the cooking process.

f. When you find the correct amount of cooking time required, make a note of it on your recipe. Then you will know the exact amount of cooking time required the next time you wish to prepare the same food in your Radarange Oven.

2. Most of the recipes in this cookbook have a yield of 4 to 6 servings. Whenever you wish to reduce the yield for lower-quantity cooking, remember to reduce the amount of cooking time. For example, if you decrease the quantity of a recipe by half, cut the cooking time approximately in half. Also, remember to reduce the dish size. Try to use a dish of approximately the same shape. (For example, if the recipe requires a large round dish, use a small round dish.)

When increasing the size of a recipe, or the amount of food, remember to **increase** the cooking time. For example, 4 potatoes require a longer cooking time than does 1 potato. A general rule to remember when increasing the size of a recipe is: When doubling a recipe, increase the cooking time to **slightly less** than 2 times as long. When tripling, increase the cooking time to slightly less than 3 times as long, etc. Again, be certain to change the dish size accordingly.

3. Your Radarange Oven is a 700-watt* microwave oven, and cooks faster than other microwave ovens on the market. When using FULL POWER, the Radarange Oven cooks at a very fast speed. Therefore, when using recipes other than those in your Amana cookbook, cooking times may be too long. Many newspapers, magazines, and other sources print microwave oven recipes. Many convenience foods, particularly frozen convenience foods, now include microwave oven cooking times. All recipes or package directions are usually written for high or full power, which on your unit is the FULL POWER setting. If the recipe requires a "one-half" or 50% cycle, use the Cookmatic Level 5 (SLO COOK) setting. If the recipe requires a "one-third-power" or 30% cycle, use the Cookmatic Level 3 (SIMMER) setting. If the recipe requires thawing, use the DEFROST pad. Frequently, recipes or package instructions will have a **range** of cooking time given. For example, a recipe may state, "Cook for 4 to 7 minutes." Since your Radarange Oven cooks at a very fast speed, the recipe should require a **minimum** amount of cooking, or, in this case, only 4 minutes. Always cook for the shortest amount of cooking time **suggested** in the "range". Then, check the food a short while **before** the **suggested** time is expired. Always use the FULL POWER setting unless otherwise stated.

Kitchen Planning with the Radarange Oven

As you become accustomed to cooking most of your foods in the Radarange Oven, you will probably want to reorganize your kitchen cupboards for microwave cooking convenience. Store any glassware which is frequently used near your Radarange Oven. Glass measures, glass casseroles and lids,

*Per 1 liter test

loaf dishes, cake dishes, and custard cups are some items you may wish to keep handy.

You may also wish to keep coverings such as plastic wrap, paper towels, or napkins nearby.

You might want to store your tableware, such as plates, cups, and saucers near the Radarange Oven for quick reheating of foods.

The Radarange Oven itself should be placed in an easily accessible location in the kitchen. After using your Radarange Oven for a period of time, you may wish to build it in, or put it on a movable cart. Special accessory built-in kits, as well as Radarange Oven carts, can be purchased from your local Amana dealer.

Reheating Cooked Foods

When reheating **cooked** foods, you can reheat a plate containing a combination of several foods.

Reheating is a great benefit when not all family members can eat at one time. "Doggie-bag" meals can also quickly be reheated and will taste as if they've just been freshly cooked.

Also, leftovers can become "planned-overs." Extra food can be prepared in the Radarange Oven, and reheated later at a minute's notice. Reheated food will always taste fresh.

There are some general guidelines to follow when reheating foods.

• **General Hints for Reheating Foods**
1. When reheating single dinner plates of food, place only one plate at a time inside the Radarange Oven. Cover each plate with heavy-duty plastic wrap or waxed paper to retain heat and moisture, before serving.

2. Arrange slow-to-heat foods around the outside edge of a plate. Examples include meats, poultry, and potatoes.

3. Place quick-heating foods in the center of a plate. Foods having low moisture, high fat or high sugar contents heat quickly. So do foods having narrow parts, or foods cut in small pieces. Examples include vegetables such as peas, fruits and some desserts.

4. Arrange irregular pieces of food with the thickest parts toward the outside edge of the plate. Examples include poultry pieces or some small cuts of meat.

5. Spread foods out, or arrange them in a thin, even layer over the plate, rather than heaping them, for faster reheating. For example, spread out scalloped potatoes or mashed potatoes. Keep a food portion size small, rather than large.

6. If the meat is served with a sauce or gravy, spoon some over the meat before reheating to avoid dehydration.

7. Reheat porous items such as breads and cakes, for a minimum amount of time. For best results, reheat these items separately.

8. Reheat fish and seafood for a minimum amount of time.

9. Cover plates with heavy-duty plastic wrap or waxed paper, before reheating. Keep covered until ready to serve.

10. Place a plate of food directly in the center of the Radarange Oven glass tray for reheating.

11. When reheating, reheat on FULL POWER for about 1 to 1-1/2 minutes per plate, or until the food is warmed as desired. Reheating times can vary, depending upon the quantity and types of food being reheated. Reheat refrigerator temperature foods longer than room temperature foods. If the plate bottom feels slightly warm, then the food is probably adequately reheated, since it is conducting heat to the bottom of the plate.

12. Foods can also be reheated in serving dishes, if desired. Do not reheat foods in dishes having a metal trim.

13. Before reheating soups, sauces or beverages, stir them vigorously.

14. For reheating small quantities of food quickly, see the "Everyday Foods Heating and Reheating Chart," located for convenience just inside the back cover of this cookbook.

15. Use the Automatic Temperature Control to reheat leftover soups, casseroles, meats, vegetables, etc., to serving temperature. Serving temperature for most foods is 150° F.

Low Calorie Cooking

Controlling calories and cooking with microwaves are natural partners. Excessive amounts of fat, butter or margarine are not needed to prevent sticking in a microwave oven. Sauces can be eliminated or kept to a minimum, and menus can be individualized to meet special diet needs.

The quick "steam-type" cooking made possible with the Radarange Oven allows foods to steam in their natural juices. Just add a touch of a favorite seasoning to enhance natural food flavors. Or, try cooking a favorite food in a little bouillon, rather than using a tempting rich sauce or butter.

Another way to reduce calories is to eat a smaller-than-normal serving. With the easy-to-reheat feature of the Radarange Oven, a single portion can be enjoyed at one meal, and any remainder can be saved for reheating at another meal.

When part of the family wishes to enjoy higher calorie foods, a calorie controlled portion of the same food can be placed separately in a small dish. Heat the calorie-controlled portion separately and quickly in the Radarange Oven.

A few of the recipes in this cookbook are designed especially for calorie watchers. Look for calorie-count information in the MICRO-TIPS.

Food Precautions for Microwave Ovens

Review this list, and do not cook these items in your microwave oven.

1. **Eggs** should not be cooked or reheated in the shell. Eggs should not be cooked with an unbroken yolk. To do so may result in a pressure build-up and eruption. Pierce the yolk with a fork or knife before cooking.

   Do not reheat previously cooked eggs in the microwave oven unless finely chopped or scrambled.

2. **Potatoes, tomatoes,** or **other foods with a "skin"** should only be cooked in the microwave oven after the skin has been pierced. You should be sure that all foods with an outer skin or membrane are pierced to allow steam to escape during cooking.

3. **Ordinary popcorn** should only be popped in the Radarange Microwave Oven in the specially designed Radarange Microwave Oven Popcorn Popper. Special popcorn in bags, designed and labeled **for microwave only** may also be used.

4. **Home canning** should not be done in a microwave oven. Home canning is generally done with metal lids. Since metal lids reflect microwaves, you cannot be assured that the food product will be heated uniformly to 212° F or above, and there is a probability of deterioration of the food product.

5. Do not leave the microwave oven unattended when drying **anything.** Foods or other items being dried can become too dry and can ignite. If anything does ignite, press the STOP switch, and open the oven door only after ignition ceases.

6. Do not use paper towels which contain nylon or other synthetic fibers since the heated synthetic could cause the paper to ignite.

EMERGENCY SUBSTITUTION CHART

1 teaspoon baking powder	= 1/2 teaspoon cream of tartar, plus 1/4 teaspoon baking soda
1 cup butter or margarine	= 7/8 to 1 cup vegetable shortening or lard, plus 1/2 teaspoon of salt
1 cup buttermilk or soured milk	= 1 tablespoon white vinegar, plus milk to equal 1 cup. (Let sit for 5 minutes.)
1 cup cake flour, sifted	= 7/8 cup sifted all-purpose flour (7/8 cup is 1 cup less 2 tablespoons.)
1 cake compressed yeast	= 1 package or 2 teaspoons active dry yeast
1 cup catsup or chili sauce	= 1 cup tomato sauce, plus 1/2 cup sugar and 2 tablespoons vinegar (for use in cooked mixtures.)
1 tablespoon fresh chives, finely chopped	= 1 teaspoon freeze-dried chives
1 oz. unsweetened chocolate (1 square)	= 3 tablespoons cocoa powder, plus 1 tablespoon butter or margarine
1 tablespoon cornstarch	= 2 tablespoons all-purpose flour or 4 teaspoons quick-cooking tapioca (for thickening)
1 cup cream (heavy, 40%)	= 3/4 cup milk, plus 1/3 cup butter or margarine (do not use for whipping)
(light, 20%)	= 7/8 cup milk, plus 3 tablespoons butter or margarine
1 teaspoon dry leaf herb	= 1 tablespoon chopped fresh herbs
1 whole egg	= 2 egg yolks, plus 1 tablespoon water
1 garlic clove	= 1 teaspoon garlic salt or: 1/8 teaspoon garlic powder
1 cup whole milk	= 1 cup skim milk, plus 2 tablespoons butter or margarine or: 1/2 cup evaporated milk, plus 1/2 cup water (use for cooking)
2 teaspoons instant, minced onion	= 1 teaspoon onion powder
1 small onion	= 1 tablespoon instant, minced onion
1 tablespoon prepared mustard	= 1 teaspoon dry mustard
1 cup dairy sour cream	= 1 tablespoon lemon juice, plus evaporated milk to make 1 cup
1 cup tomato juice	= 1/2 cup tomato sauce, plus 1/2 cup water

EQUIVALENCY CHART

Butter, Chocolate

2 tablespoons butter or margarine	= 1 oz.
1 stick or 1/4 lb. butter or margarine	= 1/2 cup
1 square chocolate	= 1 oz.

Cheese and Cream

1/4 lb. American cheese, shredded	= 1 cup
1/4 lb. blue cheese, crumbled	= 1 cup
1 cup whipping cream	= 2 cups whipped

Crumbs

1 slice bread	= 1/4 cup fine dry crumbs
1-1/2 slices bread	= 1 cup soft crumbs
14 squares graham crackers	= 1 cup fine crumbs
22 vanilla wafers	= 1 cup fine crumbs

Nuts

1 lb. walnuts (in shell)	= 1-1/2 to 1-3/4 cups, shelled

Extras

1 envelope gelatin, unflavored	= 1 tablespoon
16 large marshmallows	= 1 cup marshmallow cream
1 lb. miniature marshmallows	= 9 cups miniature marshmallows

Fruit and Vegetables

1 medium apple, sliced	= 1 cup
1 lb. (3 to 4) bananas, mashed	= 2 cups
1 lb. (3 to 4) bananas, sliced	= 2-1/2 cups
1 small cabbage, shredded	= 4 cups
1 lb. raw carrots, sliced	= 2-1/2 cups
1, 3-1/2 oz. (can) coconut, flaked	= 1-1/3 cups
1, 4 oz. (can) coconut, shredded	= 1-1/2 cups
1 lb. coconut, shredded	= 5 cups
1 medium lemon	= 1 teaspoon grated lemon peel = 2 tablespoons lemon juice
1 medium onion, chopped	= 1/2 cup
1 medium orange	= 4 teaspoons grated orange peel
1 medium orange	= 1/3 cup orange juice
1 lb. pitted dates	= 2-1/2 cups
1 medium potato, sliced	= 1 cup
1 lb. (3 to 4) peaches, peeled and sliced	= 2 to 2-1/2 cups
1 pint strawberries, hulled	= 1-1/2 cups

Sugar

1 lb. confectioners' sugar	= 4 cups, unsifted
1 lb. brown sugar	= 2-1/4 cups, firmly packed

Once you cook a few foods in the Radarange Oven, you will soon want to combine foods to make a meal. Usually, meal preparation requires cooking food items in a sequence, one after another. However, some foods can be cooked **together,** or "all-at-once" with excellent results. In this chapter, you will find meals prepared either in a sequence, or cooked all-at-once! Both types of meal preparation can be easily accomplished in your Radarange Oven.

Until you become more familiar with microwave oven cooking, you might want to do a little extra planning when you prepare your first few microwave oven meals, just as you planned more carefully when preparing your first "conventional oven meals". In fact, planning is the key to good microwave oven meals. The extra planning will be well worth your time, because you will save a considerable amount of cooking time by using your Radarange Oven, rather than your conventional oven.

Before you prepare entire meals in your Radarange Oven, you will want to familiarize yourself with the general meal planning hints.

General Hints for Meal Planning

1. BEFORE BEGINNING
    Allow yourself plenty of time when you're planning your first few meals, so you are completely at ease, and won't feel rushed.

    If you are planning a menu of your own, consider the following points as you do when cooking conventionally:

    • Contrast of color and texture of the foods

    • Nutritional balance of foods

    • Flavors of foods . . . do they blend well?

    Before starting, think through the entire meal. Assemble all of the utensils and ingredients required in the recipes. Also, **carefully read each recipe** before starting, so you are familiar with all of the instructions.

2. SEQUENCING
    Sequencing is one type of meal preparation. Foods are arranged in a certain cooking **sequence.** That is, one food will be cooked first, another will be cooked second, and so on. To determine in what order or sequence you should prepare foods, consider the following:
    • Can any of the foods be prepared ahead of time? Some desserts should be prepared hours ahead, or even the day before, in order to cool before serving. They can generally be reheated quickly, just before serving, if desired. It is usually better to reheat these items rather than to try to completely cook them at the last minute.

    Other foods can be prepared ahead, and then easily reheated. Remember, Radarange Oven reheated foods maintain a fresh flavor. Spaghetti sauce, for example, can be made the day before a big dinner, and can be quickly reheated before serving time.
    • How long of a cooking time does each food require? Some foods, such as meats or main dishes, require a longer cooking time than other foods, such as vegetables. Generally, a good rule to remember when planning the sequence or order of cooking is: Cook the food having the longest cooking time first.

    Usually foods which require a longer cooking time retain or hold heat well. Some dishes, such as casseroles, will actually improve in flavor when they are allowed to stand for a few minutes. Some foods require a "carry-over" cooking time, during which the food will actually finish its cooking without microwaves. Foods which do retain heat well, or which do require a carry-over cooking time, should be prepared first. While these foods stand, other foods can be cooked in the Radarange Oven. Therefore, proper sequencing of foods will often result in a **shorter overall cooking time** than preparing a meal "all-at-once."

    Items which are generally cooked first or sometimes hours or a day ahead, include the following:

    • Desserts (which can be reheated later or need to be served cooled or chilled)
    Examples: pies, cakes, puddings, cookies

- Sauces (which can be reheated later, if necessary) Examples: salad dressings, main dish sauces, dessert sauces

- Appetizers (some can be made ahead, or even frozen to reheat later)
Examples: meat balls, dips, spreads

- Long-Cooking Foods (which retain heat and may require carry-over cooking)
Examples: large cuts of meat or poultry, meat items that require simmering, casserole mixtures

Foods which should be prepared later in a sequence include the following:

- Foods which don't reheat well
Examples: fish and seafood, eggs, small meat items

- Foods having a shorter cooking time
Examples: breads, fish and seafood, vegetables

- Foods which need WARMING or reheating
Examples: rolls, sauces, beverages

Actual Meal Preparation Using Sequencing

Now that you're familiar with some of the "rules", let's consider an actual menu, and how the foods should be sequenced.

A sample menu might include the following:

Meat Loaf or Roast
Baked Potatoes
Green Beans
Tossed Salad with Hot Dressing
Dinner Rolls

Chocolate Pie
Coffee

The chocolate pie should be baked early in the day, or even the day before. It can then be chilled before serving. The dinner rolls can also be baked ahead.

The meat loaf (or roast) requires the longest amount of cooking time, so it should be cooked first in the sequence. It will retain heat well, if it is covered or wrapped in aluminum foil, **after** it is removed from the Radarange Oven. Next, bake the potatoes. They, also, will retain heat well if they are wrapped in aluminum foil, **after** they are removed from the Radarange Oven. The green beans should be cooked third. Cover them with a glass lid or plastic wrap, after removing them from the Radarange Oven.

A hot salad dressing can be quickly heated fourth and the quick-heating rolls are last. Cover rolls with a linen or paper napkin, during and after heating. Instant coffee can be heated while the pie is being cut for serving.

While one food is cooking, be preparing the other foods so they can be placed in the Radarange Oven immediately. Start a food cooking as quickly as possible. Remember, **always** have some food inside the Radarange Oven at all times, so no cooking time is wasted. Also, while foods are cooking, the table can be set.

You will notice that foods are always **covered** after they are removed from the Radarange Oven. Foods are covered so they will stay moist and retain their heat. By covering foods, they will all be "piping hot" when served. You can also put foods in a warm place after removing them from the Radarange Oven, such as inside your insulated conventional oven. You may wish to slightly undercook some foods, such as eggs or meats so they won't overcook while covered.

Some coverings are better than others. Roasts and other meats can be wrapped with aluminum foil, or they can be kept inside a baking dish, having a glass lid. Baked potatoes can be wrapped in aluminum foil. (Remember, use aluminum foil as a wrapping **only** after removing the food from the Radarange Oven.)

Glass lids or heavy-duty plastic wrap are good for covering foods, since they are water-vapor-proof. Paper towels, or cotton and linen napkins are good for covering baked goods, such as breads and cakes.

3. MEALS "ALL-AT-ONCE"
Some foods can be prepared "all-at-once" in the Radarange Oven with excellent results. Often, less-dense foods, such as dinner rolls, can be placed in the Radarange Oven during the final minute of the main dish's cooking so the rolls are hot and ready-to-serve with the rest of the meal.

Some foods which cook especially well "all-at-once" are:

Pot roast cooked with vegetables
Main-dish casserole cooked with a vegetable
Main-dish casserole cooked with a dessert
Two similar vegetables cooked together with a
main dish

Some of the menus in this chapter, designated as "All-at-Once" Meals will give you some ideas about how to prepare meals using this method of preparation in the Radarange Oven. If you have a favorite menu which is similar to one of the "All-at-Once" Meals menus in this chapter, you can prepare your own menu, using the "All-at-Once" Meal menu as a guide.

4. START TIME AND AUTOMATIC TEMPERATURE CONTROL SYSTEM

You can use the START TIME feature on your Touchmatic II to help with meal planning. Foods which require a longer cooking time, such as roasts, can be frozen ahead with a plastic straw inserted. You can then place the frozen meat in the Radarange Oven, insert the temperature probe in the straw, and program the Radarange Oven to start at any time of the day desired. The main dish will be ready for serving when you arrive home. For more information concerning the START TIME feature, see Session 6 in the Use and Care Manual.

5. QUANTITY COOKING

When preparing an extremely large meal, such as a holiday dinner, you may wish to use both the Radarange Oven and conventional oven. Foods which can be done in the Radarange Oven include the foods that take too long to cook conventionally such as a beef roast, a ham or a turkey. Foods such as rice, pasta, or boiled potatoes can be prepared conventionally and reheated if necessary in the Radarange Oven. Or, these foods can be prepared a day in advance and easily reheated in the Radarange Oven before serving.

6. LATE ARRIVALS

If guests are a few minutes late, don't fret. Foods can be quickly returned to the Radarange Oven to be reheated, if necessary. A good serving temperature for most foods is 150° F. Foods can also be reheated quickly before serving second helpings. Don't reheat foods in serving dishes having a metal trim. Remember, remove aluminum foil before reheating.

7. SUMMARY

Here is a list of brief reminders to consult before preparing a Radarange Oven meal:

BEFORE MEAL PREPARATION

- Know your menu and recipes well.
- Plan a logical cooking sequence or plan to cook the meal "all-at-once."
- Prepare foods ahead, if possible.

DURING MEAL PREPARATION

- If sequencing, cook the food having the longest cooking time first. Prepare each food in sequence, ending with the food having the shortest cooking or heating time. If cooking a meal "all-at-once," place all foods together in the Radarange Oven.
- Cover foods after removing them from the Radarange Oven, to keep the foods warm.
- If sequencing, always have a food ready to cook in the Radarange Oven so when one food finishes cooking, another is ready to be cooked. When you start meal preparation, begin cooking a food as quickly as possible. If preparing foods "all-at-once," you may wish to add a food such as dinner rolls in the final minutes of cooking.
- While food is cooking, set the table, and do any other extra duties.
- Reheat foods, if necessary, for late arrivals, just before serving.

Complete meals can be easily prepared in the Radarange Oven. Start with simple meals, and think through the sequence or "all-at-once" possibilities. Always remember that no matter what unexpected interruption develops, the foods will reheat beautifully. Begin with the menu ideas on the next pages. Use these menus as a guide in cooking your own menus in the Radarange Oven. All of the menus use recipes found throughout this cookbook. For information concerning how to adapt your own favorite recipes, see page 18 in the Introduction chapter. Soon you will be preparing your own favorite meals with ease in the Radarange Oven.

Dinner for Company

(For 6)

Menu

Hot Cheesy Clam Dip
with Crackers

Beef Rib Roast
Party Potatoes
Asparagus Royale
Lettuce Wedge
with Sour Cream Dressing
Herb Bread

Grasshopper Pie
Coffee

Early in the Morning or the Day Before

1. Prepare and bake the pie. Chill. See the recipe on page 332.

2. While the pie is baking, prepare the salad dressing. See the recipe on page 278. Cook the dressing. Chill. Fold in the sour cream just before serving.

3. While the dressing is cooking, begin to prepare the bread. See the recipe on page 101. Bake the bread. Cover the bread when cooled, with plastic wrap to retain the moisture.

4. While the bread is baking, prepare the cheesy clam dip. See the recipe on page 49. Heat the cheese dip. Refrigerate.

Before Serving

5. Prepare and bake the potatoes. See the recipe on page 260. Cover the potatoes with a glass lid or plastic wrap to retain the heat, until ready to serve.

6. While the potatoes are baking, prepare the roast. See the instructions on page 174. Cook the roast. Slightly undercook the roast so it won't overcook during a standing time. Wrap the roast in aluminum foil to retain the heat, until ready to serve.

7. While the roast is cooking, prepare the asparagus. See the recipe on page 250. Set the table. Prepare the cheese dip for reheating. Fold the sour cream into the salad dressing.

8. Reheat the cheesy clam dip. Serve the appetizer.

9. Cook the asparagus. Cover the asparagus with a glass lid or plastic wrap, to retain the moisture.

10. Reheat the potatoes, if necessary.

11. Water for instant coffee can be heated while the pie is being served. (If "perking" your coffee, plug in the coffee pot just before dinner so the coffee will be ready to serve with the dessert.)

Breakfast

(For 4)

Menu
Baked Grapefruit

Wake-Up Special
Cranberry Muffins

Instant Hot Chocolate

Early in the Morning or the Day Before

1. Prepare and bake the muffins. See the recipe on page 87. Store in a covered container or cover with plastic wrap, when cooled.

2. Mix together the ingredients for the hot chocolate. See the recipe on page 56. Store in a covered container, until ready to serve.

Before Serving

3. Prepare and bake the grapefruit. See the recipe on page 296. (Note: The quantity of this recipe, and therefore, also the cooking time, needs to be doubled for this menu.) Cover grapefruit loosely with waxed paper to retain the heat until ready to serve.

4. While grapefruit is cooking, prepare the eggs. See the recipe on page 144. Cook the eggs. Slightly undercook the eggs, so they won't overcook during the standing time. Keep the eggs covered with a glass lid or plastic wrap to retain the heat until ready to serve.

5. While the eggs are cooking, set the table.

6. The water for the hot chocolate can be heated while the grapefruit is being eaten.

7. The muffins may be heated, if desired. The muffins can be heated in a straw basket, wrapped with a napkin. Keep the muffins covered with the napkin to retain their heat for serving.

Brunch

(For 2)

Menu
Chilled Fruit Cup

Biscuit Breakfast Ring
Hash 'N' Egg Nests

Coffee

The Day Before

1. Prepare and cook the fruit cup. Chill. See the recipe on page 297.

Before Serving

2. Prepare and bake the bread ring. See the recipe on page 91. While bread ring is baking, add oranges and bananas to the fruit cup, if it was prepared the day before. Place the fruit cup in individual serving dishes, if desired, and return any left-overs to the refrigerator. (Note: You may wish to divide the fruit cup recipe in half for this menu.) Invert the bread ring on a serving platter, leaving the dish on top to retain moisture and heat until ready to serve.

3. Prepare and cook the hash and eggs. See the recipe on page 143.

4. Water for instant coffee can be heated while the fruit cup is being served. (If "perking" your coffee, plug in the coffee pot just before brunch so the coffee will be ready to serve.)

"All-at-Once" Meal

Colorful Luncheon

(For 4)

Menu
Stuffed Peppers
Herb Rolls
Fruit Crisp (Cherry)
Russian Tea

Early in the Morning or the Day Before
1. Prepare the mix for the tea, according to the recipe on page 58.

Before Serving
2. Prepare the peppers, according to the recipe on page 202. Place the peppers on an 8-1/2-inch diameter plate. Cover the peppers with plastic wrap.
3. Prepare the fruit crisp, according to the recipe on page 297. Use any pie filling desired and divide into 4, 6-oz. custard cups. Prepare 1/2 of the recipe for "Fruit Crisp Topping", on page 297 and divide the topping among the custard cups.
4. Prepare the rolls, according to the recipe on page 89, through step #3.
5. Place the dish of stuffed peppers in the center of the Radarange Oven. Place a dish of fruit crisp in each of the 4 corners of the Radarange Oven. Cook all in the Radarange Oven on FULL POWER for 4 minutes.
6. Add the rolls to the Radarange Oven, placing them under the plate of stuffed peppers, so that the plate of peppers rests on the inverted custard cup in the dish of rolls. Cook all in the Radarange Oven on FULL POWER for 6 to 7 minutes, or until the rolls and stuffed peppers are done.*
7. Water for the tea can be heated while the dessert is being served.

   *MICRO-TIP: You may want to turn dish of rolls halfway through cooking time.

"All-at-Once" Meal

Family Dinner

(For 4)

Menu
Bacon-Topped Meat Loaf
Baked Potatoes
Peas & Carrots
Tossed Salad with
Creamy French Dressing
Coffee

Early in the Morning or the Day Before
1. Prepare the salad dressing, according to the recipe on page 277. Chill.

Before Serving
2. Select 4, uniformly shaped, medium-size potatoes. Scrub and pierce each.
3. Prepare the meat loaf, according to the recipe on page 208.
4. Put the meat loaf and potatoes in the Radarange Oven. Place the 4 potatoes in a circle on the left side of the Radarange Oven. Place the meat loaf on the right side of the Radarange Oven. Cook in the Radarange Oven on FULL POWER for 10 minutes, or until the foods are warmed.
5. While the potatoes and meat loaf are cooking, place 1 (10 oz.) package of frozen peas and carrots in a 1-quart casserole. Add 2 tablespoons of water. Cover with a glass lid or plastic wrap. Place the frozen peas and carrots in the Radarange Oven in the middle of the circle of potatoes. Rotate the potatoes.
6. Cook all in the Radarange Oven on FULL POWER for an additional 10 minutes. Stir the vegetable halfway through the cooking time. When stirring the vegetable, remove the potatoes if done and wrap them in foil to keep them warm. During the final minutes of cooking, prepare the salad and add the dressing.
7. The water for instant coffee can be heated while serving the dinner. (If "perking" your coffee, plug in the coffee pot just before dinner so the coffee will be ready to serve.)

"All-at-Once" Meal

Basic Breakfast

(For 4)

Menu
Baked Grapefruit (4)
Hash 'N' Egg Nests
Quick Caramel Rolls
Coffee

Before Serving

1. Prepare the grapefruit, according to the recipe on page 296, through step #1. Place the 4 halves in 4, 6-oz. custard cups.

2. Prepare the rolls, according to the recipe on page 90, through step #3.

3. Prepare the hash and eggs, according to recipe on page 143, through step #2.

4. Place the 4 dishes containing the hash and eggs in a circle in the center of the Radarange Oven. Cover the dishes with a large piece of plastic wrap. Place the dish of rolls on top of the 4 dishes. Place a grapefruit half in each corner of the Radarange Oven.

5. Cook all in the Radarange Oven on FULL POWER for 6 to 7 minutes, or until the rolls are done.* After the 6 to 7 minutes of cooking, remove the rolls and grapefruit. Invert rolls on a serving plate, keeping the 9 x 2-inch dish over the top of the rolls until the eggs are done.

6. Cook the hash and eggs in the Radarange Oven on Cookmatic Level 8 (MEDIUM HIGH) for 2 to 4 minutes. **

7. The water for instant coffee can be heated while the hash and eggs are being served. (If "perking" your coffee, plug in the coffee pot just before breakfast so the coffee will be ready to serve.)

MICRO-TIPS:

*You may want to turn dish of rolls halfway through cooking time.

**You may want to rearrange eggs halfway through cooking time.

"All-at-Once" Meal

"Light" Luncheon

(For 3)

Menu
Chicken 'N' Rice
Herbed Broccoli
Rolls
Coffee

Before Serving

1. Prepare Steps #1 and #2 of the chicken dish, according to the recipe on page 232.

2. Prepare the broccoli in a 9 x 5 x 2-inch loaf dish, according to the recipe on page 252, through step #1.

3. Put the chicken in the left side of the Radarange Oven, and the broccoli on the right side. Cook in the Radarange Oven on FULL POWER for 10 minutes. Separate the broccoli. Cook in the Radarange Oven on FULL POWER for an additional 7 minutes.

4. Place 6 rolls in a plastic bag, leaving the bag open. Place the rolls in the Radarange Oven, on top of the chicken and broccoli dishes for the last 1 minute of cooking. (Use the Automatic Timer to remind you when to put in the rolls.)

Something Special

(For 6)

Menu

Bacon-Wrapped Olives

Chicken Parmesan
Baked Potatoes
Mandarin Carrots

Boston Cream Pie
Coffee or Tea

Early in the Morning or the Day Before

1. Prepare and bake the dessert. Chill. See the recipe on page 312.

2. While the dessert is baking, prepare the appetizers. Refrigerate. See the recipe on page 42. (Note: You may wish to double this recipe for this menu.)

Before Serving

3. Prepare and cook the chicken. See the recipe on page 235. Keep the chicken covered with a glass lid or plastic wrap to retain the heat until ready to serve.

4. While the chicken is cooking, wash and pierce the potatoes. See the recipe on page 261. Bake the potatoes. Wrap the potatoes in aluminum foil after they finish baking to retain their heat until ready to serve.

5. While the potatoes are baking, prepare the carrots. See the recipe on page 254. Cook the carrots. Keep the carrots covered with a glass lid or plastic wrap to retain the heat until ready to serve.

6. Heat appetizers as guests arrive. Chicken may be reheated on FULL POWER for 2 to 2-1/2 minutes before serving, if necessary.

7. Water for instant coffee or tea can be heated while the dessert is being served. (If "perking" your coffee, plug in the coffee pot just before dinner so the coffee will be ready to serve with the dessert.)

Candlelight Dinner

(For 4)

Menu

Beef Stroganoff and Noodles

Brussels Sprouts
Tossed Salad
with Creamy Blue Cheese Dressing
Rye Bread

Pineapple Bridge Dessert
Coffee

Early in the Morning or the Day Before

1. Prepare and bake the dessert. Chill. See the recipe on page 289.

2. While the dessert is cooking, prepare the salad dressing. See the recipe on page 277. Cook the dressing. Chill.

3. While the dressing is cooking, begin to prepare the bread. See the recipe on page 99. Bake the bread. Cover the bread, after cooled, with plastic wrap to retain moisture.

Before Serving

4. Cook enough noodles for 4. See the chart on page 120. While the noodles are cooking, prepare the Beef Stroganoff. See the recipe on page 197. Keep the noodles covered with a glass lid, or plastic wrap to retain the heat until ready to serve. Cook the stroganoff.

5. While the stroganoff is cooking, prepare the brussels sprouts. See the instructions on page 242. Cook the brussels sprouts. Keep the brussels sprouts covered with a glass lid or plastic wrap to retain the moisture until ready to serve.

6. While the brussels sprouts are cooking, prepare the tossed salad and set the table.

7. Reheat the bread, if desired. Cover with a napkin. Keep the bread covered to retain the heat and moisture until ready to serve.

8. Water for instant coffee can be heated while the dessert is being served. (If "perking" your coffee, plug in the coffee pot just before dinner so the coffee will be ready to serve with the dessert.)

Are you curious about how microwave cooking began, how your Radarange Microwave Oven operates, and how your Radarange Oven will benefit you?

Every year hundreds of thousands of homemakers are adding the fastest, most modern cooking device to their kitchens—the microwave oven. They like its convenience, its speed of operation, its energy-saving economy, and its compact beauty.

While microwave ovens are now considered to be an essential part of American kitchens by many homemakers, this was not always so.

HOW MICROWAVE COOKING BEGAN

The first microwave oven was produced in Raytheon Company laboratories in 1945.

The discovery of the principle of microwave cooking resulted from wartime research in radar. During World War II (and ever since) Raytheon was one of the leading producers of radar equipment. In 1945, the late Dr. Percy L. Spencer of Raytheon, while testing a radar vacuum tube, realized that the microwave energy it generated produced heat. He thought it might cook food. He sent out for a chocolate bar, it was said, and put it in front of the radar tube. The chocolate immediately melted.

So Raytheon developed and patented a microwave oven which it trademarked "Radarange". The microwave oven was designed for use in hospitals and other mass-feeding situations. These first microwave ovens were large and expensive to build.

Amana Refrigeration, Inc., became a subsidiary of Raytheon in 1965. Working with Raytheon engineers, Amana introduced the world's first 115-volt countertop domestic model in 1967, the Amana Radarange Microwave Oven.*

Since then, consumer interest in microwave cooking has soared. Happy owners have found that their microwave ovens far exceed their original expectations and provide them with a wide range of delicious foods.

HOW YOUR RADARANGE OVEN OPERATES

The Radarange Oven cooks with high energy, high frequency microwaves. Microwaves are electromagnetic waves of energy, similar to heat and light waves. The Amana Radarange Oven operates on a frequency of 2,450 megacycles. This frequency is very close to the frequency used by radio and television.

---

*"Radarange" is the registered trademark of Amana Refrigeration, Inc., for all of its microwave oven products.

For this reason, the Federal Communications Commission limits or controls the design of microwave ovens. Without these limitations, it would be possible for microwaves to interfere with household reception of radio and television programs.

Microwaves have many of the same characteristics as light waves. Both types of waves travel in straight lines and can be generated, reflected, transmitted and absorbed. The basic differences between microwaves and light waves are in what materials reflect, transmit and absorb them, and in the different way in which microwaves are generated.

In the microwave oven, the generator for producing the microwaves is called a Magnetron. The Magnetron is a vacuum tube which operates as an oscillator to generate microwaves.

Although microwaves can be reflected in the same manner as light, the materials that reflect them differ. For example, the perforated metal screen in the door of the Radarange Oven reflects microwaves, yet it transmits light. Glass, china and paper products transmit microwaves, or allow microwaves to "pass through" them. These same materials absorb or reflect light.

The selective "personality" of microwaves makes it possible to cook in the Radarange Oven and still have the oven cavity and cooking utensil remain cool. However, both the cavity and utensils may warm up slightly due to the transfer of heat from the food itself.

When you cook in a conventional oven, you cook by conduction. The oven cavity is preheated, the food is placed inside, and over a period of time this heat penetrates in toward the center of the food and cooks it.

Cooking with microwaves differs from conventional cooking in that it does not utilize the direct application of heat to cook food. In the Radarange Oven, foods are cooked by the absorption of microwave energy. This energy causes the food molecules to move very rapidly, generating heat within the food itself. Because the mi-

crowaves are transmitted by the cooking utensil, they can strike the food from all sides and cook it very rapidly throughout.

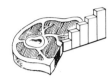

As the microwaves penetrate the food, they lose approximately half of their power every 3/4 of an inch. This means that the food is not cooked from the inside out, but is cooked **throughout at the same time** with more cooking taking place on the exterior of the food. Therefore, it is possible to prepare a roast that is brown on the exterior and rare, medium or well-done in the center. Let's look inside the Radarange Oven. Below is a diagram of how microwaves operate within the Radarange Oven.

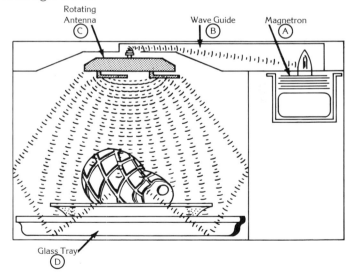

The Magnetron (A) generates microwaves which travel in straight lines down the waveguide (B). The microwaves are broadcasted into the oven by the rotating antenna (C). The antenna beams the microwaves directly at the food in a uniform pattern.

The food is placed on the Radarange Oven glass tray (D) about 1 inch above the bottom of the oven. The microwaves pass through this glass tray and are reflected off the bottom of the oven to enter the bottom side of the food. Utensils of glass, paper, plastic, and ceramic are used since they transmit microwaves, allowing them to easily reach the food.

SAFETY FEATURES

Safety features are built into each Radarange Oven. One safety feature is that you cannot operate the unit when the door is open. Cooking will stop when you push the STOP switch.

All models have two safety features which keep the microwaves inside the oven. The first feature is the primary door seal that keeps microwaves from passing around the door.

The second feature is the door gasket, which is made from a special vinyl containing carbon black. If any microwaves should pass by the primary door seal, this gasket has the ability to absorb them.

In addition to stop-start or latch switches, all models have "back-up" interlock switches that operate from door motion. These switches are located behind the door hinge arms.

ADVANTAGES OF COOKING WITH MICROWAVES

Microwave cooking is not just an improvement in conventional cooking methods. It is an entirely new cooking concept, a new process of introducing heat to foods. Amana calls it "the greatest cooking discovery since fire". Cooking with microwaves has several advantages.

Saves Times

Radarange Oven cooking can literally take hours out of kitchen chores. Most foods—even some complete meals—can be cooked in one-fourth of the time it normally takes in a conventional range! The time required to cook food in the Radarange Oven depends upon the size, shape, weight, density, and starting temperature of the food, plus the Cookmatic power level selected.

Your new Amana Radarange Oven will cook a family-size Thanksgiving turkey in just 5 to 6 minutes per pound! Dinner rolls require just a few seconds of heating time. The Radarange Oven can cook a 2-1/2 pound chicken in 12-1/2 to 15 minutes. Five ears of corn-in-the-husk will cook in 8 to 9 minutes, and no boiling water is needed!

But there is more time-saving with a Radarange Oven than just the fast cooking time.

No After-Meal Clean-Up of Metal Pots and Pans

As long as you cook with microwaves, you will never have to scour another metal pot or pan. These are never used.

Cook and Serve on Dinnerware

You can prepare food in almost any container that is not metal or that does not have metal trim or hardware. You can use glassware, ceramic dinnerware, paper plates, or plastic containers. The microwaves pass right through these materials to concentrate all the energy on the food. The "cooking" dishes can be used as "serving" dishes. Take dishes directly from the Radarange Oven to the table. You will have fewer dishes to wash after a meal.

Easy Oven Clean-Up

The sides, top, and bottom of the Radarange Oven cooking cavity do not get excessively hot. That means that splatters or spills will not burn themselves on to the sides of the oven. Use only a damp cloth with a mild detergent for cleaning. The "cool cooking" of the Radarange Oven allows for great time savings in clean-up.

Food Appearance

Foods cooked in the Radarange Oven have a bright, natural look. Only very small amounts of water are required in microwave cooking for most foods. Therefore, water-soluble colors, such as chlorophyll in green vegetables, are not lost in the cooking liquid as in conventional cooking. Also, water-soluble vitamins, such as the B Vitamins and Vitamin C, are not lost in cooking liquid since little liquid, if any, is required for microwave cooking.

Freezer to Table
Food freezers, either as part of refrigerator-freezer combinations or as separate appliances, are commonplace. Frozen foods are part of our everyday life. Now you can take hard-frozen food from the freezer, thaw and cook it in the Radarange Oven, and serve it in a matter of minutes.

Saves Energy
Because the microwaves heat only the food, and not the oven or the air around the food, your kitchen stays far cooler during microwave cooking than it does during conventional cooking. This "cool cooking" reduces the work of your air conditioner, and in turn reduces your electric bill.

Cooking in a microwave oven is fast and efficient. Energy is consumed only while food is actually cooking, and the cooking is fast!

A conventional range, whether gas or electric, is a major consumer of energy. The basic reason is that the conventional cooking process itself is relatively inefficient. When a surface element is heated, the element heats the bottom of the pan (some heat is lost into the air), which then heats the food. In the case of boiled foods, the water is heated, and then usually thrown away.

A conventional oven is preheated to heat the air, which heats the outside of the food, and, eventually heats the inside of the food to the temperature required to cook it. Heat is lost and power is wasted every time the oven door is opened.

Compared to cooking in a microwave oven, the conventional way is slow and inefficient. The microwave oven, of course, does not heat the air. There is no preheating of an empty oven, and the utensil is not heated first, except when preheating a browning skillet. Instead, the microwave energy is absorbed by the food and converted directly into heat.

Extensive tests by major electric utilities and the Amana Test Kitchen show energy savings from 50 percent to 75 percent for the Amana Radarange Oven, compared to conventional electric ranges. These savings are based upon food cooked on the FULL POWER setting in the Radarange Oven.

If a family uses the microwave oven extensively to replace other cooking means, the microwave oven can quickly pay for itself in electrical savings alone. Plus, there is no installation cost. **Regular 120-volt household current is all the Radarange Oven requires.** It just plugs in; there is no costly special wiring required.

As you begin cooking with your Radarange Oven, you will soon appreciate all of the many benefits of microwave cooking. You will undoubtedly discover many advantages of microwave cooking that are not mentioned in this chapter. All members of the family will enjoy cooking in the Radarange Oven. Your Radarange Oven will quickly become your "best friend in the kitchen".

The Radarange Oven enables a host or hostess to prepare food for a party, and still have time left for many last-minute details.

Some appetizers can be prepared ahead and then heated, as needed, when guests arrive. Some appetizers such as meat balls, can be frozen ahead, and then defrosted for a quick, spur-of-the-moment party.

Most appetizers can be quickly and easily heated on FULL POWER. Others require a lower setting for more delicate ingredients, such as cheese or mushrooms.

Read the general hints for heating appetizers and snacks before preparing them in your Radarange Oven.

General Hints for Heating Appetizers and Snacks

1. Use serving dishes for heating appetizers. Be certain dishes are Radarange Oven-safe. By using only one dish for both heating and serving, you can save precious time when entertaining.
2. Arrange appetizers in a single layer when heating, for best results. In most cases, cover with waxed paper or a paper towel to prevent spattering. Stir dips before serving.
3. Use lower settings for delicate ingredients such as cheese, mushrooms or shellfish, as recommended in the recipes. Cheese can become stringy or rubbery if heated at too high a setting. Mushrooms can "pop" if heated on FULL POWER. Seafood in the shell tends to become somewhat tough and it may also "pop" if heated at too high a setting.
4. Whenever possible, prepare appetizers ahead, and then quickly heat when guests arrive. Freeze meat balls ahead, if desired. Quickly defrost and heat when needed.
5. Don't place spreads on crackers until ready to heat to prevent sogginess.
6. Ordinary popcorn should only be popped in the Radarange Microwave Oven in the specially designed Radarange Microwave Oven Popcorn Popper. Special popcorn in bags, designed and labeled **for microwave only** may also be used.
7. Shellfish may be heated directly in the shell, since shells allow microwaves to transmit through them. Shells make attractive and unique "serving dishes".
8. Stale or soggy potato chips, crackers, or other snacks can be freshened in the Radarange Oven. Heat in Radarange Oven on FULL POWER for about 30 seconds to 1 minute.
9. Blocks of cheese can be heated for serving. Heat for only 30 seconds to 1 minute on Cookmatic Level 5 (SLO COOK).
10. Heat most appetizers and snacks on the FULL POWER setting. Appetizers which include the melting of cheese, a delicate ingredient, should be heated on Cookmatic Level 5 (SLO COOK). Appetizers containing mushrooms can be quickly heated on Cookmatic Level 8 (MEDIUM HIGH) to avoid "popping" during heating. When heating your own favorite appetizers and snacks, select a similar recipe from this chapter as a guide. Use approximately the same amount of time recommended, and use the same setting.

Oysters Casino (page 44), Escargot (page 43), Clams-in-the-Shell (page 44), and Coquilles (page 43)

APPETIZERS AND SNACKS FROZEN CONVENIENCE FOODS CHART

APPETIZER OR SNACK	PKG. SIZE	PROGRAMMING INSTRUCTIONS			
Frozen Snack Tacos	6 oz.	1	COOKING PROGRAM	3:00	DEFROST ☐
		2	COOKING PROGRAM	1:00	HOLD ☐
		3	COOKING PROGRAM	1:00 to 1:30	COOK ☐
Frozen Egg Rolls	6 oz.	1	COOKING PROGRAM	3:00	DEFROST ☐
		2	COOKING PROGRAM	1:00	HOLD ☐
		3	COOKING PROGRAM	1:00 to 1:30	COOK ☐
Frozen Pizza Rolls	6 oz.	1	COOKING PROGRAM	3:00	DEFROST ☐
		2	COOKING PROGRAM	1:00	HOLD ☐
		3	COOKING PROGRAM	1:00 to 1:30	COOK ☐
Frozen Snack Pizzas	7 to 8 oz.	1	COOKING PROGRAM	2:00	DEFROST ☐
		2	COOKING PROGRAM	1:00	HOLD ☐
		3	COOKING PROGRAM	1:00	COOK ☐

General Instructions for Cooking Frozen Appetizers and Snacks Convenience Foods

1. Place appetizers or snacks on cooking grill. Cover with paper towel.

2. Defrost, hold, and cook, according to timings in chart. Cook until hot.

FROZEN PIZZA CHART

PIZZA SIZE	1ST TIME	1ST SETTING	2ND TIME	2ND SETTING
5-1/3 oz. (Snack Size Pizza)	1-1/2 min.	DEFROST	1 to 2 min.	FULL POWER
9 oz. (7 to 8-inch round pizza)	3 min.	DEFROST	1 to 2 min.	FULL POWER
13-1/2 oz. (10" round pizza)	3 min.	DEFROST	2 to 2-1/2 min.	FULL POWER
18 oz. (7 x 8-inch Pan Style Pizza)	4 min.	DEFROST	2-1/2 to 4 min.	FULL POWER

General Instructions for Preparing Frozen Pizza

1. Place pizza on paper plate or plastic rack.
2. Thaw according to time and setting on chart.
3. Preheat large browning skillet or grill, empty, according to manufacturer's instructions. Place pizza firmly against bottom of browning skillet for maximum heat contact.
4. Heat, according to 2nd time and setting on chart.

Caramel Popcorn Balls

Yield: 12 balls

1 (14 oz.) pkg. caramels
3 tablespoons water
1 tablespoon butter or margarine

2-1/2 to 3 quarts popped popcorn, salted*

1. Combine caramels, water and butter in 1-quart casserole. Heat in Radarange Oven on Cookmatic Level 8 (MEDIUM HIGH) for 4 to 5 minutes, or until melted. Stir halfway through heating.
2. Pour over popcorn, tossing lightly to coat evenly. Grease or moisten hands, and form mixture into balls.

   *MICRO-TIP: Ordinary popcorn should only be popped in the Radarange Microwave Oven in the specially designed Radarange Microwave Oven Popcorn Popper. Special popcorn in bags, designed and labeled **for microwave only** may also be used.

Hot Crab Meat Canapes

Yield: 25 canapes

6 ozs. crab meat, shredded
1 cup mayonnaise
1 teaspoon lemon juice

1 egg white

Melba toast rounds

1. Combine crab meat with mayonnaise in small mixing bowl. Season with lemon juice.
2. Beat egg white until stiff but not dry. Fold into crab meat mixture.
3. Place approximately 1 teaspoon of crab mixture on each Melba toast round. Arrange 12 on serving dish.
4. Cook in Radarange Oven on FULL POWER for 45 to 60 seconds, or until heated through. Serve immediately. Repeate with remaining canapes.

Bacon-Wrapped Olives

Yield: 12 appetizers

3 slices bacon
12 pimento-stuffed olives,
   drained

1. Cut bacon into quarters. Wrap each piece around one olive. Secure each with toothpick. Place on dish or cooking grill. Cover with paper towel.
2. Cook in Radarange Oven, covered, on FULL POWER for 2 to 2-1/2 minutes, or until bacon is crisp and lightly browned. Serve hot.

MICRO-TIP: Black pitted olives may be substituted for pimento-stuffed olives.

Chinese Hors D'Oeuvres

Yield: 3 dozen appetizers

12 bacon strips
1 (8 oz.) can water chestnuts,
   halved

Teriyaki sauce

1. Cut each bacon strip in thirds. Wrap each water chestnut with bacon strip. Secure each with toothpick.
2. Dip in teriyaki sauce. Arrange 12 in circle on cooking grill. Cover with paper towel.
3. Cook in Radarange Oven, covered, on FULL POWER for 3 to 5 minutes, or until bacon is crisp. Repeat with remaining appetizers.

MICRO-TIP: Dip in additional teriyaki sauce or in heated "Sweet-Sour Sauce", on page 268, when serving.

Tater Wrap-Ups

Yield: 10 appetizers

5 slices bacon
10 Tater Tots®, frozen

1. Cut bacon slices in half. Cook in Radarange Oven on FULL POWER for 2 to 2-1/2 minutes, or until partially cooked. Wrap each bacon piece around Tater Tot® and secure with toothpick.
2. Place on cooking grill, or on plate lined with paper towel. Cover with paper towel. Cook in Radarange Oven, covered, on FULL POWER for 2 minutes, or until heated through.

MICRO-TIP: This appetizer is good served with "Hot Catsup Sauce", on page 268.

Glazed Bacon

Yield: 14 appetizers

1/2 lb. bacon
1/2 to 1 cup brown sugar, firmly
   packed

1. Cut each slice bacon in half. Spread brown sugar on waxed paper or plate. Lay each piece bacon on brown sugar. Pat firmly to coat sides with sugar.
2. Arrange bacon on cooking grill. Cover with waxed paper. Cook in Radarange Oven, covered, on FULL POWER for 4-1/2 to 5 minutes, or until bacon is crisp, as desired. Cool on brown paper bag to absorb grease. Bacon will stick to most other types of paper.

Hot Roquefort Canapes

Yield: 2-1/2 to 3 dozen appetizers

1 (3 oz.) pkg. cream cheese
1/4 cup Roquefort cheese,
   crumbled
1/4 cup pecans, finely chopped
1/2 teaspoon Worcestershire sauce
Dash Tabasco sauce
Butter crackers

1. Blend together first 5 ingredients. Spread mixture on crackers, using about 1 teaspoon for each cracker. Arrange 12 crackers in circle on piece of waxed paper on paper plate in Radarange Oven.

2. Heat in Radarange Oven on Cookmatic Level 5 (SLO COOK) for 45 to 60 seconds, or until cheese spread begins to bubble. Serve warm. Repeat with remaining appetizers.

Coquilles

Yield: 6 to 8 servings

1 lb. scallops, fresh or frozen,
and defrosted

1 lb. fresh mushrooms
2 tablespoons butter or margarine
2 tablespoons lemon juice

1 cup dry white wine**
1/4 teaspoon savory
1 bay leaf
1/2 teaspoon salt
1/8 teaspoon pepper

3 tablespoons butter or margarine
3 tablespoons all-purpose flour
1 cup light cream

1/2 cup toasted bread crumbs
Paprika

1. If large, cut scallops into fourths. Set aside.

2. Wash, drain and slice mushrooms. Place butter in 1-1/2-quart casserole. Heat in Radarange Oven on FULL POWER for 30 to 45 seconds, or until melted. Stir in lemon juice. Add mushrooms and toss to coat. Cook in Radarange Oven, covered, on Cookmatic Level 8 (MEDIUM HIGH) for 4 minutes. Stir halfway through cooking time. Drain.

3. Combine wine, savory, bay leaf, salt and pepper in 1-1/2-quart casserole. Add scallops. Cook in Radarange Oven, covered, on FULL POWER for 3 minutes. Remove bay leaf. Drain, reserving 1 cup of liquid.

4. Place butter in 2-quart casserole. Heat in Radarange Oven on FULL POWER for 45 seconds, or until melted. Blend in flour until smooth. Gradually stir in reserved liquid, and then cream. Cook in Radarange Oven on FULL POWER for 3 to 4 minutes, or until thickened. Stir occasionally during cooking.

5. Stir scallops and mushrooms into sauce. Cook in Radarange Oven on Cookmatic Level 8 (MEDIUM HIGH) for 4 to 5 minutes, or until temperature of 150°F is reached.* Stir halfway through cooking time.

6. Spoon into sea shells or ramekins to serve. Garnish with sprinkling of bread crumbs and paprika, as desired.

   MICRO-TIPS:

   *Use the Temperature-Hold to maintain 150° F until ready to serve. For best results, stir occasionally.

   **If salted cooking wine is used, omit salt from recipe.

Escargot

Yield: 1 to 1-1/2 dozen

1/2 cup butter or margarine
1/2 teaspoon instant, minced garlic
1 teaspoon parsley flakes

1 (4-1/2 oz.) can snails
White wine
Snail shells

1. Place butter in 1-cup glass measure. Heat in Radarange Oven on FULL POWER for about 1 to 1-1/2 minutes, or until melted. Add garlic and parsley flakes.

2. Place snails in shells. Half-fill shells with seasoned butter. Add 1/2 teaspoon white wine to each shell. Place 6 snails on plate. Cover loosely with plastic wrap.

3. Cook in Radarange Oven, covered, on Cookmatic Level 6 (ROAST) for 45 to 60 seconds, or until snails are heated. Be careful not to overcook. Repeat with remaining snails.

Clams-In-The-Shell

Yield: 4 appetizers

4 fresh clams

1. Wash and scrub clams with brush in cold water. Arrange in circle in 9-inch glass pie plate. Cover with plastic wrap.
2. Cook in Radarange Oven, covered, on FULL POWER for 2-1/2 to 4 minutes, or until clams have relaxed and opened.

MICRO-TIP: Delicious served with butter sauce.

Oysters Casino

Yield: 1 dozen appetizers

2 dozen oysters, freshly opened

3 slices bacon, cooked and crumbled
1/4 cup seasoned bread crumbs
2 tablespoons onion, minced
2 tablespoons green pepper, minced
2 tablespoons parsley, minced
2 tablespoons celery, minced
1 tablespoon butter or margarine, melted
1 teaspoon Worcestershire sauce
Dash Tabasco sauce

Paprika

1. Place 2 oysters in deep half of one shell. Repeat to fill 12 shells. Arrange filled shells on plastic tray or paper plate.
2. Combine remaining ingredients, except paprika. Spoon over oysters.
3. Cook in Radarange Oven on FULL POWER for 3 to 4 minutes, or until oysters are heated through. Sprinkle with paprika, as desired. Serve hot.

MICRO-TIP: Custard cups may be substituted for oyster shells. Place 2 oysters in each custard cup. Cover with remaining ingredients. Arrange 6 custard cups in circular arrangement in Radarange Oven. Cook in Radarange Oven on FULL POWER for about 2 minutes, or until oysters are heated through. Repeat with remaining oysters.

Oyster Cracker Snax

Yield: 6 cups

1 cup butter or margarine
1-1/2 teaspoons celery salt
1-1/2 teaspoons garlic salt
1-1/2 teaspoons onion salt
1 teaspoon paprika
1/2 cup grated Parmesan cheese

1 (10 oz.) pkg. oyster crackers (6 cups)

1. Place butter in 2-quart utility dish. Heat in Radarange Oven on FULL POWER for 1 minute to 1 minute 15 seconds, or until melted. Blend in seasonings and cheese.
2. Stir in crackers. Toss until well-coated.
3. Heat in Radarange Oven on FULL POWER for 3 to 3-1/2 minutes, or until heated through. Stir halfway through cooking time. Cool, and store in plastic bag or airtight container.

Savory Sausage Canapes

Yield: 16 appetizers

1/2 lb. pork sausage, country-style
1/4 cup dairy sour cream
1 tablespoon horseradish
2 teaspoons fresh or frozen chives

4 slices pumpernickel or rye bread, toasted
Paprika

1. Place sausage in 1-quart casserole. Cook in Radarange Oven on FULL POWER for 2 minutes, or until no longer pink. Stir halfway through cooking time. Drain. Stir in sour cream, horseradish and chives.

2. Cut toast into fourths. Spread sausage mixture on toast. Sprinkle with paprika, as desired. Arrange 8 on plastic rack, over 2-quart utility dish or on plate lined with paper towel.

3. Heat in Radarange Oven on FULL POWER for 30 to 45 seconds, or until heated through. Repeat with remaining appetizers.

Calico Crackers

Yield: 32 to 36 appetizers

1 (3 oz.) pkg. cream cheese
1 egg
1 teaspoon lemon juice
1 teaspoon frozen chives
Dash pepper
2/3 cup Cheddar cheese, shredded
1/4 cup bacon bits

32 to 36 crackers

1. Beat cream cheese, egg, lemon juice, chives and pepper until well-mixed. Stir in Cheddar cheese and bacon bits. Chill 1/2 hour.

2. Top each cracker with 1 teaspoon cheese mixture. Place 9 in circle on paper plate. Heat in Radarange Oven on Cookmatic Level 5 (SLO COOK) for 30 to 45 seconds, or until cheese is just beginning to melt. Repeat with remaining appetizers.

Nachos

Yield: 3-1/2 dozen appetizers

1 (1 lb.) can refried beans, or 1 (10-1/2 oz.) can jalapeño bean dip
1 (5-1/2 oz.) pkg. tortilla chips
4 ozs. Cheddar cheese, shredded
14 pimento-stuffed olives, sliced in thirds

1. Spread 1 teaspoon refried beans or bean dip on each tortilla chip. Top with one teaspoon cheese and one thin slice of olive. Place 8 in circle on paper plate.

2. Heat in Radarange Oven on Cookmatic Level 5 (SLO COOK) for 30 to 45 seconds, or until cheese is melted. Serve warm. Repeat with remaining appetizers.

Bacon-Cheese Puffs

Yield: 30 appetizers

1 (8 oz.) pkg. cream cheese, softened
1 egg yolk
1 teaspoon instant, minced onion
1 teaspoon baking powder
2-1/2 tablespoons imitation bacon pieces

30 round butter crackers

1. Combine cream cheese, egg yolk, onion and baking powder in large mixing bowl. Beat until smooth and blended.

2. Add bacon pieces. Blend well.

3. Place 6 crackers in circle on paper plate. Top each cracker with 1 teaspoon of cheese mixture. Heat in Radarange Oven on Cookmatic Level 6 (ROAST) for 25 to 30 seconds, or until slightly risen. Serve hot.

MICRO-TIP: Bacon-cheese mixture may be covered and stored in refrigerator until ready to serve. Slightly increase heating time, due to refrigerator temperature.

Hot Herbed Pretzels

Yield: 2 cups

2 tablespoons butter or margarine

1/2 teaspoon tarragon, crumbled
2 teaspoons parsley flakes
1/4 teaspoon celery salt
1/4 teaspoon onion powder
2 cups pretzels

1. Place butter in 2-quart utility dish. Heat in Radarange Oven on FULL POWER for 30 to 40 seconds, or until melted.
2. Blend in seasonings. Add pretzels and toss to coat.
3. Heat in Radarange Oven on FULL POWER for 1-1/2 minutes, or until heated through. Stir halfway through cooking time.

Nibbles Snack

Yield: Approximately 2 to 2-1/2 quarts

3/4 cup butter or margarine
2 teaspoons garlic salt
2 teaspoons onion salt
2 teaspoons celery salt
3 tablespoons Worcestershire sauce

1 10 oz. box thin pretzel sticks
1 (6-3/4 oz.) can cocktail peanuts
1 (6-3/4 oz.) can mixed nuts or cashews
2 cups toasted wheat cereal squares
2 cups toasted rice cereal squares
2 cups round toasted oat cereal

1. Place butter in 3-quart casserole. Heat in Radarange Oven on FULL POWER for 1 minute to 1 minute 15 seconds, or until melted. Add salts and Worcestershire sauce. Mix well.
2. Stir in remaining ingredients. Toss until well-coated.
3. Heat in Radarange Oven on FULL POWER for 6 to 7 minutes, or until uniformly heated. Mix thoroughly halfway through cooking time. Cool. Store in airtight plastic or tin container.

Teriyaki Strips

Yield: 30 to 36 appetizers

1 lb. sirloin steak, 1/4 to 1/2-inch thick

1/2 teaspoon ginger
1/2 cup bottled teriyaki sauce
1/4 cup dry sherry

1. Cut beef into 30 to 36 thin strips. Spread in 2-quart utility dish.
2. Combine ginger, sauce and sherry. Pour over meat strips. Refrigerate for 1 hour, basting several times. Drain.
3. Thread meat strips on 8 wooden skewers. Arrange 4 skewers on cooking grill. Cook in Radarange Oven on FULL POWER for 2 minutes, or until steak is cooked, as desired. Turn skewers over halfway through cooking time. Repeat with remaining meat. Remove meat from skewers to serve.

MICRO-TIP: Serve hot with buttered slices of party rye bread.

Stuffed Mushrooms

Yield: 2 to 2-1/2 dozen appetizers

1 lb. large fresh mushrooms of uniform size

1/4 lb. ground beef
1 clove garlic, minced
1/4 cup onion, minced
1 tablespoon parsley, finely chopped
1 teaspoon bottled browning sauce
1/2 teaspoon salt

1/4 cup dairy sour cream

2 tablespoons lemon juice

1. Remove stems from mushrooms. Chop stems.

2. Combine chopped mushroom stems, ground beef, garlic, onion, parsley, bottled browning sauce and salt in 1-quart casserole.

3. Cook in Radarange Oven on Cookmatic Level 8 (MEDIUM HIGH) for 2-1/2 to 3 minutes, or until beef is no longer pink. Stir halfway through cooking time. Drain. Stir in sour cream.

4. Dip each mushroom cap in lemon juice and fill with meat mixture. Arrange 10 to 12 mushrooms on plate.

5. Bake in Radarange Oven on Cookmatic Level 8 (MEDIUM HIGH) for 2-1/2 to 3 minutes, or until hot. Serve immediately. Repeat with remaining mushrooms.

Hawaiian Ham Balls

Yield: 36 appetizers

1/2 lb. ground ham
3/4 lb. ground pork sausage
1 cup bread crumbs
1 egg
1/2 cup milk
2 teaspoons fresh or frozen chives
1/4 teaspoon garlic powder
Dash salt
Dash pepper

1 (15-1/4 oz.) can pineapple chunks, with liquid
3/4 cup brown sugar, firmly packed
1/2 teaspoon dry mustard
1/8 teaspoon instant, minced onion
Salt
Pepper

1 tablespoon cornstarch
2 tablespoons water

1. Combine meats, crumbs, egg, milk, chives and garlic powder. Season with salt and pepper, as desired. Form into 1-inch diameter meat balls.

2. Place on cooking grill. Cook in Radarange Oven on FULL POWER for 5 minutes.

3. Combine pineapple and remaining ingredients. Season with salt and pepper, as desired. Pour over meat balls in 2-1/2 to 3-quart casserole. Cover with waxed paper. Cook in Radarange Oven, covered, on FULL POWER for 4 minutes, or until simmering.

4. Blend together cornstarch and water. Add to sauce. Cook in Radarange Oven on FULL POWER for 3 minutes, or until sauce is thickened. Stir halfway through cooking time.

MICRO-TIP: May be served in chafing dish with toothpicks, or serve as a main dish over rice.

Sweet-Sour Meat Balls

Yield: 20 to 24 meat balls

1 onion, finely chopped
3/4 teaspoon seasoned salt
1 (10-3/4 oz.) can tomato soup
3 tablespoons lemon juice
1/4 cup brown sugar, firmly packed

1 lb. ground beef

1 (13-1/4 oz.) can pineapple chunks, drained

1. Combine onion, salt, soup, lemon juice and brown sugar in 9 x 9 x 2-inch glass dish. Cook in Radarange Oven on FULL POWER for 3 to 5 minutes, or until simmering. Stir halfway through cooking time.

2. Roll ground beef into 1-inch diameter meat balls. Place meat balls in above sauce. Spoon some sauce over meat balls. Cook in Radarange Oven on FULL POWER for 6 to 7 minutes, or until meat is cooked through.

3. Stir in pineapple. Heat in Radarange Oven on FULL POWER for 1 minute. Serve with toothpicks.

MICRO-TIP: These meat balls are also good served as main dish. Accompany with cooked rice or whipped potatoes, as desired.

Spicy Meat Ball Appetizers

Yield: 30 meat balls

1 lb. ground beef
1/2 cup dry bread crumbs
1/2 cup onion, chopped
1 egg
2 tablespoons milk
1 teaspoon garlic salt
1/2 teaspoon parsley flakes
1/2 teaspoon salt
1/4 teaspoon pepper

SAUCE
3/4 cup hickory flavored barbecue sauce
1/2 cup tomato sauce
1 teaspoon Worcestershire sauce
1/4 teaspoon garlic salt
1/4 teaspoon onion salt

1. Combine all ingredients, except for sauce, and form into 1-1/2-inch diameter meat balls.

2. Place meat balls on cooking grill or in 2-quart dish. Cook in Radarange Oven on FULL POWER for 5 to 7 minutes, or until beef is no longer pink. Drain excess grease.

3. While meat balls are cooking, prepare sauce. Place cooked meat balls in 2-quart utility dish and cover with sauce. Cook in Radarange Oven on Cookmatic Level 3 (SIMMER) for 20 minutes. Stir once during cooking time.

MICRO-TIPS:

• May be served in chafing dish with toothpicks.

• May be served as a main dish as filling for hot dog buns.

Frank Kabobs

Yield: 4 appetizers

8 cocktail frankfurters or sausages*
8 pimento-stuffed olives
8 pineapple chunks

4 teaspoons vegetable oil
2 teaspoons soy sauce
2 teaspoons pineapple juice
2 teaspoons brown sugar

1. Cut each frankfurter in half. Thread onto 4 wooden skewers, alternating with olives and pineapple.

2. Combine oil, soy sauce, pineapple juice and brown sugar. Brush mixture on appetizers.

3. Lay kabobs across 2-quart glass utility dish. Cook in Radarange Oven on FULL POWER for 1-1/2 to 2 minutes. Turn kabobs over. Baste with remaining sauce. Cook in Radarange Oven on FULL POWER for 2 minutes, or until cooked as desired. Cook 1 additional minute if sausage is used.

MICRO-TIPS:

*Regular-size frankfurters or sausages may be used. Cut in quarters instead of halves.

*Substitute luncheon meat for frankfurters. Cook for same amount of cooking time as for frankfurters.

Hot Cheesy Clam Dip

Yield: 2 cups dip

1/4 large green pepper, finely chopped*
1/2 bunch green onions, minced
2 (5 oz. each) jars sharp pasteurized process cheese spread
1 (7 oz.) can clams, drained, minced
2 to 4 dashes Tabasco sauce
1/8 teaspoon garlic powder

1. Combine all ingredients in 1-1/2-quart casserole.

2. Heat in Radarange Oven, uncovered, on Cookmatic Level 5 (SLO COOK) for about 3 to 4 minutes, or until cheese is melted. Stir halfway through cooking time.

MICRO-TIPS:

•May be served very hot with crisp corn chips for dippers.

*1/4 cup celery may be substituted for green pepper.

Prepare-Ahead Crab Balls

Yield: 18 appetizers

1 (6-1/2 or 7 oz.) can crab meat, drained
1 egg
1/3 cup dry bread crumbs
3 tablespoons dairy sour cream
2 tablespoons onion, finely chopped
1 teaspoon prepared horseradish

3 tablespoons cornflake crumbs

1. Combine all ingredients except cornflake crumbs. Form mixture into 18, 1-inch diameter balls.

2. Coat each ball with crumbs. Place in single layer in shallow dish. Freeze until firm. Store in heavy plastic bag.

3. Arrange frozen balls on glass plate. Cook in Radarange Oven on FULL POWER for 3 to 3-1/2 minutes, or until heated through.

Shrimp Dip

Yield: 2-1/4 cups dip

1 (8 oz.) pkg. cream cheese
1 (10-3/4 oz.) can cream of
  shrimp soup
4 green onions, sliced

1. Place cream cheese in 1-quart casserole. Heat in Radarange Oven on Cookmatic Level 5 (SLO COOK) for 2-1/2 to 3 minutes, or until melted. Stir halfway through melting. Stir in soup and onions.

2. Heat in Radarange Oven on Cookmatic Level 5 (SLO COOK) for 2-1/2 to 3 minutes, or until heated through. Stir halfway through cooking time.

   MICRO-TIP: Serve warm with crackers or fresh vegetables.

Hot Crab Dip

Yield: 2 cups dip

1 (8 oz.) pkg. cream cheese
1 tablespoon milk
1 teaspoon Worcestershire sauce

1 (5-1/2 oz.) can crab meat, drained
2 tablespoons chives, chopped
1/8 teaspoon onion salt
Dash cayenne pepper

1. Blend cheese, milk and Worcestershire sauce with electric mixer in small bowl.

2. Stir in remaining ingredients. Pour into 1-quart casserole.

3. Cook in Radarange Oven on Cookmatic Level 5 (SLO COOK) for 3 to 4 minutes, or until hot. Stir halfway through cooking time. Serve while warm.

   MICRO-TIP: Serve as dip with crackers or fresh vegetables.

Fresh Mushroom Dip

Yield: 2 cups dip

2 cups fresh mushrooms, chopped
1/2 cup onion, chopped
2 tablespoons butter or margarine, melted

1/4 cup all-purpose flour
3/4 cup heavy cream
1 tablespoon parsley flakes
1/2 teaspoon salt
Dash cayenne pepper

1. Place mushrooms and onions in butter in 1-quart bowl. Cook in Radarange Oven on Cookmatic Level 8 (MEDIUM HIGH) for 2 to 3 minutes, or until onion is tender.

2. Stir in flour, blending well. Gradually stir in cream and remaining ingredients.

3. Cook in Radarange Oven on Cookmatic Level 8 (MEDIUM HIGH) for 2 to 3 minutes, or until thickened. Stir once or twice during cooking time.

   MICRO-TIP: Serve with crisp crackers or celery. If desired, let dip cool and then drop by rounded teaspoons onto crackers. Heat 12 to 15 crackers on plate in Radarange Oven on Cookmatic Level 8 (MEDIUM HIGH) for 1-1/2 to 2 minutes.

Ham Nibbles

Yield: 20 appetizers

1 cup cooked ham, ground or
  minced
3 tablespoons mayonnaise
2 teaspoons prepared mustard

Melba toast rounds
Sweet pickle relish

1. Mix together ham, mayonnaise and mustard.

2. Spread mixture on toast rounds. Top with sweet pickle relish, as desired.

3. Place 10 "Nibbles" on plate. Heat in Radarange Oven on FULL POWER for 45 to 60 seconds. Serve hot.

Swiss Cheese Fondue

Yield: 4 servings

1-1/2 cups Swiss cheese, shredded
1 tablespoon cornstarch
1/2 teaspoon dry mustard
1/2 teaspoon garlic powder
1/4 teaspoon salt
1/4 teaspoon pepper

1 cup beer

1. Combine cheese, cornstarch and spices.

2. Place beer in 1-quart casserole. Heat in Radarange Oven on FULL POWER for 3 minutes.

3. Add cheese mixture gradually to hot beer, stirring constantly with wire whip until smooth.

4. If necessary, heat in Radarange Oven on Cookmatic Level 5 (SLO COOK) for about 2 minutes, or until cheese is completely melted.

MICRO-TIP: May be served with French bread cubes, if desired.

Pizza Fondue

Yield: 1 quart

1 lb. ground beef
2/3 cup onion, chopped

3 (8 oz. each) cans pizza sauce with cheese
1 tablespoon cornstarch
3/4 teaspoon leaf oregano
1/4 teaspoon garlic powder

1 cup Mozzarella cheese, shredded
2 (5 oz. each) jars sharp pasteurized process cheese spread
French bread cubes or chips

1. Place meat and onion in 2-quart casserole. Cook in Radarange Oven on FULL POWER for 3 to 4 minutes, or until meat is no longer pink. Break meat apart with fork during cooking time. Drain any fat.

2. Blend together sauce, cornstarch, oregano and garlic powder. Add to meat mixture. Cook in Radarange Oven on Cookmatic Level 6 (ROAST) for 13 to 15 minutes, or until bubbling and thickened.

3. Add cheeses by thirds, stirring well. Heat in Radarange Oven on Cookmatic Level 6 (ROAST) for 7 to 8 minutes, or until cheese melts and is no longer stringy. Stir occasionally. Serve hot with French bread cubes or chips.

MICRO-TIP: Ground sausage may be substituted for beef. This recipe may also be used for a lunch when served over toasted English muffins or hamburger buns.

Party Tuna Balls

Yield: 12 to 18 appetizers

1 (6 or 7 oz.) can tuna, drained and flaked
1 egg, beaten
1 cup bread crumbs
2 tablespoons parsley, snipped
1/4 cup onion, finely chopped
1/2 (10-1/2 oz.) can condensed consommé
1/4 cup mayonnaise
1 tablespoon prepared mustard
1 teaspoon poultry seasoning

1 cup corn flake crumbs

1. Combine all ingredients, except corn flake crumbs. Chill.

2. Form mixture into 1-inch diameter balls. Roll in corn flake crumbs. Arrange 12 balls in circle on sheet of waxed paper on paper plate.

3. Heat in Radarange Oven on FULL POWER for 1-1/2 to 2 minutes, or until very hot. Serve immediately.

MICRO-TIP: Tuna balls may be prepared ahead and frozen. In that case, defrost 12 balls in Radarange Oven on FULL POWER for 4 to 4-1/2 minutes.

Beverages can be quickly heated or reheated in the Radarange Oven. Individual servings can be heated directly in cups or mugs, so you avoid washing sticky pans. Handles of cups and mugs stay cool, even though the beverage gets hot. Larger quantities of a beverage can be heated in a serving pitcher, if the pitcher is not too tall, and if it is Radarange Oven-safe. Check the utensil tests in the Introduction chapter to see how you can determine whether your cups, mugs or pitchers are safe for Radarange Oven use. Remember that styrofoam cups and other "disposable" cups can also be used. Be sure that any cups used are suitable for hot beverages. Avoid using mugs or cups with glued-on handles.

Beverages can be quickly reheated. Save leftover coffee in a glass measure or serving cup, and refrigerate. Later, reheat it in the Radarange Oven. The coffee will taste as if it has just been freshly brewed! There's no need to keep your coffee pot plugged in for an entire day. **Remember, however, to always vigorously stir a beverage before it is reheated.**

Many beverages are quickly prepared using FULL POWER. Others, however, contain "special" or "delicate" ingredients which are better heated using a lower Cookmatic Level setting. Milk tends to boil over easily, and a lower setting helps to avoid boil-overs. Since the alcohol in wine, rum or sherry will evaporate if allowed to boil, which is more likely to happen when using FULL POWER, most of the recipes for punches that include these ingredients require a lower setting.

Be sure to read the general hints before preparing beverages in your Radarange Oven. In this chapter, "heating" refers to the heating of a beverage for the first time. "Reheating" means to heat a beverage, **again,** after it has already been **heated.**

General Hints for Heating Beverages

1. If you're in a hurry, you may wish to use hot tap water when heating water to make instant coffee, tea, or other mixes. Hot tap water will boil faster than cold.
2. Refrigerator-temperature beverages will require a longer heating or reheating time than room-temperature beverages. Adjust times accordingly. Times for heating milk are based upon refrigerator temperature.
3. When heating or reheating a beverage in 3 or more serving cups, arrange the cups in a circle.
4. If heating 4 or more cups of a beverage at one time, you may wish to heat the beverage in a large serving bowl, glass measure, or pitcher, rather than in individual cups or mugs. Be sure that bowls or pitchers contain no metal trim. Check to see whether the container is too tall before pouring in the beverage. By using one container for a beverage, you eliminate the fuss of placing and removing several cups in and out of the Radarange Oven. Use a ladle to serve punch or other beverages from a large bowl. Try thawing frozen fruit juice in a serving pitcher.
5. To avoid boil-overs, only fill a cup 2/3 to 3/4 full. Most coffee cups are 6-ounce cups. Some larger mugs may hold 8 ounces. Be sure to alter heating times for different sizes of cups, accordingly.
6. Always stir a beverage vigorously before reheating.
7. Milk should not be allowed to boil. Heat milk until it is just warmed. Since milk will boil over easily, use Cookmatic Level 8 (MEDIUM HIGH) when heating milk or a beverage containing milk. Add a marshmallow to a cup of hot chocolate halfway through the heating time, if desired, and it will melt just the right amount.
8. When reheating coffee and tea, for the best taste, do not allow them to boil. Most reheated beverages taste better when reheated to **almost** boiling. When preparing a beverage and heating it for the first time, it should be heated until it is approximately 190° F, or below boiling. Use the Temperature-Control to stop the Radarange Oven at 190° F.
9. Always add instant coffee or tea to hot water to avoid a bitter flavor and boil-overs. Water will not boil over as easily as pre-mixed coffee and tea.
10. Some persons prefer their beverage to be served at a warmer or cooler temperature. Beverages can be heated in the Radarange Oven, as desired, by in-

Mulled Wine Punch (page 62)

creasing or decreasing heating times, accordingly.
11. When converting your own favorite beverage recipes to Radarange Oven timings, select a similar recipe from this section, and use the setting and time given as a guide. Usually 1 cup of any beverage will heat in 1 to 1-1/2 minutes on FULL POWER, with the exception of beverages containing "special" or "delicate" ingredients, which should be heated on Cookmatic Level 8 (MEDIUM HIGH) for 1-1/2 to 2 minutes per cup.

FROZEN BEVERAGE CHART

TYPE OF BEVERAGE	CARTON OR CAN SIZE	UTENSIL*	HEATING TIME	SETTING	SPECIAL INSTRUCTIONS
Frozen Juice Concentrate	6 oz. can	1-quart casserole or glass measure	35 to 40 sec.	FULL POWER	Place frozen juice concentrate in utensil. Heat, according to time and setting, or until thawed.
	12 oz. can	2-quart casserole or glass measure	1 to 1-1/2 min.	FULL POWER	
	16 oz. can	2-1/2-quart casserole	2 to 2-1/2 min.	FULL POWER	
Frozen Non-Dairy Creamer	1 pint carton	Thaw in carton	9 to 11 min.	DEFROST	Open carton. Heat, according to time and setting, or until thawed. Shake or stir occasionally during heating.

*Frozen juice concentrate can be placed directly in the serving pitcher and heated in the Radarange Oven. Be certain the pitcher is Radarange Oven-safe and fits inside the Radarange Oven.

Hot Egg Nog

Yield: 4 servings

1 quart milk

4 egg yolks
1/3 cup sugar
1/4 teaspoon cinnamon
1/4 teaspoon nutmeg
1/4 teaspoon vanilla

1. Place milk in 2-quart casserole. Heat in Radarange Oven, covered, on Cookmatic Level 8 (MEDIUM HIGH) for 8 to 9 minutes, or until temperature of 160° F is reached.* Do not boil.

2. Beat egg yolks lightly, with sugar, spices and vanilla. Stir one cup of hot milk into egg mixture, and then gradually blend all of egg mixture into milk.

3. Heat in Radarange Oven, covered, on Cookmatic Level 8 (MEDIUM HIGH) for 2 to 3 minutes, or until warmed. Stir halfway through cooking time.

MICRO-TIPS:
* Use Automatic Temperature Control System to cook to 160° F, if your Radarange Oven has this feature.

• For maximum blending of flavors, heat on Cookmatic Level 3 (SIMMER) for 10 minutes in step #3, rather than on Cookmatic Level 8 (MEDIUM HIGH) for 5 to 6 minutes.

French Chocolate

Yield: 4 servings

3 tablespoons chocolate syrup
2 tablespoons light corn syrup
1-1/2 tablespoons water
1/4 teaspoon vanilla

1/2 cup whipping cream, chilled

2 cups milk

1. Combine syrups, water and vanilla. Heat in Radarange Oven on FULL POWER for 30 seconds, or until heated through.

2. In chilled bowl, beat cream until stiff, adding chocolate mixture gradually. Beat until mixture forms mounds when dropped from spoon.

3. Place milk in 1-quart glass measure. Heat in Radarange Oven on Cookmatic Level 8 (MEDIUM HIGH) for 2 to 3 minutes, or until warmed. Do not boil. Fill serving cups half-full of cream mixture. Finish filling cups with warm milk. Stir before serving.

Mexican Chocolate

Yield: 1 serving

1 tablespoon chocolate syrup
1/2 teaspoon instant coffee
1 cup milk
1 tablespoon cream (optional)
1/4 teaspoon vanilla
1/4 teaspoon cinnamon

1. Combine all ingredients in large mug or 2-cup measure.

2. Heat in Radarange Oven on Cookmatic Level 8 (MEDIUM HIGH) for 2 to 3 minutes, or until warmed, and temperature of 160° F is reached. Stir halfway through cooking time. Do not boil. Serve immediately.

Hot Chocolate Ukrainian Style

Yield: 5 servings

1 (1 oz.) square unsweetened chocolate
1/4 cup sugar
1/8 teaspoon salt
1-1/4 cups boiling water
3/4 cup milk
3/4 cup light cream

1 teaspoon vanilla
2 cups coffee, freshly brewed

1. Place chocolate in 2-quart casserole. Heat in Radarange Oven on Cookmatic Level 6 (ROAST) for 2 minutes, or until melted.

2. Stir in sugar, salt and water. Heat in Radarange Oven on FULL POWER for 2 minutes.

3. Add milk and light cream. Stir. Heat in Radarange Oven on Cookmatic Level 8 (MEDIUM HIGH) for 4 to 6 minutes, or until warmed.

4. Mix in vanilla and coffee. Heat in Radarange Oven on FULL POWER for 2 minutes, or until warmed, and temperature of 160° F is reached.

Peppermint Milk Shake

Yield: 2 to 3 servings

2 cups milk
1/4 cup peppermint candy, crushed

3 scoops ice cream

1. Combine milk and crushed candy in 1-quart casserole. Cook in Radarange Oven on Cookmatic Level 8 (MEDIUM HIGH) for 2 to 2-1/2 minutes, or until candy is dissolved. Stir halfway through cooking time. Chill.

2. Add ice cream to peppermint mixture and mix in blender until frothy.

MICRO-TIP: To make a malt, add 3/4 cup malted milk powder with the ice cream.

Hot Chocolate

Yield: 1 serving

3/4 cup milk
1 tablespoon chocolate syrup

1. Pour milk into ceramic or glass mug. Stir in chocolate syrup.

2. Heat in Radarange Oven on Cookmatic Level 8 (MEDIUM HIGH) for 1 minute, 45 seconds, or until warmed, and temperature of 160° F is reached.

Hot Chocolate Malted

Yield: 1 serving

1 cup milk
2 tablespoons chocolate syrup
1 tablespoon malted milk powder

1. Pour milk into ceramic or glass mug. Stir in chocolate syrup and malted milk powder.

2. Heat in Radarange Oven on Cookmatic Level 8 (MEDIUM HIGH) for 2 minutes, or until warmed, and temperature of 160° F is reached.

MICRO-TIP: Don't forget to use the utensil test in the Introduction chapter to determine whether mugs are Radarange Oven-safe.

Cocoa

Yield: 4 servings

1/4 cup warm water
3 tablespoons sugar
2-1/2 tablespoons cocoa

3 cups milk
Dash salt

1. Place cocoa, sugar and water in 1-1/2-quart casserole. Heat in Radarange Oven on FULL POWER for 30 to 60 seconds, or until mixture boils.

2. Stir in milk and salt. Heat in Radarange Oven on Cookmatic Level 8 (MEDIUM HIGH) for 8 to 9 minutes, or until warmed, and temperature of 160° F is reached.

Instant Hot Chocolate Mix

Yield: 1 gallon dry mix

1-1/2 cups (or 6 oz. jar) powdered non-dairy coffee creamer
10-2/3 cups non-fat dry milk (enough to make 8 quarts milk)
1/2 cup confectioners' sugar
1 lb. instant cocoa mix

Water

1. Combine all ingredients, except water, in large mixing bowl. (Mix may be stored in air-tight 1-gallon container.)

2. Fill serving mug half-full of mixture. Finish filling with water. Stir to blend. Heat in Radarange Oven on Cookmatic Level 8 (MEDIUM HIGH) for 1-1/2 to 2 minutes, or until warmed, and temperature of 160° F is reached. Do not boil.

MICRO-TIP: To make a larger amount, mix one part mix to two parts water. Increase cooking time proportionately for each additional serving.

Honey Cocoa

Yield: 3 to 4 servings

6 tablespoons cocoa
3/4 cup water
1/3 cup honey
Dash salt

3-1/4 cups milk
1 teaspoon vanilla

1. Blend cocoa, water, honey and salt in 2-quart casserole. Cook in Radarange Oven on FULL POWER for 2 to 3 minutes, or until heated through. Stir halfway through cooking time.

2. Gradually blend in milk. Cook in Radarange Oven on Cookmatic Level 8 (MEDIUM HIGH) for 7 to 9 minutes, or until hot and temperature of 160°F is reached.* Stir halfway through cooking time. Stir in vanilla before serving.

*MICRO-TIP: Use the Temperature-Control to stop the Radarange Oven at 160° F.

VARIATIONS FOR HOT CHOCOLATE CHART

HOT CHOCOLATE VARIATION	AMOUNT HOT CHOCOLATE**	ADDITIONAL INGREDIENTS	PREPARATION INSTRUCTIONS	HEATING TIME* COOKMATIC LEVEL 8 (MEDIUM HIGH)
Skier's Cocoa	1 cup	1-1/2 ozs. Galliano	Stir Galliano into cocoa.	30 seconds to 1 minute, as needed.
Cocoa Grasshopper	1 cup	2 teaspoons white Creme de Menthe 1 peppermint stick or candy cane	Stir Creme de Menthe into cocoa. Use candy as stirrer.	30 seconds to 1 minute, as needed.
Cocoa Eggnog	2 cups	2 eggs 1/2 teaspoon vanilla	Gradually beat eggs and vanilla into cocoa.	30 seconds to 1 minute, as needed.
Molasses Hot Chocolate	1 cup	1 teaspoon molasses	Stir molasses into cocoa.	30 seconds to 1 minute, as needed.
Hot Chocolate Schnapps	1 cup	1 tablespoon peppermint schnapps	Stir schnapps into cocoa.	30 seconds to 1 minute, as needed.
Cocoa Alexander	2 cups	1/4 cup cream 2 teaspoons brandy	Beat cream and brandy together. Stir into cocoa.	30 seconds to 1 minute, as needed.
Spicy Marshmallow Cocoa	1 cup	1 large marshmallow Dash ground cloves	Sprinkle cloves into cocoa. Add marshmallow.	30 seconds to 1 minute, as needed.
Cocoa Tahiti	1 cup	1/4 teaspoon coconut extract Toasted coconut	Stir in coconut extract. Sprinkle coconut over top.	30 seconds to 1 minute, as needed.
Cocoa Float	1 cup	1/8 teaspoon cinnamon 1 scoop vanilla ice cream	Stir cinnamon into cocoa. Top with scoop of ice cream.	30 seconds to 1 minute, as needed.

*Use Cookmatic Level 8 (MEDIUM HIGH) for heating hot chocolate beverages. Do not boil.
**Prepare amount of hot chocolate given using "Instant Hot Chocolate Mix" recipe, page 56.

Instant Breakfast Drink

Yield: 1 serving

1 (1.24 oz.) pkg. instant breakfast drink mix
1 cup milk

1. Place instant breakfast drink in 1-cup glass measure or serving cup. Mix in milk.

2. Heat in Radarange Oven on Cookmatic Level 8 (MEDIUM HIGH) for 1-1/2 to 2 minutes, or until warmed and temperature of 160°F is reached.

Instant Tea

Yield: 1 serving

3/4 cup water

1/2 to 1 teaspoon instant tea (to taste)

1. Place water in serving cup. Heat in Radarange Oven on FULL POWER for 1 to 1-1/2 minutes, or until almost boiling.
2. Stir in instant tea.

   MICRO-TIP: 1 cup tea may be reheated in Radarange Oven on FULL POWER for 1 minute to 1 minute, 15 seconds, or until hot. Do not boil. Stir vigorously before reheating.

Russian Tea

Yield: 30 to 40 servings

1 cup powdered orange flavor instant drink
1 cup sugar
1/2 cup instant tea
1 teaspoon ground cinnamon
1 teaspoon ground cloves

3/4 cup water

1. Combine all ingredients, except water, in large mixing bowl.

2. Place water in ceramic or glass mug with 2 to 3 teaspoons of tea mixture. Stir. Heat in Radarange Oven on FULL POWER for 1-1/2 to 2 minutes, or until warmed, and temperature of 160° F is reached.

   MICRO-TIP: Mix may be stored in air-tight container for future use.

Easy Spiced Tea

Yield: 3 servings

2 cups water
2 tablespoons sugar
1 teaspoon lemon juice
1/3 cup orange juice
2 teaspoons instant tea
4 whole cloves
Dash cinnamon (optional)

1. Combine all ingredients in 1-quart casserole or liquid measure.

2. Heat in Radarange Oven on FULL POWER for 4 minutes, or until warmed, and temperature of 160° F is reached. Stir well before serving.

Moroccan Mint Tea

Yield: 4 servings

4 cups water

1/4 to 1/2 cup fresh mint leaves
1/4 cup sugar
2 teaspoons green tea

1. Place water in 1-1/2-quart casserole. Heat in Radarange Oven on FULL POWER for 6 to 7 minutes, or until almost boiling.
2. Add mint leaves, sugar and tea. Strain before serving.

Hot Coconut Mocha

Yield: 1 serving

1 (1 oz.) pkg. instant hot cocoa mix
1 teaspoon instant coffee

3/4 cup water
1/4 teaspoon coconut extract

1. Combine cocoa mix and instant coffee in coffee cup, mug or 1-cup measure.

2. Blend in water and coconut extract. Cook in Radarange Oven on Cookmatic Level 8 (MEDIUM HIGH) for 1-1/2 to 2 minutes, or until heated through, and temperature of 160° F is reached.* Do not boil.

   *MICRO-TIP: Use the Temperature-Control to stop the Radarange Oven at 160° F in step #2. 1/4 cup Instant Cocoa Mix, page 56, may be substituted for the instant hot cocoa mix.

Instant Coffee

Yield: 1 serving

3/4 cup water

1/2 to 1 teaspoon instant coffee

1. Place water in serving cup. Heat in Radarange Oven on FULL POWER for 1 to 1-1/2 minutes, or until almost boiling.
2. Stir in instant coffee.

MICRO-TIP: 1 cup coffee may be reheated in Radarange Oven on FULL POWER for 1 minute to 1 minute, 15 seconds, or until hot. Do not boil. Stir coffee vigorously before reheating.

Egg Coffee

Yield: 6 to 8 servings

6 cups water

1 egg
2 tablespoons water
3/4 cup ground coffee

1. Place water in 2-quart casserole. Heat in Radarange Oven, covered, on FULL POWER for 12 minutes, or until almost boiling.
2. Beat egg and 2 tablespoons water. Stir 2 tablespoons egg mixture into coffee grounds. Add enough cold water to completely moisten grounds. Pour into hot water.
3. Heat in Radarange Oven on FULL POWER for 4 minutes, or until almost boiling. Strain before serving.

MICRO-TIP: Because of the egg, this recipe makes very **clear** coffee.

Mexican Coffee

Yield: 4 servings

4 cups water
1/3 cup brown sugar, firmly packed
2 (3-inch each) sticks cinnamon

3 tablespoons instant coffee

1. Combine all ingredients except coffee in 2-quart casserole. Heat in Radarange Oven on FULL POWER for 8 to 10 minutes, or until almost boiling.
2. Pour over coffee. Stir. Strain before serving.

MICRO-TIP: This recipe makes a **strong** cup of coffee. The amount of coffee used can be adjusted, as desired.

Irish Coffee

Yield: 1 serving

1 cup strong, hot coffee
1 jigger Irish whiskey
1 teaspoon sugar

1 tablespoon whipped cream

1. Place ingredients, except whipped cream, in large ceramic or glass mug.
2. Heat in Radarange Oven on Cookmatic Level 8 (MEDIUM HIGH) for 2 to 2-1/2 minutes, or until warmed. Do not boil. Add whipped cream.

Hot Mocha

Yield: 4 to 6 servings

1-1/2 ozs. unsweetened chocolate
1/2 cup sugar
1/4 cup instant coffee
1/4 teaspoon salt
1 cup hot water

4 cups milk

1. Combine chocolate, sugar, instant coffee and salt. Stir in hot water. Cook in Radarange Oven on FULL POWER for 2 to 3 minutes, or until mixture boils and chocolate is melted.
2. Gradually stir in milk. Cook in Radarange Oven on Cookmatic Level 8 (MEDIUM HIGH) for 9 to 11 minutes, or until hot and temperature of 160° F is reached.*

MICRO-TIPS:

*Use the Temperature-Control to stop the Radarange Oven at 160° F.

•Top each serving with whipped cream and nutmeg.

Fruit Cubes

Yield: 10 to 12 servings, or 28 cubes

1 cup sugar
2 cups water

1 cup orange juice
2 tablespoons lemon juice
2 teaspoons grated orange peel
1/2 teaspoon grated lemon peel

Ginger ale

1. Mix sugar and water in 1-1/2-quart casserole. Heat in Radarange Oven on FULL POWER for 5 minutes, or until sugar is dissolved.
2. Stir in remaining ingredients, except ginger ale. Pour mixture into 2 ice cube trays and freeze.
3. When frozen, place 2 to 3 cubes in each serving glass. Fill glasses with ginger ale.

   MICRO-TIP: After freezing, cubes may be stored in plastic freezer bags in freezer until ready to use.

Hot Spiced Cider

Yield: 4 servings

1 quart apple cider
1/2 teaspoon whole cloves
1/2 teaspoon whole allspice
1, 3-inch stick cinnamon

1. Combine all ingredients in 2-quart casserole.
2. Heat in Radarange Oven, covered, on FULL POWER for 9-1/2 to 10 minutes, or until mixture boils.
3. Heat in Radarange Oven on Cookmatic Level 3 (SIMMER) for 4 minutes. Remove spices and serve.

   MICRO-TIP: This is a nutritious after-school beverage that is simple for children to prepare when the weather is cool.

Tangy Tomato Twister

Yield: 4 servings

4 cups tomato juice
1 cup water
1/2 cup celery leaves, firmly packed
1/4 cup onion, diced
3 whole cloves
1 bay leaf
1/2 teaspoon salt
1/4 teaspoon pepper

1. Combine all ingredients in 2-1/2-quart casserole.
2. Heat in Radarange Oven on FULL POWER for 15 minutes, or until warmed, and temperature of 160° F is reached. Strain before serving.

   MICRO-TIP: 1 teaspoon horseradish will give zip to this cocktail.

Steamy Fruit Punch

Yield: 16, 4 oz. servings

1 cup sugar
2 cups water
1-1/2 cups pineapple juice
1 (8 oz.) can crushed pineapple

1-1/2 cups grapefruit juice
1-1/2 cups orange juice

1. Combine sugar, water, pineapple juice and pineapple in 4-quart casserole. Heat in Radarange Oven on FULL POWER for 10 to 12 minutes, or until bubbling. Stir.
2. Add grapefruit and orange juices. Heat in Radarange Oven on FULL POWER for 4 minutes, or until temperature of 160°F is reached.* Serve warm.

   *MICRO-TIP: Use the Temperature-Control to stop the Radarange Oven at 160°F.

Rhubarb Punch

Yield: 22, 4 oz. servings

1-1/2 lbs. fresh rhubarb, cut in 1-inch pieces
1 quart water

1-1/2 cups sugar

1/2 cup orange juice
1/4 cup lemon juice
1 quart dry ginger ale or club soda

1. Place rhubarb in 3-quart casserole. Cover with water.

2. Cook in Radarange Oven, covered, on FULL POWER for 14 to 15 minutes, or until rhubarb is tender. Strain through double thickness of damp cheesecloth.

3. Stir in sugar. Heat in Radarange Oven on FULL POWER for 5 minutes, or until sugar is completely dissolved. Cool.

4. Stir in juices. Chill. Add ginger ale just before serving.

MICRO-TIPS:

• Punch may be poured over ice in a large punch bowl or pitcher for serving.

• To use frozen rhubarb, defrost in Radarange Oven on DEFROST for 7 to 9 minutes.

• For something special, serve with a scoop of lemon sherbet.

Tea-base Fruit Punch

Yield: 15 to 17, 4 oz. servings

1-1/2 cups water
3 tea bags

1-1/2 cups sugar
1 cup water
6 to 8 ice cubes

2 cups orange juice
1-1/2 cups lemon juice
1/8 teaspoon salt
1 quart ginger ale

1. Place water in 3-quart casserole. Heat in Radarange Oven on FULL POWER for 4 minutes, or until almost boiling. Immerse tea bags in water. Steep 5 minutes.

2. Dissolve sugar in water in large mixing bowl. Heat in Radarange Oven on FULL POWER for 2 to 3 minutes, or until boiling. Add ice cubes to cool.

3. Mix in tea from Step #1, fruit juices and salt. Stir well. Add ginger ale just before serving.

MICRO-TIP: A sprig of mint may be placed in each glass as it is served.

Hot Lemon-Grape Punch

Yield: 10, 4 oz. servings

1 (6 oz.) can frozen lemonade
1 (6 oz.) can frozen grape juice
4-1/2 cups water

2 tablespoons brown sugar
2 sticks cinnamon

1. Combine lemonade, grape juice, and water in 2-quart casserole.

2. Stir in brown sugar and cinnamon. Heat in Radarange Oven on FULL POWER for 5 to 6 minutes, or until warmed, and temperature of 160° F is reached. Serve warm.

Mulled Wine Punch

Yield: 15 to 17, 4 oz. servings

2 tablespoons whole cloves
2 tablespoons whole allspice
2 (2-inch each) cinnamon sticks
4 cups boiling water
3 to 4 tablespoons instant tea
1 (6 oz.) can frozen orange or tangerine juice concentrate
1 (6 oz.) can frozen Hawaiian Punch concentrate

2 (25 oz. each) bottles rosé wine

1. Combine all ingredients, except wine, in 3 to 3-1/2-quart casserole.

2. Heat in Radarange Oven, covered, on Cookmatic Level 3 (SIMMER) for 20 minutes, or until warmed, and temperature of 160° F is reached. Remove spices by straining. Stir in wine. Serve warm or cold.

MICRO-TIP: Garnish with lemon or orange slices. Liquid refreshments can always be reheated quickly in the Radarange Oven. Stir vigorously before reheating. Reheat in Radarange Oven on FULL POWER for 1 to 1-1/2 minutes per serving.

Spicy Fruit Punch Mix

Yield: 8 servings

1 (3 oz.) pkg. sweetened lemonade mix
1 (3 oz.) pkg. sweetened orange drink mix
3 (2-inch each) cinnamon sticks
1/2 teaspoon whole cloves
1 teaspoon whole allspice

Water

1. Combine all ingredients.

2. Fill ceramic or glass mugs with water.

3. Heat in Radarange Oven on FULL POWER for 1-1/2 minutes per mug, or until steaming hot. Stir in 2 rounded teaspoons of mix per cup.

MICRO-TIPS:

• Hot tap water will heat faster than cold.

• Mix may be stored in air-tight container for future use.

Hot Rum Lemonade

Yield: 1 serving

3/4 cup water
1/3 cup lemon juice
1 jigger rum
1 teaspoon honey

1. Combine all ingredients in 2-cup glass measure, or in ceramic or glass mug.

2. Heat in Radarange Oven on Cookmatic Level 8 (MEDIUM HIGH) for 1-1/2 to 2 minutes, or until warmed. Do not boil.

MICRO-TIP: Remember to increase each ingredient and the heating time proportionately when increasing the number of servings.

Holiday Wassail

Yield: 4-1/2 cups or 9, 1/2-cup servings

3 cups apple cider
1-1/4 cups unsweetened pineapple juice
2 tablespoons honey
1 (2-inch) cinnamon stick
1 tablespoon lemon juice
1/8 teaspoon nutmeg
1 teaspoon whole cloves

1. Combine all ingredients in 2-1/2 to 3-quart casserole.

2. Heat in Radarange Oven, covered, on FULL POWER for 10 to 12 minutes, or until mixture boils. Stir halfway through cooking time.

3. Heat in Radarange Oven on Cookmatic Level 5 (SLO COOK) for 3 minutes.

   MICRO-TIP: The last 3 minutes of cooking time on the lower setting allow the spices more time to flavor the beverage. Garnish with orange or lemon slices. A cinnamon stick may be used in each cup as a stirrer.

Hot Spiced Cranberry Punch

Yield: 14, 4 oz. servings

1 quart cranberry juice
1 quart unsweetened pineapple juice
1 teaspoon whole cloves
1/2 teaspoon whole allspice
2 (2-inch each) cinnamon sticks
1/2 cup brown sugar, firmly packed

1. Combine all ingredients in 3-quart casserole.

2. Heat in Radarange Oven, covered, on FULL POWER for 17 to 20 minutes, or until mixture is bubbly. Pour hot punch into mugs before serving.

   MICRO-TIPS:

   • 2 cups apple cider may be substituted for 2 cups pineapple juice.
   • Each mug may be garnished with an orange slice.
   • Punch may be reheated in serving mugs on FULL POWER for about 2 minutes per cup. Stir liquid vigorously before reheating.
   • Punch may be served hot or cold. When served cold, chilled club soda may be added for extra zest.

Raspberry Cooler

Yield: 6 to 8 servings

1/4 cup sugar
1/2 cup mint leaves
1 cup water

1 (10 oz.) pkg. frozen raspberries
1 (6 oz.) can frozen limeade or lemonade concentrate

2 cups club soda

1. Combine sugar, leaves and water in 2-quart casserole. Cook in Radarange Oven on FULL POWER for 2-1/2 to 4 minutes, or until mixture boils. Stir halfway through cooking time. Let stand for 5 minutes.

2. Add frozen raspberries and limeade. Stir until raspberries are thawed.

3. Gradually stir in club soda, just before serving. Serve on ice.

   MICRO-TIP: Frozen strawberries may be substituted for raspberries. Water may be added instead of club soda, if the beverage will be stored in the refrigerator for several days.

Soups and stews are quickly heated in the Radarange Oven. Soups can be heated directly in serving bowls or mugs, so there are fewer dishes to wash.

Many soups are prepared on FULL POWER, with good results. The fast cooking speed allows soups and stews to maintain a "fresh" flavor. Other soups or stews, which contain "delicate" ingredients such as milk or cheese, should be heated at a lower power setting. Soups can be allowed to "simmer" in the Radarange Oven to blend flavors. Use the Temperature-Hold feature to keep a soup at 150° F to 160° F until ready for serving.

Read the general hints for heating soups and stews.

General Hints for Heating Soups and Stews

1. Vegetables and meat can be pre-cooked before adding to soups and stews to shorten heating time.
2. Fat may be trimmed from meat, if desired, so soup or stew is less greasy.
3. Use a container which is 2 to 3 times larger than the amount of soup or stew being heated, to avoid boil-overs. Soups and stews will expand slightly during heating.
4. Soup or stew may be heated directly in serving bowls or mugs. Do not use containers having a metal trim.
5. Cook soups and stews, covered, as recommended in recipes for faster, more even cooking. Cover with a glass lid or heavy-duty plastic wrap, since these types of coverings are the most water-vapor-proof. Pierce plastic wrap slightly before heating. Remove coverings from soups and stews carefully to avoid steam burns.
6. Soup may be stirred during cooking, if desired.
7. Allow soups or stews to stand, as recommended in recipes, for "carry-over" cooking or added thickening. Stir well before serving for uniform thickening.
8. Use the Temperature-Hold feature to keep a soup or stew at 150° F or 160° F, a good temperature range for serving.
9. When reheating soups or stews, stir the liquid vigorously, or pour from a container into serving bowls or casserole before reheating.
10. Leftover soup can become "planned-over" soup. Freeze any leftover soup. It can later be prepared in the Radarange Oven. Soup can be frozen in cubes, and transferred for long-term storage to plastic bags. A quick mug of soup can easily be made from 2 to 3 "soup cubes".
11. Generally, less liquid is required in "Radarange Oven stews" than in conventionally-prepared stews. Adjust your own favorite stew recipes, accordingly.
12. Most soups and stews are cooked on FULL POWER. Some soups and stews contain delicate ingredients, such as mushrooms or cheese, and are best prepared using a lower power setting. When preparing your own favorite homemade soups or stews, heat, covered, on the same setting and for about the same amount of time as a similar recipe in this chapter. If you wish to let a soup or stew "slow cook" to blend flavors, cook on Cookmatic Level 5 (SLO COOK). Cut the amount of time required for a **conventional** recipe in half. If using a **microwave** recipe, use **slightly less** than double the amount of **microwave** cooking time required for FULL POWER cooking.

Fresh Zucchini Soup (page 71)

CANNED SOUPS AND STEWS HEATING CHART

SOUP OR STEW	YIELD	SIZE CAN	HEATING TIME	COOKMATIC LEVEL	SPECIAL INSTRUCTIONS
Beef Stew	2 to 3 servings	15 oz.	2-1/2 to 3 min.	FULL POWER	— — —
	4 to 5 servings	24 oz.	4-1/2 to 5 min.	FULL POWER	
Chili with Beans	2 servings	15 oz.	2 to 2-1/2 min.	FULL POWER	— — —
Condensed Soup (add water)	2 servings	10 to 11 oz.	3 to 4 min.	FULL POWER	Combine 1 soup can of water with soup in casserole before heating. Stir halfway through cooking time.
(add milk)	2 servings	10 to 11 oz.	4 to 5 min.	Cookmatic Level 8 (MEDIUM HIGH)	Combine 1 soup can of milk with soup in casserole before heating. Stir halfway through cooking time.
Uncondensed (Chunky-style)	1 serving	10 to 11 oz.	1-1/2 to 2 min.	FULL POWER	— — —

General Instructions for Heating Canned Soups and Stews

1. Place soup or stew in 1 to 1-1/2-quart casserole.

2. Read "Special Instructions" before heating. Heat, on recommended Cookmatic Level, according to recommended time, or until heated through.

3. Stir halfway through cooking time, or as needed.

Frozen Soup

Yield: 1 serving

7 ozs. frozen, semi-condensed soup
1/2 cup water

1. Remove frozen soup from container and place in 1-quart casserole. Add water.

2. Heat in Radarange Oven, covered, on FULL POWER for 4 to 6 minutes, or until hot. Stir halfway through cooking time.

Single-Serving Instant Soup Mix

Yield: 1 serving

3/4 cup water

1 packet instant soup

1. Place water in 1-cup glass measure. Heat in Radarange Oven on FULL POWER for 1 to 1-1/2 minutes, or until boiling.

2. Add water to instant soup. Stir and serve.

Chili Mix

Yield: 6 to 8 servings

1 lb. ground beef

1 (1-3/4 oz.) pkg. chili
    seasoning mix
1 (1 lb.) can tomatoes
1 (1 lb.) can kidney or pinto beans
1/2 cup water

1. Place beef in 1-1/2-quart casserole. Cook in Radarange Oven on FULL POWER for 3 to 4 minutes, or until beef is no longer pink. Stir halfway through cooking time. Drain.

2. Blend in remaining ingredients listed, or those listed in package instructions. Cook in Radarange Oven on FULL POWER for 10 minutes, or until heated through, and temperature of 160° F is reached. Stir halfway through cooking time.

Vegetable Beef Soup

Yield: 8 to 10 servings

1 lb. ground beef

1 cup potatoes, diced
1/2 cup onion, chopped
1/2 cup celery, chopped
1/2 cup carrots, sliced
1/2 cup frozen peas, or
    1/2 cup frozen green beans
1/4 cup water

5 cups water
1 tablespoon parsley flakes
1 (16 oz.) can tomato wedges
1 tablespoon salt
1/4 teaspoon pepper

1. Crumble beef in 1-1/2-quart casserole. Cook in Radarange Oven on FULL POWER for 3 to 4 minutes, or until beef is no longer pink. Stir halfway through cooking time. Drain.

2. Combine potatoes, onion, celery, carrots, peas and 1/4 cup water in 4-quart casserole. Cook in Radarange Oven, covered, on FULL POWER for 8 to 10 minutes, or until vegetables are tender. Stir halfway through cooking time.

3. Stir in 5 cups water, parsley flakes, tomatoes, salt and pepper. Add beef. Cook in Radarange Oven, covered, on FULL POWER for 11 to 13 minutes, or until temperature of 160° F is reached.*

*MICRO-TIP: Use Temperature-Hold to maintain 160° F until ready to serve.

European Vegetable Soup

Yield: 8 servings

1 cup potatoes, pared and cubed
2 medium carrots, thinly sliced
3 cups cabbage, coarsely shredded

1 (1 lb.) ham slice with bone
1 (1 lb.) can kidney beans, drained
1 (8 oz.) can tomato sauce with
    onion
1/8 teaspoon instant, minced
    garlic
1 tablespoon salt
1/2 teaspoon pepper
1 quart water

1. Combine potatoes, carrots and cabbage in 4-quart casserole. Cook in Radarange Oven, covered, on FULL POWER for 6 to 8 minutes, or until vegetables are tender.

2. Cut meat from bone in cubes. Add meat, bone and remaining ingredients to vegetables. Cook in Radarange Oven on FULL POWER for 20 minutes, or until heated through. Stir halfway through cooking time. Remove bone before serving.

French Onion Soup

Yield: 4 servings

2 medium onions, thinly sliced
2 tablespoons butter or margarine

2 (14 oz. each) cans beef broth
1/2 cup water
1 teaspoon Worcestershire sauce

4 slices French bread, toasted
Grated Parmesan cheese
4 slices Mozzarella cheese, halved
    or shredded

1. Place onion and butter in 3-quart casserole. Cook in Radarange Oven, covered, on FULL POWER for 8 to 10 minutes, or until onion is tender.

2. Add beef broth, water and Worcestershire sauce. Cook in Radarange Oven, covered, on FULL POWER for 5 to 7 minutes, or until mixture boils.

3. Toast French bread. Place on paper towels or plastic rack. Sprinkle with Parmesan cheese. Top with Mozzarella cheese. Heat in Radarange Oven on Cookmatic Level 5 (SLO COOK) for 30 seconds, or until cheese is softened.

4. Place one slice of bread in each serving bowl. Pour soup over bread.

Cream of Tomato and Rice Soup

Yield: 6 to 8 servings

1 medium onion, thinly sliced
1/4 cup butter or margarine

1 small carrot, grated

3 tablespoons all-purpose flour
2 cups tomatoes, pureed

2 cups milk
3/4 cup evaporated milk
1 cup cooked rice
1 teaspoon salt
1/8 teaspoon pepper

1. Place onion and butter in 3-quart casserole. Cook in Radarange Oven on FULL POWER for 3 minutes, or until onion is tender.
2. Add carrot. Cook in Radarange Oven on FULL POWER for 1-1/2 minutes, or until carrot is tender.
3. Blend in flour. Add tomato puree gradually. Cook in Radarange Oven on FULL POWER for 4 minutes, or until thickened.
4. Slowly add milks, rice and seasonings. Cook in Radarange Oven on Cookmatic Level 5 (SLO COOK) for 6 to 8 minutes, or until heated through. Stir halfway through cooking time.

Iced Fresh Tomato Soup

Yield: 6 servings

2 tablespoons vegetable oil
1 cup onion, chopped
6 medium tomatoes, chopped

1 (10-1/2 oz.) can condensed beef broth
1/4 cup catsup

3 cups ice, crushed
1 tablespoon dry dill weed
1 teaspoon salt
Dash Tabasco sauce

1/2 cup heavy cream

1. Place oil, onion and tomatoes in 3-quart casserole. Heat in Radarange Oven on FULL POWER for 2-1/2 to 3 minutes, or until onion is tender.
2. Stir in beef broth and catsup. Heat in Radarange Oven on FULL POWER for 2 minutes. Pour into blender. Process until smooth.
3. Return mixture to casserole. Stir in ice and seasonings. Chill until cold. Blend with rotary beater before serving.
4. Whip cream until it stands in soft peaks. Top each soup serving with whipped cream.

Burgundy Beef Stew

Yield: 8 to 10 servings

1 cup water
1/2 cup red cooking wine
2 tablespoons all-purpose flour
1 tablespoon bottled browning sauce
1 bay leaf
1 teaspoon salt
1/4 teaspoon pepper
1/4 teaspoon marjoram

2 lbs. stew beef

1 cup carrots, chopped
1 cup celery, diced
1 large onion, chopped
4 medium potatoes, cut in eighths

1. Combine water, wine, flour, browning sauce and spices in 3-quart casserole. Mix well.
2. Add beef. Cook in Radarange Oven, covered, on Cookmatic Level 5 (SLO COOK) for 11 to 13 minutes, or until beef is no longer pink.
3. Add vegetables. Cook in Radarange Oven, covered, on Cookmatic Level 5 (SLO COOK) for 40 to 60 minutes, or until meat and vegetables are tender. Stir halfway through cooking time.

Irish Lamb Stew

Yield: 6 to 8 servings

2 tablespoons butter or margarine
2-1/2 to 3 lbs. lamb stewing meat
   or neck slices

2 cups water
2 teaspoons seasoned salt
1/4 teaspoon pepper
1/4 teaspoon dried thyme
1 teaspoon dried parsley
1 large onion, chopped
3 medium potatoes, peeled and
   chopped

1 (17 oz.) can green peas, drained

1 (5-1/3 oz.) can evaporated milk
1/4 cup cornstarch
2 tablespoons bottled
   browning sauce

1. Place butter in 3-quart casserole. Heat in Radarange Oven on FULL POWER for 30 to 45 seconds, or until melted. Add lamb pieces. Cook in Radarange Oven on FULL POWER for 6 minutes, or until lamb is no longer pink.

2. Stir in water, salt, pepper, thyme, parsley, onion and potatoes. Cook in Radarange Oven, covered, on Cookmatic Level 5 (SLO COOK) for 45 to 60 minutes, or until meat is tender.

3. Stir in peas. Cook in Radarange Oven, covered, on Cookmatic Level 5 (SLO COOK) for 15 minutes.

4. Blend together evaporated milk, cornstarch, and browning sauce in small bowl. Stir into stew. Cook in Radarange Oven on FULL POWER for 5 to 8 minutes, or until thickened. Stir halfway through cooking time.

Leftover Stew

Yield: 2 to 3 servings

1/2 cup carrots, sliced
1/2 cup celery, sliced
1/2 cup onion, chopped
2 tablespoons water

1 to 1-1/2 cups leftover, cooked
   meat
3/4 cup water
1 teaspoon bottled browning
   sauce
1/2 teaspoon salt
1/4 teaspoon pepper

1 tablespoon cornstarch
1 tablespoon water

1. Place carrots, celery, onion and water in 1-quart casserole. Cook in Radarange Oven, covered, on FULL POWER for about 4 to 5 minutes, or until vegetables are tender.

2. Add meat, water, browning sauce, salt and pepper. Cook in Radarange Oven on FULL POWER for 3 to 4 minutes, or until mixture is bubbling.

3. Combine cornstarch and water. Stir into stew. Cook in Radarange Oven on FULL POWER for 2 minutes, or until thickened. Stir before serving.

MICRO-TIP: Stew may be served over biscuits, or mashed potatoes.

Flounder Stew

Yield: 4 to 6 servings

1 cup onion, coarsely chopped
1 cup celery, sliced in 1/2-inch
   pieces
1 cup carrots, sliced in
   1/2-inch pieces
2 medium potatoes, pared and
   diced
1/4 cup water

1 (1 lb.) can tomatoes
1 lb. flounder fillets, cut in
   bite-size pieces
1 teaspoon salt
1/2 teaspoon thyme
1 tablespoon parsley flakes
Dash pepper

1. Combine onion, celery, carrots, potatoes and water in 3-quart casserole. Cook in Radarange Oven, covered, on FULL POWER for 8 to 10 minutes, or until vegetables are tender.

2. Add remaining ingredients. Cook in Radarange Oven, covered, on FULL POWER for 4 to 6 minutes, or until fish flakes easily with fork.

Meat Ball Stew

Yield: 6 servings

2 lbs. ground beef
2/3 cup applesauce
2 eggs
1 cup bread crumbs

1. Combine beef, applesauce, eggs and bread crumbs. Form into medium-size meat balls. Place in 2-quart utility dish. Cover with waxed paper. Cook in Radarange Oven, covered, on FULL POWER for 10 to 12 minutes, or until beef is no longer pink.

1 green pepper, chopped
1/2 cup celery, chopped
1/2 cup carrots, chopped
1 onion, chopped
1/4 cup tomato juice

2. Combine green pepper, celery, carrots, onion and 1/4-cup tomato juice in 4-quart casserole. Cook in Radarange Oven, covered, on FULL POWER for 8 to 10 minutes, or until vegetables are tender.

2-3/4 cups tomato juice
2 teaspoons instant beef bouillon
1 tablespoon cornstarch
Salt
Pepper

3. Add remaining tomato juice, bouillon, cornstarch and meat balls. Season with salt and pepper, as desired. Cook in Radarange Oven, covered, on FULL POWER for 12 minutes, or until temperature of 160° F is reached. Stir halfway through cooking time.

Old-Fashioned Beef Stew

Yield: 6 to 8 servings

1 lb. stew beef

1. Place beef in 4-quart casserole. Cook in Radarange Oven on FULL POWER for 5 minutes, or until beef is no longer pink.

4 medium carrots, sliced in 1/2-inch pieces
4 medium potatoes, cut in eighths
1 cup water
1 (8 oz.) can tomato sauce
3/4 cup dry red wine, or 3/4 cup beef broth
1 bay leaf
1 clove garlic, minced
1/2 teaspoon monosodium glutamate
1/2 teaspoon salt
1/2 teaspoon pepper
Dash thyme

2. Stir in remaining ingredients, except onions, cornstarch and water. Cook in Radarange Oven, covered, on Cookmatic Level 5 (SLO COOK) for 60 minutes.

1 (16 oz.) jar boiled, whole onions, drained

3. Stir in onions. Cook in Radarange Oven on Cookmatic Level 5 (SLO COOK) for 10 minutes, or until vegetables and meat are tender.

2 tablespoons cornstarch
2 tablespoons water

4. Combine cornstarch and water. Stir into stew. Cook in Radarange Oven on FULL POWER for 2 to 3 minutes, or until thickened. Remove bay leaf and stir before serving.

Russian Borscht

Yield: 4 servings

1/2 cup onion, finely chopped
2 tablespoons butter or margarine

1. Place onion and butter in 3-quart casserole. Cook in Radarange Oven on FULL POWER for 3 minutes, or until onion is tender.

1 (16 oz.) can diced beets, drained
2 cups hot water
3 teaspoons instant beef bouillon
1/2 teaspoon salt
Dash Tabasco sauce
1 tablespoon lemon juice
Dairy sour cream

2. Place beets and onion in blender. Process until smooth. Return mixture to casserole. Mix in water, instant bouillon, salt and Tabasco sauce. Heat in Radarange Oven on FULL POWER for 5 minutes, or until temperature of 160° F is reached.* Stir in lemon juice. Pour into individual serving bowls. Add sour cream to each serving, as desired.

*MICRO-TIP: Use the Temperature-Control to stop the Radarange Oven at 160° F.

Chili Con Carne

Yield: 4 to 6 servings

1 cup onion, chopped
1/2 cup green pepper, chopped
1 tablespoon vegetable oil

1 lb. ground beef

1 (1 lb.) can tomatoes
1 (8 oz.) can tomato sauce
1/3 cup catsup
1 (1 lb.) can chili beans,
　drained
1/2 teaspoon chili powder*
Dash cayenne pepper
1 bay leaf
1/4 teaspoon oregano
1 teaspoon salt

1. Place onion, green pepper, and oil in 2-quart casserole. Cook in Radarange Oven on FULL POWER for 4 to 5 minutes, or until onion and green pepper are tender.

2. Add ground beef. Cook in Radarange Oven on FULL POWER for 4 to 5 minutes, or until beef is no longer pink. Stir halfway through cooking time.

3. Blend in remaining ingredients. Cook in Radarange Oven on FULL POWER for 10 minutes, or until heated through. Stir halfway through cooking time. Remove bay leaf.

*MICRO-TIP: The amount of chili powder can be increased or decreased, as desired.

Fresh Zucchini Soup

Yield: 4 to 6 servings

3 cups (1-1/2 lbs.) zucchini

1-1/3 cups water
2/3 cup condensed consommé
1/4 cup onion, coarsely chopped
2 slices bacon, cooked and
　crumbled
1 small clove garlic
2 tablespoons parsley, chopped
1/2 teaspoon basil
1/2 teaspoon salt
1/2 teaspoon seasoning salt
1/8 teaspoon pepper

Grated Parmesan cheese

1. Trim both ends of zucchini. Cut into 1-inch chunks. Place in 2-quart casserole.

2. Mix in remaining ingredients except cheese. Cook in Radarange Oven, covered, on FULL POWER for 13 to 15 minutes, or until zucchini is tender. Stir halfway through cooking time. Cool slightly.

3. Process zucchini mixture in blender, 2 cups at a time, until smooth. Return to casserole. Heat in Radarange Oven on FULL POWER for 5 minutes, or until temperature of 160° F is reached.* Separate into individual servings. Sprinkle cheese over each serving, as desired.

* MICRO-TIP: Use the Temperature-Control to stop the Radarange Oven at 160° F.

Hearty Hamburger Soup

Yield: 10 to 12 servings

1 lb. ground beef

3 medium onions, sliced
3 medium carrots, sliced
3 medium stalks celery, sliced
1/4 cup water

7 cups water
1 (16 oz.) can stewed tomatoes
1/2 cup quick-cooking barley
1/4 cup quick-cooking rice
1 tablespoon instant beef
  bouillon
1 tablespoon salt
1 teaspoon monosodium glutamate

1. Crumble beef in 1-1/2-quart casserole. Cook in Radarange Oven on FULL POWER for 3 to 4 minutes, or until beef is no longer pink. Stir halfway through cooking time. Drain.

2. Combine onions, carrots, celery and 1/4 cup water in 4-quart casserole. Cook in Radarange Oven, covered, on FULL POWER for 9 to 12 minutes, or until vegetables are tender. Stir halfway through cooking time.

3. Mix in remaining ingredients. Cook in Radarange Oven, covered, on FULL POWER for 30 to 35 minutes, or until temperature of 160° F is reached.* Let stand, covered, 5 minutes before serving.

* MICRO-TIP: Use the Temperature-Control to stop the Radarange Oven at 160° F.

Corn and Potato Chowder

Yield: 8 to 10 servings

1/2 lb. bacon
1 cup onion, chopped

5 cups potatoes, peeled and cubed
1/4 cup water

1 (1 lb.) can whole corn, drained
2-1/2 cups milk
1 cup water
1 teaspoon salt
1/4 teaspoon pepper

1. Cut bacon into small pieces. Combine bacon and onion in 4-quart casserole. Cook in Radarange Oven on FULL POWER for 9 to 11 minutes, or until bacon is cooked and onion is tender. Stir halfway through cooking time. Drain.

2. Add potatoes and 1/4 cup water. Stir. Cook in Radarange Oven, covered, on FULL POWER for 10 to 12 minutes, or until potatoes are tender. Stir halfway through cooking time.

3. Add remaining ingredients. Cook in Radarange Oven, covered, on Cookmatic Level 8 (MEDIUM HIGH) for 9 to 11 minutes, or until heated through, and temperature of 160° F is reached.* Do not boil. Stir halfway through cooking time.

* MICRO-TIP: Use the Temperature-Control to stop the Radarange Oven at 160° F.

Salmon Bisque

Yield: 4 to 6 servings

1/2 cup celery, finely diced
1 small carrot, shredded
1/2 cup onion, chopped
2 tablespoons butter or margarine

3 tablespoons all-purpose flour
3 cups milk
1 cup evaporated milk

2 (7 oz. each) cans salmon or
  tuna, flaked
1 bay leaf
1/8 teaspoon salt
1/8 teaspoon pepper

1 cup (4 ozs.) Cheddar cheese,
  shredded
Dash cayenne pepper
1 teaspoon parsley flakes

1. Combine celery, carrot, onion and butter in 3-quart casserole. Cook in Radarange Oven on FULL POWER for 4 minutes, or until vegetables are tender.

2. Blend in flour. Add milks gradually. Cook in Radarange Oven on Cookmatic Level 8 (MEDIUM HIGH) for 5 to 6 minutes, or until thickened.

3. Add salmon, bay leaf, salt and pepper. Cook in Radarange Oven on Cookmatic Level 8 (MEDIUM HIGH) for 4 minutes.

4. Add cheese, cayenne pepper and parsley flakes. Cook in Radarange Oven on Cookmatic Level 8 (MEDIUM HIGH) for 2 minutes, or until cheese is melted, and temperature of 160° F is reached.*

* MICRO-TIP: Use the Temperature-Control to stop the Radarange Oven at 160° F.

Manhattan Clam Chowder

Yield: 6 servings

2 strips bacon
1/2 cup onion, chopped
1 cup celery, chopped

3 tablespoons all-purpose flour
1 (16 oz.) can tomatoes
1 (10 oz.) can clams, minced,
   with liquid
1/2 teaspoon powdered thyme
1 teaspoon parsley flakes
1 cup potatoes, peeled and diced
2 cups water
Salt
Pepper

1. Place bacon in 3-quart casserole. Cover with paper towel. Cook in Radarange Oven, covered, on FULL POWER for 2 minutes, or until crisp. Crumble bacon. Stir in onion and celery. Cook in Radarange Oven on FULL POWER for 3 to 4 minutes, or until onion and celery are tender.

2. Blend in flour until smooth. Mix in remaining ingredients. Season with salt and pepper, as desired.

3. Cook in Radarange Oven on FULL POWER for 20 minutes, or until potatoes are tender. Stir halfway through cooking time.

MICRO-TIP: For extra flavor add 8 ounces clam juice.

Easy New England Clam Chowder

Yield: 8 servings

1 cup onion, chopped
1/4 cup butter or margarine

1 (10 oz.) can clams, with liquid
2 (10-3/4 oz. each) cans New
   England-Style clam chowder
2 (10-3/4 oz. each) cans cream of
   potato soup
2-2/3 cups milk
1 (13 oz.) can evaporated milk
Salt
Pepper

1. Place onion and butter in 4-quart casserole. Cook in Radarange Oven on FULL POWER for 3 to 4 minutes, or until onion is tender.

2. Stir in remaining ingredients. Season with salt and pepper, as desired. Cook in Radarange Oven on FULL POWER for 15 minutes, or until heated through. Stir halfway through cooking time.

Shrimp Vegetable Soup

Yield: 6 to 8 servings

1/2 cup green pepper, chopped
1-1/2 cups celery, thinly sliced
1 cup carrots, thinly sliced
1/2 cup onion, chopped
1/4 cup water

2 (13 ozs. each) cans chicken
   broth
1 (1 lb., 12 oz.) can tomatoes
12 ozs. frozen shrimp, thawed
1/2 teaspoon basil leaves
1/8 teaspoon thyme
1 bay leaf
1 teaspoon salt
1 tablespoon parsley flakes
Dash cayenne pepper

1. Combine green pepper, celery, carrots, onion and water in 3 or 4-quart casserole. Cook in Radarange Oven, covered, on FULL POWER for 8 to 10 minutes, or until vegetables are tender.

2. Add remaining ingredients. Cook in Radarange Oven, covered, on FULL POWER for 10 to 12 minutes, or until shrimp is cooked. Remove bay leaf before serving.

MICRO-TIP: Fresh shrimp may be substituted for frozen.

Peanutty Corn Chowder
Yield: 4 servings

3/4 cup celery, chopped
1/3 cup onion, chopped
2 tablespoons vegetable oil

3/4 cup peanut butter, chunky style
2 tablespoons cornstarch
2 cups chicken broth
1 (1 lb.) can cream style corn
Dash cayenne pepper
1/4 teaspoon salt

1-1/2 cups milk
1 tablespoon parsley flakes

1. Combine celery, onion and oil in 2-quart casserole. Cook in Radarange Oven on FULL POWER for 4 to 5 minutes, or until celery and onion are tender.

2. Stir in peanut butter. Blend in cornstarch, and gradually add broth. Add corn and seasonings. Cook in Radarange Oven on FULL POWER for 5 minutes, or until thickened and heated through.

3. Add milk and parsley flakes. Cook in Radarange Oven on Cookmatic Level 8 (MEDIUM HIGH) for 7 minutes, or until temperature of 160° F is reached.*

 * MICRO-TIP: Use the Temperature-Control to stop the Radarange Oven at 160° F.

Shrimp and Crab Gumbo
Yield: 6 servings

1 (10 oz.) pkg. frozen okra

1/2 cup celery, chopped
1/3 cup green onion, chopped
1/4 cup water
1 teaspoon salt
1/4 teaspoon instant, minced garlic
1/4 teaspoon leaf oregano
1/4 teaspoon pepper
1 bay leaf
4 to 5 drops Tabasco sauce

2 (1 lb. each) cans tomato wedges, with liquid
12 ozs. shrimp, cleaned
6 to 8 ozs. crab meat
1-1/2 cups cooked rice

1. Place frozen okra, in opened package, in Radarange Oven. Cook in Radarange Oven on FULL POWER for 1 minute, or until pieces can be separated. Slice while still slightly frozen. Place slices in 3-quart casserole.

2. Add celery, green onion, water and seasonings to okra. Blend well. Cook in Radarange Oven, covered, on FULL POWER for 5 to 6 minutes, or until vegetables are tender.

3. Add tomatoes with liquid, shrimp and crab meat. Cook in Radarange Oven, covered, on FULL POWER for about 13 to 15 minutes, or until shrimp is cooked and temperature of 160° F is reached.* Remove bay leaf. Place 1/4 cup rice in each of 6 individual serving bowls. Fill each bowl with gumbo mixture.

 *MICRO-TIP: Use the Temperature-Hold to maintain 160° F until ready to pour over rice and serve.

Mulligatawny Soup

Yield: 6 to 8 servings

1/4 cup carrots, diced
1/4 cup celery, diced
1/4 cup onion, diced
1 tart apple, peeled and diced
2 tablespoons water

1 tablespoon cornstarch
1/8 teaspoon ground cloves
1/8 teaspoon curry powder
1/8 teaspoon mace (optional)
1 tablespoon parsley flakes
2 cups cooked chicken, diced
2 (13-3/4 oz. each) cans chicken
  broth
1 cup stewed tomatoes, drained
Salt
Pepper

1. Combine carrots, celery, onion, apple and water in 3-quart casserole. Cook in Radarange Oven, covered, on FULL POWER for 7 to 9 minutes, or until vegetables and apple are tender.

2. Blend in cornstarch, seasonings and parsley flakes. Add chicken, broth and tomatoes. Cook in Radarange Oven, covered, on FULL POWER for 8 to 10 minutes, or until mixture boils. Season with salt and pepper, as desired.

Minestrone Soup

Yield: 8 to 10 servings

1/2 cup carrots, thinly sliced
1-1/2 cups celery, thinly sliced
1 tablespoon water

1 lb. pork sausage, country style
1/2 medium onion, chopped

1 (28 oz.) can tomatoes, undrained
1 cup kidney beans
1 teaspoon garlic salt
1/4 teaspoon salt
Dash pepper
2 tablespoons parsley, chopped
1 bay leaf
1/4 teaspoon basil leaves
3 cups hot water

6 ozs. spaghetti rings, cooked
1/2 cup spinach, or celery tops,
  coarsely chopped
Grated Parmesan cheese

1. Combine carrots, celery and water in 4-quart casserole. Cook in Radarange Oven, covered, on FULL POWER for 6 to 7 minutes, or until vegetables are tender.

2. Add sausage and onion. Cook in Radarange Oven on FULL POWER for 7 to 8 minutes, or until sausage is no longer pink, and onion is tender. Stir halfway through cooking time.

3. Add tomatoes, beans, salts, pepper, parsley, bay leaf, basil leaves and water. Cook in Radarange Oven on FULL POWER for 15 minutes. Stir halfway through cooking time.

4. Add spaghetti and spinach. Cook in Radarange Oven on FULL POWER for 5 minutes, or until temperature of 160° F is reached. Remove bay leaf before serving. Sprinkle servings with Parmesan cheese, as desired.

Cheddar Chowder

Yield: 4 to 6 servings

2 cups potatoes, diced
2 carrots, sliced
3/4 cup onion, chopped
1/2 cup celery, diced
1/2 cup water

1. Combine potatoes, carrots, onion, celery and water in 2-quart casserole. Cook in Radarange Oven, covered, on FULL POWER for 8 to 10 minutes, or until vegetables are tender.

1/4 cup butter or margarine
1/4 cup all-purpose flour
1 teaspoon seasoned salt
1/4 teaspoon pepper
1/2 teaspoon dry mustard
1 tablespoon Worcestershire sauce
2 cups milk
3/4 cup Cheddar cheese, shredded

2. Place butter in 4-cup glass measure. Heat in Radarange Oven on FULL POWER for 45 to 60 seconds, or until melted. Stir in flour. Blend in salt, pepper, mustard, Worcestershire sauce and milk. Blend thoroughly. Cook in Radarange Oven on Cookmatic Level 8 (MEDIUM HIGH) for 3 to 5 minutes, or until smooth and thickened. Add cheese. Stir until smooth.

1 teaspoon parsley flakes
1 cup canned tomatoes, drained

3. Add sauce to vegetables. Stir in parsley flakes and tomatoes. Cook in Radarange Oven on Cookmatic Level 8 (MEDIUM HIGH) for 1-1/2 to 2-1/2 minutes, or until heated through.

Lentil-Ham Soup

Yield: 8 to 10 servings

1-1/2 cups lentils
1 quart water

1. Soak lentils in 1 quart water overnight in refrigerator. Drain. Place lentils in 4-quart casserole.

2 quarts water
1 cup potatoes, peeled and diced
1/2 cup onion, chopped
1/2 cup carrots, thinly sliced
1/2 cup celery, thinly sliced
2 cups cooked ham, diced
2 tablespoons parsley flakes
1/2 teaspoon oregano
1/2 teaspoon pepper
2 teaspoons salt
1 teaspoon bottled browning sauce

2. Add remaining ingredients.

3. Cook in Radarange Oven, covered, on FULL POWER for 35 to 40 minutes, or until vegetables are tender.

MICRO-TIP: If thickening is desired, stir 1 cup hot broth into 1/4 cup all-purpose flour. Add to soup. Cook in Radarange Oven, covered, on FULL POWER for about 5 minutes, or until boiling.

Split Pea Soup

Yield: 8 servings

1 lb. (2 cups) dry, split green
  peas
1-1/2 quarts water

1 carrot, diced
1 small potato, peeled and cubed
1 small onion, chopped
1 ham bone
1 lb. smoked ham, cubed*
2 quarts hot water
Salt
Pepper

1. Soak peas in 1-1/2 quarts water overnight. Drain. Place peas in 4-quart casserole.

2. Add remaining ingredients. Season with salt and pepper, as desired.

3. Cook in Radarange Oven, covered, on FULL POWER for 35 to 40 minutes, or until vegetables are tender. Stir halfway through cooking time.
   MICRO-TIPS:

   * If ham bone is not available, use 3-inch square smoked bacon, cubed and 1/2 lb. smoked ham instead of 1 lb.
   • For creamy soup, after cooked, blend 2 tablespoons cornstarch with 1 cup evaporated milk. Add to soup. Cook in Radarange Oven on FULL POWER for about 5 minutes, or until thickened.

Bloody Mary "Warm-Up"

Yield: 4 to 6 servings

1/4 cup butter or margarine
1/2 lb. mushrooms, sliced

2 (16 oz. each) cans clam and
  tomato juice
2 tablespoons Worcestershire
  sauce
1 tablespoon seasoned salt

1/2 cup vodka
8 ozs. French onion chip dip

1. Place butter and mushrooms in 1-quart casserole. Cook in Radarange Oven on Cookmatic Level 8 (MEDIUM HIGH) for 4 to 5 minutes, or until mushrooms are tender.

2. Combine mushrooms, juice, Worcestershire sauce and salt in 2-quart casserole. Cook in Radarange Oven on FULL POWER for 4 to 5 minutes, or until heated through.

3. Stir in vodka. Cook in Radarange Oven on Cookmatic Level 8 (MEDIUM HIGH) for 1-1/2 to 2 minutes, or until heated. Do not boil. Top each serving with chip dip.

   MICRO-TIP: Canned mushrooms may be substituted for fresh. 1/2-cup of the liquid from the canned mushrooms, or water, can be substituted for the vodka, if desired. If canned mushrooms are used, omit butter and Step #1.

Chilled Pea Soup

Yield: 6 servings

2 (10 oz. each) pkgs. frozen
  green peas
1/2 cup green onion, finely chopped
3/4 cup water
1/2 teaspoon salt
  Dash nutmeg

1 cup condensed chicken broth,
  undiluted
1/2 cup heavy cream

1. Combine peas, onion, water, salt and nutmeg in 3-quart casserole. Cook in Radarange Oven, covered, on FULL POWER for 10 minutes. Stir halfway through cooking time. Pour into blender. Process until smooth.

2. Return mixture to casserole. Mix in broth. Cover and refrigerate. Stir in cream just before serving.

Breads are easily prepared in the Radarange Oven with good results. Breads baked at lower power settings are evenly cooked and very tender. In yeast breads, lower settings allow the yeast to stay alive and active long enough to make breads light. Quick breads are baked with good results on FULL POWER.

Breads baked in the Radarange Oven are very moist, and have a good eating quality. Due to short cooking times, you can bake a "spur-of-the-moment" coffee cake for a coffee break with a neighbor. When overnight guests arrive unexpectedly, surprise them with fresh hot muffins in the morning. Breads baked in the Radarange Oven are great for toast, too.

Before getting started, review the general hints for baking breads.

General Hints for Baking Breads

1. UTENSILS & COVERINGS

Plastic or glass dishes can be used when baking or proofing (rising) breads. In most cases, dishes should be greased before baking. During **rising** of yeast breads, cover the bread dough with a damp cotton cloth, such as a dishcloth, or plastic wrap. Breads are generally **baked,** uncovered.

Several recipes in this chapter require an 8-1/2-inch glass ring mold. You can create your own "ring mold" by simply placing a 6 oz. custard cup in an 8 or 9 x 2-inch round glass dish. For easy removal of bread from a bread ring, run a knife along the edge of the dish. Place a serving platter over the top of the dish, and invert. Usually the custard cup is removed more easily **after** inverting the bread ring on the serving platter. Some recipes require a larger 10-cup glass ring mold. You can place a 2 to 3-inch diameter drinking glass in a 3 or 4-quart glass casserole. The glass should be the same height as the casserole dish used. Usually it is easier to remove the glass **before** inverting the bread ring on the serving platter. Note: When a plastic or ceramic utensil is used, cooking times may need to be shortened or lengthened, respectively.

2. BROWNING

Breads won't brown in a microwave oven as they do in a conventional oven. For color, use toppings or ingredients which supply color. Some examples include rye flour, whole wheat flour, brown sugar or dark spices, such as cinnamon. In some recipes, there may seem to be extra topping ingredients leftover. Use all ingredients, since the bread will expand during baking. All ingredients will be needed.

3. RISING OR PROOFING

The process of rising yeast breads is delicate. But this process can be quickly and easily accomplished by using the Cookmatic Level 1 (WARM) setting. Use the rising (proofing) instructions in the recipes as a guide for proofing your own favorites.

4. MUFFINS

When baking muffins, use 6 oz. glass custard cups or a 6-cupcake capacity plastic tray. When a plastic or ceramic utensil is used, cooking times may need to be shortened or lengthened, respectively. Line custard cups or plastic tray compartments with paper liners. Fill liners half-full of batter to avoid having the muffins rise over the edges. Arrange custard cups in a circle, rather than in rows, according to the recipe. Remove muffins from custard cups and plastic tray, immediately, to avoid soggy "bottoms". Most plastic cupcake trays have holes in the compartment bottoms which allow moisture to escape, and help to eliminate sogginess.

5. AFTER BAKING

Breads are usually fully baked when:

a. A toothpick inserted in the center comes out clean (generally recommended for quick breads).

b. The top springs back when lightly pressed with a finger. (generally recommended for yeast breads). Recipe instructions in this chapter will indicate the recommended test for the particular recipe.

Some breads will look slightly moist when first removed from the Radarange Oven. Look through bottom of glass dish to see if bread is fully cooked. Breads should be allowed to stand for a few minutes after baking. During this time, the breads will "carryover" cook. After 3 to 5 minutes, remove the bread

From Top: Pumpkin Bread Ring (page 95), Whole Wheat Pumpkin Muffins (page 85), Cranberry Muffins (page 87), Quick Sweet Rolls (page 98), Herb Bread (page 101), Pecan Rolls (page 98), and Herb Rolls (page 89)

from the glass dish so the bottom won't become soggy. Invert the bread on a serving platter, or turn it out on a cooling rack.

If the bottom of the bread is slightly underdone, return the bread to the Radarange Oven, upside-down, on FULL POWER for 30 seconds to 1 minute, to allow the bottom to dry.

6. WRAPPING BREADS

After baking or reheating, breads should be covered tightly with plastic wrap or stored in an air-tight container to keep them moist and fresh. Keep warm breads on a serving table covered with a cloth, napkin or paper towel to keep them warm and moist.

Warm bread is very delicate when fresh, and should be handled carefully. An electric knife will help to prevent tearing when cutting. When bread is cooled, it cuts more easily and can be cut with a regular, serrated knife.

7. REHEATING BREADS

When reheating baked bread, heat for only a **few** seconds. Over-heated bread will become tough, rubbery, and hard. As a general rule, reheat only as much bread as is needed for each meal. Wrap the bread in a paper towel or napkin when reheating to capture steam and help keep the bread moist. You may heat bread in a straw basket, if desired, as long as there is no metal trim. Bread should still be covered by a linen napkin, cotton cloth, or paper towel, to retain moisture. Bread can also be reheated, wrapped in a paper towel and placed on a plastic rack. Breads can be reheated in a plastic wrapper or plastic bag. Loosen the end of the wrapper or bag and remove any metal fasteners before heating.

Moist fillings inside coffee cakes or rolls, as well as frostings, will reheat more rapidly and to higher temperatures than the dough part of the bread. Be certain the entire bread is warmed before serving.

When reheating a group of rolls or muffins, either heat in a basket, or place them in a circle in the Radarange Oven, rather than in rows. Left-over breads can be freshened, if stale. Reheat them, covered, for only a few seconds. Eat them immediately.

8. EXTRAS

Bread crumbs and croutons can be made quickly and economically in the Radarange Oven. See the chapter, "Radarange Oven Extras".

9. ADAPTING RECIPES

When converting your own favorite bread recipes, select a similar recipe from this chapter and use it as a guide. Yeast breads are baked on Cookmatic Level 7 (BAKE). Use the same recommended setting and approximately the same amount of time for baking your own favorite breads. When you find the correct amount of time for your recipe, jot it down for future use.

FROZEN BREADS CHART

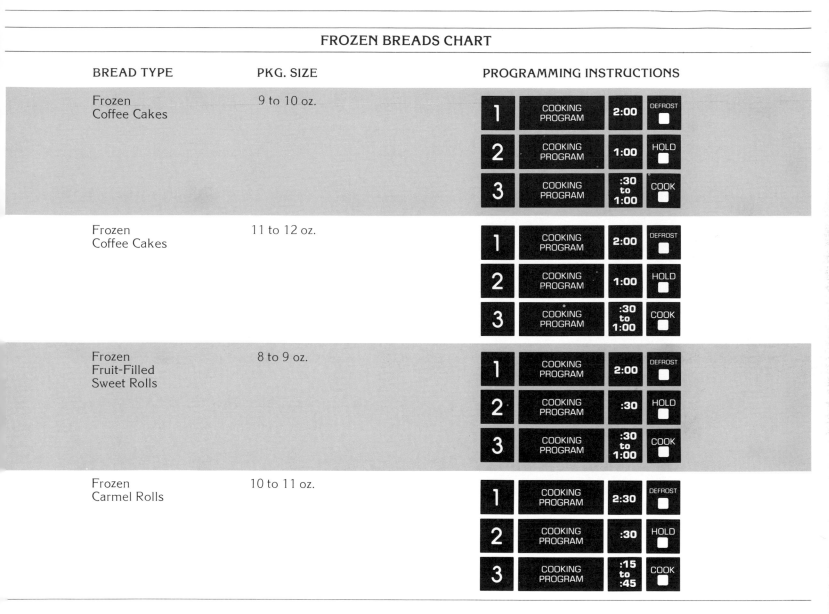

BREAD TYPE	PKG. SIZE	PROGRAMMING INSTRUCTIONS			
Frozen Coffee Cakes	9 to 10 oz.	1 COOKING PROGRAM	2:00	DEFROST ☐	
		2 COOKING PROGRAM	1:00	HOLD ☐	
		3 COOKING PROGRAM	:30 to 1:00	COOK ☐	
Frozen Coffee Cakes	11 to 12 oz.	1 COOKING PROGRAM	2:00	DEFROST ☐	
		2 COOKING PROGRAM	1:00	HOLD ☐	
		3 COOKING PROGRAM	:30 to 1:00	COOK ☐	
Frozen Fruit-Filled Sweet Rolls	8 to 9 oz.	1 COOKING PROGRAM	2:00	DEFROST ☐	
		2 COOKING PROGRAM	:30	HOLD ☐	
		3 COOKING PROGRAM	:30 to 1:00	COOK ☐	
Frozen Carmel Rolls	10 to 11 oz.	1 COOKING PROGRAM	2:30	DEFROST ☐	
		2 COOKING PROGRAM	:30	HOLD ☐	
		3 COOKING PROGRAM	:15 to :45	COOK ☐	

General Instructions for Defrosting and Cooking Breads

1. Remove the coffee cake or sweet rolls from the metal container. Place on a plastic rack or paper plate. Cover with a paper towel.

2. Defrost, hold, and cook, according to the directions in the "Frozen Breads Chart".

FROZEN CONVENIENCE BREADS DEFROST CHART

BREAD TYPE	PKG. SIZE	DEFROST TIME	SETTING	SPECIAL INSTRUCTIONS
Frozen Bread Dough	1 lb. loaf	4 to 6 min.	DEFROST	Wrap dough loosely in waxed paper, or keep in plastic wrapper. Bake frozen bread dough conventionally.
Frozen Donuts	2 donuts	45 sec. to 1 min.	DEFROST	Place donuts on plastic rack or paper plate. Cover with paper towel.
	4 donuts	1 min., 15 sec. to 1 min., 45 sec.	DEFROST	
Frozen French Bread	1 lb. loaf	3 to 4 min.	DEFROST	Defrost in plastic wrapper.
Frozen French Toast (4 slices)	9 oz. pkg.	2-1/2 to 3 min.	FULL POWER	Place slices on plastic rack, paper plate, or paper towel. Cover with paper towel.
Frozen Jelly Donuts	2 donuts	2 to 2-1/2 min.	DEFROST	Place donuts on plastic rack or paper plate. Cover with paper towel.
	4 donuts	2 min., 45 sec. to 3 min., 15 sec.	DEFROST	Place donuts on plastic rack or paper plate. Cover with paper towel.
Frozen Pancake Batter	17 oz. carton	3 to 6 min.	DEFROST	Open carton before defrosting. Defrost in carton. Stir occasionally during defrosting. Grill pancakes conventionally, or on browning grill.
Frozen Sandwich Bread Loaf	1-1/2 lb. loaf	5 to 6 min.	DEFROST	Defrost in plastic wrapper.
Frozen Sweet Rolls	2 individual rolls	2 to 2-1/2 min.	DEFROST	Remove rolls from metal container. Place on plastic rack or paper plate. Cover with paper towel.
Frozen Waffles*	5-1/2 x 7-inch waffle	45 sec. to 1 min.	FULL POWER	Place waffle in preheated browning skillet or grill. Turn over halfway through cooking time.

*Preheat large browning skillet or grill in Radarange Oven on FULL POWER, according to manufacturer's instructions for breads. Add waffles to hot skillet. For repeated usage of the browning skillet, re-preheat each time the skillet is reused.

General Instructions for Defrosting Frozen Convenience Breads

1. Read the "Special Instructions" before defrosting the frozen convenience bread.

2. A bread may be defrosted in the plastic wrapper. Loosen the end of the wrapper before defrosting.

CONVENIENCE BREAD MIX COOKING CHART

BREAD MIX	PKG. SIZE	QUANTITY	COOKING TIME ON FULL POWER
Coffee Cake Mix	14 to 16 ozs.	8 x 8 x 2-inch, or 9-inch round	3-1/2 to 4 min.*
	17 to 19 ozs.	8 x 8 x 2-inch, or 9-inch round	4 to 5 min.*
Corn Bread Muffin Mix	8 to 9 oz.	6 muffins	1 min. to 1 min., 15 sec.
		4 muffins	45 sec. to 55 sec.
Blueberry Muffin Mix	12 to 14 oz.	6 muffins	1 min., 15 sec. to 1 min., 30 sec.
Honey Date Muffin Mix	7 oz.	6 muffins	1 min., 15 sec. to 1 min., 30 sec.
		2 muffins	20 sec. to 30 sec.
Quick Bread Mix	16 to 17 oz.	1, 9 x 5 x 2-inch loaf	3 min., 45 sec. to 4 min., 15 sec.
Gingerbread Mix	14 to 15 oz.	1, 8 x 8 x 2-inch, or 1, 9-inch round loaf	5 min., 30 sec. to 6 min.

*You may want to turn dish halfway through cooking time.

General Instructions for Cooking Convenience Bread Mixes

1. Follow the package instructions for mixing specific breads. Use the recommended utensil size. Use a glass utensil. (If a plastic or ceramic utensil is used, cooking times may need to be shortened or lengthened, respectively.) For muffins, use 2 tablespoons of batter per muffin.

2. Breads are done when a toothpick inserted in the center comes out clean, or when the top springs back when pressed lightly with a finger. Some breads may look slightly moist on the surface. Look at bottoms when possible.

Stuffing Mix

Yield: 4 to 6 servings

1 (6 oz.) pkg. stuffing mix
1-3/4 cups water
1/4 cup butter or margarine, melted

1. Combine contents of seasoning packet, water and butter in 1-1/2-quart casserole. Cook in Radarange Oven, covered, on FULL POWER for 4 to 6 minutes, or until all ingredients are tender.

2. Add stuffing crumbs. Stir to moisten. Cover, and let stand 5 minutes. Fluff and serve.

Perpetual Muffins

Yield: 6 dozen muffins

2 cups boiling water
4 cups all-bran cereal
2 cups 100% Bran Flakes
1 quart buttermilk
3 cups sugar
4 eggs, beaten
1 cup soft shortening or vegetable oil
5 cups all-purpose flour
5 teaspoons baking soda
1 teaspoon salt

1. Pour hot water over cereals in large mixing bowl. Stir in buttermilk, sugar, eggs, shortening, flour, baking soda and salt. Mix until just blended.

2. Spoon 2 tablespoons of batter into plastic muffin tray (or 6, 6 oz. glass custard cups) lined with paper liners.* Arrange 6 muffins in circle in Radarange Oven if using custard cups.

3. Bake half-dozen in Radarange Oven on FULL POWER for 1 minute, 10 seconds to 1 minute, 20 seconds, or until tops spring back when lightly pressed with finger. Remove muffins from tray or custard cups, and place on cooling rack immediately. Repeat with remaining muffins.

MICRO-TIPS:
• To bake 4 muffins, bake in Radarange Oven on FULL POWER for 40 to 50 seconds. To bake 2 muffins, bake in Radarange Oven on FULL POWER for 25 seconds to 35 seconds.

• This batter can be refrigerated for up to 3 to 4 weeks. Baking directions for refrigerator temperature are: Bake in Radarange Oven on FULL POWER for:

QUANTITY	COOKING TIME*
6 muffins	1 min., 20 sec. to 1 min., 30 sec.
4 muffins	1 min. to 1 min., 10 sec.
2 muffins	35 to 45 sec.

*If a plastic tray is used, the cooking time may need to be shortened.

Whole Wheat Pumpkin Muffins

Yield: about 2 dozen muffins

3/4 cup canned pumpkin
2 eggs
1/2 cup honey
1/2 cup brown sugar, firmly packed
1/2 cup vegetable oil
1-1/2 cups whole wheat flour
1 teaspoon pumpkin pie spice
3/4 teaspoon baking powder
1/2 teaspoon baking soda
1/2 teaspoon salt

1/2 cup walnuts, chopped
1/2 cup raisins

1. Combine pumpkin, eggs, honey, brown sugar and oil. Add to combined dry ingredients in large mixing bowl. Mix until just blended.

2. Stir in nuts and raisins. Spoon 2 tablespoons of batter into plastic muffin tray (or 6, 6 oz. glass custard cups) lined with paper liners.* Arrange 6 muffins in circle in Radarange Oven if using custard cups.

3. Bake half-dozen in Radarange Oven on FULL POWER for 1 minute, 10 seconds to 1 minute, 20 seconds, or until tops spring back when lightly pressed with finger. Remove muffins from tray or custard cups, and place on cooling rack immediately. Repeat with remaining muffins.

   MICRO-TIPS:

   •Serve warm with butter or cream cheese.

   *If a plastic tray is used, the cooking time may need to be shortened.

Spiced Apple Muffins

Yield: 14 to 16 muffins

1 (13-14 oz.) pkg. applesauce-raisin spice snack cake mix
1 cup water

2-1/2 tablespoons butter or margarine
1/3 cup sugar
2 teaspoons cinnamon

1. Prepare mix according to package instructions by mixing water with cake mix.

2. Spoon 2 tablespoons of batter into plastic muffin tray (or 6, 6 oz. glass custard cups) lined with paper liners.* Arrange 6 muffins in circle in Radarange Oven if using custard cups.

3. Bake half-dozen in Radarange Oven on FULL POWER for 1 minute, 10 seconds to 1 minute, 20 seconds, or until tops spring back when lightly pressed with finger. Remove muffins from tray or custard cups, and place on cooling rack immediately. Repeat with remaining muffins.

4. When cooled, brush top of each muffin with butter. Generously sprinkle each muffin with cinnamon-sugar mixture. Tip each muffin to remove excess.

   *MICRO-TIP: If a plastic tray is used, the cooking time may need to be shortened.

Blueberry Muffins

Yield: about 1-1/2 to 2 dozen muffins

2 cups all-purpose flour
1/2 cup sugar
1 tablespoon baking powder
1/2 teaspoon salt
1 cup milk
1/4 cup vegetable oil
1 egg

1 cup fresh blueberries, washed and drained*

CRUMB TOPPING

3 tablespoons all-purpose flour
3 tablespoons sugar
1 teaspoon cinnamon
3 tablespoons butter or margarine

1. Combine flour, sugar, baking powder and salt in large mixing bowl. Combine milk, oil and egg. Add to combined dry ingredients. Mix until just blended.

2. Fold in blueberries. Spoon 2 tablespoons of batter into plastic muffin tray (or 6, 6 oz. glass custard cups), lined with paper liners.**

3. For crumb topping, cut butter into dry ingredients. Sprinkle over muffin batter. Arrange 6 muffins in circle in Radarange Oven if using custard cups.

4. Bake half-dozen in Radarange Oven on FULL POWER for 1 minute, 10 seconds to 1 minute, 20 seconds, or until tops spring back when lightly pressed with finger. Remove muffins from tray or custard cups, and place on cooling rack immediately. Repeat with remaining muffins.

MICRO-TIPS:

*Canned, or frozen and defrosted blueberries may be used.

**If a plastic tray is used, the cooking time may need to be shortened.

Granola Muffins

Yield: 18 muffins

1-3/4 cups all-purpose flour
1-3/4 cups granola with raisins*
1/2 cup brown sugar, firmly packed
1 tablespoon baking powder
1/4 teaspoon salt
1 egg, slightly beaten
1 cup milk
1/4 cup butter or margarine, melted

1. Combine flour, 1-1/2 cups granola, brown sugar, baking powder and salt in large mixing bowl. Mix thoroughly. Combine egg, milk and butter. Add to combined dry ingredients. Mix until just blended.

2. Spoon 2 tablespoons of batter into plastic muffin tray (or 6, 6 oz. glass custard cups) lined with paper liners.** Sprinkle remaining granola over top of muffins. Arrange 6 muffins in circle in Radarange Oven if using custard cups.

3. Bake half-dozen in Radarange Oven on FULL POWER for 1 minute, 10 seconds to 1 minute, 20 seconds, or until tops spring back when lightly pressed with finger. Remove muffins from tray or custard cups, and place on cooling rack immediately. Repeat with remaining muffins.

MICRO-TIPS:

*You can use the "Granola" recipe on page 117.

**If a plastic tray is used, the cooking time may need to be shortened.

Cranberry Muffins

Yield: about 2 dozen muffins

2 cups all-purpose flour
1/2 cup sugar
1 tablespoon baking powder
1/2 teaspoon salt
1 cup milk
1/4 cup vegetable oil
1 egg, beaten

1 cup cranberries, coarsely chopped
1/2 cup nuts, chopped
1 tablespoon orange peel, grated
2 tablespoons sugar
1 teaspoon cinnamon
2 tablespoons nuts, chopped

1. Combine flour, sugar, baking powder and salt in large mixing bowl. Combine milk, oil and egg. Add to combined dry ingredients. Mix until just blended.

2. Fold in cranberries, nuts and 2 teaspoons orange peel. Spoon 2 tablespoons of batter into plastic muffin tray (or 6, 6 oz. glass custard cups) lined with paper liners.* Combine remaining ingredients and sprinkle over muffins. Arrange 6 muffins in circle in Radarange Oven if using custard cups.

3. Bake half-dozen in Radarange Oven on FULL POWER for 1 minute, 10 seconds to 1 minute, 20 seconds, or until tops spring back when lightly pressed with finger. Remove muffins from tray or custard cups, and place on cooling rack immediately. Repeat with remaining muffins.

   MICRO-TIPS:

   •To bake 4 muffins, bake in Radarange Oven on FULL POWER for 40 to 50 seconds.

   •To bake 2 muffins, bake in Radarange Oven on FULL POWER for 25 to 35 seconds.

   *If a plastic tray is used, the cooking time may need to be shortened.

Mexicorn Bread

Yield: 1, 9-inch round loaf

1 cup yellow cornmeal
1 cup all-purpose flour
1/4 cup sugar
4 teaspoons baking powder
1/2 teaspoon salt
1/4 teaspoon chili powder

2 eggs, beaten
1 cup milk
1/4 cup vegetable oil
1 (12 oz.) can Mexicorn® niblets, drained

1. Combine cornmeal, flour, sugar, baking powder, salt and chili powder in large mixing bowl.

2. Stir in eggs, milk and oil. Beat with rotary beater until smooth. Mix in corn. Pour batter into greased, 9 x 2-inch round glass dish.

3. Bake in Radarange Oven on FULL POWER for 8-1/2 to 10-1/2 minutes, or until top springs back when lightly pressed with finger.* Let stand 5 minutes. Invert on platter.

   *MICRO-TIP: You may want to turn dish halfway through cooking time.

Quick Corn Bread Ring

Yield: 1 ring

1 (8-1/2 oz.) pkg. corn muffin mix
2/3 cup biscuit baking mix
2/3 cup milk
1 egg

Spray-on vegetable coating
3 tablespoons cornflake crumbs

1. Mix together corn muffin mix and biscuit baking mix in large mixing bowl. Blend in milk and egg.

2. Spray inside of 9 x 2-inch round glass dish and outside of 6 oz. glass custard cup with spray-on vegetable coating. Coat both with cornflake crumbs. Invert custard cup in center of dish to form ring mold. Pour batter into dish.

3. Bake in Radarange Oven on FULL POWER for 3 to 4 minutes, or until toothpick inserted in center comes out clean.* Let stand 10 minutes. Invert ring on serving platter, and remove custard cup.

   *MICRO-TIP: You may want to turn dish halfway through cooking time.

Carolina Corn Bread

Yield: 1, 9-inch round loaf

1 cup yellow cornmeal
1 cup all-purpose flour, sifted
1/4 cup sugar
4 teaspoons baking powder
1/2 teaspoon salt

1 egg
1 cup milk
1/4 cup shortening, softened

Spray-on vegetable coating
3 tablespoons cornflake crumbs

1. Sift together cornmeal, flour, sugar, baking powder and salt in large mixing bowl.

2. Stir in egg, milk and shortening. Beat with rotary beater until smooth.

3. Spray inside of 9 x 2-inch round glass dish with spray-on vegetable coating. Coat with cornflake crumbs. Pour batter into dish.

4. Bake in Radarange Oven on FULL POWER for 4 to 5 minutes, or until toothpick inserted in center comes out clean. Let stand 10 minutes. Invert on serving platter.

   MICRO-TIP: For a ring shape, invert 6 oz. glass custard cup in center of 9 x 2-inch round dish to form ring mold. Spray custard cup with spray-on vegetable coating, and coat with cornflake crumbs before inverting in dish.

Banana Nut Bread

Yield: 1 loaf

3/4 cup brown sugar, firmly packed
1/3 cup vegetable oil
2 eggs
1 teaspoon vanilla

3 bananas, mashed (1-1/2 cups)
1/3 cup walnuts, chopped
1-1/4 cups all-purpose flour
1/3 cup all-bran cereal
3/4 teaspoon baking soda
1/2 teaspoon salt

1. Combine sugar, oil, eggs and vanilla in large mixing bowl.

2. Stir in bananas, nuts, and then remaining ingredients. Pour into greased, 9 x 5 x 2-inch glass loaf dish.

3. Bake in Radarange Oven on FULL POWER for 6 to 7 minutes, or until toothpick inserted in center comes out clean.* Let stand 5 minutes. Turn out onto cooling rack.

Date Nut Bread

Yield: 1 loaf

1 cup dates, chopped
1 cup pecans, chopped
1/2 teaspoon salt
3/4 cup milk
1/4 cup shortening, melted
1 egg

1-1/2 cups all-purpose flour
1/2 cup brown sugar, firmly packed
2 teaspoons baking powder
1/2 teaspoon vanilla

1. Combine dates, pecans and salt in large mixing bowl. Stir in milk, shortening and egg.

2. Stir in remaining ingredients. Pour into greased, 9 x 5 x 2-inch glass loaf dish.

3. Bake in Radarange Oven on FULL POWER for 5 to 6 minutes, or until top springs back when lightly pressed with finger. Let stand 5 minutes. Turn out onto cooling rack.

Refrigerator Cinnamon Rolls

Yield: 1 ring

1 (8 to 9.5 oz.) pkg. refrigerator cinnamon rolls

2 tablespoons sugar (optional)
1/4 teaspoon cinnamon (optional)

1. Invert 6 oz. glass custard cup in center of lightly greased, 9 x 2-inch round glass dish to form ring mold, or use 8-1/2-inch glass ring mold.

2. Arrange rolls around custard cup.

3. Bake in Radarange Oven on FULL POWER for 2 to 2-1/2 minutes, or until top springs back when lightly pressed with finger. Invert ring on serving platter, and remove custard cup. Sprinkle with cinnamon, and sugar, if desired, or spread with icing. Serve immediately.

   MICRO-TIP: Prepare 1 (10 to 11 oz.) pkg. refrigerator cinnamon rolls the same as above. Bake in Radarange Oven on FULL POWER for 2-1/2 to 3 minutes, or until top springs back when lightly pressed with finger. (You may want to turn dish halfway through cooking time.)

Herb Rolls

Yield: 1 ring

1/4 cup butter or margarine, melted
1 tablespoon grated Parmesan cheese
1 teaspoon paprika
1/8 teaspoon instant, minced garlic
1 teaspoon sesame seeds

10 refrigerator biscuits

1. Combine Parmesan cheese, paprika, garlic and sesame seed in small bowl.

2. Invert 6 oz. glass custard cup in center of 9 x 2-inch round glass dish to form ring mold, or use 8-1/2-inch glass ring mold.

3. Cut each biscuit into halves. Dip in melted butter. Roll each half in cheese and spice mixture. Arrange around custard cup. Sprinkle any remaining spice mixture over top.

4. Bake in Radarange Oven on FULL POWER for 1 minute, 45 seconds to 2 minutes, or until top springs back when lightly pressed with finger.* Invert ring on serving platter, and remove custard cup. Serve immediately.

   *MICRO-TIP: You may want to turn dish halfway through cooking time.

Upside-Down Cherry Pineapple Ring

Yield: 1 ring

3 tablespoons butter or margarine
1/4 cup brown sugar, firmly packed
4 maraschino cherries, halved
8 pineapple chunks
1/2 cup walnuts or pecans, chopped

3/4 cup water
1 (1/4 oz.) pkg. active dry yeast

1/4 cup brown sugar, firmly packed
1 teaspoon salt
2-1/2 cups all-purpose flour
1 egg
1/4 cup vegetable oil

1. Place butter and brown sugar in 10-cup ring mold or 2-quart glass Bundt® dish.* Heat in Radarange Oven on FULL POWER for 30 to 45 seconds, or until melted. Arrange cherry halves and pineapple chunks over butter and sugar mixture. Sprinkle with nuts.

2. Place water in 2-quart glass measure or mixing bowl. Heat in Radarange Oven on FULL POWER for about 30 to 60 seconds, or until temperature of 105°F to 115°F, is reached.** Dissolve yeast in water.

3. Stir brown sugar, salt, and half of flour into yeast mixture. Mix well. Add egg and oil. Beat in remaining flour until smooth.

4. Drop dough by spoonfuls over nut mixture. Let rise in Radarange Oven on Cookmatic Level 1 (WARM) for 10 to 15 minutes, or until almost doubled.

5. Bake in Radarange Oven on Cookmatic Level 7 (BAKE) for 5-1/2 to 7 minutes, or until top springs back when lightly pressed with finger.*** Turn out onto serving platter.

MICRO-TIPS:

*If a plastic or ceramic utensil is used, cooking times may need to be shortened or lengthened, respectively.

**Use the Temperature-Control to stop the Radarange Oven at 110°F.

***You may want to turn dish halfway through cooking time.

Quick Caramel Rolls

Yield: 12 rolls

2 tablespoons butter or margarine
1/2 cup caramel sundae topping
1/4 cup raisins, or 1/4 cup nuts, chopped

1 (8 oz.) can refrigerator crescent rolls

1. Place butter in 8 x 2-inch round dish. Heat in Radarange Oven on FULL POWER for 30 to 45 seconds, or until melted. Add caramel topping and raisins. Mix well.

2. Invert 6 oz. glass custard cup in center of 8 x 2-inch round glass dish to form ring mold, or use 8-1/2-inch glass ring mold.

3. Remove crescents from can. Separate into 2 rolled sections. (Do not unroll.) Slice each of the 2 rolled sections into 6 rolls. Arrange around custard cup.

4. Bake in Radarange Oven on FULL POWER for 3 to 4 minutes, or until top springs back when lightly pressed with finger.* Invert ring on serving platter, and remove custard cup. Serve immediately.

*MICRO-TIP: You may want to turn dish halfway through cooking time

Biscuit Breakfast Ring

Yield: 1 ring

1/3 cup brown sugar, firmly packed
3 tablespoons butter or margarine
1 tablespoon water

1/3 cup nuts, chopped
10 refrigerator biscuits

1. Place sugar, butter and water in 1-cup glass measure. Heat in Radarange Oven on FULL POWER for 1 minute. Stir until butter is melted.

2. Invert 6 oz. glass custard cup in center of 9 x 2-inch round glass dish to form ring mold, or use 8-1/2-inch glass ring mold.

3. Sprinkle nuts evenly around custard cup. Cut each biscuit into halves. Stir into sugar mixture, coating each piece. Arrange around custard cup.

4. Bake in Radarange Oven on FULL POWER for 2-1/2 to 3 minutes, or until top springs back when lightly pressed with finger.* Let stand 2 minutes. Invert ring on serving platter, and remove custard cup. Serve immediately.

   *MICRO-TIP: You may want to turn dish halfway through cooking time.

Toffee Coffee Cake

Yield: 1, 9-inch round coffee cake

1/3 cup coconut, flaked
1/4 cup nuts, chopped
1/3 cup semi-sweet chocolate morsels
1/4 cup brown sugar, firmly packed
1 tablespoon butter or margarine, melted

2 cups biscuit baking mix
1/4 cup brown sugar, firmly packed
1 egg
2/3 cup milk
2 tablespoons vegetable oil

1. Combine coconut, nuts, chocolate morsels, brown sugar and butter in greased, 9 x 2-inch round glass dish. Mix well.

2. Combine remaining ingredients. Pour over nut mixture.

3. Bake in Radarange Oven on FULL POWER for 4 to 4-1/2 minutes, or until top springs back when lightly pressed with finger.* Turn dish once or twice during cooking time. Invert on serving platter immediately.

   MICRO-TIPS:

   •This cake makes a good dessert when served with vanilla ice cream.

   *You may want to turn dish halfway through cooking time.

Apple-Raisin Bread

Yield: 1 ring

1/2 cup butter or margarine, softened
1/2 cup brown sugar, firmly packed
1/2 cup sugar
1/2 cup dairy sour cream
2 eggs
1-1/2 cups apples, peeled, cored and grated
3/4 cup raisins

2 cups all-purpose flour
1/2 teaspoon salt
1 teaspoon cinnamon
2-1/2 teaspoons baking powder
1/2 cup walnuts or pecans, chopped (optional)

1. Cream butter, sugars and sour cream in large mixing bowl. Add eggs. Stir in apples and raisins.

2. Combine remaining ingredients. Add to apple mixture. Mix until just blended.

3. Invert 2-inch diameter glass in center of greased 2-quart casserole to form ring mold, or use greased, 10-cup Bundt® dish.* Pour batter into dish.

4. Bake in Radarange Oven on FULL POWER for 7 to 7-1/2 minutes, or until top springs back when lightly pressed with finger.** Let stand 10 minutes. Remove glass, and invert ring on serving platter.

MICRO-TIPS:

•Be sure waxed paper remains flat in dish.

*If a plastic or ceramic utensil is used, cooking times may need to be shortened or lengthened, respectively.

**You may want to turn dish halfway through cooking time.

Gingerbread Coffee Cake

Yield: 1, 9-inch round coffee cake

1 cup all-purpose flour
1/2 cup sugar
1/2 teaspoon baking soda
1/4 teaspoon salt
1/4 teaspoon cinnamon
1/4 teaspoon ground ginger
1/4 cup shortening, softened

1 egg, beaten
1/2 cup buttermilk
1 tablespoon dark molasses

1. Sift together flour, sugar, soda and spices in large mixing bowl.

2. Cut in shortening until mixture is crumbly. Reserve 1/2 cup for topping.

3. Stir in egg, buttermilk and molasses. Mix until blended. Spread batter in greased, 9 x 2-inch round glass dish. Sprinkle reserved crumb mixture on top.

4. Bake in Radarange Oven on FULL POWER for 3-1/2 to 4-1/2 minutes, or until top springs back when lightly pressed with finger.*

*MICRO-TIP: You may want to turn dish halfway through cooking time.

Peanut Butter And Jelly Coffee Cake

Yield: 1, 9-inch round coffee cake

2 cups biscuit baking mix
2 tablespoons brown sugar
1/4 cup chunky peanut butter
2/3 cup milk
1 egg

1/2 cup jelly or jam

1. Mix together all ingredients, except jelly, in large mixing bowl with electric mixer, until well-blended. Spread in greased, 9 x 2-inch round glass dish.

2. Place jelly in 1-cup glass measure. Heat in Radarange Oven on FULL POWER for 30 seconds to 1 minute, or until softened. Drizzle over batter. Draw knife through batter several times to marble.

3. Bake in Radarange Oven on FULL POWER for 4-1/2 to 5-1/2 minutes, or until top springs back when lightly pressed with finger.*

   *MICRO-TIP: You may want to turn dish halfway through cooking time.

Cherry Crumb Coffee Cake

Yield: 2, 9-inch round coffee cakes

1/4 cup butter or margarine
1 cup sugar
2 eggs

1 cup dairy sour cream
2 cups all-purpose flour
1-1/2 teaspoons baking powder
1/2 teaspoon baking soda
1/2 teaspoon salt
1/4 teaspoon vanilla extract
1/4 teaspoon almond extract

1 (1 lb.) can cherry pie filling

TOPPING

1/2 cup all-purpose flour
1/4 cup dark brown sugar, firmly packed
1 teaspoon cinnamon
2 tablespoons butter or margarine
1/2 cup nuts, chopped

1. Cream butter and sugar in large mixing bowl. Add eggs one at a time. Mix well.

2. Add remaining ingredients except pie filling. Beat well.

3. Spread 1/4 of batter in each of 2, greased, 9 x 2-inch round glass dishes. Spread 1/2 can of cherry pie filling in each dish over batter. Spread each with remaining batter.

4. For topping, combine all ingredients, except butter and nuts, in small mixing bowl. Cut in butter. Stir in nuts. Sprinkle topping over batter in both dishes. Bake each coffee cake separately.

5. Bake in Radarange Oven on FULL POWER for 6 to 7 minutes, or until top springs back when lightly pressed with finger.* Repeat with remaining coffee cake.

   MICRO-TIPS:

   •Eat one coffee cake now, and freeze the other.

   *You may want to turn dish halfway through cooking time.

Swedish Tea Ring

Yield: 1 ring

1 cup milk

1 (1/4 oz.) pkg. active dry yeast
1/4 cup sugar
1 teaspoon salt
1 egg
1/4 cup vegetable oil

3 to 3-1/2 cups all-purpose flour

2 tablespoons butter or margarine, softened
1/3 cup brown sugar, firmly packed
1/3 cup raisins
1/3 cup nuts, chopped
2 teaspoons cinnamon

ICING

1 cup confectioners' sugar
1/2 tablespoon milk
1 tablespoon butter or margarine, melted
1/2 teaspoon vanilla

1. Place milk in 2-cup glass measure. Heat in Radarange Oven on Cookmatic Level 8 (MEDIUM HIGH) for 1-1/2 to 2 minutes, or until temperature of 105°F to 115°F is reached.*

2. Dissolve yeast, sugar and salt in milk in large mixing bowl. Stir in egg and oil.

3. Stir in flour, 1 cup at a time until dough is moderately stiff.

4. Turn dough out onto lightly floured board. Knead until smooth and elastic, or about 5 minutes. Roll into 9 x 18-inch rectangle.

5. Spread dough with butter, and sprinkle with mixture of sugar, raisins, nuts and cinnamon. Roll up dough, beginning at wide side. Put sheet of waxed paper on Radarange Oven glass tray. Place dough on waxed paper. Shape into ring, pinching ends together. With scissors, make cuts on outside of ring 2/3-way through dough at 1-inch intervals. Turn each section on its side, overlapping adjacent sections. Use the Radarange Oven glass tray for rising and baking.

6. Let rise in Radarange Oven on Cookmatic Level 1 (WARM) for 10 to 15 minutes, or until doubled.

7. Bake in Radarange Oven on Cookmatic Level 7 (BAKE) for 5 to 6 minutes, or until top springs back when lightly pressed with finger.

8. For icing, mix together sugar, milk, butter and vanilla until smooth. Drizzle over bread ring.

*MICRO-TIP: Use the Temperature-Control to stop the Radarange Oven at 110° F.

Pumpkin Bread Ring

Yield: 1 ring

1/2 cup butter or margarine
3/4 cup sugar
3/4 cup brown sugar, firmly
   packed
1/2 cup water
2 eggs
1 cup canned pumpkin

2 cups all-purpose flour
1/2 cup raisins (optional)
2 teaspoons pumpkin pie spice
1 teaspoon baking powder
3/4 teaspoon salt

1. Cream butter and sugars in large mixing bowl. Add water, eggs and pumpkin.

2. Combine dry ingredients. Add to liquid ingredients. Mix until smooth.

3. Place 2-inch diameter glass in center of waxed paper-lined 2-quart glass casserole to form ring mold.* Pour batter into dish.

4. Bake in Radarange Oven on FULL POWER for 8 to 9 minutes, or until top springs back when lightly pressed with finger.** Let stand 10 minutes. Remove glass, and invert ring on serving platter.

GLAZE

1-1/2 ozs. cream cheese
1 tablespoon butter or margarine
1/2 teaspoon vanilla
1/2 cup confectioners' sugar
1 to 2 teaspoons milk
Pumpkin pie spice (optional)
Walnuts, chopped (optional)

5. For glaze, combine cream cheese, butter and vanilla. Add confectioners' sugar slowly. Blend in milk, and stir until smooth. Drizzle over cooled bread. Sprinkle lightly with pumpkin pie spice or chopped walnuts, if desired.

MICRO-TIPS:

*Be sure waxed paper remains flat in dish.

**You may want to turn dish halfway through cooking time.

Refrigerator Hot Loaf Bread

Yield: 1 loaf

2 (8 oz. each) pkgs. refrigerator
   hot loaf dough
Butter or margarine, melted

1. Place two dough rolls side by side in greased, 9 x 5 x 2-inch glass loaf dish. Brush with melted butter, as desired.

2. Bake in Radarange Oven on FULL POWER for 3 to 4 minutes, or until top springs back when lightly pressed with finger.

MICRO-TIP: Roll each piece of dough in melted butter and then in shredded cheese, cinnamon and sugar or a mixture of seasonings, such as paprika, instant minced garlic and grated Parmesan cheese.

Sticky Apple Buns

Yield: 8 large buns

3/4 cup water
1 (1/4 oz.) pkg. active dry yeast

1/4 cup sugar
1 teaspoon salt
1/2 teaspoon cinnamon
1/2 teaspoon baking powder
2-1/4 cups all-purpose flour
1 egg
1/4 cup vegetable oil

1/4 cup butter or margarine
1/3 cup brown sugar, firmly packed
1 tablespoon milk
1 teaspoon cinnamon
1 cup apples, chopped (about 2
   medium apples)
1/4 cup raisins

1. Place water in 2-quart glass measure or large mixing bowl. Heat in Radarange Oven on FULL POWER for 1 minute, or until temperature of 105° F to 115° F is reached.* Dissolve yeast in water.

2. Add sugar, salt, cinnamon, baking powder and 1 cup of flour. Beat until batter drops from spoon in sheets. Add egg, oil and remaining flour. Beat until smooth.

3. Place butter, brown sugar, milk and cinnamon in 2-quart utility dish. Heat in Radarange Oven on FULL POWER for 1 to 2 minutes, or until butter is melted. Stir in apples and raisins.

4. Drop batter from Step #2 to make 8 buns over apple mixture. Cover with damp cotton cloth, such as dishcloth. Let rise in Radarange Oven on Cookmatic Level 1 (WARM) for 10 to 15 minutes, or until almost doubled.

5. Bake in Radarange Oven, uncovered, on Cookmatic Level 7 (BAKE) for 4-1/2 to 6-1/2 minutes, or until top springs back when lightly pressed with finger.** Invert on serving platter. Serve immediately.

MICRO-TIPS:

   *Use the Temperature-Control to stop the Radarange Oven at 110°F.

   **You may want to turn dish halfway through cooking time.

Zucchini Bread

Yield: 1 loaf

1/2 cup vegetable oil
2 eggs, well-beaten
1 teaspoon vanilla
1 cup brown sugar, firmly packed

1 cup zucchini, grated
1 cup nuts, chopped
1-1/2 cups all-purpose flour
1/2 teaspoon baking soda
1/8 teaspoon baking powder
1 teaspoon cinnamon
1/2 teaspoon allspice

1. Combine oil, eggs, vanilla, and brown sugar in large mixing bowl.

2. Add remaining ingredients. Mix well. Pour into greased, 9 x 5 x 2-inch glass loaf dish.

3. Bake in Radarange Oven on FULL POWER for 5 to 6 minutes, or until toothpick inserted in center comes out clean. The top will appear slightly moist. Turn out onto cooling rack.

Cheese Spoon Bread

Yield: 1 round loaf

1 cup yellow cornmeal
1/2 teaspoon salt
1 tablespoon brown sugar

1-1/2 cups milk
1/4 cup vegetable oil
1-1/2 cups sharp Cheddar cheese, shredded

4 eggs, separated

1 teaspoon baking powder

Butter or margarine

1. Combine cornmeal, salt and sugar in large mixing bowl.

2. Place milk and oil in 1-quart glass measure. Heat in Radarange Oven on Cookmatic Level 8 (MEDIUM HIGH) for 4 to 6 minutes, or until warmed. Stir once during cooking. Add cheese. Stir until cheese is melted. Stir into cornmeal mixture.

3. Beat egg whites until stiff peaks form. Beat yolks until thick and lemon colored.

4. Fold yolks, whites and baking powder into cornmeal mixture. Pour into greased, 2-quart glass casserole.

5. Bake in Radarange Oven on Cookmatic Level 6 (ROAST) for 8 to 10 minutes, or until toothpick inserted in center comes out clean. Serve immediately with butter, as desired.

White Bread

Yield: 2 loaves

1 cup milk
1 cup water
2 (1/4 oz. each) pkgs. active dry yeast
2 tablespoons sugar

1 egg
1/4 cup butter or margarine, melted
1 teaspoon salt
6 to 6-1/2 cups all-purpose flour

1. Place milk and water in large mixing bowl. Heat in Radarange Oven on Cookmatic Level 8 (MEDIUM HIGH) for about 2 minutes, or until temperature of 105° F to 115° F is reached.* Dissolve yeast in water and milk. Stir in sugar.

2. Add egg, butter, salt and 2 cups of flour. Stir in enough remaining flour to make soft dough.

3. Turn dough out onto lightly floured board. Knead until smooth and elastic, or about 8 to 10 minutes.

4. Place in greased bowl. Grease top of dough. Cover with damp cotton cloth, such as dishcloth. Let rise in Radarange Oven on Cookmatic Level 1 (WARM) for 10 to 15 minutes, or until doubled.

5. Punch down dough. Divide in half. Roll each half into 9 x 18-inch rectangle. Roll each, starting with narrow sides. Press each end to seal. Tuck ends under loaves. Place loaves, seam-side-down in 2, greased, 9 x 5 x 2-inch glass loaf dishes. Cover each dish with damp cotton cloth, such as dishcloth. Let each loaf rise and bake separately. Let rise in Radarange Oven on Cookmatic Level 1 (WARM) for 10 to 15 minutes, or until doubled.

6. Bake in Radarange Oven, uncovered, on Cookmatic Level 7 (BAKE) for 4 to 5 minutes, or until top springs back when lightly pressed with finger. Turn out onto cooling rack. Repeat with remaining loaf.

*MICRO-TIP: Use the Temperature-Control to stop the Radarange Oven at 110° F.

Quick Sweet Rolls

Yield: 3 batches of about 1 dozen rolls each.

2 cups warm water
2 (1/4 oz. each) pkgs. active dry yeast
1/3 cup sugar
1 tablespoon salt

1/3 cup vegetable oil
2 eggs, beaten
6 to 6-1/2 cups all-purpose flour

Butter or margarine, softened
1/2 cup sugar
1 tablespoon cinnamon
1/3 cup raisins (optional)

1. Place water in 1-quart mixing bowl. Heat in Radarange Oven on FULL POWER for 1-1/2 to 2 minutes, or until temperature of 105°F to 115°F is reached.* Dissolve yeast in water. Stir in sugar and salt.

2. Blend in oil and eggs. Mix in flour, 2 cups at a time. Scrape dough from sides of bowl to center. Cover. Let stand for 20 minutes. Knead dough until smooth and elastic, or about 5 minutes.

3. Turn dough out onto lightly floured board. Divide dough into thirds. Roll each third into 1/4-inch thick rectangle. Spread each, with butter, as desired. Sprinkle each with mixture of sugar and cinnamon. Sprinkle raisins, on each, if desired. Roll each starting with narrow sides. Cut rolls into 3/4-inch slices. Evenly distribute slices among 3, greased, 9 x 2-inch round glass dishes. Let each dish of rolls rise and bake separately. Let rise in Radarange Oven on Cookmatic Level 1 (WARM) for 10 to 15 minutes, or until almost doubled.

4. Bake in Radarange Oven, uncovered, on Cookmatic Level 7 (BAKE) for 3 to 4 minutes, or until tops spring back when lightly pressed with finger.*** Invert on serving platter. Repeat with remaining rolls.

ICING**

3 tablespoons butter or margarine, melted
1 tablespoon milk
1/2 teaspoon vanilla
1 cup confectioners' sugar

5. For icing**, add butter, milk and vanilla to confectioners' sugar. Stir until smooth. Drizzle over rolls.

MICRO-TIPS:

*Use the Temperature-Control to stop the Radarange Oven at 110° F.

**This icing will cover 1, 9-inch round glass dish of sweet rolls. Triple recipe to make icing for 3 dishes.

***You may want to turn dish halfway through cooking time.

VARIATION FOR QUICK SWEET ROLLS

You may wish to try this recipe variation with 1/3 of the dough. You can prepare a different variety of rolls in each of the three dishes.

PECAN ROLLS: Prepare as "Quick Sweet Rolls", except place the 3/4-inch slices into dish prepared as follows

1/4 cup butter or margarine*
1/4 cup brown sugar, firmly packed*
1/4 cup pecan pieces*

1. Place butter in 9 x 2-inch round glass dish. Heat in Radarange Oven on FULL POWER for about 45 to 60 seconds, or until melted.

2. Stir in brown sugar, and sprinkle with pecans. Place rolls in dish. Bake for same amount of time as in original recipe.

*MICRO-TIP: If you wish to make "Pecan Rolls" with all of the dough, triple the amount of ingredients in this recipe. Icing is not used with this recipe variation.

ORANGE ROLLS: Prepare as "Quick Sweet Rolls", except for following alterations:

3-1/2 teaspoons orange peel, grated

1. Mix 1 tablespoon orange peel with cinnamon-sugar mixture in Step #3. Sprinkle on dough.

2. Proceed as in original recipe. Use remaining 1/2 teaspoon of orange peel in icing.

MICRO-TIP: If you wish to make "Orange Rolls" with all of the dough, triple the amount of ingredients in this recipe. For 1, 9 x 2-inch round glass dish of rolls, make icing used in original recipe.

Rye Bread

Yield: 1 round loaf

1 cup water
1 (1/4 oz.) pkg. active dry yeast
2 tablespoons molasses

1. Place water in 2-quart glass measure or large mixing bowl. Heat in Radarange Oven on FULL POWER for about 1 minute, or until temperature of 105° F to 115° F is reached.* Dissolve yeast in water. Stir in molasses.

2 tablespoons brown sugar
1/2 teaspoon salt
1 tablespoon butter or margarine, melted
1-1/2 teaspoons caraway seed
3/4 cup rye flour

2. Dissolve brown sugar and salt in yeast mixture. Add butter, caraway seeds and rye flour. Mix well. Stir in enough flour to make moderately stiff dough.

1-3/4 to 2 cups all-purpose flour

3. Turn dough out onto floured board. Let stand 5 to 10 minutes. Knead dough until smooth and elastic, or about 5 minutes. Place in greased bowl. Grease top of dough. Cover with damp cotton cloth, such as dishcloth. Let rise in Radarange Oven on Cookmatic Level 1 (WARM) for 10 to 15 minutes, or until almost doubled.

Cornmeal

4. Punch down dough and shape into round loaf. Place dough on piece of waxed paper sprinkled with cornmeal. Let rise in Radarange Oven on Cookmatic Level 1 (WARM) for 10 to 15 minutes, or until doubled.

5. Bake in Radarange Oven, uncovered, on Cookmatic Level 7 (BAKE) for 3-1/2 to 4 minutes, or until top springs back when lightly pressed with finger. Remove from waxed paper onto cooling rack.

*MICRO-TIP: Use the Temperature-Control to stop the Radarange Oven at 110° F.

Sally Lunn Bread

Yield: 1 ring

1/4 cup water
1 (1/4 oz.) pkg. active dry yeast

1/2 cup milk

2/3 cup butter or margarine, softened
1/4 cup sugar
1/2 teaspoon salt

2 cups all-purpose flour
2 eggs, well-beaten

3 tablespoons graham cracker crumbs

Butter or margarine

1. Place water in 1-cup glass measure. Heat in Radarange Oven on FULL POWER for 20 to 30 seconds, or until temperature of 105° F to 115° F is reached.* Dissolve yeast in water.

2. Place milk in 1-cup glass measure. Heat in Radarange Oven on Cookmatic Level 8 (MEDIUM HIGH) for 1-1/2 minutes, or until temperature of 190° F is reached. Use Temperature-Hold to keep milk at 190° F for 3 minutes, or until milk is scalded.

3. Combine butter, sugar, and salt in large mixing bowl. Add scalded milk. Stir, until butter is melted. Cool to lukewarm.

4. Beat in 1/2-cup flour, until smooth. Add yeast. Beat in 3/4-cup flour, until smooth. Beat in eggs and remaining flour until smooth, or about 5 minutes.

5. Scrape dough from sides of bowl. Cover with damp cotton cloth, such as dishcloth. Let rise in Radarange Oven on Cookmatic Level 1 (WARM) for 10 minutes. Let rest additional 10 minutes, or until almost doubled.

6. Place 2-inch diameter glass in center of generously greased, 3-quart glass casserole to form ring mold, or use greased, 10-cup glass Bundt* dish.** Sprinkle with graham cracker crumbs.

7. Beat dough for 5 minutes. Pour dough into prepared dish. Cover with damp cotton cloth, such as dishcloth. Let rise in Radarange Oven on Cookmatic Level 1 (WARM) for 10 minutes. Let rest additional 10 minutes.

8. Bake in Radarange Oven, uncovered, on Cookmatic Level 7 (BAKE) for 6 to 8 minutes, or until top springs back when lightly pressed with finger. Remove glass, and invert ring on serving platter. Serve immediately with butter, as desired.

MICRO-TIPS:

*Use the Temperature-Control to stop the Radarange Oven at 110° F.

**If a plastic or ceramic utensil is used, cooking times may need to be shortened or lengthened, respectively.

Herb Bread

Yield: 1, 9-inch round ring

4 to 4-1/2 cups all-purpose flour
2 tablespoons sugar
1-1/2 teaspoons salt
1 (1/4 oz.) pkg. active dry yeast

1-1/4 cups milk
2 tablespoons vegetable oil
1 egg

2 tablespoons butter or margarine, melted
1 teaspoon onion salt
2 tablespoons grated Parmesan cheese
1/2 teaspoon paprika

1. Combine 1 cup flour, sugar, salt and yeast in large mixing bowl.

2. Place milk and oil in 2-cup glass measure. Heat in Radarange Oven on Cookmatic Level 8 (MEDIUM HIGH) for 2 minutes, or until just warm. Add to flour mixture along with egg.

3. Beat 1/2 minute on low speed, and then 3 minutes on medium speed. Gradually stir in enough flour to make a soft dough.

4. Turn dough out onto lightly floured board. Knead until smooth and elastic, or about 5 to 8 minutes. Shape dough into ball and place in bowl. Cover with damp cotton cloth, such as dishcloth. Let rise in Radarange Oven on Cookmatic Level 1 (WARM) for 10 to 15 minutes, or until almost doubled.

5. Punch down dough and divide into thirds. Roll into strips about 1-1/2 feet long. Brush dough strips with melted butter. Combine spices, and roll dough strips in spices. Braid strips.

6. Place 2-inch diameter glass in center of 3-quart glass casserole to form ring mold, or use 8-1/2-inch glass ring mold.* Arrange braided dough around glass. Let rise in Radarange Oven on Cookmatic Level 1 (WARM) for 10 to 14 minutes, or until almost doubled.

7. Bake in Radarange Oven, uncovered, on Cookmatic Level 7 (BAKE) for 6 to 7 minutes, or until top springs back when lightly pressed with finger.** Invert ring on serving platter, and remove glass.

MICRO-TIPS:

• Try rolling the dough strips in following mixture for variation:

   1/2 cup Cheddar cheese, shredded
   1 tablespoon cornmeal
   1 teaspoon onion salt
   1 teaspoon poppy or sesame seed

• May also bake Herb Bread on Radarange Oven glass tray. Put sheet of waxed paper on glass oven tray. Place dough on waxed paper. Shape into ring, pinching ends together. Let rise and bake as above.

*If a plastic or ceramic utensil is used, cooking times may need to be shortened or lengthened, respectively.

**You may want to turn dish halfway through cooking time.

Pumpkin-Raisin Bread

Yield: 2 loaves

1-1/2 cups water
1 (1/4 oz.) pkg. active dry yeast

2/3 cup brown sugar, firmly
    packed
1-1/2 teaspoons salt
2/3 cup vegetable oil
2 eggs
1 cup canned pumpkin
1-1/2 teaspoons pumpkin pie spice
7 to 7-1/2 cups all-purpose flour
1/2 cup raisins

Cinnamon
Butter or margarine, melted

ICING

1 cup confectioners' sugar
1/4 cup butter or margarine, melted
1 tablespoon milk
1/2 teaspoon vanilla
1/2 teaspoon pumpkin pie spice

1. Place water in 2-quart glass measure or large mixing bowl. Heat in Radarange Oven on FULL POWER for 1 to 1-1/2 minutes, or until temperature of 105° F to 115° F is reached.* Dissolve yeast in water.

2. Stir in brown sugar, salt, oil, eggs, pumpkin, pumpkin pie spice and 3 cups of flour. Add raisins. Add enough of remaining flour to make dough easy to handle.

3. Turn dough out onto lightly floured board. Knead until smooth and elastic, or about 5 minutes. Place in greased bowl. Grease top of dough. Cover with damp cotton cloth, such as dishcloth. Let rise in Radarange Oven on Cookmatic Level 1 (WARM) for 10 to 15 minutes, or until almost doubled.

4. Punch down dough. Divide in half. Roll each half into 9 x 18-inch rectangle. Sprinkle with cinnamon, as desired. Roll each, starting with narrow sides. Press each end to seal. Tuck ends under loaves. Place loaves, seam-sides-down in 2, greased, 9 x 5 x 2-inch glass loaf dishes. Brush loaves lightly with melted butter. Cover with damp cotton cloth, such as dishcloth. Let each loaf rise and bake separately. Let rise in Radarange Oven on Cookmatic Level 1 (WARM) for 10 to 15 minutes, or until doubled.

5. Bake in Radarange Oven, uncovered, on Cookmatic Level 7 (BAKE) for 5-1/2 to 6-1/2 minutes, or until top springs back when lightly pressed with finger. Turn out onto cooling rack. Repeat with remaining loaf.

6. For icing, mix together confectioners' sugar, butter, milk, vanilla, and pumpkin pie spice. Drizzle over cooled loaves.

*MICRO-TIP: Use the Temperature-Control to stop the Radarange Oven at 110° F.

Raisin-Wheat Bread

Yield: 1 loaf

1 (1/4 oz.) pkg. active dry yeast
2-3/4 to 3 cups all-purpose flour

1-1/4 cups milk
2 tablespoons brown sugar
2 tablespoons dark molasses
1 tablespoon vegetable oil
1/2 teaspoon salt
3/4 cup shredded wheat, crumbled

1 cup raisins

2 to 3 teaspoons cinnamon

1. Combine yeast and 1-1/2 cups of flour in large mixing bowl.

2. Mix together milk, sugar, molasses, oil and salt in 4-cup glass measure. Heat in Radarange Oven on Cookmatic Level 8 (MEDIUM HIGH) for 2 to 3 minutes, or until just warm. Stir once or twice during heating. Add shredded wheat to milk mixture. Let stand 2 minutes.

3. Add milk mixture to flour and yeast mixture. Beat on low speed for 1/2 minute, and then on high speed for 3 minutes. Stir in raisins and enough remaining flour to make moderately stiff dough.

4. Turn dough out onto lightly floured board. Knead until smooth and elastic, or about 5 to 8 minutes. Place in greased bowl. Grease top of dough. Cover with damp cotton cloth, such as dishcloth. Let rise in Radarange Oven on Cookmatic Level 1 (WARM) for 10 to 15 minutes, or until almost doubled.

5. Punch down dough. Roll into 9 x 18-inch rectangle. Sprinkle with cinnamon, as desired. Roll, starting with narrow side. Press each end to seal. Tuck ends under loaf. Place loaf seam-side-down in greased, 9 x 5 x 2-inch glass loaf dish. Cover with damp cotton cloth, such as dishcloth. Let rise in Radarange Oven on Cookmatic Level 1 (WARM) for 10 to 15 minutes, or until doubled.

6. Bake in Radarange Oven, uncovered, on Cookmatic Level 7 (BAKE) for 4 to 5 minutes, or until top springs back when lightly pressed with finger. Turn out onto cooling rack.

Cranberry Coffee Loaf

Yield: 1 loaf

2 cups all-purpose flour
1/2 cup sugar
1/2 cup brown sugar, firmly packed
1-1/2 teaspoons baking powder
1 teaspoon salt
1/2 teaspoon baking soda

1 orange

Hot water
2 tablespoons shortening, melted
1 egg, beaten

1 cup raw cranberries, coarsely chopped
1 cup nuts, chopped

TOPPING

2 tablespoons brown sugar
1 teaspoon cinnamon
2 tablespoons nuts, chopped
1 teaspoon orange peel, grated

1. Blend together flour, sugar, brown sugar, baking powder, salt and baking soda in large mixing bowl.

2. Grate the orange. Reserve grated peel.

3. Combine juice of orange and enough hot water to measure 3/4 cup liquid. Stir in shortening and egg. Add to dry ingredients. Mix until just blended.

4. Stir in cranberries, nuts and 1 tablespoon of orange peel. Spread batter in greased, 9 x 5 x 2-inch glass loaf dish.

5. For topping, combine all ingredients. Sprinkle topping over batter.

6. Bake in Radarange Oven on FULL POWER for 5-1/2 to 6-1/2 minutes, or until toothpick inserted in center comes out clean. Invert on serving platter immediately.

Rice, cereals, and pastas are easy to prepare. These foods can be cooked directly in serving dishes when cooked in the Radarange Oven, avoiding hard-to-clean pans. Also, cooking can be done without scorching.

Before preparing these three foods in the Radarange Oven, note the few basic hints that are given. Consult the charts in this section for accurate cooking instructions.

General Hints for Cooking Rice

1. When preparing rice in the Radarange Oven, the size of the dish is important to consider. If too small a dish is used for the amount of rice, water will boil over slightly, due to the expansion of the rice as it cooks. Choose a glass cooking dish which is of an adequate size to allow water to boil vigorously. The addition of oil will help to prevent boil-overs.

2. It's very important to cook rice in a covered dish. This allows for faster cooking. Glass lids or heavy-duty plastic wrap are the best coverings to use since they are the most water-vapor-proof. After rice is added to boiling water, the lid may be left slightly off-center to avoid boil-overs. You may wish to stir rice halfway through the cooking time to avoid boil-overs. Use hot pads when removing rice from the Radarange Oven.

3. Rice should require virtually no stirring during cooking. In fact, less stirring is better, since over-stirring can cause a "mushy" texture. Even after rice is cooked, avoid too much tossing.

4. The standing time, after cooking, allows the rice to finish its own cooking, and to absorb all of the moisture.

5. Long grain white rice begins cooking at FULL POWER, but finishes cooking at a lower setting. This slower cooking helps to give the rice a fluffier texture.

6. Quick-cooking rice can be simply rehydrated. Bring the required amount of water to a boil in the serving dish. Stir in quick-cooking rice, cover with glass lid or heavy-duty plastic wrap, and let stand, according to the amount of time required on the package. (See the "Rice Cooking and Convenience Food Chart" on pages 106 and 107.)

7. Wild rice is actually not a cereal grain, but is a grass seed. Wild rice cooking instructions are, however, included in the "Rice Cooking and Convenience Food Chart" on pages 108 and 109. If wild rice is presoaked before cooking, it will be more tender.

8. Rice can be reheated quickly in the Radarange Oven. Rice should be reheated on FULL POWER in a covered casserole, until it is steaming hot. Again, a glass lid or heavy-duty plastic wrap covering is best. It is not necessary to add liquid for reheating. However, for a large quantity you may wish to add 1 to 2 tablespoons of water. If rice has been refrigerated, stir once or twice during reheating. Since rice is easily reheated, rice can be cooked ahead and later reheated quickly for casserole dishes requiring rice.

RICE YIELD CHART

UNCOOKED RICE	COOKED RICE
1 cup raw, long grain white rice	3 to 3-1/2 cups
1 cup raw, brown rice	4 cups
1 cup raw, wild rice	3-1/2 cups
1 cup quick-cooking rice	2 cups

RICE TYPE	AMOUNT OR PKG. SIZE	DISH SIZE	AMOUNT HOT TAP WATER	AMOUNT OIL, BUTTER OR MARGARINE	AMOUNT SALT	EXTRA INGRED.	1ST COOKING TIME
Brown Rice	1 cup rice	3-quart casserole	3 cups	1 teaspoon oil	1 teaspoon	—	5 to 7 min.
Canned Spanish Rice	15 oz. can	1-quart casserole	—	—	—	—	2-1/2 to 3 min.
Long Grain White Rice	1 cup rice	3-quart casserole	2 cups**	1 teaspoon oil	1 teaspoon	—	4 to 5 min.
Quick Brown Rice	1 cup rice	3-quart casserole	1-1/2 cups	1 teaspoon oil	1/2 teaspoon	—	3 to 5 min.
Quick-Cooking Rice	Amount rice equal to amt. water	Twice as large as amt. water	Equal to amt. rice	1/2 teaspoon butter or margarine per serving, optional	1/8 teaspoon per serving	—	1 cup water — 1 to 1-1/2 min. 2 cups water — 4 to 5 min.

*Chart is continued on pages 108 and 109. See the "General Instructions for Cooking Rice and Rice Convenience Foods" on page 108.

**Use amount of ingredients recommended in package instructions.

Rice-Stuffed Tomatoes

Yield: 6 servings

6 large firm, ripe tomatoes

1/2 cup green onion, chopped
1/4 cup celery, chopped
2 tablespoons butter or margarine

2/3 cup cooked rice
1/2 cup Cheddar cheese, shredded
1 (4 oz.) can mushrooms, drained
1 teaspoon salt
1/8 teaspoon pepper
1/4 teaspoon basil
Dash cayenne pepper

1. Cut 1/4-inch slice off top of each tomato. Scoop out pulp, drain and reserve.

2. Place onion, celery and butter in 1-quart casserole. Heat in Radarange Oven on FULL POWER for 2 to 3 minutes, or until onion and celery are tender.

3. Add tomato pulp and remaining ingredients to onion and celery. Spoon mixture into tomatoes. Place in 9 x 2-inch round dish. Cover with plastic wrap.

4. Bake in Radarange Oven, covered, on FULL POWER for 3 to 4 minutes, or until heated through.

CONVENIENCE FOOD CHART*

1ST SETTING	2ND COOKING TIME	2ND SETTING	3RD COOKING TIME	3RD SETTING	SPECIAL INSTRUCTIONS
FULL POWER	25 to 30 min.	FULL POWER	—	—	Stir salt and oil into hot tap water. Heat, covered, according to 1st time and setting, or until water boils. Stir in rice. Cook, covered, according to 2nd time and setting, or until rice is tender. Allow a 5-minute standing time, if necessary, after the rice finishes cooking.
FULL POWER	—	—	—	—	Place canned ingredients in casserole. Cook until heated through. Stir and serve.
FULL POWER	1-1/2 to 2-1/2 min.	FULL POWER	12 to 14 min.	Cookmatic Level 3 (SIMMER)	Stir salt and oil into hot tap water. Heat, covered, according to 1st time and setting, or until water boils. Stir in rice. Cook, covered, according to 2nd time and setting, or until water boils. Cook, covered, according to 3rd time and setting, or until rice is tender. Allow a 5-minute standing time, if necessary, after the rice finishes cooking.
FULL POWER	10 to 12 min.	FULL POWER	—	—	Stir salt and oil into hot tap water. Heat, covered, according to 1st time and setting, or until water boils. Stir in rice. Cook, covered, according to 2nd time and setting, or until rice is tender. Allow a 5-minute standing time, if necessary, after the rice finishes cooking.
FULL POWER	—	—	—	—	Heat water, salt, and butter according to 1st setting, or until water boils. (Use equal measures of rice and water.) Stir in rice. Let stand, covered, for amount time recommended on pkg. Fluff with fork to serve. For firmer rice, use 1 tablespoon less water per serving.

Swedish Rice Pudding

Yield: 5 to 6 servings

1-1/2 cups cooked rice
3 cups milk

3 eggs, beaten
3/4 cup sugar
1 teaspoon vanilla
1/2 teaspoon ground cardamon
1/4 teaspoon salt

2 tablespoons sugar
1 teaspoon cinnamon

1. Combine rice and milk in 1-1/2-quart casserole.

2. Combine eggs, sugar, vanilla, cardamon and salt. Add to rice mixture.

3. Cook in Radarange Oven, covered, on Cookmatic Level 4 (MEDIUM) for 30 to 35 minutes, or until knife inserted in center comes out clean. Sprinkle with sugar and cinnamon.

MICRO-TIPS:

•This is a good way to use left-over rice.

•Serve hot. Sprinkle individual servings with additional sugar and cinnamon, if desired.

RICE TYPE	AMOUNT OR PKG. SIZE	DISH SIZE	AMOUNT HOT TAP WATER	AMOUNT OIL, BUTTER OR MARGARINE	AMOUNT SALT	EXTRA INGRED.	1ST COOKING TIME
Long Grain White and Wild Rice Mix	6-3/4 oz. pkg.	3-quart casserole	2-1/2 cups*	1 tablespoon oil	—	—	15 to 20 min.
Rice Oriental Main Dish Mix	8 oz. pkg.	3-quart casserole	4 cups	—	—	1 lb. ground beef	4 to 5 min.
Rice-Vermicelli Mix	8 oz. pkg.	Large browning skillet	2-3/4 cups	2 tablespoons butter or margarine	—	—	8 to 11 min.
Spanish Rice Mix	6 oz. pkg.	1-quart casserole	1 cup	2 tablespoons butter or margarine	—	1 (16 oz.) can tomatoes	7 to 9 min.
Wild Rice**	4 oz. pkg.	3-quart casserole	2-1/2 cups	1 teaspoon oil	1 teaspoon	—	5 to 6 min.

*Use amount of ingredients recommended in package instructions.
*Pre-soak wild rice before cooking, for a more tender product.

General Instructions for Cooking Rice and Rice Convenience Foods

1. Read the "Special Instructions" in the chart before cooking.

2. When water is used, be certain to use hot tap water, since it will boil faster than cold. Water also boils faster in a covered utensil.

3. Be sure to cook, covered, if the "Special Instructions" state to do so. Cooking is accomplished faster in a covered utensil. Let stand for 5 minutes, covered, in most cases, before serving. Fluff with fork.

CONVENIENCE FOOD CHART (Continued)

1ST SETTING	2ND COOKING TIME	2ND SETTING	3RD COOKING TIME	3RD SETTING	SPECIAL INSTRUCTIONS
FULL POWER	—	—	—	—	Stir butter into hot tap water. Add packaged ingredients. Cook, according to 1st time and setting, or until rice is tender, and water is absorbed. Allow a 5-minute standing time, if necessary, after the rice finishes cooking.
FULL POWER	20 min.	FULL POWER	—	—	Place beef in casserole and cook according to 1st setting, or until beef is no longer pink. Stir halfway through cooking time. Drain. Add mix and water. Cook according to 2nd setting, or until rice is tender. Stir occasionally during cooking time.
Cookmatic Level 3 (SIMMER)	—	—	—	—	Preheat browning skillet, according to manufacturer's instructions. Add butter and rice mix, stirring to coat and brown. Add water and soup base envelope. Stir. Cover. Cook, according to 2nd time and setting, or until all water is absorbed.
FULL POWER	—	—	—	—	Combine water, tomatoes, contents of seasoning packet in casserole. Cook. Stir halfway through cooking time. Stir in rice, cover and let stand 12 minutes. Stir and serve.
FULL POWER	20 to 25 min.	FULL POWER	—	—	Stir salt and oil into hot tap water. Heat, covered according to 1st time and setting, or until water boils. Stir in rice. Cook, covered, according to 2nd time and setting, or until rice is tender. Allow a 5-minute standing time, if necessary, after the rice finishes cooking.

Chicken, Bacon and Rice

Yield: 4 to 6 servings

6 slices bacon, cut in 1/2-inch pieces

1 onion, chopped

2 cups cooked chicken, diced
2 cups cooked rice
1/2 cup strong chicken bouillon
1 tablespoon parsley flakes
1/2 teaspoon salt
1/4 teaspoon pepper

1/2 cup dairy sour cream
2 tablespoons grated Parmesan cheese
1/2 teaspoon paprika

1. Place bacon in 1-1/2-quart casserole. Cook in Radarange Oven on FULL POWER for 3 to 4 minutes, or until crisp. Remove bacon and drain all but one tablespoon of grease.

2. Add onion to bacon grease. Cook in Radarange Oven on FULL POWER for 2 to 3 minutes, or until onion is tender.

3. Add bacon, chicken, rice, bouillon, parsley flakes, salt and pepper. Heat in Radarange Oven on FULL POWER for 2 minutes.

4. Combine remaining ingredients, and stir into rice mixture. Heat in Radarange Oven on Cookmatic Level 5 (SLO COOK) for 1 minute, or until heated through.

Orange Rice

Yield: 4 servings

1/4 cup onion, chopped
1 cup celery, chopped
2 tablespoons vegetable oil

1-1/4 cups water
2 tablespoons orange juice
concentrate, undiluted
1/2 teaspoon salt
1-1/3 cups quick-cooking rice

1. Combine onion, celery and oil in 2-quart casserole. Cook in Radarange Oven on FULL POWER for 3 to 4 minutes, or until onion and celery are tender.

2. Stir in water, orange juice concentrate and salt. Cook in Radarange Oven, covered, on FULL POWER for 3 to 4 minutes, or until mixture boils. Mix in rice. Cover, and let stand 5 minutes, or until water is absorbed. Stir and serve.

Fiesta Rice

Yield: 6 to 8 servings

1 tablespoon butter or margarine
2 cups celery, chopped
1 cup green pepper, chopped
1 cup onion, chopped

1 lb. ground beef

3 cups cooked rice
1 (8 oz.) can tomato sauce
1 teaspoon garlic salt
1/2 to 1 teaspoon chili powder
1/2 teaspoon cumin powder
1/2 teaspoon oregano

1. Place butter and vegetables in 2-quart casserole. Cook in Radarange Oven, covered, on FULL POWER for 4 to 6 minutes, or until vegetables are almost tender.

2. Add beef. Cook in Radarange Oven on FULL POWER for 4 to 5 minutes, or until beef is no longer pink. Stir halfway through cooking time. Drain.

3. Add remaining ingredients. Cook in Radarange Oven on FULL POWER for 4 to 6 minutes, or until heated through.

Wild Rice and Mushrooms

Yield: 4 to 5 servings

1 (6-3/4 oz.) pkg. long grain and wild rice mix

1 (4 oz.) can sliced mushrooms, drained
1 tablespoon fresh or frozen chives
1/4 cup dairy sour cream or
1/4 cup Cheddar cheese soup

1. Prepare rice according to package directions. Place in 3-quart casserole. Cook in Radarange Oven, covered, on FULL POWER for about 15 to 20 minutes, or until all water is absorbed.

2. Add mushrooms, chives and sour cream. Heat in Radarange Oven on FULL POWER for about 1 minute, or until heated through.

"Souper" Rice & Mushrooms

Yield: 6 servings

1-1/4 cups water
3/4 teaspoon instant beef bouillon
1-1/4 cups quick-cooking rice

1 (10-3/4 oz.) can golden cream of mushroom soup

1. Combine water and instant bouillon in 1-quart casserole. Cook in Radarange Oven on FULL POWER for 2 to 3 minutes, or until mixture boils. Stir in rice. Let stand, covered, until water is absorbed.

2. Stir in soup, until well-blended. Cook in Radarange Oven on FULL POWER for 2 to 3 minutes, or until heated through.

Quick Fried Rice

Yield: 4 to 5 servings

2 tablespoons butter or margarine
2 tablespoons onion, chopped

2 cups quick-cooking rice
1-2/3 cups water
2 teaspoons instant beef
    bouillon
1/2 teaspoon salt
Dash pepper

2 eggs, slightly-beaten
1/4 cup green onion, sliced
2 teaspoons soy sauce

1. Place butter in 2-quart casserole. Heat in Radarange Oven on FULL POWER for 20 to 30 seconds, or until melted. Add onion. Cook in Radarange Oven on FULL POWER for 1 to 2 minutes, or until onion is tender.

2. Stir in rice, water, instant bouillon, salt and pepper. Cook in Radarange Oven, covered, on FULL POWER for about 3 to 4 minutes, or until rice is tender. Stir halfway through cooking time. Stir and let stand, covered, until water is absorbed, or about 4 to 5 minutes.

3. Mix in eggs, green onion and soy sauce. Cook in Radarange Oven on Cookmatic Level 8 (MEDIUM HIGH) for 2 to 3 minutes, or until eggs are set. Stir halfway through cooking time. Stir in soy sauce.

Apple 'N' Rice Casserole

Yield: 4 servings

1/4 cup butter or margarine

2 cups cooked rice
2 cups apples, pared, cored and
    thinly sliced
1 tablespoon lemon juice
1/4 cup sugar
1 teaspoon cinnamon
2 tablespoons dairy sour cream

1. Place butter in 1-quart casserole. Heat in Radarange Oven on FULL POWER for 20 to 30 seconds, or until melted.

2. Stir in rice, apples, lemon juice, sugar, cinnamon and sour cream.

3. Bake in Radarange Oven, covered, on FULL POWER for 4-1/2 to 5 minutes, or until apples are tender.

MICRO-TIP: Add 1/2 cup raisins, if desired. Great to serve with pork.

Hopping John

Yield: 4 to 6 servings

3 strips bacon

1/3 cup onion, chopped

1-1/2 cups cooked, black eyed
    beans
1-1/2 cups cooked rice
1 cup ham, diced
1/2 teaspoon salt
1/4 teaspoon pepper

1. Place bacon in 1-1/2-quart utility dish. Cover with paper towel. Cook in Radarange Oven, covered, on FULL POWER for 2 to 3 minutes, or until crisp. Remove bacon and all but 1 tablespoon of bacon grease.

2. Add onion to bacon grease. Cook in Radarange Oven on FULL POWER for 2 minutes, or until onion is tender.

3. Stir in remaining ingredients, except bacon. Cook in Radarange Oven, covered, on FULL POWER for 3 to 4 minutes, or until hot. Crumble bacon, and sprinkle over top.

Rice and Spinach Deluxe

Yield: 6 servings

2 tablespoons butter or margarine
1 cup onion, chopped

1-1/2 cups quick-cooking rice
1/2 teaspoon salt
1-1/2 cups water

1 (10 oz.) pkg. frozen spinach, chopped
1 (5 oz.) jar sharp process cheese spread*

1 (10-3/4 oz.) can cream of mushroom soup
1/8 teaspoon nutmeg (optional)

1. Place butter in 1-1/2-quart casserole. Heat in Radarange Oven on FULL POWER for 20 to 30 seconds, or until melted. Stir in onion. Cook in Radarange Oven on FULL POWER for 3 to 4 minutes, or until onion is tender.

2. Add rice, salt and water. Cook in Radarange Oven, covered, on FULL POWER for 2 to 3 minutes, or until boiling. Let stand, covered, until moisture is absorbed.

3. Place frozen spinach in 1-quart casserole or leave in package.*** Cook in Radarange Oven on FULL POWER for 2-1/2 to 3 minutes, or until thawed. Drain, and add to rice along with cheese spread. Stir until cheese spread melts.

4. Stir in soup. Add nutmeg, if desired. Cook in Radarange Oven on Cookmatic Level 5 (SLO COOK) for about 8 to 10 minutes, or until temperature of 150° F is reached. ****

MICRO-TIPS:

*Place jar of cheese spread, without lid, in Radarange Oven on Cookmatic Level 5 (SLO COOK) for 1 to 2 minutes, to easily remove cheese from jar.

**Remember to make a 1-inch slit with a knife in the pouch or box before cooking.

***Use the Temperature-Control to stop the Radarange Oven at 150° F.

Savory Rice Ring

Yield: 6 servings

2-1/4 cups hot water
2 teaspoons instant chicken bouillon
3/4 teaspoon salt

1 tablespoon instant, minced onion
2-1/4 cups quick-cooking rice

1/4 cup butter or margarine, melted
1/8 teaspoon saffron (optional)
1 tablespoon parsley flakes

1. Combine water, bouillon, and salt in 4-cup glass measure. Cook in Radarange Oven on FULL POWER for about 4 to 5 minutes, or until mixture boils.

2. Stir in onion and rice. Cover, and let stand 7 minutes, or until water is absorbed.

3. Place butter and saffron in 1-cup glass measure. Heat in Radarange Oven on FULL POWER for about 45 to 60 seconds, or until melted. Stir into rice with parsley flakes.

4. Pat rice mixture into 8-1/2-inch ring mold with back of spoon. Press firmly. Turn out onto serving plate.

MICRO-TIP: Center of ring may be filled with creamed chicken or other meat.

Fruited-Rice Cream

Yield: 6 servings

1-1/2 cups cooked rice
1 (16 oz.) can fruit cocktail, drained

1 cup heavy cream
1/4 cup confectioners' sugar
1 teaspoon vanilla
1/4 teaspoon cinnamon

1. Cook rice, according to directions on pages 106 and 107. Combine rice and fruit cocktail.

2. Beat cream with confectioners' sugar, vanilla and cinnamon, until stiff. Fold into rice and fruit mixture. Spoon into dessert cups. Chill.

Crab Creole Casserole

Yield: 6 servings

1 cup onion, chopped
1/4 cup green pepper, chopped
1/4 cup celery, chopped
1/4 cup butter or margarine

1 (16 oz.) can tomatoes
1 teaspoon salt
1/4 teaspoon pepper
1/8 teaspoon chili powder

3/4 cup cooked rice
1 cup Cheddar cheese, shredded
2 (6-1/2 oz. each) cans crab meat
1 tablespoon Worcestershire sauce

2/3 cup Cheddar cheese, shredded
1/2 cup potato chips, crushed

1. Combine onion, green pepper, celery and butter in 2-quart casserole. Cook in Radarange Oven on FULL POWER for 4 to 5 minutes, or until vegetables are tender. Stir twice during cooking time.

2. Add tomatoes, salt, pepper and chili powder to vegetables. Cook in Radarange Oven on FULL POWER for 3 minutes.

3. Stir in rice, 1 cup cheese, crab meat and Worcestershire sauce. Cook in Radarange Oven on FULL POWER for 5 minutes. Stir halfway through cooking time to blend in cheese.

4. Sprinkle on cheese, and then chips. Heat in Radarange Oven on Cookmatic Level 5 (SLO COOK) for 2 minutes, or until cheese is melted.

Jambalaya

Yield: 4 to 6 servings

1/2 cup onion, chopped
1/3 cup green pepper, chopped
1/8 teaspoon instant, minced garlic
1 tablespoon vegetable oil

1/2 cup boiling water
1 teaspoon instant chicken bouillon

1 (12 oz.) pkg. shrimp, frozen*
1 (8 oz.) can stewed tomatoes
1 cup ham, cubed
1/2 teaspoon salt
1/8 teaspoon pepper

1-1/2 cups cooked rice

1. Place onion, green pepper, garlic and oil in 2-quart casserole. Cook in Radarange Oven on FULL POWER for 2 to 3 minutes, or until onion and green pepper are tender.

2. Dissolve bouillon in water. Add to onion and green pepper.

3. Add remaining ingredients, except rice. Cook in Radarange Oven, covered, on FULL POWER for 7 to 8 minutes, or until hot. Stir halfway through cooking time.

4. Add rice. Cook in Radarange Oven on FULL POWER for 3 to 5 minutes, or until heated through. Stir before serving.

    *MICRO-TIP: When substituting fresh shrimp for frozen, slightly decrease cooking time in step #3.

Bacon 'N' Rice Salad

Yield: 6 to 8 servings

3 cups cooked rice

8 slices bacon, cooked and crumbled
1 cup cooked green peas
1/4 cup chives, snipped
1 cup celery, thinly sliced
1/2 teaspoon salt
1/4 teaspoon pepper
1/2 cup thousand island salad dressing

1. Cook rice, according to directions on pages 106 and 107.
2. Combine all ingredients. Chill.

MICRO-TIP: May be served on lettuce leaves, and garnished with olives.

Rice and Spice Hamburger Casserole

Yield: 6 servings

1/2 cup onion, chopped
1/2 cup celery, chopped
1 tablespoon butter or margarine

1 lb. ground beef

1 (10-3/4 oz.) can golden cream
  of mushroom soup
1 (10-3/4 oz.) soup can water
1 cup cooked rice
1 cup carrot, thinly sliced
2 tablespoons soy sauce
1 teaspoon instant chicken bouillon
1/4 teaspoon ground thyme

1. Place onion, celery and butter in 1-1/2-quart casserole. Heat in Radarange Oven on FULL POWER for 1-1/2 minutes, or until onion and celery are tender.

2. Add beef. Cook in Radarange Oven on FULL POWER for 3 to 4 minutes, or until beef is no longer pink. Stir halfway through cooking time. Drain.

3. Add remaining ingredients. Cook in Radarange Oven on FULL POWER for 9 to 10 minutes, or until heated through and temperature of 150° F is reached.*

*MICRO-TIP: Use the Temperature-Hold to maintain 150° F until ready to serve.

Beef-Rice Bake

Yield: 4 to 6 servings

1 cup onion, chopped
1-1/2 cups celery, chopped
1 tablespoon vegetable oil

1 lb. ground beef

1-1/2 cups cooked rice
1 (10-3/4 oz.) can cream of
  mushroom soup
2 tablespoons soy sauce

1 (3 oz.) can chow mein noodles

1. Combine onion, celery and oil in 2-quart casserole. Cook in Radarange Oven on FULL POWER for 4 to 5 minutes, or until onion and celery are tender.

2. Add beef. Cook in Radarange Oven on FULL POWER for 3 to 4 minutes, or until beef is no longer pink. Stir halfway through cooking time. Drain.

3. Blend in rice, soup and soy sauce. Cook in Radarange Oven on FULL POWER for 4 minutes. Stir after cooking time.

4. Sprinkle chow mein noodles over top. Cook in Radarange Oven on FULL POWER for 3 minutes, or until heated through and temperature of 150° F is reached.*

*MICRO-TIP: Use the Temperature-Hold to maintain 150° F until ready to serve.

Tangy Rice Salad

Yield: 6 servings

1-1/3 cups tomato juice
1-1/3 cups quick-cooking rice

1/2 cup celery, chopped
1/4 cup green onion, thinly sliced
1/2 cup mayonnaise
1/4 cup sweet pickle relish
1/2 teaspoon salt

1. Place tomato juice in 1-1/2-quart casserole. Heat in Radarange Oven on FULL POWER for 2-1/2 to 3 minutes, or until boiling. Stir in rice and cover.

2. When rice has absorbed all liquid, stir in remaining ingredients. Chill.

Tuna-Rice Casserole

Yield: 8 servings

1/4 cup onion, chopped
1 medium green pepper, chopped
6 tablespoons butter or margarine

1/4 cup all-purpose flour
1 cup milk

2 cups cooked rice
2 (7 oz. each) cans tuna, drained
1 (10-3/4 oz.) can cream of chicken soup
1 (10-3/4 oz.) can cream of mushroom soup*
1 (4 oz.) can sliced mushrooms, drained
1 (2 oz.) jar pimentos (optional)
Salt (optional)

1. Place onion, green pepper and butter in 2-quart casserole. Heat in Radarange Oven on FULL POWER for 2 to 3 minutes, or until onion and green pepper are tender.

2. Blend in flour. Stir in milk gradually, until smooth. Cook in Radarange Oven on FULL POWER for 2 minutes, or until slightly thickened. Stir halfway through cooking time.

3. Mix in rice, tuna, soups, mushrooms and pimentos. Season with salt, as desired. Cook in Radarange Oven on FULL POWER for 10 minutes, or until heated through and temperature of 150° F is reached.**

MICRO-TIPS:

*For richer color and flavor, use golden cream of mushroom soup, instead of cream of mushroom soup.
**Use the Temperature-Control to stop the Radarange Oven at 150° F.

Shrimp-Rice Casserole

Yield: 6 servings

2 tablespoons green pepper, chopped
2 tablespoons onion, chopped
1 teaspoon vegetable oil

1 (10-3/4 oz.) can cream of mushroom soup
2 cups cooked rice
1 tablespoon lemon juice
1/2 teaspoon Worcestershire sauce
1/2 teaspoon dry mustard
1/4 teaspoon pepper
1/2 lb. shrimp, cleaned
2 tablespoons cornflake crumbs
1 to 2 tablespoons butter or margarine
Paprika

1. Combine green pepper, onion and oil in 1-1/2-quart casserole. Cook in Radarange Oven on FULL POWER for 1 to 2 minutes, or until onion and green pepper are tender.

2. Blend in soup, rice, lemon juice, Worcestershire sauce, mustard, pepper and shrimp. Top with crumbs. Dot with butter. Sprinkle with paprika, as desired.

3. Cook in Radarange Oven, covered, on FULL POWER for 6 to 8 minutes, or until temperature of 150° F is reached.*

*MICRO-TIP: Use the Temperature-Hold to maintain 150° F until ready to serve.

Saucy Chops and Rice

Yield: 4 servings

1 tablespoon vegetable oil
4 (1-3/4 to 2 lbs.) pork chops

2 (8 oz. each) cans tomato sauce
1 cup long-grain rice
1-1/2 cups water
1/2 cup onion, chopped
1 teaspoon salt

1. Preheat large browning skillet for maximum amount of time, according to manufacturer's instructions. Place oil and pork chops in skillet. Cook in Radarange Oven on FULL POWER for 5 minutes. Turn chops over halfway through cooking time.

2. Add remaining ingredients. Cook in Radarange Oven, covered, on Cookmatic Level 5 (SLO COOK) for 20 to 30 minutes, or until chops are tender. Turn chops over, and stir sauce halfway through cooking time.

Tetrazzini Bake

Yield: 10 to 12 servings

1/4 cup onion, chopped
1/4 cup green pepper, chopped
1 tablespoon vegetable oil

1 (10-3/4 oz.) can golden cream of mushroom soup
1 (10-3/4 oz.) can cream of celery soup
2-1/2 cups cooked macaroni, noodles, or spaghetti
3/4 cup evaporated milk
2 cups cooked chicken or turkey, cubed
1 (4 oz.) can mushrooms, drained
1/4 cup ripe olives, chopped
1/4 cup grated Parmesan cheese
Paprika

1. Combine onion, green pepper and oil in 2-1/2-quart casserole. Cook in Radarange Oven on FULL POWER for 2 to 3 minutes, or until onion and green pepper are tender.

2. Add remaining ingredients. Cook in Radarange Oven on FULL POWER for 10 to 12 minutes, or until heated through, and temperature of 150° F is reached.* Stir halfway through cooking time and just before serving. Sprinkle with cheese and paprika, as desired.

*MICRO-TIP: Use the Temperature-Control to stop the Radarange Oven at 150° F.

Creamy Rice Bake

Yield: 4 to 5 servings

1 onion, chopped
1-1/2 tablespoons butter or margarine
1-1/2 cups cooked rice
1 (4 oz.) can mushrooms, drained
1 cup leftover meat, diced, or 1 (6 oz.) can tuna or ham
1 teaspoon parsley flakes
1/2 teaspoon salt
1/4 teaspoon pepper

1/2 cup dairy sour cream
1 egg yolk

1/4 cup Cheddar cheese, shredded

1. Place onion and butter in 1-1/2-quart casserole. Cook in Radarange Oven on FULL POWER for 2 to 3 minutes, or until onion is tender. Add rice, mushrooms, meat, parsley flakes, salt and pepper.

2. Combine sour cream and egg yolk. Stir into rice mixture. Cook in Radarange Oven on Cookmatic Level 8 (MEDIUM HIGH) for 2 to 3 minutes, or until heated through.

3. Sprinkle cheese on top. Heat in Radarange Oven on Cookmatic Level 5 (SLO COOK) for 1 to 2 minutes, or until cheese is melted.

General Hints for Cooking Cereals

1. Cereals can be simply prepared in the Radarange Oven. Each family member, even each child, can fix his or her own cereal directly in the serving bowl, with no worry of scorching. Clean-up following breakfast is easy, too, since there is no sticky pan to wash.

2. Large cereal bowls or casserole dishes are best-suited for cooking cereals in the Radarange Oven. With large bowls, there is less chance for cereals to spill over into the Radarange Oven cavity. Stirring during the cooking time will help to prevent boil-overs and lumping.

Granola
Yield: 6 cups

3 cups quick-cooking or old-fashioned oats, uncooked

1/3 cup wheat germ
1/3 cup coconut, shredded
1/3 cup sesame seeds
1/3 cup nuts, chopped
1/3 cup brown sugar, firmly packed
1/2 teaspoon cinnamon

1/3 cup vegetable oil, or
   1/3 cup butter or margarine, melted
1/4 cup honey
1 teaspoon vanilla

1/2 cup raisins

1. Place oats in ungreased, 2-quart utility dish. Heat in Radarange Oven on FULL POWER for 2-1/2 minutes.

2. Add wheat germ, coconut, sesame seeds, nuts, brown sugar, and cinnamon to oats. Stir to blend.

3. Add oil, honey and vanilla to dry ingredients. Toss lightly, until coated. Cook in Radarange Oven on Cookmatic Level 7 (BAKE) for about 6 minutes, or until heated through. Stir twice during cooking.

4. Add raisins. Cook in Radarange Oven on Cookmatic Level 7 (BAKE) for 2 minutes, or until ingredients are heated through. Press granola firmly against bottom of dish. Cool. Break into pieces, and store in tightly-covered container in refrigerator.

Bran-Oatmeal
Yield: 1 serving

3/4 cup water
1/8 teaspoon salt

1/4 cup quick-cooking, rolled oats
2 tablespoons all-bran cereal
1/8 teaspoon cinnamon

1. Combine water and salt in 1-quart casserole. Heat in Radarange Oven on FULL POWER for 1 to 1-1/2 minutes, or until boiling.

2. Stir in remaining ingredients. Cook in Radarange Oven on FULL POWER for 30 to 60 seconds, or until cereal is thickened, as desired.

CEREAL TYPE & SERVINGS	UTENSIL	AMOUNT HOT TAP WATER	AMOUNT SALT	AMOUNT CEREAL	1ST COOKING TIME
Bulgar Wheat (4 to 6 servings)	3-quart casserole	2 cups	1/2 teaspoon	1 cup bulgar wheat	10 to 13 min.
Cornmeal Mush (6 to 8 servings)	2-quart casserole	4 cups	1-1/2 teaspoons	1 cup white or yellow cornmeal	7 to 9 min.
Cracked Wheat Cereal (1 serving)	large serving bowl or 2-cup measure	1 cup	1/8 teaspoon	1/3 cup cracked wheat cereal	1-1/2 to 2-1/2 min.
(2 servings)	1-quart casserole	2 cups	1/4 teaspoon	2/3 cup cracked wheat cereal	4 to 5 min.
(3 to 4 servings)	1-1/2-quart casserole	3 cups	1/2 teaspoon	1 cup cracked wheat cereal	6 to 7 min.
Grits (Instant) (1 serving)	1-cup glass measure	1/2 cup	—	.8 oz. pkg.	1 min.
Hot Malted Wheat Cereal (4 servings)	1-quart casserole	2-1/2 cups	1/2 teaspoon	1/2 cup hot malted wheat cereal	5 to 6 min.
Oatmeal (Quick-Cooking Oats) (1 serving)	serving bowl	1/2 cup	1/8 teaspoon	1/4 cup quick, rolled oats	1 min.
(4 to 6 servings)	2-quart casserole	3 cups	3/4 teaspoon	1-1/2 cups quick, rolled oats	5 to 7 min.
Oatmeal (Old-Fashioned Oats) (4 to 6 servings)	3-quart casserole	4 cups	1 teaspoon	2 cups old-fashioned rolled oats	7 to 8 min.

General Instructions for Cooking Cereals

1. Read the "Special Instructions" in the chart before cooking each cereal.

2. Use hot tap water, since it boils faster than cold.

3. Let each cereal stand, covered, about 5 minutes before serving if necessary for all water to be absorbed. Stir before serving

CHART

1ST SETTING	2ND COOKING TIME	2ND SETTING	SPECIAL INSTRUCTIONS
FULL POWER	—	—	Place cereal, water and salt in casserole. Cover. Cook, according to 1st time and setting, or until water is absorbed.
FULL POWER	—	—	Place cornmeal, water, and salt in casserole. Cook, according to 1st time and setting, or until cereal is cooked, as desired. Stir, as needed, to prevent boiling over.
FULL POWER	6 to 8 min.	Cookmatic Level 3 (SIMMER)	Place water and salt in utensil. Heat, according to 1st time and setting, or until water boils. Stir in cereal gradually. Heat, according to 2nd time and setting, or until cereal reaches desired thickness. Stir occasionally during cooking.
FULL POWER	9 to 11 min.	Cookmatic Level 3 (SIMMER)	
FULL POWER	12 to 14 min.	Cookmatic Level 3 (SIMMER)	
FULL POWER	—	—	Place water in utensil. Heat, according to 1st time and setting, or until water boils. Stir into instant grits.
FULL POWER	1 min.	FULL POWER	Place water and salt in casserole. Heat, according to 1st time and setting, or until water boils. Stir in cereal. Cook, according to 2nd time and setting, or until cereal is cooked, as desired. Stir, as needed, to prevent boiling over. 1/2 cup raisins may be added to cereal before serving. May be served with brown sugar and milk.
FULL POWER	15 sec.	FULL POWER	Place water and salt in utensil. Heat in Radarange Oven, according to 1st time and setting, or until water boils. Stir in cereal. Cook, according to 2nd time and setting, or until cereal is cooked, as desired. Be careful not to boil over. (Alternate method: Place cereal, water, and salt in utensil. Cook, according to 1st cooking time and setting, or until cereal is cooked as desired. This method makes a thicker cereal.)
FULL POWER	—	—	Place oats, water and salt in casserole. Cook, according to 1st time and setting, or until cereal is cooked, as desired.
FULL POWER	4 min.	Cookmatic Level 5 (SLO COOK)	Place water and salt in casserole. Cook, according to 1st time and setting, or until water boils. Stir in oats. Cook, according to 2nd time and setting. Stir often during cooking time, to prevent boiling over. Let stand, covered, until thickened.

PASTA CONVENIENC[...]

CONVENIENCE FOOD TYPE & PKG. SIZE	DISH SIZE AND YIELD	AMOUNT HOT TAP WATER	AMOUNT SALT	1ST COOKING TIME (TO BOIL WATER)	1ST SETTING	2ND COOKING TIME	2ND SETTING	3RD COOKING TIME
Macaroni and Cheese Dinner Mix (7-1/4 oz. pkg.)	3 to 4-quart casserole (4 to 6 servings)	6 cups	1 teaspoon	8 to 10 min.	FULL POWER	1-1/2 to 2 min.	FULL POWER	3 to 5 min.
Macaroni and Cheese Deluxe Dinner Mix (14 oz. pkg.)	casserole (4 to 6 servings)	2 quarts	1 teaspoon	10 to 12 min.	FULL POWER	1-1/2 to 2 min.	FULL POWER	5 to 7 min.
Noodles Romanoff (5.5 oz. pkg.) OR Noodles Stroganoff (5.25 oz. pkg.)	2-quart casserole (5 servings)	3 cups	1/2 teaspoon	6 to 7 min.	FULL POWER	5 to 7 min.	FULL POWER	—
Noodles, Cheese Sauce and Tuna Mix (7.75 oz. pkg.) and Creamy Noodles and Tuna Main Dish Mix (8.75 oz. pkg.)	3-quart casserole (4 to 6 servings)	3-2/3 to 4 cups	—	10 to 12 min.	FULL POWER	—	—	—
Lasagna Dinner Mix (23-7/8 oz. pkg.)	3 to 4-quart casserole (6 servings)	1-1/2 quarts	2 teaspoons	8 to 10 min.	FULL POWER	15 to 17 min.	FULL POWER	8 to 10 min.
Spaghetti and Sauce Dinner Mix (8 oz. pkg.)	4-quart casserole (4 servings)	2-1/2 cups	2 teaspoons	5 to 6 min.	FULL POWER	7 to 8 min.	FULL POWER	4 to 5 min.

*Use 2/3 cup of milk for Noodles Stroganoff.

General Instructions For Cooking Pasta Convenience Foods

1. Read package instructions and add any extra ingredients not suggested in chart.
2. Read the "Special Instructions" in the chart before cooking each convenience food.
3. Use hot tap water since it boils faster than cold. Water will boil faster if the dish is covered.

OODS CHART

3RD SETTING	EXTRA INGREDIENTS	AMOUNT OIL	SPECIAL INSTRUCTIONS
Cookmatic Level 3 (SIMMER)	1/4 cup butter or margarine 1/4 cup milk	—	Combine water and salt in casserole. Cook, covered, according to 1st time and setting, or until water boils. Stir in macaroni. Cook, covered, according to 2nd time and setting, or until water boils. Cook, covered, according to 3rd time and setting, or until macaroni is tender. Stir halfway through cooking time. Drain. Add butter. Stir until melted. Add milk and cheese mix. Blend well.
Cookmatic Level 3 (SIMMER)	—	—	Combine water and salt in casserole. Cook, covered, according to 1st time and setting, or until water boils. Stir in macaroni. Cook, covered, according to 2nd time and setting, or until water boils. Cook according to 3rd time and setting, or until macaroni is tender. Stir occasionally. Drain. Blend in cheese sauce.
—	2 tablespoons butter or margarine 1/3 cup milk*	—	Place water and salt in casserole. Cook, covered, according to 1st time and setting, or until water boils. Add noodles. Cook, uncovered, according to 2nd time and setting, or until noodles are tender. Stir halfway through cooking time. Drain. Stir in sauce mix, and extra ingredients. Blend well.
—	1 (6-1/2 oz.) can tuna, drained	—	Combine all ingredients in casserole. Cook, according to 1st time and setting, or until noodles are tender. Stir occasionally.
FULL POWER	—	— 1 tablespoon	Combine water and salt in casserole. Cook, covered, according to 1st time and setting, or until water boils. Add oil and lasagna noodles. Cook, covered, according to 2nd time and setting, or until noodles are tender. Stir halfway through cooking time. Follow pkg. instructions and assemble dinner mix in 1-1/2-quart utility dish. Cook, according to 3rd time and setting, or until heated through.
FULL POWER	1 (6 oz.) can tomato paste 2 cans water 1 tablespoon butter or margarine	1 tablespoon	Combine water and salt in casserole. Cook, covered, according to 1st time and setting, or until water boils. Add spaghetti noodles. Cook, covered, according to 2nd time and setting, or until noodles are tender. Stir occasionally. Allow to stand in hot water. Combine sauce mix, tomato paste, water, and margarine in 1-quart casserole. Cook, according to 3rd time and setting. Stir occasionally. Drain spaghetti noodles. Toss lightly with oil. Pour sauce over and serve.

PASTA COOKING CHART

PASTA TYPE	DISH SIZE	AMOUNT HOT TAP WATER	AMOUNT SALT	AMOUNT PASTA	AMOUNT OIL	1ST COOKING TIME	1ST SETTING	2ND COOKING TIME	2ND SETTING
Egg Noodles	3-quart casserole	4 cups	1 teaspoon	2 cups	2 tablespoons	5 to 7 min.	FULL POWER	—	—
Lasagna Noodles	5-quart casserole	6 cups	1 teaspoon	8 ozs.	2 tablespoons	6 min.	FULL POWER	4 to 7 min.	Cookmatic Level 5 (SLO COOK)
Macaroni	4-quart casserole	4 cups	1 teaspoon	2 cups	2 tablespoons	3 min.	FULL POWER	2 to 4 min.	Cookmatic Level 3 (SIMMER)
Spaghetti	4-quart casserole	4 cups	1 teaspoon	8 ozs.	2 tablespoons	3 min.	FULL POWER	2 to 4 min.	Cookmatic Level 3 (SIMMER)

General Instructions for Cooking Pasta

1. Place water and salt in a covered casserole. Be certain to cover the casserole, so the water will boil faster. Cook in Radarange Oven on FULL POWER for 7 to 9 minutes, or until water boils. Hot tap water will boil faster than cold.

2. Stir in the pasta and oil. Cover. Be certain to cover, so the pasta will cook faster. Cook, according to 1st and 2nd cooking times and settings recommended on the chart. The 1st and 2nd settings and times may be programmed in the following way:

Example:
Macaroni
(1st & 2nd Settings)

1	COOKING PROGRAM	3:00	COOK ☐		
2	COOKING PROGRAM	2:00 to 4:00	COOK ☐	**3**	COOKMATIC LEVEL ☐

3. Cook all pasta until it reaches the desired tenderness. Allow a 5 minute, covered, standing time, if necessary, after the pasta finishes cooking. (Pastas can vary slightly in the amount of cooking time they require.)

4. Sample the pasta before draining the liquid. If it is not tender, it can be quickly returned to the Radarange Oven for 1 to 2 additional minutes of cooking. Drain after the pasta has reached the desired tenderness. Rinse with hot tap water before serving.

General Hints for Cooking Pastas

1. The amount of oil in the water is important when cooking pasta, as it helps to keep the water from boiling over.

2. It's very important to cook pasta in a covered dish. This allows for faster cooking. Glass lids or heavy-duty plastic wrap are the best coverings to use since they are the most water-vapor-proof.

3. Use a large enough dish so that water can completely cover pasta. Pasta can be more completely tenderized when covered with water.

4. Pasta can be reheated quickly in the Radarange Oven.

Pasta should be reheated on FULL POWER in a covered casserole until it is steaming hot. Again, a glass lid or plastic wrap covering is best. For a large quantity, you may wish to add 1 to 2 tablespoons of liquid before reheating. If pasta has been refrigerated, stir once or twice during reheating.

PASTA YIELD CHART

UNCOOKED PASTA	COOKED PASTA
1 (7 oz.) pkg. macaroni	4 cups
1 (7 oz.) pkg. spaghetti	4 cups
1 cup egg noodles	1 to 1-1/2 cups

Roman Noodles

Yield: 4 to 5 servings

1/2 cup onion, chopped
1 green pepper, chopped
2 tablespoons vegetable oil

1 (4 oz.) can sliced mushrooms,
    with liquid
2 (8 oz. each) cans tomato sauce
1/4 teaspoon powdered thyme
1/2 teaspoon salt
1/8 teaspoon pepper

8 ozs. medium noodles, uncooked
3/4 cup water

1 (8 oz.) can peas, drained
    (1 cup)
1/4 cup grated Parmesan cheese

1. Combine onion, green pepper and oil in 2-quart casserole. Cook in Radarange Oven on FULL POWER for 2 to 3 minutes, or until onion and green pepper are tender.

2. Stir in mushrooms with liquid, tomato sauce and seasonings. Cook in Radarange Oven, covered, on FULL POWER for 3 minutes, or until heated through.

3. Stir in noodles and water. Cook, in Radarange Oven, covered, on FULL POWER for 9 to 12 minutes, or until noodles are tender. Stir halfway through cooking time.

4. Stir in peas. Sprinkle with Parmesan cheese before serving.

Macaroni and Cheese

Yield: 6 servings

2 tablespoons butter or margarine
2 tablespoons all-purpose flour
1/2 teaspoon salt
1/4 teaspoon pepper

1-1/2 cups milk
1-1/2 cups sharp Cheddar cheese,
    shredded

3 cups cooked macaroni
1/4 cup bread crumbs
1/2 teaspoon paprika

1. Place butter in 1-quart glass measure. Heat in Radarange Oven on FULL POWER for 20 to 30 seconds, or until melted. Stir in flour, salt and pepper.

2. Add milk slowly. Cook in Radarange Oven on Cookmatic Level 8 (MEDIUM HIGH) for 6 to 7 minutes, or until thickened. Stir in cheese, stirring until melted.

3. Stir sauce into cooked macaroni in 1-1/2-quart casserole. Top with mixture of bread crumbs and paprika. Heat in Radarange Oven on Cookmatic Level 8 (MEDIUM HIGH) for 3 to 4 minutes, or until bubbling.

Macaroni Supreme

Yield: 4 servings

1/4 cup onion, chopped
1 tablespoon butter or margarine

1 (10-3/4 oz.) can condensed
    cream of celery soup
2 cups cooked macaroni
1/2 cup milk

1 cup Cheddar cheese, shredded

1. Combine onion and butter in 1-quart casserole. Cook in Radarange Oven on FULL POWER for 2 minutes, or until onion is tender.

2. Stir in soup, macaroni and milk. Cook in Radarange Oven, covered, on Cookmatic Level 8 (MEDIUM HIGH) for 6 minutes, or until heated through.

3. Mix in cheese. Stir until cheese is melted.

All-At-Once Spaghetti

Yield: 6 servings

1 tablespoon butter or margarine
1 cup onion, chopped

1 lb. ground beef

1 teaspoon salt
1/4 teaspoon pepper
2 (8 oz. each) cans tomato sauce
1-1/2 cups water
1/2 teaspoon ground oregano
1/2 teaspoon basil

1/4 lb. spaghetti, uncooked
Grated Parmesan cheese

1. Place butter and onion in 2-quart casserole. Heat in Radarange Oven on FULL POWER for about 3 to 4 minutes, or until onion is tender.

2. Add beef. Cook in Radarange Oven on FULL POWER for 3 to 4 minutes, or until beef is no longer pink. Stir halfway through cooking time. Drain.

3. Add salt, pepper, tomato sauce, water, oregano and basil. Cook in Radarange Oven, covered, on FULL POWER for 4 minutes.

4. Break spaghetti in half and stir into sauce. Cook in Radarange Oven, covered, on FULL POWER for 18 to 20 minutes, or until spaghetti is tender. Stir twice during cooking time. Sprinkle with Parmesan cheese, as desired.

Italian Spaghetti

Yield: 8 servings

1 cup onion, chopped
1/2 cup celery, chopped
1 clove garlic, minced
1 tablespoon vegetable oil

1-1/2 lbs. ground chuck

1 (28 oz.) can tomatoes, with liquid
1 (10-3/4 oz.) can tomato soup
1 (8 oz.) can tomato sauce
1 (6 oz.) can tomato paste
1 (4 oz.) can mushrooms, drained
1 tablespoon sugar
1 bay leaf
1 teaspoon salt
1/4 teaspoon pepper
1/4 teaspoon oregano
1/2 teaspoon basil
1 lb. spaghetti, cooked
Grated Parmesan cheese

1. Mix together onion, celery, garlic and oil in 4-quart casserole. Cook in Radarange Oven on FULL POWER for 4 to 5 minutes, or until onion and celery are tender.

2. Add beef. Cook in Radarange Oven on FULL POWER for 4 to 5 minutes, or until beef is no longer pink. Drain.

3. Add remaining ingredients, except spaghetti and cheese.

1	COOKING PROGRAM	15:00	COOK ☐		
2	COOKING PROGRAM	45:00	COOK ☐	5	COOKMATIC LEVEL ☐

(For best results, stir every 20 minutes and remove lid for last 20 minutes.) Serve over cooked spaghetti. Sprinkle with Parmesan cheese, as desired.

MICRO-TIPS:

• For extra flavor, refrigerate overnight and reheat next day in Radarange Oven on FULL POWER for 10 to 15 minutes.

• Prepare the spaghetti after cooking the sauce. Keep the sauce covered, while the spaghetti is cooking, to keep it warm.

Beef-Noodle Casserole
Yield: 8 to 10 servings

1/2 cup onion, chopped
1/2 cup celery, chopped
1/4 cup green pepper, diced
1 tablespoon vegetable oil

1-1/2 lbs. ground beef

10 to 12 ozs. cooked noodles
1 (10-3/4 oz.) can cream of mushroom soup
1 (10-3/4 oz.) can cream of chicken soup
1 (4 oz.) can mushrooms, drained (optional)
1/2 cup milk
1/2 cup cashews (optional)
1-1/2 teaspoons salt
1/4 teaspoon pepper

1. Combine onion, celery, green pepper and oil in 3-quart casserole. Cook in Radarange Oven on FULL POWER for 3 to 4 minutes, or until vegetables are tender.

2. Add beef. Cook in Radarange Oven on FULL POWER for 4 to 5 minutes, or until beef is no longer pink. Stir halfway through cooking time. Drain.

3. Blend in remaining ingredients. Cook in Radarange Oven on FULL POWER for 10 to 12 minutes, or until heated through, and temperature of 150° F is reached.* Stir halfway through cooking time.

*MICRO-TIP: Use the Temperature-Hold to maintain 150° F until ready to serve.

Tuna Tetrazzini
Yield: 6 servings

4 ozs. spaghetti, broken into 2-inch lengths and cooked
1 (10-3/4 oz.) can cream of mushroom soup
1/2 cup milk
1 (6-1/2 to 7 oz.) can tuna, drained
1 (3 oz.) can sliced mushrooms, drained
1/3 cup onion, finely chopped
1 cup Cheddar cheese, shredded

1. Combine spaghetti, soup and milk in 1-1/2-quart casserole. Blend in tuna, mushrooms, onion and 1/2 cup cheese. Mix lightly.

2. Cook in Radarange Oven on FULL POWER for 8 minutes, or until temperature of 150°F is reached.* Stir halfway through cooking time. Sprinkle on remaining cheese. Heat in Radarange Oven on Cookmatic Level 5 (SLO COOK) for 1 to 2 minutes, or until cheese is melted.

*MICRO-TIP: Use the Temperature-Hold to maintain 150° F until ready to serve.

Noodles Au Gratin
Yield: 4 servings

2 cups cooked noodles
1/2 cup dairy sour cream
1/2 cup Cheddar cheese, shredded
2 tablespoons milk
1 tablespoon parsley flakes
1/4 teaspoon salt

1. Combine all ingredients in 1-quart casserole. Blend well.

2. Cook in Radarange Oven, covered, on Cookmatic Level 5 (SLO COOK) for 6 to 8 minutes, or until cheese is melted. Stir 1 to 2 times during cooking time.

Beef Corkscrew Bake

Yield: 4 to 6 servings

1/2 cup green onion, chopped
1 tablespoon butter or margarine

1 lb. ground beef

1 (10-3/4 oz.) can golden cream
    of mushroom soup
1/2 cup catsup
4 ozs. cooked corkscrew macaroni

1/2 cup Cheddar cheese, shredded

1. Place onion and butter in 1-1/2-quart casserole. Heat in Radarange Oven on FULL POWER for 1-1/2 minutes, or until onion is tender.

2. Add beef. Cook in Radarange Oven on FULL POWER for 3 to 4 minutes, or until beef is no longer pink. Stir halfway through cooking time. Drain.

3. Add remaining ingredients, except cheese. Cook in Radarange Oven on FULL POWER for 4 to 5 minutes, or until heated through and temperature of 150° F is reached.* Stir halfway through cooking time.

4. Mix in cheese before serving.

   *MICRO-TIP: Use the Temperature-Hold to maintain 150° F until ready to serve.

Goulash

Yield: 4 to 6 servings

1 medium onion, chopped
1 tablespoon butter or margarine

1 lb. ground beef

1 (15 oz.) can stewed tomatoes
1 cup cooked elbow macaroni
1 teaspoon salt
1/4 teaspoon pepper

1 tablespoon cornstarch
1 tablespoon water

1. Combine onion and butter in 1-1/2-quart casserole. Cook in Radarange Oven on FULL POWER for 2 minutes, or until onion is tender.

2. Add beef. Cook in Radarange Oven on FULL POWER for 3 to 4 minutes, or until beef is no longer pink. Stir halfway through cooking time. Drain.

3. Add tomatoes, noodles, salt and pepper. Cook in Radarange Oven on FULL POWER for 4 to 5 minutes, or until bubbling. Stir halfway through cooking time.

4. Blend together cornstarch and water. Add to casserole. Cook in Radarange Oven on FULL POWER for 1 minute, or until thickened and temperature of 150° F is reached.*

   *MICRO-TIP: Use the Temperature-Hold to maintain 150° F until ready to serve.

Macaroni Salad

Yield: 6 servings

1 cup macaroni, uncooked

1 cup Cheddar cheese, cubed
3/4 cup celery, chopped
1/4 cup pimento-stuffed green
    olives, sliced
1/4 cup green pepper, diced
1/4 cup green onion, sliced
2 tablespoons pimentos, diced
2 teaspoons lemon juice
1/4 teaspoon salt
1/2 cup mayonnaise or salad
    dressing

1. Cook macaroni, according to instructions on page 122 using only 1 cup of macaroni. Use the same amount of all other ingredients as when cooking 2 cups of macaroni. Drain.

2. Add remaining ingredients. Mix well. Chill.

Lasagna

Yield: 10 to 12 servings

1 lb. ground beef or Italian sausage
1 clove garlic, minced

1 (1-1/2 oz.) pkg. dry onion soup mix
1-1/2 cups water
1 (6 oz.) can tomato paste
1 (8 oz.) can tomato sauce
1/2 teaspoon salt
1/4 teaspoon pepper
1/2 teaspoon sugar
1 teaspoon oregano
1/2 teaspoon basil

1/2 lb. lasagna noodles, cooked
1/2 lb. Mozzarella cheese, shredded
1 lb. cottage cheese or ricotta cheese
Grated Parmesan cheese

1. Combine meat and garlic in 2-quart casserole. Cook in Radarange Oven on FULL POWER for 3 to 4 minutes. Stir 1 to 2 times during cooking time. Drain.

2. Blend in onion soup, water, tomato paste, tomato sauce, salt, pepper, sugar, oregano and basil. Cook in Radarange Oven, covered, on FULL POWER for 10 minutes. Stir halfway through cooking time.

3. Layer meat mixture, noodles, Mozzarella cheese and cottage cheese in 2-quart utility dish. Repeat layers, ending with meat sauce. Sprinkle top generously with Parmesan cheese, as desired.

4. Cover loosely with plastic wrap. Cook in Radarange Oven, covered, on FULL POWER for 12 to 14 minutes, or until heated through.

Lasagna Casserole

Yield: 6 servings

1 lb. ground beef
1/2 cup onion, chopped
2 (8 oz. each) cans tomato sauce
1/2 teaspoon salt
1/2 teaspoon basil
1/4 teaspoon ground oregano

1 (12 oz.) pkg. cottage cheese
1 (3 oz.) pkg. cream cheese, softened
1/4 cup dairy sour cream
1/4 cup Mozzarella cheese

2 cups egg noodles, cooked
Grated Parmesan cheese

1. Place ground beef and onions in 1-quart casserole. Cook in Radarange Oven on FULL POWER for 3 to 4 minutes, or until beef is no longer pink. Stir halfway through cooking time. Drain. Add tomato sauce, salt, basil and oregano.

2. Combine remaining ingredients, except noodles and Parmesan cheese.

3. In 2-quart casserole, put about 1/4 cup meat sauce, half of noodles, half of cheese mixture, half of sauce and repeat again. Sprinkle Parmesan cheese on top, as desired.

4. Bake in Radarange Oven on FULL POWER for 8 to 10 minutes, or until temperature of 150°F is reached.*

   *MICRO-TIP: Use the Temperature-Control to stop the Radarange Oven at 150°F.

Sandwiches can be heated instantly in the Radarange Oven for a quick lunch. You can be creative in making sandwich fillings; some leftover casseroles or salads often make great fillings. Clean-up is easy, too, since sandwiches can be heated in paper towels, which are disposable.

Most sandwiches can be heated in the Radarange Oven on FULL POWER. Sandwiches having fillings which contain cheese, however, are usually heated on Cook-matic Level 5 (SLO COOK). Cheese is a "special" or "delicate" ingredient which tends to become tough and "rubbery" when heated using a higher setting.

Read the general tips before heating sandwiches in your Radarange Oven.

General Hints for Heating Sandwiches

1. Sandwiches should be covered with a paper towel when heated in buns or bread, to prevent the buns or bread from losing moisture and becoming too dry. Sandwiches should be placed on a paper towel or a plastic or ceramic rack during heating to prevent the bottoms from becoming soggy.

2. Whenever possible, heat the sandwich filling before spreading it inside the bun. Then heat the entire sandwich, just until the bun is warmed. Again, this will prevent moisture loss in the bun. Also, the shorter amount of time a filling is inside a bun, the less chance there is for sogginess to occur.

3. Toasted bread or day-old bread make great bases for Radarange Oven sandwiches, since they do not tend to become soggy as readily as fresh bread or buns. Also, day-old bread will tend to "freshen" during the heating time.

4. Heat sandwiches just until the bread is warmed, or until cheese, a "delicate" ingredient, is melted.

5. Sandwiches spread with a "thin" layer of filling will heat faster than sandwiches with thicker fillings. When heating meat sandwiches, use thin, rather than thick, slices of meat.

6. For heating your own favorite sandwich "creations," use FULL POWER. Heat 1 sandwich, inside a bun or bread, for approximately 1 to 2 minutes, or until warmed, depending upon the size of the sandwich. If the sandwich filling includes cheese as a main ingredient, heat on Cookmatic Level 5 (SLO COOK), until the cheese is melted.

"Left-Over" Turkey In Buns

Yield: 4 servings

4 hamburger buns, toasted
1 cup cooked turkey, chopped*
1 tablespoon instant, minced onion
1 teaspoon parsley flakes
1/4 cup salted peanuts, chopped (optional)
1 egg, hard-cooked and chopped**
1/2 cup mayonnaise
1/3 cup sharp Cheddar cheese, shredded
Salt
Pepper

1. Place bottom halves of buns on paper towel-lined plate. Combine remaining ingredients. Season with salt and pepper, as desired. Spread filling on buns. Add bun tops to make 4 "bunwiches."

2. Heat in Radarange Oven on Cookmatic Level 5 (SLO COOK) for 2 to 3 minutes, or until heated through.

MICRO-TIPS:

*Any leftover cooked poultry or meat may be used.

**Remember, do not hard-cook eggs in the Radarange Oven.

Iced Fresh Tomato Soup (page 68) & "Left-Over" Turkey In Buns (See this page

FROZEN SANDWICH PROGRAMMED DEFROSTING & HEATING CHART*

SANDWICH TYPE	SIZE OF SANDWICH	PROGRAMMING INSTRUCTIONS		
(Any) Frozen* Sandwich (with buns)	1 sandwich (3-1/2 to 4 oz.)	**1** COOKING PROGRAM	1:30	DEFROST ☐
		2 COOKING PROGRAM	:30	HOLD ☐
		3 COOKING PROGRAM	:45 to 1:00	COOK ☐
(Any) Frozen* Sandwich (with buns)	1 sandwich (4-1/2 to 5 oz.)	**1** COOKING PROGRAM	1:45	DEFROST ☐
		2 COOKING PROGRAM	:30	HOLD ☐
		3 COOKING PROGRAM	:30 to :45	COOK ☐
Frozen Fish Burgers (without buns)	1 pattie (3 oz.)	**1** COOKING PROGRAM	2:00	DEFROST ☐
		2 COOKING PROGRAM	1:30	HOLD ☐
		3 COOKING PROGRAM	1:00 to 2:00	COOK ☐
Frozen Fish Burgers (without buns)	2 patties (3 oz. each)	**1** COOKING PROGRAM	2:30	DEFROST ☐
		2 COOKING PROGRAM	1:30	HOLD ☐
		3 COOKING PROGRAM	2:00 to 3:00	COOK ☐
Frozen Fish Burgers (without buns)	4 patties (3 oz. each)	**1** COOKING PROGRAM	4:00	DEFROST ☐
		2 COOKING PROGRAM	2:00	HOLD ☐
		3 COOKING PROGRAM	2:30 to 4:00	COOK ☐

*These sandwich timings were based upon purchased sandwiches. Timings for defrosting and heating your "home-made" sandwiches are similar. You may heat unfrozen refrigerator temperature sandwiches for about the same amount of time given in one of the #3 Cooking Programs. For defrosting, as well as heating, use all 3 cooking programs.

CONVENIENCE SANDWICH FILLING SEASONING MIX COOKING CHART

MIX TYPE	1ST COOKING TIME ON FULL POWER*	2ND COOKING TIME ON FULL POWER**	ADDITIONAL INGREDIENTS	SPECIAL INSTRUCTIONS
Sloppy Joe Seasoning Mix (1-1/2 oz.) (8 servings)	3 to 4 min.	3 to 4 min.	1 lb. ground beef 1 (6 oz.) can tomato paste 1-1/4 cups water 8 hamburger buns	Crumble beef in 1-1/2-quart casserole. Cook, according to 1st Cooking Time. Drain. Blend in remaining ingredients. Cook, according to 2nd Cooking Time. Spoon 1/4 cup mixture into each hamburger bun.
Taco Seasoning Mix (1-3/4 oz.) (4 to 6 servings)	4 to 5 min.	7 to 8 min.	1 lb. ground beef 1 cup water	Crumble beef in 1-1/2-quart casserole. Cook, according to 1st Cooking Time. Drain. Blend in remaining ingredients. Cook, according to 2nd Cooking Time. Follow package instructions for serving.

*Stir halfway through cooking time.
**Stir 1 to 2 times during cooking time.

CONVENIENCE CANNED SANDWICH FILLING HEATING CHART

FILLING TYPE	CAN SIZE	UTENSIL	HEATING TIME ON FULL POWER	SPECIAL INSTRUCTIONS
Beef Taco Filling (2 to 4 servings)	7 to 8 oz.	1-quart casserole	1-1/2 to 2 min.	Place filling in small bowl or casserole. Heat, according to time on chart. Spoon into taco shells.
Sloppy Joe Filling (4 servings)	15 to 16 oz.	1-quart casserole	2 to 2-1/2 min.	Place filling in casserole. Heat, according to time on chart. Spoon into hamburger buns.

General Instructions for Cooking Convenience Sandwich Fillings

1. Read the "Special Instructions" on the charts before cooking or heating the sandwich filling.

2. Heat in the Radarange Oven, according to the times in the charts.

Salami-Kraut Roll-Ups

Yield: 4 servings

4 slices dark rye bread, toasted
1/2 cup sauerkraut, drained
4 slices Swiss cheese, halved
4 slices Cheddar cheese, halved
8 slices Cotto salami

1. Cut each slice bread in half lengthwise. Place 1 tablespoon sauerkraut on each piece.

2. Center one-half slice Swiss cheese and one-half slice Cheddar cheese on each slice salami. Roll up and secure with toothpick. Lay one salami roll on each piece of bread.

3. Place sandwiches on plastic rack or paper towels. Heat in Radarange Oven on Cookmatic Level 5 (SLO COOK) for 2 to 3 minutes, or until cheese is slightly melted.

Grilled Cheese Sandwich

Yield: 1 or 2 servings

ONE SANDWICH

Butter or margarine
2 slices bread
1 slice cheese

1. Preheat browning skillet or grill in Radarange Oven, according to manufacturer's instructions. Spread desired amount of butter evenly on one side of each slice bread. Place cheese between unbuttered sides. Place sandwich in hot browning skillet.

2. Cook in Radarange Oven on Cookmatic Level 5 (SLO COOK) for 1 to 1-1/2 minutes, or until cheese is melted. Turn sandwich over halfway through cooking time.

TWO SANDWICHES

Butter or margarine
4 slices bread
2 slices cheese

1. Preheat browning skillet or grill in Radarange Oven, according to manufacturer's instructions. Spread desired amount of butter evenly on one side of each slice bread. Place one slice cheese between 2 unbuttered sides. Place sandwiches in hot browning skillet.

2. Cook in Radarange Oven on Cookmatic Level 5 (SLO COOK) for 1 to 2 minutes, or until cheese is melted. Turn sandwiches over after 30 seconds.

MICRO-TIP: Spread butter evenly for even browning. Press sandwiches firmly against bottom of browning skillet for maximum browning. Don't cover with glass lid, or sandwiches will taste "steamed" and will be soggy. If sandwiches are not browned as desired, increase or decrease preheat time as needed.

French Dip Sandwiches

Yield: 4 servings

2 cups water
2 teaspoons instant beef bouillon
2 tablespoons dry onion soup mix

3/4 to 1 lb. roast beef, cooked and thinly sliced

4 French rolls

1. Combine water, instant bouillon, and soup mix in 1-quart casserole or glass measure. Cook in Radarange Oven on FULL POWER for 4 to 6 minutes, or until mixture boils and bouillon is dissolved.

2. Place meat on plate. Cover with paper towel. Heat in Radarange Oven covered, on FULL POWER for 3 to 5 minutes, or until hot.

3. Place roast beef in rolls or buns. Serve with hot beef broth dip.

Made-Right Mushroom Burgers

Yield: 6 to 8 servings

1 cup celery, chopped
1 cup onion, chopped
1 tablespoon vegetable oil

1 lb. ground beef

1 (10-3/4 oz.) can cream of onion soup
1 (4 oz.) can sliced mushrooms, drained
3/4 cup catsup
1 teaspoon chili powder
1 teaspoon salt
6 to 8 hamburger buns

1. Combine celery, onion and oil in 1-1/2-quart casserole. Cook in Radarange Oven on FULL POWER for 3 to 4 minutes, or until celery and onion are tender.

2. Add beef. Cook in Radarange Oven on FULL POWER for 3 to 4 minutes, or until beef is no longer pink. Stir halfway through cooking time. Drain.

3. Combine remaining ingredients and add to meat. Heat in Radarange Oven on FULL POWER for 7 to 8 minutes, or until heated through, and temperature of 150° F is reached.* Spoon into split hamburger buns.

*MICRO-TIP: Use the Temperature-Control to stop the Radarange Oven at 150° F.

Hot Swiss Chicken Salad Sandwiches

Yield: 8 sandwiches

1 cup cooked chicken, diced
2/3 cup celery, diced
1/2 cup Swiss cheese, cubed
1/4 teaspoon salt
1/4 cup mayonnaise
1/2 teaspoon lemon juice
8 hamburger buns

1. Combine all ingredients, except buns. Fill each bun with 1/4 cup mixture. Place 4 sandwiches on plastic rack.

2. Heat in Radarange Oven on Cookmatic Level 5 (SLO COOK) for 1 minute, 45 seconds, to 2 minutes, or until heated through.

   MICRO-TIPS:

   • Heat 1 sandwich in Radarange Oven on Cookmatic Level 5 (SLO COOK) for 30 to 60 seconds. For 2 sandwiches, heat in Radarange Oven on Cookmatic Level 5 (SLO COOK) for 1 to 1-1/4 minutes.

   • 1 (6-1/2 oz.) can tuna, drained, may be substituted for chicken, if desired.

   • 4 split and toasted English muffins may be substituted for buns, if desired.

Ham Salad Sandwiches

Yield: 4 sandwiches

1 cup cooked ham, ground
1/2 cup celery, finely chopped
2 tablespoons pickle relish, drained
1/4 cup mayonnaise
4 hamburger buns

1. Combine all ingredients, except buns. Divide ham mixture and spread in 4 buns. Place 4 sandwiches on plastic rack or paper towels.

2. Heat in Radarange Oven on FULL POWER for 1-1/2 to 2 minutes, or until heated through.

   MICRO-TIP: Sandwiches can be made on toasted rye bread or English muffins, if desired.

Peanut Butter and Bacon Sandwiches

Yield: 4 sandwiches

5 slices bacon
1/2 cup chunky peanut butter

2 English muffins, split and toasted

1. Cut bacon in 1-inch pieces. Place on plastic rack or paper plate. Cover with paper towel. Cook in Radarange Oven, covered, on FULL POWER for 3 to 4 minutes, or until crisp. Stir hot bacon into peanut butter.

2. Spread mixture on 4 muffin halves. Place 4 halves on plastic rack or paper towels. Heat in Radarange Oven on FULL POWER for 1 to 2 minutes, or until hot.

Hot Dog Wrap-Ups

Yield: 5 sandwiches

1 (4 oz.) roll hot dog bake-arounds
1/2 lb. frankfurters

1. Separate dough into 5 rectangles. Place one frankfurter lengthwise on each rectangle. Roll each up, sealing edges.

2. Place "wrap-ups" in greased, 2-quart utility dish, so they are not touching each other.

3. Cook in Radarange Oven on Cookmatic Level 7 (BAKE) for 4 to 5 minutes, or until dough is cooked but still slightly moist.

Egg Salad Sandwiches

Yield: 4 to 5 servings

4 hard-cooked eggs, chopped*
2 tablespoons pimento-stuffed olives, chopped
3 tablespoons mayonnaise
2 teaspoons prepared mustard
1/4 teaspoon salt
Dash pepper

2 to 3 English muffins, split and toasted
Paprika

1. Blend together eggs, olives, mayonnaise and mustard. Season with salt and pepper, as desired.

2. Spread 1/4 cup mixture on each muffin half. Sprinkle with paprika, as desired. Place 4 halves on plastic rack or paper towels. Heat in Radarange Oven on FULL POWER for 1-1/2 to 2 minutes, or until heated through.

   MICRO-TIPS:

   • To heat 1 muffin half, heat in Radarange Oven on FULL POWER for 30 to 45 seconds.
   • Substitute 4 to 5 hamburger buns for muffins.
   * Remember, do not hard-cook eggs in the Radarange Oven.

Turkey, Bacon and Tomato Sandwiches

Yield: 6 servings

6 slices bacon

1/4 cup mayonnaise
1/4 cup dairy sour cream
1 tablespoon lemon juice
Dash cayenne pepper
6 English muffins, split and toasted

12 slices turkey
12 slices tomato

6 slices American process cheese

1. Place bacon on plastic rack or paper plate. Cover with paper towel. Cook in Radarange Oven, covered, on FULL POWER for 4 to 5 minutes, or until crisp. Crumble.

2. Blend together mayonnaise, sour cream, lemon juice and cayenne pepper. Spread mixture on each muffin half.

3. Place one slice turkey, and then one slice tomato on each muffin half. Sprinkle with bacon.

4. Cut each slice cheese in 4 strips. Crisscross 2 strips over each sandwich. Place 6 muffin halves on plastic rack or paper towels.

5. Heat in Radarange Oven on Cookmatic Level 5 (SLO COOK) for 2 to 3 minutes, or until cheese is melted. Repeat with remaining muffin halves.

Barbecued Hamburgers

Yield: 4 servings

1/2 cup onion, chopped
1 tablespoon vegetable oil

1 lb. ground beef

1/3 cup catsup
1 tablespoon brown sugar
2 teaspoons vinegar
1 teaspoon prepared mustard
1/2 teaspoon Worcestershire sauce
1/2 teaspoon salt
4 hamburger buns

1. Combine onion and oil in 2-quart casserole. Cook in Radarange Oven on FULL POWER for 3 to 4 minutes, or until onion is tender.

2. Add crumbled beef to onion. Cook in Radarange Oven on FULL POWER for 3 to 4 minutes, or until beef is no longer pink. Stir halfway through cooking time. Drain.

3. Add remaining ingredients, except buns. Blend well. Heat in Radarange Oven on FULL POWER for 3 minutes, or until heated through, and temperature of 150° F is reached. Spoon into hamburger buns and serve.

Chili Dogs

Yield: 4 to 6 servings

1 cup onion, chopped
1/2 cup green pepper, chopped
1 tablespoon vegetable oil

1 lb. ground beef
1 (1 lb.) can chili beans, drained
1 (8 oz.) can tomato sauce
1 (8 oz.) can tomatoes
1/3 cup catsup
1 teaspoon salt
1/2 teaspoon chili powder*
1 bay leaf (optional)
Dash cayenne pepper

1 lb. frankfurters

4 to 6 buns, split

1. Place onion, green pepper and oil in 1-1/2-quart casserole. Cook in Radarange Oven on FULL POWER for 4 to 5 minutes, or until onion and green pepper are tender.

2. Add beef. Cook in Radarange Oven on FULL POWER for 3 to 4 minutes, or until beef is no longer pink. Stir halfway through cooking time. Drain. Add remaining ingredients, except frankfurters and buns. Blend well.

3. Cook in Radarange Oven on FULL POWER for 10 minutes, or until heated through. Stir 2 to 3 times during cooking. Remove bay leaf. Cover to keep hot.

4. Pierce skins of frankfurters with fork. Place on cooking grill. Cover with paper towel.

5. Cook in Radarange Oven, covered, on FULL POWER for 2 to 4 minutes, or until heated through. Place 1 or 2 frankfurters on each opened bun. Pour about 3/4 cup chili over each.

*MICRO-TIP: Increase or decrease amount of chili powder, as desired.

Tangy Tunawiches

Yield: 8 sandwiches

1 (6-1/2 or 7 oz.) can tuna, drained
2/3 cup celery, chopped
1/2 cup Swiss cheese, cubed
1/4 teaspoon salt
1/4 cup mayonnaise
1/2 teaspoon lemon juice
2 tablespoons catsup

8 hamburger buns

1. Combine all ingredients, except buns.

2. Fill buns with 1/4 cup mixture. Place 4 sandwiches on plastic rack or paper towels. Heat in Radarange Oven on Cookmatic Level 5 (SLO COOK) for 1-1/2 to 2 minutes, or until heated through.

MICRO-TIPS:

- To heat one sandwich, heat in Radarange Oven on Cookmatic Level 5 (SLO COOK) for 30 to 40 seconds.

- 4 split and toasted English muffins may be substituted for buns, if desired. Sprinkle each with paprika or parsley flakes for extra color.

Pizzawiches

Yield: 8 sandwiches

1 cup onion, chopped
1 tablespoon vegetable oil

1 lb. ground beef

1 (8 oz.) can tomato sauce
1 (2-1/2 oz.) jar sliced mushrooms, drained
1/2 teaspoon oregano
1/2 teaspoon basil
1/2 teaspoon salt
1/8 teaspoon pepper

4 English muffins, split and toasted
4 ozs. (1 cup) Mozzarella cheese, shredded

1. Place onion in oil in 1-1/2-quart casserole. Cook in Radarange Oven on FULL POWER for 2 minutes, or until onion is tender.

2. Add meat. Cook in Radarange Oven on FULL POWER for 3 to 4 minutes, or until beef is no longer pink. Stir halfway through cooking time. Drain.

3. Blend in remaining ingredients except muffins and cheese. Cook in Radarange Oven on FULL POWER for 4 to 6 minutes, or until heated through. Stir 2 to 3 times during cooking time.

4. Spoon 1/4 cup hot mixture on each muffin half. Top with cheese. Place 4 muffin halves on plastic rack or paper towels. Heat in Radarange Oven on Cookmatic Level 5 (SLO COOK) for 1 to 2 minutes, or until cheese is melted. For one muffin half, heat on Cookmatic Level 5 (SLO COOK) for 30 seconds. For two, heat on Cookmatic Level 5 (SLO COOK) for 1 to 1-1/2 minutes.

MICRO-TIPS:

• Sliced French bread may be used instead of muffins. May be topped with green pepper, crumbled bacon, or olives, as desired.

• If meat mixture is chilled before using, remember to allow slightly longer cooking time.

Surf and Turfwiches

Yield: 6 servings

1 (6 oz.) can crab meat, flaked
1 cup cooked chicken, diced
1/3 cup celery, finely diced
1/3 cup mayonnaise
1 teaspoon prepared mustard

6 English muffins, split and toasted

6 slices bacon, cooked and crumbled
6 slices Swiss cheese, halved

1. Mix together crab meat, chicken, celery, mayonnaise and mustard.

2. Spread mixture on muffin halves. Place 6 halves on plastic rack or on paper towels.

3. Heat in Radarange Oven on FULL POWER for 1-1/2 to 2 minutes, or until hot. Top each half with bacon and one slice cheese.

4. Heat in Radarange Oven on Cookmatic Level 5 (SLO COOK) for 1-1/2 to 3 minutes, or until cheese is almost completely melted. Repeat with remaining 6 halves.

Eggs and Hamwich

Yield: 4 sandwiches

2 hard-cooked eggs, chopped*
1/2 cup cooked ham, cubed
1/4 cup mayonnaise
8 slices bread, toasted
4 slices process cheese

1. Blend together eggs, ham and mayonnaise. Spread mixture on 4 slices toasted bread. Place one slice cheese over each. Top with second slice of bread. Place all sandwiches on plastic rack or paper towels. Cover with paper towel.

2. Heat in Radarange Oven, covered, on Cookmatic Level 5 (SLO COOK) for 1-1/2 to 2 minutes, or until cheese is melted.

*MICRO-TIP: Remember, do not hard-cook eggs in the Radarange Oven.

Hot Crab Meat Sandwiches

Yield: 6 sandwiches

1 cup crab meat, flaked
3 hard-cooked eggs, chopped*
1/4 cup mayonnaise
1 teaspoon instant, minced onion
1 teaspoon Worcestershire sauce
1/4 teaspoon lemon juice
3/4 teaspoon salt
1/8 teaspoon pepper

1. Mix together crab meat, eggs, mayonnaise, onion, Worcestershire sauce, lemon juice, salt and pepper.

6 slices bread, or English
   muffins, split
1/4 cup Cheddar cheese, shredded
Paprika

2. Toast bread or muffins. Spread crab meat mixture on toast. Sprinkle with cheese and then paprika, as desired. Place 6 sandwiches on plastic rack or paper towels. Heat in Radarange Oven on Cookmatic Level 5 (SLO COOK) for 2 to 3 minutes, or until cheese is melted. Serve immediately.

   *MICRO-TIP: Remember, do not hard-cook eggs in the Radarange Oven.

Reuben Sandwich

Yield: 1 serving

1 slice cooked, corned beef
2 slices rye bread, toasted
2 tablespoons sauerkraut
1 slice Swiss cheese

1. Place corned beef slice on one slice of bread. Drain sauerkraut well. Place sauerkraut and Swiss cheese on corned beef.

1 teaspoon thousand island
   dressing

2. Spread second piece of bread with dressing and place on top. Place sandwich on paper plate. Cover with paper towel.

3. Heat in Radarange Oven, covered, on Cookmatic Level 5 (SLO COOK) for 45 to 60 seconds, or until cheese is melted.

Taco Heroes

Yield: 6 servings

1/2 cup onion, finely chopped
1/4 cup celery, finely chopped
1 tablespoon vegetable oil

1. Place onion, celery, and oil in 1-1/2-quart casserole. Cook in Radarange Oven on FULL POWER for 2 to 3 minutes, or until onion and celery are tender.

1-1/2 lbs. ground beef

2. Add beef. Cook in Radarange Oven on FULL POWER for 4 to 5 minutes, or until beef is no longer pink. Stir halfway through cooking time. Drain.

1 (1-3/4 oz.) pkg. taco seasoning
   mix
1 (8 oz.) can tomato sauce

3. Add taco mix and tomato sauce. Heat in Radarange Oven on FULL POWER for 4 minutes, or until heated through, stirring halfway through cooking time.

6 English muffins or hamburger
   buns, split and toasted
12 slices tomato
1 cup Cheddar cheese, shredded

4. Spread 1/2 cup of meat mixture on each muffin half. Top each with tomato slice and sprinkle with cheese. Place 6 halves on cooking grill.

3/4 cup lettuce, shredded
   (optional)
12 ripe olives, chopped (optional)

5. Heat in Radarange Oven on Cookmatic Level 5 (SLO COOK) for 2 to 3 minutes, or until cheese is melted. Top with lettuce and olives, if desired.

Les Oeufs (eggs) can be prepared in endless ways. In this chapter we'll show you how the Radarange Oven can make fluffy scrambled eggs in seconds. Breakfast will never be dull again after using this variety of scrambled egg recipes. Also, there will never be any "hard-to-wash" pans or skillets.

In this chapter, you will find custards, omelets, soufflés, and many other "Eggs and Cheese" dishes. Be sure to try one of the quiche recipes. A quiche (pronounced kēesh) is a savory, rather than sweet, custard pie. It is served as an hors d'oeuvre in a French meal, but it can be used as a brunch or supper dish. If you are proud of your custard-baking ability, this is a great way to "show it off." Dessert custards are found in the Desserts chapter.

When using one of the charts in this chapter, be sure to read the general cooking instructions for valuable cooking information. Be certain to read all of the general hints for cooking eggs and cheese before preparing them in your Radarange Oven. Fondue recipes are found in the "Appetizers and Snacks" chapter, and Rarebit recipes are found in the "Sauces, Jams and Relishes" chapter. Since eggs and cheese both cook best on Cookmatic Level 8 (MEDIUM HIGH), these two food items can be easily combined in recipes.

General Hints for Cooking Eggs

1. **Do not** hard-cook eggs or boil eggs in the shell in a microwave oven. Yolks cook faster than whites, and the rapid heat generated through microwave cooking expands the air inside the shell, causing it to burst. **Do not reheat** eggs which have been prepared conventionally or in the Radarange Oven unless they are finely chopped or scrambled before heating. Pressure can build up in reheated eggs and cause them to burst.
2. The size, temperature and age of the eggs can affect cooking times. Large eggs require a slightly longer cooking time than small eggs. Large-size eggs were used in developing the recipes in this chapter. Room temperature eggs cook faster than refrigerator temperature eggs. Recipes in this chapter are based upon refrigerator-temperature eggs. Older eggs should be used for scrambling, rather than for poaching or frying. Yolk membranes become weak in older eggs and tend to break during cooking when fried or poached. Use fresh eggs for frying and poaching.
3. Egg yolks and whites cook at different rates of speed. Egg yolks cook faster than egg whites, due to the fat content. Egg dishes which require the mixing of egg whites and yolks, such as omelets or scrambled eggs, cook evenly and easily. Fried eggs and poached eggs require special handling. Read the tips on pages 139, 141, and 142, for preparing scrambled, fried and poached eggs.
4. Use the exact utensils recommended for cooking eggs in the recipes. Cooking times can vary due to the types and shapes of utensils.
5. Eggs can be prepared in individual serving dishes. Remember, do not use dishes which have a metal trim.
6. Before frying or poaching eggs, gently pierce or puncture the yolk membrane with a knife or the tines of a fork. This will slightly break the membrane and prevent the yolk from erupting during cooking.
7. Cook eggs covered. Glass lids or heavy-duty plastic wrap are the best coverings to use since they are the most water-vapor-proof of all coverings. Since egg yolks cook faster than egg whites, a yolk can become tough or may "pop," while the white is still undercooked, if cooked uncovered. A lid will retain steam which cooks the egg white. Steam will also help keep the yolk tender.
8. Remove eggs and egg dishes while they are still slightly moist and slightly underdone. Let them stand a few minutes, covered, to complete the cooking process, as recommended in the recipes. Eggs may be stirred during or after cooking, for a fluffier product.
9. Be careful not to overcook eggs. Overcooking can cause eggs to become tough and "rubbery." Check eggs at the minimum amount of cooking time recommended in the recipe to see if they are done.
10. Use Cookmatic Level 8 (MEDIUM HIGH) when preparing most egg dishes. Eggs are best when cooked at a lower power setting than FULL POWER. When converting your own favorite egg recipes, use Cookmatic Level 8 (MEDIUM HIGH). Select a similar

recipe in this chapter and use approximately the same amount of cooking time. Check eggs early during cooking to see if they are done. If not, cook slightly longer. Be careful not to overcook. Make a note of the correct time for your recipe for future reference.

General Hints for Cooking Cheese
1. Use the type of cheese that is recommended in the recipe. If you wish to substitute cheeses, substitute another cheese of the same general type. Example: substitute a hard cheese, for another hard cheese, and not with a soft cheese.
2. When recipes require a covering, use a glass lid or heavy-duty plastic wrap, since they are the most water-vapor-proof of all coverings.
3. Cheese can be easily and rapidly softened or melted, due to its fat content. Melt cheese using Cookmatic Level 5 (SLO COOK). Soften cheese using Cookmatic Level 3 (SIMMER).
4. Cheese should be cooked using Cookmatic Level 8 (MEDIUM HIGH) so it will cook quickly, but below the boiling point to avoid a tough "rubbery" product. Prepare your own favorite recipes using this setting. Select a similar recipe in this chapter and use approximately the same amount of cooking time.

SCRAMBLED EGGS CHART

NO. OF EGGS	BOWL SIZE	AMOUNT OF BUTTER*	AMOUNT OF MILK** OR WATER (OPTIONAL)	COOKING TIME	COOKMATIC LEVEL
1	1-pt. bowl	1 teaspoon	2 teaspoons	50 sec. to 1 min., 10 sec.	Cookmatic Level 8 (MEDIUM HIGH)
2	1-pt. bowl	1 teaspoon	1 tablespoon	1 min., 15 sec. to 1 min., 30 sec.	Cookmatic Level 8 (MEDIUM HIGH)
4	1-qt. bowl	2 teaspoons	1-1/2 tablespoons	2 min., 15 sec. to 2 min., 30 sec.	Cookmatic Level 8 (MEDIUM HIGH)
6	1-1/2-qt. bowl	1 tablespoon	2 tablespoons	3 min., 30 sec. to 3 min., 45 sec.	Cookmatic Level 8 (MEDIUM HIGH)

*Spray-on vegetable coating may be used instead of butter. Spray to cover entire dish.
**When using milk, increase cooking time about 10 to 15 seconds.

General Instructions for Cooking Scrambled Eggs
1. Melt butter in bottom of bowl (see chart for bowl size) in Radarange Oven on FULL POWER for 20 to 30 seconds. Swirl bowl so melted butter covers entire dish bottom. Butter will help to keep eggs from sticking to bowl and thus aids in clean-up.
2. Stir eggs vigorously with fork in butter-coated bowl. Add milk, or water if desired, for a smooth texture.
3. Cook in Radarange Oven, covered, on Cookmatic Level 8 (MEDIUM HIGH) for the time specified in the "Scrambled Eggs Chart," depending upon the quantity of eggs used. Eggs may be covered loosely with waxed paper. For fluffier eggs, stir halfway through cooking time, or several times during cooking.
4. Eggs are cooked when they look done, but are still slightly moist. Stir or fluff with fork before serving. Be careful not to overcook. Season with salt and pepper, as desired.

FRIED EGGS CHART

NO. OF EGGS	AMOUNT OF BUTTER OR MARGARINE*	COOKING TIME**	COOKMATIC LEVEL
1	2 teaspoons	40 sec., to 1 min.	Cookmatic Level 8 (MEDIUM HIGH)
2	2 teaspoons	1 min., to 1 min., 10 sec.	Cookmatic Level 8 (MEDIUM HIGH)
4	1 tablespoon	1 min., 15 sec. to 1 min., 30 sec.	Cookmatic Level 8 (MEDIUM HIGH)
6	1 tablespoon	1 min., 30 sec. to 1 min., 45 sec.	Cookmatic Level 8 (MEDIUM HIGH)

*Spray-on vegetable coating may be used instead of butter or margarine.
**Cooking times for these eggs are based upon refrigerator temperatures.

Fried Eggs
Fried eggs should be cooked in a browning skillet for best results. Without a browning skillet, eggs are really "baked", rather than fried. See the section on browning, page 17, for hints on using browning skillets.

General Instructions for Cooking Fried Eggs
1. Preheat the browning skillet for the proper amount of time according to manufacturer's instructions. Always preheat the skillet **completely** empty. Skillet should have a slight "yellow" color when eggs are added.

2. Melt butter in browning skillet before adding egg(s), according to the amount required as indicated on the "Fried Eggs Chart".

3. Add eggs quickly to browning skillet to avoid scorching butter. Pierce yolk(s) with knife or tines of fork. For more tender eggs, 1 to 2 teaspoons of water can be added with eggs.

4. **Cover** eggs with glass lid, so the eggs will cook evenly. (The glass lid will retain steam for even cooking.)

5. Cook eggs in the Radarange Oven for the amount of time indicated in the "Fried Eggs Chart." The shorter cooking time will produce soft-cooked yolks. The longer cooking time in the chart is for more hard-cooked yolk(s). If eggs have been standing at room temperature, decrease cooking time slightly since cooking times are based upon refrigerator-temperature eggs. The lower power setting helps to keep yolks intact during cooking.

6. Let eggs stand, covered, 1 minute before serving. Season with salt and pepper, as desired.

7. When frying 4 to 6 eggs, slightly undercook. Let stand, covered, for about 5 minutes. The egg whites will finish cooking without overcooking the yolks.

8. **We do not recommend reheating leftover fried eggs in a microwave oven.**

POACHED EGGS CHART

NO. OF EGGS	UTENSIL	AMOUNT OF WATER	COOKING TIME*	COOKMATIC LEVEL
1	1 pt. bowl	1 cup	30 sec. to 1 min.	Cookmatic Level 8 (MEDIUM HIGH)
2	1 qt. bowl	1 cup	1 min. to 1 min., 45 sec.	Cookmatic Level 8 (MEDIUM HIGH)
4	1-1/2-qt. bowl	1-1/2 cups	1 min., 45 sec. to 2 min., 15 sec.	Cookmatic Level 8 (MEDIUM HIGH)
6	1-1/2-qt. bowl	1-1/2 cups	2 min., 30 sec. to 3 min.	Cookmatic Level 8 (MEDIUM HIGH)

*Cooking times for these eggs are based upon refrigerator temperatures.

Poached Eggs

Poached eggs cook beautifully in the Radarange Oven. Consult the "Poached Eggs Chart" for specific cooking instructions.

General Instructions for Cooking Poached Eggs

1. Bring the required amount of water to a boil in a glass measure in the Radarange Oven on FULL POWER.

2. Break egg(s) into size of utensil indicated on "Poached Eggs Chart". Be sure to use a bowl having rather steep sides so water won't "spread out" too much in dish.

3. Pierce yolk(s) with knife or tines of fork.

4. Pour boiling water **slowly over** eggs. Be sure that water covers eggs. If more water is needed to cover eggs, slightly increase cooking time. 1 tablespoon of vinegar can be added to the water to help egg(s) hold its (their) shape.

5. Cook egg(s) according to time on "Poached Egg Chart". Egg(s) may be covered loosely with plastic wrap. The shorter cooking time in the chart will produce soft-cooked yolks. The longer cooking time in the chart is for more hard-cooked yolk(s). For soft yolks, eggs can be removed from Radarange Oven while slightly undercooked. Allow to stand, covered. Whites will finish cooking without overcooking yolks. If eggs have been standing at room temperature, decrease cooking time slightly since cooking times are based upon refrigerator-temperature eggs. The lower setting helps to keep yolk(s) intact during cooking. Remove eggs after cooking with slotted spoon. Season with salt and pepper, as desired.

6. **We do not recommend reheating leftover poached eggs in a microwave oven.**

Eggs Benedict

Yield: 2 servings

4 eggs, poached
1/2 cup hollandaise sauce
4 thin slices Canadian bacon or ham
2 English muffins, split

1. Poach eggs according to timing in above chart. Let stand in water, covered. Prepare Hollandaise sauce according to recipe on page 271. Let stand, covered. Place Canadian bacon on plate. Heat in Radarange Oven on FULL POWER for 45 seconds.

2. Arrange 2 muffin halves, cut-side up, on each serving plate. Top each half with slice of Canadian bacon or ham. Remove eggs from water, using slotted spoon. Place eggs on bacon. Spoon sauce over eggs. Heat one plate at a time. Heat in Radarange Oven on FULL POWER for 15 seconds, or until heated through.

Hash 'N' Egg Nests

Yield: 2 to 4 servings

1 (15-1/2 oz.) can hash*

4 eggs

1. Divide hash evenly among 4, 6-oz. custard cups, spreading hash up the sides of cups.
2. Break egg into each hash-lined cup, and pierce each yolk with knife or tines of fork. Place cups on plate. Cover with plastic wrap.
3. Cook in Radarange Oven, covered, on Cookmatic Level 8 (MEDIUM HIGH) for 4-1/2 to 5 minutes, or until eggs are cooked as desired.***

   MICRO-TIPS:
   - You can cook one at a time to achieve either soft or hard-cooked egg yolks for different personal preferences. Increase or decrease cooking time, accordingly.

   *Any type of hash may be used.

   ***You may want to turn dish halfway through cooking time.

Bacon and Eggs for One

Yield: 1 serving

2 slices bacon

1 egg
Salt
Pepper

1. Cut bacon in half and place in 1-quart dish or skillet. Cover with paper towel. Cook in Radarange Oven, covered, on FULL POWER for 1 minute.
2. Arrange bacon at edge of dish. Break egg into center of dish. Pierce yolk with knife or tines of fork.
3. Cook in Radarange Oven, covered, on Cookmatic Level 8 (MEDIUM HIGH) for 40 seconds to 1 minute, or until egg is cooked as desired. Season with salt and pepper, as desired.

   MICRO-TIP: If cooking 2 eggs, increase time in step #3 to 1-1/4 to 1-1/2 minutes, or until eggs are cooked as desired.

Chinese Scramble

Yield: 3 to 4 servings

1 tablespoon butter or margarine

6 eggs
1 (10 oz.) can Chinese vegetables, drained
1/2 cup cooked rice
1/4 cup onion, finely chopped
1/4 cup green pepper, finely chopped
2 tablespoons soy sauce

1. Place butter in 1-1/2-quart casserole. Heat in Radarange Oven on FULL POWER for 20 seconds, or until melted.
2. Break eggs into casserole. Beat with fork. Stir in remaining ingredients.
3. Cook in Radarange Oven, covered, on Cookmatic Level 8 (MEDIUM HIGH) for 6 to 7 minutes, or until eggs are cooked, but still slightly moist. Stir halfway through cooking time.

Wake-Up Special

Yield: 4 to 6 servings

6 slices bacon

1. Place bacon strips side by side in 1-quart casserole. Cover with paper towel. Cook in Radarange Oven, covered, on FULL POWER for 4 to 5 minutes, or until crisp. Remove bacon and crumble. Reserve 1 tablespoon of grease.

1/4 cup green pepper, chopped

2. Add green pepper to bacon grease. Cook in Radarange Oven on FULL POWER for 60 seconds, or until green pepper is tender.

4 eggs
1/2 (10-3/4 oz.) can cream of chicken soup

3. Combine eggs and soup. Pour into casserole with green pepper. Cook in Radarange Oven, covered, on Cookmatic Level 8 (MEDIUM HIGH) for 3-1/2 to 4 minutes, or until eggs are cooked as desired. Stir halfway through cooking time, for fluffier eggs.

Salt
Pepper

4. Sprinkle crumbled bacon over top. Season with salt and pepper, as desired.

MICRO-TIP: If desired, mix remaining soup with 1/2 cup milk. Heat in Radarange Oven on Cookmatic Level 8 (MEDIUM HIGH) for 2-1/2 to 3 minutes, or until warmed. Use as sauce for eggs.

Eggs Delicious

Yield: 4 servings

1/2 cup milk

1. Place milk in 1-cup glass measure. Heat in Radarange Oven on Cookmatic Level 8 (MEDIUM HIGH) for 1 minute, or until warmed.

1 (3 oz.) pkg. cream cheese
6 medium eggs

2. Beat cream cheese until fluffy in large mixing bowl. Beat in milk and eggs.

1 cup cooked ham, diced
1 large ripe tomato, cut in wedges
Salt
Pepper

3. Stir in ham and tomato. Season with salt and pepper, as desired.

2 tablespoons butter or margarine

4. Place butter in 10-inch glass pie plate. Heat in Radarange Oven on FULL POWER for 20 to 30 seconds, or until melted. Pour egg mixture into pie plate. Cook in Radarange Oven, covered, on Cookmatic Level 8 (MEDIUM HIGH) for 8 to 10 minutes, or until firm, but moist. Stir 2 to 3 times during cooking time.

Toast-Framed Egg

Yield: 1 serving

1 slice bread, toasted and buttered
1 egg

1. Cut 3-inch diameter circle in toast with biscuit cutter or knife. Place toast on plate. Break egg into hole. Pierce yolk with knife or tines of fork. Cover with plastic wrap.

2. Cook in Radarange Oven, covered, on Cookmatic Level 8 (MEDIUM HIGH) for 45 seconds to 1 minute, or until egg is cooked as desired.

Puffy Omelet

Yield: 2 to 3 servings

4 egg whites
3 tablespoons water
1/4 teaspoon cream of tartar
1/4 teaspoon salt

4 egg yolks
1/8 teaspoon pepper

Spray-on vegetable coating

1. Beat egg whites, water, cream of tartar and salt until egg whites are stiff, but not dry.

2. Beat together yolks and pepper until yolks are thick and lemon-colored. Fold into egg whites.

3. Preheat large browning skillet in Radarange Oven, according to manufacturer's instructions. Spray with vegetable coating. Pour omelet mixture into skillet. Cook in Radarange Oven on Cookmatic Level 8 (MEDIUM HIGH) for 3-1/2 to 4 minutes, or until knife inserted in center comes out clean. To serve, make cut across middle of omelet but don't cut completely through. Fold omelet over and slide out of dish onto warm platter.

MICRO-TIPS:

• Sprinkle center of omelet with shredded cheese before folding, if desired.

• For Fruit-Filled Dessert Omelet Variation, follow original "Puffy Omelet" recipe except the following:

FRUIT FILLED DESSERT OMELET VARIATION:

1/4 cup sugar

1/2 cup strawberries, sliced, or other fruit
1/2 cup whipped cream

1. Omit pepper in Step #2. Add sugar to egg yolks before beating.

2. Blend together strawberries and whipped cream. Spread half on omelet before folding. Spread remaining mixture over top before serving.

Savory Bacon Omelet

Yield: 4 servings

9 to 10 strips (1/2 lb.) bacon

1/2 cup green onions, thinly sliced

8 eggs, beaten
1/4 cup heavy cream
2 teaspoons prepared mustard
1/4 teaspoon pepper
Salt

1. Place bacon slices on 10-inch glass pie plate side by side. Cover with paper towel. Cook in Radarange Oven, covered, on FULL POWER for 8 to 9 minutes, or until crisp.

2. Remove bacon and crumble. Remove all of grease, reserving 1 tablespoon. Add green onions to grease. Cook in Radarange Oven on FULL POWER for 1 minute, or until green onions are almost tender.

3. Mix together eggs, bacon, green onions, cream and seasonings. Season with salt, as desired. Pour into pie plate. Cook in Radarange Oven on Cookmatic Level 8 (MEDIUM HIGH) for 6 to 7 minutes, or until firm but moist. Lift outer edge once or twice during cooking, to allow uncooked portion to touch outside of dish. Serve immediately.

Cheese Soufflé

Yield: 4 to 6 servings

2 tablespoons butter or margarine
2 tablespoons all-purpose flour
1/2 teaspoon salt
1/2 teaspoon dry mustard
1/8 teaspoon paprika
1 cup evaporated milk

1. Place butter in 1 to 1-1/2-quart casserole. Heat in Radarange Oven on FULL POWER for 20 to 30 seconds, or until melted. Stir in flour, salt, mustard and paprika. Gradually add evaporated milk.

1-1/2 cups sharp Cheddar cheese, shredded

2. Cook in Radarange Oven on Cookmatic Level 8 (MEDIUM HIGH) for 2-1/2 to 3 minutes, or until thickened. Stir with wire whip until smooth. Stir in cheese until melted. If necessary, heat in Radarange Oven on Cookmatic Level 5 (SLO COOK) for 1 to 2 minutes, or until cheese is completely melted.

4 eggs, separated
1/4 teaspoon cream of tartar

3. Beat egg whites with cream of tartar until stiff, but not dry. Beat egg yolks until thick and lemon-colored. Beat cheese mixture slowly into egg yolks, beating until well-blended. Fold cheese mixture into egg whites thoroughly, but gently. Turn into 2-quart soufflé dish.

4. Cook in Radarange Oven on Cookmatic Level 8 (MEDIUM HIGH) for 6-1/2 to 7-1/2 minutes, or until top seems dry.* Serve immediately.

*MICRO-TIP: You may want to turn dish halfway through cooking time.

Egg and Sausage Scramble

Yield: 4 to 6 servings

6 eggs, slightly-beaten
6 slices bread, cubed
1 cup Cheddar cheese, shredded
1 teaspoon salt
1 teaspoon dry mustard
12 ozs. pork sausage (or smokies), fully cooked and cut into pieces
2 cups milk

1. Mix all ingredients together in 1-1/2-quart casserole. Refrigerate 4 to 6 hours or overnight.

2. Cook in Radarange Oven, covered, on Cookmatic Level 8 (MEDIUM HIGH) for 12 to 14 minutes, or until knife inserted in center comes out clean. Serve immediately.

Cholesterol-Free Scrambled Eggs

ONE SERVING

1/2 (8oz.) carton cholesterol-free egg substitute (1/2 cup), thawed*

1. Pour egg substitute into small bowl.

2. Cook in Radarange Oven on Cookmatic Level 8 (MEDIUM HIGH) for 1-1/4 to 1-1/2 minutes, or until firm. Stir halfway through cooking time. Season, as desired.

TWO SERVINGS

1 (8 oz.) carton cholesterol-free egg substitute (1 cup), thawed*

1. Pour egg substitute into 1-quart casserole.

2. Cook in Radarange Oven on Cookmatic Level 8 (MEDIUM HIGH) for 2 to 2-1/2 minutes, or until firm. Stir occasionally during cooking time. Season, as desired.

*MICRO-TIP: Defrost 1, 8 oz. carton in Radarange Oven on DEFROST for 5 to 6 minutes, or until thawed. Stir occasionally during defrosting. Do not allow to cook.

Crustless Quiche Lorraine

Yield: 4 servings

9 to 10 (1/2 lb.) slices bacon, cooked and crumbled*
1 cup Swiss cheese, shredded
1/4 cup onion, minced

4 eggs
1 cup evaporated milk
3/4 teaspoon salt
1/4 teaspoon sugar
1/8 teaspoon cayenne pepper

1. Sprinkle bacon, cheese and onion into 9-inch glass pie plate.

2. Beat eggs, milk and seasonings in large mixing bowl with rotary beater, until well-blended. Pour over bacon mixture.

3. Bake in Radarange Oven on Cookmatic Level 8 (MEDIUM HIGH) for 9-1/2 to 11 minutes, or until knife inserted near center comes out clean.** Let stand, 1 minute, before serving.

   MICRO-TIPS:

   *Prepare bacon, according to instructions, on page 178.

   **You may want to turn dish halfway through cooking time.

Wheat Crusted Quiche

Yield: 6 servings

3/4 cup wheat germ
3/4 cup all-purpose flour
1/4 teaspoon salt
1/2 cup shortening
2 to 3 tablespoons cold water

9 to 10 (1/2 lb.) slices bacon, cooked and crumbled
3/4 cup Swiss cheese, shredded
1/4 cup onion, minced

3 eggs
1/2 cup evaporated milk
1/2 teaspoon salt
1/8 teaspoon cayenne pepper

1. Combine wheat germ, flour and salt. Cut in shortening. Stir in water. Press dough firmly against bottom and sides of 9-inch glass pie plate. Prick bottom and sides with tines of fork. Bake in Radarange Oven on FULL POWER for 1-1/2 to 2 minutes, or until cooked but slightly moist.

2. Sprinkle bacon, cheese and onion on crust.

3. Beat together eggs, evaporated milk and seasonings until well-blended. Pour into shell. Bake on Cookmatic Level 8 (MEDIUM (HIGH) for 6 to 8 minutes, or until knife inserted near center comes out clean.*

   *MICRO-TIP: You may want to turn dish halfway through the cooking time.

Fancy Scrambled Eggs

Yield: 6 to 8 servings

3 tablespoons butter or margarine
8 eggs
1/2 cup milk
1 teaspoon chives, chopped
1/2 teaspoon salt
1/4 teaspoon dry mustard

1. Place butter in 1-quart casserole. Heat in Radarange Oven on FULL POWER for 30 to 40 seconds, or until melted. Add remaining ingredients. Beat vigorously with fork until well-mixed.

2. Cook in Radarange Oven, covered, on Cookmatic Level 8 (MEDIUM HIGH) for 6 to 7 minutes, or until eggs are cooked as desired. Stir halfway through cooking time, for fluffier eggs.

Whether you're fishing for flattery, or just preparing fish, a few guidelines will help you catch compliments. This chapter includes instructions and recipes for cooking a variety of fish and seafood which can be prepared in your Radarange Oven. You can serve the seafood with one of the sauces found in the "Sauces, Jams, and Relishes" chapter.

Fish and seafood are delicate food items to prepare, so follow recipe instructions carefully. Fish and seafood are more flaky and moist when prepared in a Radarange Oven instead of in a conventional oven. Since fish is delicate and has no tough tissues, the cooking time will be short. Weight-watchers will love Radarange Oven-prepared fish and seafood since oils and fats can be eliminated. Shellfish are easily prepared, since the huge quantities of water necessary in conventional cooking of shellfish are not required. The "Appetizers and Snacks" chapter includes several seafood appetizers. Read the following tips before preparing fish and seafood.

General Hints for Cooking Fish and Seafood

1. In most cases, fish should be defrosted, before cooking, unless otherwise specified in a recipe. Consult the "Fish and Seafood Defrosting Chart" for complete instructions. When fish is not completely thawed after defrosting, rinse with cold running water to complete the defrosting process.
2. Most fish and seafood require a cooking time of 3 to 4 minutes per pound on FULL POWER. When "delicate" ingredients, such as cheese, are cooked with seafood, sometimes a recipe will suggest cooking at a lower power setting. A lower setting, for example, will prevent such ingredients as cheese from becoming "rubbery."
3. Always cook fish and seafood in a covered utensil, so steam and moisture will be retained. The use of coverings also decreases the cooking time as well as prevents dehydration. Glass lids or heavy-duty plastic wrap are the best coverings to use since they retain more moisture than other types of coverings.

If a dish doesn't have a glass lid, heavy-duty plastic wrap can easily be substituted. Plastic wrap should be pierced, by making a 1-inch slit with a knife.
4. Place larger and thicker pieces of fish and seafood near the edge of the dish for more even cooking.
5. Cook fish only until it may be easily flaked with a fork. Make certain that the center of large fish flakes easily as well as the edges. Shellfish meat will look opaque, and the shell will have a pink color when it is completely cooked. The flesh of all seafood, such as shrimp, crab and lobster, will look opaque and firm. Always try to cook fish and seafood for the minimum amount of time, since it is easily overcooked. Be careful not to overcook. Cover all fish and seafood during the standing time to:
   a) Keep it hot.
   b) Keep it moist and prevent dehydration.
   c) Finish its cooking process. (For example, the center may need to finish cooking.)
6. Always cook fish last when preparing an entire meal. Fish and seafood won't reheat as easily as some foods, and overcooking can occur during reheating. Other foods, such as vegetables, will keep a better texture longer after cooking and can be reheated more easily. If necessary, however, fish and seafood can be quickly reheated before serving. Be certain to cover during reheating.
7. One kind of fish required in a recipe can easily be substituted for another. For example, snapper, flounder, perch, halibut, and sole can be used interchangeably in the following recipes. Fish steaks can also be substituted for fillets, but they may require slightly longer cooking and defrosting times.
8. Shellfish can be prepared right in the shell. Shells make very attractive and unusual serving "dishes." Shellfish cooked in the shell will have the same cooking time as fish cooked out of the shell since shells do not absorb microwaves.
9. Seafood can be attractively garnished by using lemon slices, parsley, almonds, tomato slices, or spices. Consult the MICRO-TIPS for other serving hints.

tuffed Red Snapper (page 160)

10. Most seafood casserole recipes can be prepared ahead of time and refrigerated. Remember to allow 4 to 7 minutes of extra cooking time, due to the refrigerator temperature. The cooking time of a refrigerated casserole will vary slightly, depending upon the size and ingredients of the casserole.

11. You can convert your own favorite seafood recipes to Radarange Oven cooking times. Use the timings of the recipes in this chapter as a general guide. Find a recipe that is approximately the same size and includes the same type of seafood. Cook most casseroles covered on FULL POWER. Follow the other cooking tips found in this section.

FISH AND SEAFOOD DEFROSTING CHART

TYPE	PKG. SIZE	PREPARATION INSTRUCTIONS	DEFROSTING TIME	SETTING
Crab Claws	12 oz.	Make 1-inch slit in pkg. Turn and rearrange claws halfway through cooking time.	6 to 8 min.	DEFROST
Crab Meat	6 oz.	Make 1-inch slit in pkg. Turn halfway through cooking time.	3-1/2 to 4-1/2 min.	DEFROST
Fillets, Flounder, Cod, Sole, Haddock, etc.	1 lb.	Unwrap pkg. and open. Turn fillets over halfway through cooking time.	8 to 12 min.	DEFROST
Lobster Tail	16 oz.	Wrap in plastic wrap or waxed paper.	7-1/2 to 9-1/2 min.	DEFROST
Shrimp	12 oz.	Make 1-inch slit in pkg. Turn halfway through cooking time.	7 to 9 min.	DEFROST

General Instructions for Defrosting Fish and Seafood

1. Frozen seafood may be thawed in its original package. Open the package slightly, or pierce it by making a 1-inch slit with a knife. Place it directly on the Radarange Oven glass tray, or on a plastic rack. Consult the "Fish and Seafood Defrosting Chart" for complete instructions.

2. Be sure to use the DEFROST cycle for thawing. This cycle operates at a low enough power to prevent cooking from starting at the outer edges.

3. Allow thawed seafood to stand for a short period of time before cooking to be certain the seafood is totally defrosted. Larger seafood pieces can be held under cold running water, if necessary, to finish the defrosting process, or to allow still-frozen fillets to be separated. Fish and seafood should be totally defrosted before cooking, so that cooking will be done evenly.

FISH AND SEAFOOD CONVENIENCE FOOD CHART

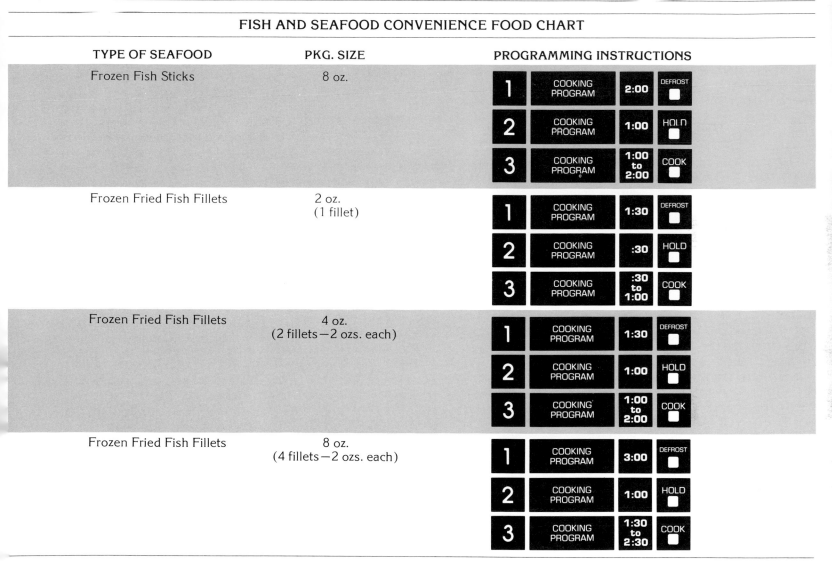

TYPE OF SEAFOOD	PKG. SIZE	PROGRAMMING INSTRUCTIONS		
Frozen Fish Sticks	8 oz.	**1** COOKING PROGRAM	2:00	DEFROST ☐
		2 COOKING PROGRAM	1:00	HOLD ☐
		3 COOKING PROGRAM	1:00 to 2:00	COOK ☐
Frozen Fried Fish Fillets	2 oz. (1 fillet)	**1** COOKING PROGRAM	1:30	DEFROST ☐
		2 COOKING PROGRAM	:30	HOLD ☐
		3 COOKING PROGRAM	:30 to 1:00	COOK ☐
Frozen Fried Fish Fillets	4 oz. (2 fillets—2 ozs. each)	**1** COOKING PROGRAM	1:30	DEFROST ☐
		2 COOKING PROGRAM	1:00	HOLD ☐
		3 COOKING PROGRAM	1:00 to 2:00	COOK ☐
Frozen Fried Fish Fillets	8 oz. (4 fillets—2 ozs. each)	**1** COOKING PROGRAM	3:00	DEFROST ☐
		2 COOKING PROGRAM	1:00	HOLD ☐
		3 COOKING PROGRAM	1:30 to 2:30	COOK ☐

General Instructions for Fish and Seafood Convenience Food Chart

1. Place the frozen seafood on a cooking grill or on a paper plate. Cover with a paper towel, waxed paper or plastic wrap.

2. DEFROST, HOLD, and COOK, according to the instructions in the chart. The HOLD period is necessary before cooking to be certain the seafood is totally defrosted.

Fresh Crab Claws

Yield: 2 to 3 servings

12 fresh crab claws

1. Place crab claws in circle in soufflé or au gratin dish with claws toward center.
2. Cook in Radarange Oven on FULL POWER for 1-1/2 to 2 minutes, or until hot.

Crunchy Crab Bake

Yield: 4 to 6 servings

1 (4 oz.) can mushrooms, drained
1/2 cup mayonnaise
1/3 cup Cheddar cheese, shredded
1 (10-3/4 oz.) can cream of shrimp soup

1 (6-1/2 oz.) can crab meat, drained
1 (8 oz.) can water chestnuts, drained and sliced
2 hard-cooked eggs, chopped*

1 (3 oz.) can French fried onion rings

1. Blend together mushrooms, mayonnaise, cheese and soup in 1-1/2-quart casserole.
2. Gently fold in crab meat, water chestnuts and eggs. Cook in Radarange Oven on FULL POWER for 5 minutes. Stir halfway through cooking time and at end of cooking time.
3. Sprinkle onion rings over casserole. Cook in Radarange Oven on FULL POWER for 2-1/2 to 3 minutes, or until heated through and temperature of 150°F is reached.**

MICRO-TIPS:

*Remember, do not hard-cook eggs in the Radarange Oven.

**Use the Temperature-Control to stop the Radarange Oven at 150°F.

Fish For One

Yield: 1 serving

1/4 lb. fish fillet
1/2 tablespoon butter or margarine
1 teaspoon lemon juice
Salt
Pepper

1. Arrange fish on glass serving plate. Dot with butter. Sprinkle with lemon juice. Season with salt and pepper, as desired. Cover with plastic wrap.
2. Cook in Radarange Oven, covered, on FULL POWER for 1 to 2 minutes, or until fish flakes easily with fork. Remove excess liquid, using paper towels, before serving.

Cooked Shrimp

Yield: 1/2 to 3/4 lb. cooked shrimp, approx. 4 servings

1 lb. shrimp, shelled and cleaned
1/4 cup hot water
2 teaspoons lemon juice
1/4 teaspoon salt
1/8 teaspoon thyme

1. Place shrimp in 1 to 1-1/2-quart casserole. Add water, lemon juice, salt and thyme.
2. Cook in Radarange Oven, covered, on FULL POWER for 2 to 3 minutes, or until shrimp is opaque and firm. Drain shrimp. Cover and chill.

MICRO-TIP: Use this shrimp for cocktails or salads.

Shrimp Creole

Yield: 4 to 5 servings

2 tablespoons butter or margarine

3/4 cup green pepper, chopped
1 cup onion, chopped
1 cup celery, chopped

2 tablespoons all-purpose flour
1 (14-1/2 oz.) can tomatoes

1 teaspoon sugar
5 to 6 drops Tabasco sauce
1 bay leaf
1 teaspoon salt
1/8 teaspoon pepper
1 lb. shrimp, shelled and cleaned

1. Place butter in 2-1/2 to 3-quart casserole. Heat in Radarange Oven on FULL POWER for 20 to 30 seconds, or until melted.

2. Stir in green pepper, onion and celery. Cook in Radarange Oven on FULL POWER for 6 to 8 minutes, or until vegetables are tender. Stir halfway through cooking time.

3. Sprinkle vegetables with flour, and stir to blend. Mix in tomatoes. Cook in Radarange Oven on FULL POWER for 4 to 6 minutes, or until heated through. Stir halfway through cooking time.

4. Blend in remaining ingredients. Cook in Radarange Oven on FULL POWER for 6 minutes, or until shrimp are fully cooked. Stir twice during cooking time. Remove bay leaf before serving.

MICRO-TIP: May be served over cooked rice.

Creamed Shrimp

Yield: 4 to 6 servings

1/4 cup onion, chopped
3/4 cup celery, chopped
1 tablespoon vegetable oil

1 (10-3/4 oz.) can cream of
   mushroom soup
1 (12 oz.) pkg. frozen shrimp
1 tablespoon lemon juice
1/2 teaspoon salt

2 eggs, hard-cooked and diced*
1/2 cup Cheddar cheese, cubed

1. Place onion, celery and oil in 1-1/2-quart casserole. Cook in Radarange Oven on FULL POWER for 3 to 4 minutes, or until onion and celery are tender.

2. Add soup, shrimp, lemon juice and salt. Cook in Radarange Oven, covered, on FULL POWER for 8 to 10 minutes. Stir halfway through cooking time.

3. Blend in eggs and cheese. Cook in Radarange Oven, covered, on Cookmatic Level 5 (SLO COOK) for 2 minutes, or until cheese is slightly melted. Stir before serving.

MICRO-TIPS:

• May be served over rice, chow mein noodles, toast or English muffins.

* Remember, do not hard-cook eggs in the Radarange Oven.

Curried Shrimp and Broccoli

Yield: 6 to 8 servings

1 (10-3/4 oz.) can cream of
   celery soup
1 to 2 teaspoons curry powder
2 teaspoons Worcestershire sauce
1/2 cup onion, finely chopped
1/2 cup milk

2 lbs. shrimp, shelled and cleaned
1 (10 oz.) pkg. frozen, chopped
   broccoli, cooked

4 cups (8 ozs.) fine egg noodles,
   cooked
Salt
1 tablespoon grated Parmesan
   cheese

1. Combine soup, curry powder, Worcestershire sauce and onion in 3-quart casserole. Stir in milk. Cook in Radarange Oven, covered, on FULL POWER for 4 to 5 minutes, or until onion is slightly tender. Stir halfway through cooking time.

2. Stir in shrimp and broccoli. Cook in Radarange Oven, covered, on FULL POWER for 4 to 5 minutes, or until shrimp is cooked and temperature of 160°F is reached.* Stir halfway through cooking time.

3. Gently combine soup mixture with noodles. Salt, as desired, and toss. Sprinkle with cheese before serving.

*MICRO-TIP: Use the Temperature-Hold to maintain 160°F until ready to serve. Toss with noodles just before serving.

Fillet of Sole with Oyster Sauce

Yield: 4 servings

1 (16 oz.) pkg. fillet of sole, defrosted
1 (10-3/4 oz.) can oyster stew
1 (4 oz.) can mushrooms, drained
1/2 teaspoon salt
Paprika

1. Separate fillets and arrange in 1-1/2-quart utility dish.

2. Blend together oyster stew, mushrooms and salt. Pour over fillets. Sprinkle with paprika, as desired. Cover with plastic wrap.

3. Cook in Radarange Oven, covered, on FULL POWER for 5 to 7 minutes, or until fish flakes easily with fork.

   MICRO-TIP: For tartness, add sprinkling of lemon juice. Fresh fillet of sole may be substituted for frozen.

French Fish Fillets

Yield: 4 servings

1 lb. fish fillets
1/4 cup French dressing
1/2 cup cracker crumbs
Paprika

1. Dip fillets in dressing. Coat with crumbs. Place fillets in greased, 1-1/2-quart utility dish. Sprinkle with paprika, as desired. Cover with plastic wrap.

2. Bake in Radarange Oven, covered, on FULL POWER for 3-1/2 to 5 minutes, or until fish flakes easily with fork.

Colorful Fillets

Yield: 4 servings

1 lb. haddock fillets, cut into serving pieces
3 green onions, sliced
1 cup fresh mushrooms, sliced
1 cup tomato, chopped
1/8 teaspoon basil
3/4 teaspoon salt
Dash pepper

1. Arrange fillets in 8 x 8 x 2-inch glass baking dish. Top with vegetables. Sprinkle with seasonings. Cover with plastic wrap.

2. Cook in Radarange Oven, covered, on FULL POWER for 3 to 4 minutes, or until fish flakes easily with fork.

   MICRO-TIP: This is a good fish recipe for weight watchers. There are approximately 136 calories per serving!

Tuna-Tomato Bake

Yield: 4 to 6 servings

1/2 cup onion, chopped
1/3 cup celery, chopped
2 tablespoons vegetable oil
1 (10-3/4 oz.) can golden cream of mushroom soup
1/2 cup milk
2 (6-1/2 to 7 oz. each) cans tuna, drained
1 cup canned tomatoes, drained and chopped
1 cup peas, cooked and drained
1/2 teaspoon salt
Herb-seasoned croutons (optional)

1. Place onion, celery and oil in 2-quart casserole. Cook in Radarange Oven on FULL POWER for 3 to 4 minutes, or until onion and celery are tender.

2. Blend in remaining ingredients. Top with croutons, if desired.

3. Cook in Radarange Oven on FULL POWER for 10 to 12 minutes, or until heated through, and temperature of 150°F is reached.

Shrimp Oriental

Yield: 4 servings

3/4 teaspoon instant chicken bouillon
1/2 cup boiling water

1/4 cup vegetable oil
1/8 teaspoon garlic powder
1/4 teaspoon ginger
1 lb. shrimp, shelled and cleaned

1 medium onion, cut in eighths
1 cup celery, diagonally cut in 3/4-inch pieces
1 medium green pepper, cut in 1-inch squares

1 (8 oz.) can tomato sauce
1 tablespoon sugar
1/4 teaspoon salt
1 tablespoon cornstarch
1/2 teaspoon monosodium glutamate
1/4 cup soy sauce

2 tomatoes, cut in eighths

1. Dissolve chicken bouillon in boiling water. Set aside.

2. Place oil, garlic powder and ginger in 10-inch ceramic skillet. Heat in Radarange Oven on FULL POWER for 1-1/2 minutes. Stir in shrimp. Toss to coat with oil. Cook in Radarange Oven on FULL POWER for 1 minute. Stir and remove from skillet to dish.

3. Stir onion, celery and green pepper into skillet. Cook in Radarange Oven on FULL POWER for 4 minutes. Stir halfway through cooking time.

4. Mix together tomato sauce, sugar, salt, cornstarch, monosodium glutamate, soy sauce and chicken bouillon. Stir into vegetable mixture.

5. Cook in Radarange Oven, covered, on FULL POWER for about 4 to 5 minutes, or until sauce is thickened. Stir halfway through cooking time. Blend in tomatoes and shrimp. Cook in Radarange Oven on FULL POWER for 1 to 2 minutes, or until heated through.

MICRO-TIP: May be served with rice.

Tuna Oriental

Yield: 4 to 5 servings

3/4 cup celery, chopped
1/4 cup onion, chopped
1 tablespoon butter or margarine

1 (10-3/4 oz.) can cream of mushroom soup
1/2 cup milk
1 (4 oz.) can sliced mushrooms, drained
1 (6-1/2 or 7 oz.) can of tuna, drained
1 (3 oz.) can chow mein noodles
1/2 cup cashews (optional)
Salt
Pepper

1. Place celery, onion and butter in 1-quart casserole. Heat in Radarange Oven on FULL POWER for 3 minutes, or until celery and onion are tender.

2. Stir in remaining ingredients, using only 1 cup of chow mein noodles. Season with salt and pepper, as desired. Top with remaining chow mein noodles.

3. Cook in Radarange Oven on FULL POWER for 6 to 7 minutes, or until heated through, and temperature of 150°F is reached.

MICRO-TIP: 1 (8 oz.) can water chestnuts, drained and sliced, may be added in Step #2.

Shoestring Tuna Casserole

Yield: 4 to 5 servings

1 (4 oz.) can cheese flavor
   shoestring potatoes
1 (10-3/4 oz.) can golden cream
   of mushroom soup
1 (6-1/2 or 7 oz.) can tuna, drained
1 (5.3 oz.) can evaporated milk
1 (3 oz.) can sliced mushrooms,
   drained
1/4 cup pimento, chopped

1. Combine all ingredients in 1-1/2-quart casserole, reserving 1 cup of shoestring potatoes. Sprinkle reserved potatoes over top.

2. Bake in Radarange Oven on FULL POWER for 10 minutes, or until temperature of 150°F is reached.*

   *MICRO-TIP: Use the Temperature-Control to stop the Radarange Oven at 150°F.

Tuna Tot Casserole

Yield: 6 to 8 servings

1/3 cup green pepper, chopped
1/2 cup onion, chopped
1 tablespoon vegetable oil

1 (10-3/4 oz.) can cream of
   mushroom soup
2 tablespoons milk
1 (2-1/2 oz.) can sliced mushrooms,
   drained (optional)
2 (6-1/2 or 7 oz. each) cans tuna,
   drained
1 (8-1/2 oz.) can peas, drained
1/2 lb. Tater Tots®

1. Combine green pepper, onion and oil in 1-1/2-quart casserole. Cook in Radarange Oven on FULL POWER for 2 minutes, or until green pepper and onion are tender.

2. Blend in soup, milk, mushrooms, tuna and peas. Top with Tater Tots.®

3. Cook in Radarange Oven on FULL POWER for 10 to 12 minutes, or until temperature of 150°F is reached.*

   *MICRO-TIP: Use the Temperature-Hold to maintain 150°F until ready to serve.

Tuna Loaf

Yield: 4 to 6 servings

3/4 cup celery, chopped
1 tablespoon butter or margarine

1 (6 oz.) pkg. (2 cups)
   seasoned stuffing mix
2 eggs
1 cup milk
1 tablespoon parsley flakes

3 (6-1/2 to 7 oz. each) cans tuna,
   drained

1. Combine celery and butter in 1-1/2-quart casserole. Cook in Radarange Oven on FULL POWER for 2 to 3 minutes, or until celery is tender.

2. Combine stuffing mix, eggs, milk and parsley in large mixing bowl. Allow stuffing to soften for 5 to 10 minutes.

3. Add tuna and blend well. Pat into greased 9 x 5 x 2-inch glass loaf dish. Cook in Radarange Oven on FULL POWER for 9 minutes, or until temperature of 150°F is reached.*

   MICRO-TIPS:

   •Use TIMER in Step #2 to remind you when stuffing has softened.

   *Use the Temperature-Control to stop the Radarange Oven at 150°F.

Tuna Tetrazzini

Yield: 6 servings

4 ozs. spaghetti, broken into
2-inch lengths and cooked
1 (10-3/4 oz.) can cream of
mushroom soup
1/2 cup milk
1 (6-1/2 to 7 oz.) can tuna, drained
1 (3 oz.) can sliced mushrooms,
drained
1/3 cup onion, finely chopped
1 cup Cheddar cheese, shredded

1. Combine cooked spaghetti, soup and milk in 1-1/2-quart casserole. Blend in tuna, mushrooms, onion and 1/2 cup cheese. Mix lightly. Cover.

2. Cook in Radarange Oven, covered, on FULL POWER for 8 minutes, or until temperature of 150°F is reached.* Stir halfway through cooking time. Sprinkle on remaining cheese. Cook in Radarange Oven on Cookmatic Level 5 (SLO COOK) for 1 to 2 minutes, or until cheese is melted.

   *MICRO-TIP: Use the Temperature-Control to stop the Radarange Oven at 150°F.

Tuna Stroganoff

Yield: 4 servings

2 (6-1/2 to 7 oz. each) cans tuna
1 (10-3/4 oz.) can cream of
mushroom soup
1 (3 or 4 oz.) can sliced
mushrooms, with liquid

1/2 cup dairy sour cream
1 tablespoon parsley, chopped
(optional)

1. Combine tuna, soup, and mushrooms in 1-1/2-quart casserole.

2. Cook in Radarange Oven on FULL POWER for 4 to 5 minutes, or until mixture begins to boil. Stir twice during cooking time. Stir in sour cream. Garnish with parsley, as desired.

   MICRO-TIP: May be served over rice or noodles.

Curried Scallops

Yield: 3 to 4 servings

1 tablespoon butter or margarine

1 lb. scallops, rinsed and
drained
1/4 cup green onions, sliced

1-1/2 teaspoons cornstarch
1/2 teaspoon curry powder
1/4 teaspoon salt

1. Place butter in 9-inch glass pie plate. Heat in Radarange Oven on FULL POWER for 20 seconds, or until melted.

2. Add scallops and onions. Cover with plastic wrap. Cook in Radarange Oven, covered, on FULL POWER for 2-1/2 to 3-1/2 minutes, or until scallops are almost opaque. Stir halfway through cooking time. Reserve 2 tablespoons liquid.

3. Combine cornstarch, curry powder and salt with 2 tablespoons reserved liquid. Stir into scallops. Cover with plastic wrap.

4. Cook in Radarange Oven, covered, on FULL POWER for 2 minutes, or until sauce is thickened and smooth. Scallops should be opaque.

   MICRO-TIP: Serve scallops over rice. Garnish with tomatoes and watercress.

Spring-time Sole

Yield: 4 servings

1 lb. sole fillets
1 (10 oz.) pkg. frozen asparagus
  or 3/4 lb. fresh asparagus,
  cooked
1/2 teaspoon salt
1/4 teaspoon leaf thyme

1/2 cup plain yogurt
1 teaspoon buttermilk salad
  dressing mix

1. Arrange fillets evenly in 1-1/2-quart utility dish. Layer asparagus over fillets. Sprinkle with salt and thyme. Cover loosely with plastic wrap. Cook in Radarange Oven, covered, on FULL POWER for 3-1/2 to 4-1/2 minutes, or until fish flakes easily with fork.

2. Combine yogurt and dressing mix. Spoon evenly over asparagus. Cook in Radarange Oven on Cookmatic Level 8 (MEDIUM HIGH) for 1-1/2 to 2 minutes, or until sauce is heated through.

   MICRO-TIP: This low-calorie recipe has only about 138 calories per serving.

Salmon-Stuffed Green Peppers

Yield: 4 servings

4 large green peppers

1. Cut off upper third of each pepper. Dice tops and reserve. Remove seeds and membranes. Place peppers in 1-1/2 to 2-quart casserole. Fill with enough water to half-cover peppers. Cover with lid or plastic wrap. Cook in Radarange Oven, covered, on FULL POWER for 4 to 5 minutes, or until partially cooked. Turn peppers over halfway through cooking time.

1 (1 lb.) can salmon, drained
1/2 cup fine bread crumbs
1/2 cup celery, finely diced
1/3 cup mayonnaise
1 egg
2 tablespoons lemon juice
2 tablespoons prepared mustard
2 tablespoons butter or margarine,
  softened
1 tablespoon instant, minced onion
1/4 teaspoon salt
1/8 teaspoon Tabasco sauce

2. Thoroughly mix diced green pepper with remaining ingredients, except cheese. Fill pepper shells with mixture.

3. Place stuffed peppers upright in greased, shallow baking dish. Cook in Radarange Oven on FULL POWER for 7 to 8 minutes, or until heated through.*

2 slices process cheese, each
  cut into 4 strips

4. Arrange cheese strips in criss-cross fashion on each pepper. Cook in Radarange Oven on Cookmatic Level 5 (SLO COOK) for 2 minutes, or until cheese is slightly melted.

   *MICRO-TIP: You may want to turn dish halfway through cooking time.

Savory Salmon Steaks

Yield: 4 servings

1 egg
1 tablespoon milk
1 tablespoon lemon juice
1/2 teaspoon salt

4 (3/4 to 1-inch thick each)
  salmon steaks
1/2 cup cornflake or bread crumbs

2 tablespoons butter or margarine

1. In shallow bowl, combine eggs, milk, lemon juice and salt. Beat well.

2. Dip each steak in egg mixture, and then into cornflake crumbs.

3. Place butter in 2-quart utility dish. Heat in Radarange Oven on FULL POWER for 20 to 30 seconds, or until melted. Arrange steaks in dish. Cover with plastic wrap. Cook in Radarange Oven, covered, on FULL POWER for 6 to 8 minutes, or until fish flakes easily with fork.

Salmon Quiche

Yield: 6 servings

1, 9-inch pastry shell, baked

2 cups salmon chunks, cooked and
  boned, or 1 (1 lb.) can salmon,
  drained
1/2 cup ripe olives, sliced
1 tablespoon parsley, snipped
1 cup Cheddar cheese, shredded

3 eggs
3/4 cup light cream, or
  3/4 cup evaporated milk
1/4 teaspoon salt
1/4 teaspoon onion powder

1. Bake pastry shell, as desired. Set aside.

2. Lightly mix salmon, olives and parsley. Place in pastry shell. Top with cheese.

3. Combine eggs with light cream, salt and onion powder. Pour over salmon.

4. Cook in Radarange Oven on Cookmatic Level 5 (SLO COOK) for 12 to 14 minutes, or until knife inserted in center comes out clean.*

   *MICRO-TIP: You may want to turn dish halfway through cooking time.

Tuna Divan

Yield: 6 to 8 servings

2 (10 oz. each) pkgs. frozen
  broccoli cuts
1/4 cup water

2 (6-1/2 to 7 oz. each) cans tuna,
  drained

1 (10-3/4 oz.) can cream of
  onion soup
1/3 cup grated Parmesan cheese
1/3 cup milk
1 (2-1/2 oz.) jar sliced mushrooms,
  drained
1 tablespoon lemon juice
Dash cayenne pepper
Paprika

1. Place broccoli in 2-quart utility dish. Pour water over broccoli. Cover with plastic wrap. Cook in Radarange Oven, covered, on FULL POWER for 9 to 11 minutes, or until broccoli is cooked as desired. Stir to break apart after 5 minutes. Drain.

2. Spread tuna evenly over broccoli.

3. Blend together soup, cheese, milk, mushrooms, lemon juice and cayenne pepper. Pour evenly over tuna. Sprinkle with paprika, as desired. Cover with plastic wrap.

4. Cook in Radarange Oven, covered, on FULL POWER for 4-1/2 to 5-1/2 minutes, or until heated through.

Stuffed Red Snapper

Yield: 6 servings

1 (2-1/2 to 3 lb.) whole red snapper
Salt
Pepper

1 egg
1/4 cup evaporated milk
2 tablespoons butter or margarine, melted
1-1/2 cups soft bread crumbs
1/2 cup celery leaves, minced
1/4 cup onion, chopped
1/4 cup parsley, minced
1 teaspoon salt
1/8 teaspoon seasoned pepper
Pinch dill weed

1. Rinse prepared whole fish and pat dry. Sprinkle interior cavity with salt and pepper, as desired.

2. Mix together egg, milk, butter, bread crumbs, celery leaves, onion, parsley, salt, pepper and dill weed to make stuffing.

3. Stuff fish. Skewer with wooden picks. Lace with string to close. Make 3 small slashes in top of fish skin. Place fish on cooking grill, or place on greased heavy brown paper or parchment paper. Fold over parchment and if necessary secure ends with rubber bands. If using cooking grill, cover with plastic wrap.

4. Cook in Radarange Oven, covered, on FULL POWER for 8 to 10 minutes, or until fish flakes easily with fork. Turn fish over halfway through cooking time.

MICRO-TIP: May be garnished with lemon wedges and watercress.

Baked Stuffed Whole Fish

Yield: 4 servings

1-1/2 lb. whole fish
1/4 cup butter or margarine, melted
1/2 teaspoon salt

2 cups bread cubes
1/4 cup boiling water
1/4 cup celery, finely chopped
1/4 teaspoon poultry seasoning
2 tablespoons onion, minced

Paprika

1. Wash dressed whole fish and wipe dry with paper towel. Brush interior of fish with half of butter. Sprinkle with salt.

2. Toss remaining ingredients together lightly for stuffing. Loosely fill cavity. Fasten with toothpicks.

3. Place stuffed fish on cooking grill. Sprinkle with paprika, as desired. Cover with plastic wrap. Cook in Radarange Oven, covered, on FULL POWER for 4-1/2 to 6 minutes, or until fish flakes easily with fork.

MICRO-TIP: Several different types of fish can be used in this recipe: lake trout, white fish and red snapper are some examples.

Creole Fish Bake

Yield: 4 servings

2 cups tomato juice
1/3 cup green pepper, diced
1 tablespoon parsley flakes
2 teaspoons onion, minced
1/4 teaspoon oregano
1/2 teaspoon salt
1/4 teaspoon pepper

1 lb. fish (halibut, cod or turbot)

1. Combine all ingredients, except fish, in 1-1/2-quart utility dish. Cook in Radarange Oven, covered, on FULL POWER for 3 minutes, or until green pepper and onion are tender.

2. Place fish in 1-1/2-quart utility dish. Spoon sauce over fish. Cover with plastic wrap. Cook in Radarange Oven, covered, on FULL POWER for 5 to 7 minutes, or until fish flakes easily with fork.

   MICRO-TIP: This recipe is good for calorie-watchers since there are only approximately 155 calories per serving.

Cod Fillets in Lime Sauce

Yield: 4 servings

1 lb. cod fillets

2 to 3 tablespoons butter or margarine
2 green onions, thinly sliced
1/4 cup lime juice
1/2 teaspoon salt
1/4 teaspoon ginger
1/8 teaspoon pepper
Dash powdered bay leaf

1. Arrange fillets in 1-1/2-quart utility dish.

2. Place 1 tablespoon butter in small dish. Heat in Radarange Oven on FULL POWER for 20 seconds, or until melted. Add onions, lime juice and spices. Pour over fillets. Dot with remaining butter. Cover with plastic wrap.

3. Cook in Radarange Oven, covered, on FULL POWER for 3-1/2 to 4-1/2 minutes, or until fish flakes easily with fork.

Sole Roll-Ups

Yield: 4 servings

1 lb. sole fillets
Paprika
Butter or margarine

1/4 cup celery, minced
1 tablespoon butter or margarine
1/2 cup bread crumbs
1 teaspoon lemon juice
2 teaspoons instant, minced onion
1 teaspoon parsley flakes
1/4 teaspoon thyme
1/8 teaspoon salt

1. Arrange fillets on large plate or waxed paper. Sprinkle with paprika, as desired. Generously butter 4, 5-oz. each, custard cups.

2. Combine celery and butter in small glass bowl. Cook in Radarange Oven on FULL POWER for 2 minutes, or until celery is tender. Blend in remaining ingredients for filling. Spread over fish. Divide seasoned fillets into 4 equal portions. Roll up fillets with stuffing, pinwheel-style, into 4 rolls. Set on sides in custard cups. Cover each lightly with plastic wrap.

3. Cook in Radarange Oven, covered, on FULL POWER for 3-1/2 to 5 minutes, or until fish flakes easily with fork.

Scalloped Oysters

Yield: 4 to 6 servings

1/4 cup butter or margarine
1/4 cup onion, chopped
1/4 cup celery, chopped
1 tablespoon parsley flakes
1 teaspoon lemon juice
1 teaspoon salt
1/8 teaspoon pepper
1/8 teaspoon instant, minced
   garlic

1. Combine butter, onion, celery, parsley flakes, lemon juice, salt, pepper and garlic in 1-1/2-quart casserole. Cook in Radarange Oven on FULL POWER for 3 to 4 minutes, or until onion and celery are tender.

1 pint oysters, drained

2. Place oysters in 1-quart casserole. Cook in Radarange Oven, covered, on FULL POWER for 2 to 3 minutes, or until edges of oysters curl.

2 cups butter flavor cracker
   crumbs
1 cup milk

3. Blend oysters, 1-1/2 cups crumbs and milk into onion and celery mixture.

1/2 cup Cheddar cheese, shredded

4. Sprinkle remaining crumbs, and then cheese, over casserole. Cook in Radarange Oven on FULL POWER for 3 to 4 minutes, or until temperature of 150°F is reached.*

   *MICRO-TIP: Use Temperature-Hold to maintain 150°F until ready to serve.

Scalloped Oysters and Corn

Yield: 8 servings

1/4 cup cracker crumbs
1 tablespoon butter or margarine,
   melted

1. Combine 1/4 cup cracker crumbs and butter. Set aside.

3/4 cup cracker crumbs
1 (1 lb.) can whole kernel corn,
   drained
1 (1 lb.) can cream-style corn
1 (10-3/4 oz.) can oyster stew
1 cup oysters, washed and drained
1/4 cup onion, finely chopped
1 teaspoon salt
1/4 teaspoon pepper

2. Combine remaining ingredients, except paprika, in 2-quart casserole. Cook in Radarange Oven on FULL POWER for 7 minutes. Stir.

Paprika (optional)

3. Sprinkle with reserved crumbs, and then with paprika, if desired. Cook in Radarange Oven on FULL POWER for 1 to 2 minutes, or until temperature of 150°F is reached.*

   *MICRO-TIP: Use Temperature-Hold to maintain 150°F until ready to serve.

Creole Halibut

Yield: 4 servings

1-1/2 lbs. halibut steaks

1 cup onion, chopped
1/2 cup green pepper, chopped
1/4 cup celery, finely chopped
1 clove garlic, minced
1/4 cup butter or margarine

1 (1 lb.) can stewed tomatoes
1 (4 oz.) can mushrooms, drained
1 teaspoon salt
1/2 teaspoon sugar
Dash Tabasco sauce

1. Arrange halibut in greased, 2-quart utility dish. Set aside.

2. Combine onion, green pepper, celery, garlic and butter in 1-quart casserole. Cook in Radarange Oven on FULL POWER for 3 to 4 minutes, or until green pepper and celery are tender. Stir halfway through cooking time.

3. Blend in tomatoes, mushrooms and seasonings. Pour over fish. Cook in Radarange Oven on FULL POWER for 6-1/2 to 8 minutes, or until fish flakes easily with fork.

MICRO-TIP: May be garnished with parsley and lemon wedges.

Halibut Teriyaki

Yield: 4 to 6 servings

1/4 cup soy sauce
1/4 cup dry white wine
1-1/2 tablespoons vegetable oil
1 tablespoon green onion, thinly sliced
2 teaspoons sugar
1/8 teaspoon garlic powder

1-1/2 lbs. halibut fillets

1. Blend together all ingredients, except halibut, in 1-cup jar. Cover with lid. Shake vigorously.

2. Arrange fish in single layer in 2-quart utility dish. Pour liquid over fish. Cover with plastic wrap and refrigerate for 30 minutes. Drain all but 2 tablespoons liquid from dish.

3. Cook in Radarange Oven, covered, on FULL POWER for 4-1/2 to 6 minutes, or until fish flakes easily with fork.

Swiss Flounder

Yield: 3 to 4 servings

1 lb. flounder fillets
1-1/2 teaspoons instant, minced onion
1/2 teaspoon salt
Dash pepper
1 medium tomato, cut in thin wedges

2/3 cup Swiss cheese, shredded

1. Place fillets in single layer in 1-1/2-quart utility dish. Sprinkle with onion, salt and pepper. Arrange tomato wedges over fillets. Cover loosely with plastic wrap. Cook in Radarange Oven, covered, on FULL POWER for 3-1/2 to 4 minutes.

2. Sprinkle cheese over fish. Cover with plastic wrap. Cook in Radarange Oven, covered, on Cookmatic Level 5 (SLO COOK) for 1 to 2 minutes, or until cheese is melted and fish flakes easily with fork.

Meats can be prepared in your Radarange Oven with excellent results. This chapter will tell you exactly how to prepare and cook meats to achieve the best results. This chapter includes many recipes which are main dishes that include meat as the basic ingredient.

Throughout this section, all cooking times given for meats are based upon completely defrosted meat items of refrigerator temperature. To determine whether a meat item is completely defrosted, insert a sharp knife in the meat. Do not cook meat before it is completely thawed.

Before cooking meats in your Radarange Oven, be sure to read this chapter introduction carefully.

General Hints for Defrosting Meats

1. Meats can remain wrapped in their original coverings during defrosting. Any metal wrapping, however, should be removed.
2. Defrosting time depends upon the **shape** of the meat, such as the meat's thickness, irregular areas, etc. For example, thinner cuts defrost more quickly than thicker cuts. Rolled roasts require longer defrosting times than flat-shaped roasts.
3. Defrosting time also depends upon how solidly a piece of meat is frozen. For example, a freezer in a combination refrigerator-freezer may not freeze meat as solidly as an individual freezer. If meat is frozen in an individual freezer, slightly increase the defrosting time.
4. The cooking grill is ideal for defrosting, since juices can drain away from the meat into the 2-quart utility dish.
5. Cover meats with heavy-duty plastic wrap during defrosting to speed the defrosting process and to defrost more evenly.
6. Large cuts of meat may need to be turned over during defrosting to ensure even defrosting.
7. If a meat is frozen in pieces, such as individual steaks, chops, hamburgers, etc., the pieces should be separated before the last half or last quarter of the defrosting time. This will allow for faster, more even, defrosting.

8. If meats are not completely defrosted after the defrost time, the Cookmatic Level 1 (WARM) setting of the Cookmatic Cycle will allow them to finish defrosting. See the "Roast Defrosting Chart" on page 167. This 10% power setting provides just enough energy to finish defrosting without starting the actual cooking process. Remember, meats should be totally defrosted before cooking begins. You can determine whether a meat is completely defrosted by inserting a sharp knife in the center of the meat to check for ice crystals, if you are in doubt.

Preparing Meats for Freezing and Defrosting with the Automatic Temperature Control System

1. Make a hole in the meat with a slender knife blade in the center of the meat. Make the hole reach to the center of the meat, where the probe will eventually be inserted. Make the hole in the thickest part of the meat. Avoid making the hole in fat or bone.

2. Insert a plastic drinking straw in the hole. Trim the straw with scissors, so that only 1/4-inch to 1/2-inch of the straw extends above the surface of the meat.

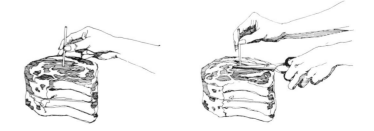

Spiced Cider Baked Ham (page 219)

3. Prepare the meat for freezing, using proper wrapping methods, and freeze.

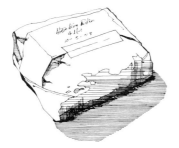

4. When ready to use, remove the meat from the freezer. For faster defrosting, allow the meat to remain wrapped, or cover with plastic wrap. Place the meat on the cooking grill. Insert the temperature probe in the straw to the center of the meat, if you plan to program the Radarange Oven to automatically defrost, and then cook the meat.

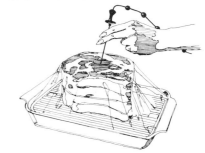

5. Defrost, according to the directions on the "Roast Defrosting Chart". Or, you may wish to automatically defrost and cook the meat in one process. See also the Beef, Pork, Lamb or Veal Cooking Charts on pages 174 and 175.

SMALL SIZE MEATS DEFROSTING CHART

MEAT TYPE	WEIGHT	DEFROSTING TIME ON DEFROST	SPECIAL INSTRUCTIONS
Bacon	16 ozs.	3 to 4 min.	Make 1-inch slit in package.
Frankfurters	12 ozs.	3 to 5 min.	Make 1-inch slit in package.
	16 ozs.	4 to 6 min.	Make 1-inch slit in package.
Ground Beef Bulk	16 ozs.	10 to 12 min.	Remove from plastic wrap. Remove outside meat as it defrosts. Break apart with fork.
Patties	16 ozs.	7 to 10 min.	Remove from plastic wrap. Arrange in circle.
Sausage	12 ozs.	4 to 6 min.	Make 1-inch slit in package.
Steaks (beef)	16 ozs.	5 to 7 min.	Remove from plastic wrap.

General Instructions for Defrosting Small Size Meats

1. Read the "Special Instructions" on the chart before defrosting small meat items.

2. Defrost the meat, according to the time on the chart. Use the DEFROST setting.

ROAST DEFROSTING CHART*

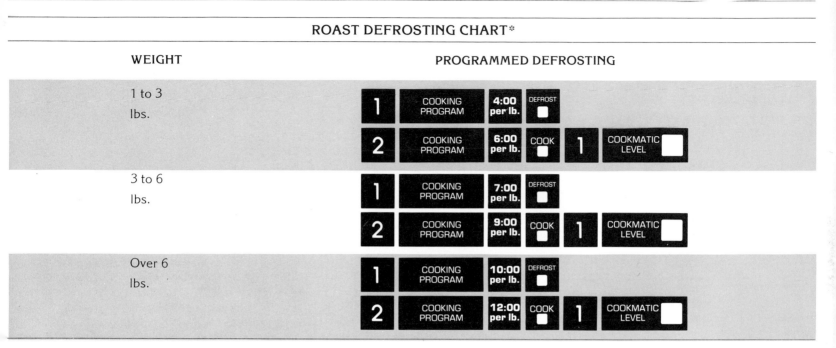

WEIGHT	PROGRAMMED DEFROSTING
1 to 3 lbs.	**1** COOKING PROGRAM — 4:00 per lb. — DEFROST ▪ **2** COOKING PROGRAM — 6:00 per lb. — COOK ▪ **1** COOKMATIC LEVEL ▫
3 to 6 lbs.	**1** COOKING PROGRAM — 7:00 per lb. — DEFROST ▪ **2** COOKING PROGRAM — 9:00 per lb. — COOK ▪ **1** COOKMATIC LEVEL ▫
Over 6 lbs.	**1** COOKING PROGRAM — 10:00 per lb. — DEFROST ▪ **2** COOKING PROGRAM — 12:00 per lb. — COOK ▪ **1** COOKMATIC LEVEL ▫

*This chart is designed for defrosting large cuts of meat. For programmed defrosting and cooking, use this chart as well as the charts on pages 174 and 175.

General Instructions for Defrosting Roasts or Large Cuts of Meat

1. Place meat on cooking grill or directly on Radarange Oven glass tray. Loosen original wrapping or cover loosely with plastic wrap. Remove all metal pieces.

2. Defrost, according to the amount of time on the chart. For example, if a meat weighs 4 pounds you would use the following programming instructions:

As shown in the "Roast Defrosting Chart", a 3 to 6 lb. roast should be defrosted for 7 minutes per pound. Therefore, a 4 pound roast should be defrosted for 28 minutes.

$$4 \text{ lbs.} \times 7 \text{ min./lb.} = 28 \text{ minutes}$$

As shown in the "Roast Defrosting Chart", a 3 to 6 lb. roast should be further defrosted on Cookmatic Level 1 (WARM) for 9 minutes per pound. Therefore, a 4 pound roast should be defrosted for an additional 36 minutes.

$$4 \text{ lbs.} \times 9 \text{ min./lb.} = 36 \text{ minutes}$$

3. To cook a roast immediately after defrosting in one automatic process, program the cooking instructions from one of the charts on pages 174 and 175 immediately following the defrosting instructions.

General Hints for Cooking Meats

1. Meats weighing 3 pounds or more will brown by themselves "naturally" in the Radarange Oven. The exterior of a meat this size becomes very hot during cooking, and it requires a longer cooking time than do smaller cuts. The long cooking time and the heat are required for browning.
2. For more browning of small cuts of meat such as steaks, chops, and hamburgers, a browning skillet or a bottled browning sauce may be used. See "Browning", on page 17.
3. Most meats are best prepared by using a cooking grill. (See the "Glossary of Microwave Cooking Terms," page 6.) A heavy duty plastic roasting bag is recommended for some meats.

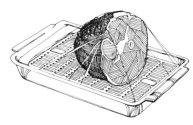

4. Do not salt meats, until after cooking or just before serving. This is especially important when cooking solid cuts of meat. Do **not** salt the raw meat surface. If, however, the meat is just one ingredient in a main dish, or if the meat is covered by a sauce, then you may add salt to the sauce or the main dish. When a raw meat surface is salted in microwave or conventional cooking, the meat surface will become dehydrated and tough, since salt draws out the meat moisture.
5. Excess fat may be trimmed from meat before cooking to decrease the amount of accumulated meat juices and to prevent spattering within the Radarange Oven.
6. Aged or ripened meat will tend to cook more quickly than fresh meat. If you are cooking an aged piece of meat, decrease the cooking time slightly.
7. Tender meat can be cooked quickly in the Radarange Oven on higher Cookmatic Levels with good results. For less tender cuts of meat, use lower Cookmatic Levels for the best results. Less tender meat needs a longer cooking in order to tenderize. Moist cooking methods are recommended for less tender cuts of meat. Tenderizing agents can also be used. For less tender cuts of meat (particularly flat cuts), such as blade steak, chuck roast, pot roast, shoulder cuts, arm cuts, or ribs, you may wish to use a tenderizing agent. Less tender cuts can also be marinated or mechanically tenderized by pounding with a meat mallet before cooking.
8. When cooking medium tender or less tender cuts of meat, you may wish to hold the meat at the final temperature, to tenderize. Use the Temperature-Hold to hold the meat at the final temperature. You can use the TIMER on the Radarange Oven, at the same time the Radarange Oven is holding, to audibly signal you when the desired amount of holding time is finished. However, if you are not in the kitchen to remove the meat when the timer indicates, the Radarange Oven will continue to hold the meat at the desired temperature, without damaging the meat. The meat will be warm when ready to serve.
9. For the best cooking results, turn most large meats over approximately halfway through the cooking time, in order to achieve even cooking throughout the meat.
10. The 2-step cooking process used in most of the meat cooking in this cookbook is designed to quickly warm the meat, and then finish the cooking slowly to the desired temperature for maximum tenderizing.
11. When barbecuing meats on an outdoor grill, barbecue a few "extras", and freeze them. Later, these meats can be defrosted and reheated quickly in the Radarange Oven.

METHODS FOR COOKING MEATS

In this cookbook, there are 3 basic methods in which meats should be cooked. These methods are easy to follow, and they are based upon whether a cut of meat is tender, medium tender, or less tender.

On the charts on pages 174 and 175, the recommended method for cooking each particular cut of meat is listed. You can check pages 169 to 172 to see how the recommended methods are accomplished. Soon, you will automatically remember these methods. You can then use the cooking method instructions in this chapter only as a handy reference.

Your Radarange Oven will allow you to cook meats with confidence and accuracy, due to the Automatic Temperature Control System feature. By using the Automatic Temperature Control, you can cook meats accurately to the desired degree, using one of the three recommended cooking methods.

Before cooking a meat, check the charts on pages 174 and 175 to be sure you have selected the proper cooking method. These charts indicate which cooking method should be used for each individual meat cut. The charts list the different sections of beef, lamb, pork, and veal. The charts further indicate from which section the individual cuts of meat are taken. In general, the section of the animal from which individual cuts are taken determines whether the cut is a tender cut or a less tender cut.

Cooking Method #1: Tender Meats

1. Place the meat fat-side-down on the cooking grill.
2. Cover the meat with heavy-duty plastic wrap. Tuck the plastic wrap beneath the edges of the plastic rack.
3. Insert the temperature probe in the center of the lean portion of the meat in the thickest part, through the plastic wrap. Avoid touching fat or bone with the probe. (If the meat is frozen, insert the probe in the plastic straw.) Be sure the plastic has been pierced well, either by inserting the probe through it, or by slitting it with a knife.
4. Cook in the Radarange Oven on Cookmatic Level 9 (HIGH) for 3 minutes per pound. Then, cook in the Radarange Oven on Cookmatic Level 6 (ROAST) until a temperature of 140°F, 150°F, 160°F, or 170°F is reached, as desired. (See the "Recommended End Temperature Chart," on page 173.) Use the Temperature-Hold to maintain a temperature until ready to serve, if desired. However, holding is not necessary for good results with tender meats. You may wish to turn large cuts of meat over halfway through the cooking time, for best results.

5. **SUMMARY:** These are the actual instructions you will "touch in". The numbers 1 and 2 for the cooking programs may become 3 and 4 if you use Cooking Programs 1 and 2 for defrosting before cooking.

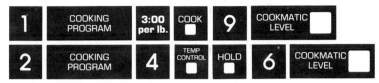

NOTE: The "4" in Cooking Program #2 = 140°F. 5, 6 or 7 for 150°F, 160°F, or 170°F may be used, as desired. The "HOLD" is optional, and may be omitted, if desired.

EXAMPLE: Frozen Standing Rib Roast (Beef) weighing 2 lbs. (under 3 lbs. category on chart) prepared to the Rare degree. See the "Beef Cooking Chart", page 174.

1. Prepare the meat, according to Cooking Method #1, as just described.

2.

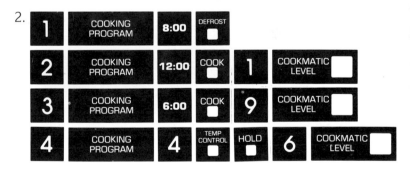

In this example, you will use 2 different charts to program the Radarange Oven. First, see the "Roast Defrosting Chart", on page 167. Since the roast in this example weighs 2 lbs., then the 1 to 3 lbs. category on the chart is used.

In Cooking Program #1, as shown in the "Roast Defrosting Chart", a 1 to 3 lb. roast should be defrosted for 4 minutes per pound. Therefore, a 2 pound roast should be defrosted for 8 minutes.

2 lbs. x 4 min./lb. = 8 minutes

In Cooking Program #2, as shown in the "Roast Defrosting Chart", a 1 to 3 lb. roast should be further defrosted on Cookmatic Level 1 (WARM) for 6 minutes per pound. Therefore, a 2 pound roast should be defrosted for an additional 12 minutes.

2 lbs. x 6 min./lb. = 12 minutes

In Cooking Program #3, as described in Cooking Method #1, the meat should be cooked on Cookmatic Level 9 (HIGH) for 3 minutes per pound. Therefore, a 2 pound roast should be cooked for 6 minutes.

2 lbs. x 3 min./lb. = 6 minutes

In Cooking Program #4, the 4 stands for 140°F or the Rare degree. The meat should be cooked on Cookmatic Level 6 (ROAST), until 140°F is reached. If you don't touch HOLD , which is optional, then the Radarange Oven will shut off. If you touch HOLD , the meat will stay warmed until ready to serve.

The entire process of defrosting and cooking will require about 1 to 1-1/2 hours, as is indicated on the "Beef Cooking Chart", page 174. Since this meat is cooked to the Rare degree, probably only 1 hour of total time will be required. Any holding time is not included in this total, as is indicated on the chart.

Cooking Method #2: Medium Tender Meats
1. Place the meat fat-side-down on the cooking grill.
2. One of the sauces for meats on page 172 may be used, if desired.
3. Cover the meat with plastic wrap. Tuck the plastic wrap beneath the edges of the plastic rack.
4. Insert the temperature probe in the center of the lean portion of the meat in the thickest part through the plastic wrap. Avoid touching fat or bone with the probe. (If the meat is frozen, insert the probe in the plastic straw.) Be sure the plastic has been pierced well, either by inserting the probe through it, or by slitting it with a knife.

5. Cook in the Radarange Oven on Cookmatic Level 8 (MEDIUM HIGH) for 3 minutes per pound. Then, cook in the Radarange Oven on Cookmatic Level 5 (SLO COOK) until a temperature of 160°F or 170°F is reached, as desired. (See the "Recommended End Temperature Chart", on page 173.) Use the Temperature-Hold to maintain the desired temperature for at least 15 to 30 minutes for good product results. You may wish to turn large cuts of meat over halfway through the cooking time for the best results.
6. **SUMMARY:** These are the actual instructions you will "touch in". The numbers 1 and 2 for the cooking programs may become 3 and 4 if you use Cooking Programs 1 and 2 for defrosting before cooking.

NOTE: The "6" in Cooking Program #2 = 160°F. 7, for 170°F may also be used, as desired. Use Temperature-Hold for at least 15 to 30 minutes to allow meats time to become tender. Set the TIMER for 15 to 30 minutes once the temperature has reached 160°F (or 170°F) to remind you when the meat has been on Temperature-Hold long enough.

EXAMPLE: Refrigerator Temperature Round (Rolled) Rump Roast (Beef) weighing 4 lbs. (3 to 6 lb. category on chart) prepared to the Medium degree. See the "Beef Cooking Chart", page 174.

1. Prepare the meat, according to Cooking Method #2, as just described.

2.

In Cooking Program #1, as described in Cooking Method #2, the meat should be cooked on Cookmatic Level 8 (MEDIUM HIGH) for 3 minutes per pound. Therefore, a 4 pound roast should be cooked for 12 minutes.

$$4 \text{ lbs.} \times 3 \text{ min./lb.} = 12 \text{ minutes}$$

In Cooking Program #2, the 6 stands for 160°F or the Medium degree. The meat should be cooked on Cookmatic Level 5 (SLO COOK), until 160°F is reached. The HOLD is recommended in this cooking

method for at least 15 to 30 minutes, in order to achieve a tender meat product. The entire process (except the holding time) will require about 45 to 70 minutes, as is indicated on the "Beef Cooking Chart", page 174. Since this meat is cooked only to the Medium degree, the full 70 minutes of total time will probably not be required. Any holding time is not included in this total, as is indicated on the chart.

Cooking Method #3: Less Tender Meats

1. Place the meat inside a heavy-duty plastic roasting bag.
2. Insert the temperature probe in the center of the lean portion of the meat in the thickest part, through the plastic bag. Avoid touching fat or bone with the probe. (If the meat is frozen, insert the probe in the plastic straw.) Inserting the probe, or "poking" it through the plastic bag, will also "pierce" the bag. Tuck the end of the plastic bag securely beneath the meat.
3. Cook in the Radarange Oven on Cookmatic Level 7 (BAKE) for 3 minutes per pound. Then, cook in the Radarange Oven on Cookmatic Level 4 (MEDIUM) until a temperature of 170°F is reached. (Usually 170°F is the desired end temperature for less tender cuts of meat. See the "Recommended End Temperature Chart," on page 173.) Use the Temperature-Hold to maintain 170°F for at least 30 to 60 minutes for good product results. You may wish to turn large cuts of meat over halfway through the cooking time, for best results.
   NOTE: If you wish to cook vegetables with a pot roast, you may put them in the cooking bag when cooking the meat. Onions, potatoes or carrots may be added. If vegetables are large, slice them into smaller pieces before cooking.

4. **SUMMARY:** These are the actual instructions you will "touch in". The numbers 1 and 2 for the cooking programs may become 3 and 4 if you use Cooking Programs 1 and 2 for defrosting before cooking.

NOTE: The "7" in Cooking Program #2 = 170°F. This is the recommended end temperature for less tender cuts of meat. Use Temperature-Hold for at least 30 to 60 minutes to allow meats time to become tender. Set the TIMER for 30 to 60 minutes once the temperature has reached 170°F, to remind you when the meat has been on Temperature-Hold long enough.

EXAMPLE: Refrigerator Temperature Round Pot Roast (Beef) weighing 2-1/2 lbs. (3 to 6 lb. category on chart) prepared to the Well-Done degree. See the "Beef Cooking Chart", page 174.

1. Prepare the meat, according to Cooking Method #3, as just described.

2.

In Cooking Program #1, as described in Cooking Method #3, the meat should be cooked on Cookmatic Level 7 (BAKE) for 3 minutes per pound. Therefore, a 2-1/2 pound pot roast should be cooked for 7 minutes, 30 seconds.

$$2\text{-}1/2 \text{ lbs.} \times 3 \text{ min./lb.} = 7\text{-}1/2 \text{ minutes or}$$
7 minutes, 30 seconds

In Cooking Program #2, the 7 stands for 170°F, or the Well-Done degree. The meat should be cooked on Cookmatic Level 4 (MEDIUM) until 170°F is reached.

The **HOLD** is recommended in this cooking method for at least 30 to 60 minutes, in order to achieve a tender meat product. The entire process (except the holding time) will require about 25 to 45 minutes, as indicated on the "Beef Cooking Chart", page 174. Any holding time is not included in this total, as is indicated on the chart.

SAUCES FOR MEATS

For some cuts of meat such as blade steak, chuck roast, pot roast, shoulder cuts, arm cuts, or ribs, you may wish to use one of these sauces, or one of your own favorites, to add flavor.

Baste the meat with the desired sauce, and cook, covered, with heavy-duty plastic wrap. Notice there are no cooking times for these sauces, since they are cooked with the meat. One of these sauces may be used in Cooking Method #2, or in the cooking bag in Cooking Method #3.

- a. Spicy Sauce
  - 1/2 cup vinegar
  - 1/2 cup water
  - 1 bay leaf
  - 1 medium onion, sliced
  - 10 whole cloves

- b. Wine Sauce
  - 1/2 cup wine
  - 1/2 cup bouillon or consomme
  - 1 teaspoon Worcestershire sauce
  - 1 bay leaf
  - 2 teaspoons seasoned salt
  - 1 tablespoon bottled browning sauce

- c. Sweet-Sour Sauce
  - 1/3 cup sherry
  - 1/3 cup soy sauce
  - 2 tablespoons honey
  - 1 clove garlic
  - 1 tablespoon sugar
  - 2 teaspoons salt
  - 1/2 teaspoon pepper

- d. Tangy Tomato Sauce
  - 3/4 cup tomato sauce
  - 1/4 cup vinegar or lemon juice
  - 1 small onion, minced
  - 1 bay leaf
  - 1/2 teaspoon oregano
  - 2 tablespoons brown sugar
  - 1 teaspoon prepared mustard
  - 2 teaspoons salt
  - 1/2 teaspoon pepper
  - 1/8 teaspoon instant, minced garlic
  - (1 (1 lb.) jar meatless spaghetti sauce can be substituted for the Tangy Tomato Sauce)

- e. Barbecue Sauce
  - 3/4 cup barbecue sauce
  - 1/4 cup water
  - 1 teaspoon salt
  - 1 teaspoon liquid smoke

NOTE: Tougher cuts of meat may require a commercial or mechanical tenderizing agent. Follow the instructions on the jar label. Mechanically tenderize meat by using a meat mallet.

EXPLANATION OF CHARTS

The charts on the following pages give directions for cooking many types of meats. The "Beef Cooking Chart", "Lamb Cooking Chart", "Pork Cooking Chart", and "Veal Cooking Chart" all recommend one of the three major cooking methods:

Cooking Method #1: Tender Meats
Cooking Method #2: Medium Tender Meats
Cooking Method #3: Less Tender Meats

The chart on the following page includes a summary of cooking instructions for the three cooking methods. Use this chart as a handy reference guide.

MEAT COOKING METHODS: SUMMARY CHART*

COOKING METHOD	SPECIAL INSTRUCTIONS	PROGRAMMING INSTRUCTIONS**
Cooking Method #1: Tender Meats	Cover meat with heavy-duty plastic wrap.	**1** COOKING PROGRAM · 3:00 per lb. · COOK · 9 · COOKMATIC LEVEL □ **2** COOKING PROGRAM · 4 · TEMP CONTROL · HOLD · 6 · COOKMATIC LEVEL □
Cooking Method #2: Medium-Tender Meats	Cover meat with heavy-duty plastic wrap.	**1** COOKING PROGRAM · 3:00 per lb. · COOK · 8 · COOKMATIC LEVEL □ **2** COOKING PROGRAM · 6 · TEMP CONTROL · HOLD · 5 · COOKMATIC LEVEL □
Cooking Method #3: Less-Tender Meats	Place meat in roasting bag.	**1** COOKING PROGRAM · 3:00 per lb. · COOK · 7 · COOKMATIC LEVEL □ **2** COOKING PROGRAM · 7 · TEMP CONTROL · HOLD · 4 · COOKMATIC LEVEL □

*Detailed instructions for these cooking methods are found on pages 168 to 172 of this cookbook.

**Cooking programs #1 and #2 may become #3 and #4 if cooking programs #1 and #2 are used for defrosting before cooking. See the "Roast Defrosting Chart", page 167.

Notice on the beef, pork, lamb, and veal charts that the "approximate total time" is given. This entire time will not actually be programmed, since the Automatic Temperature Control System will shut the Radarange Oven off at the appropriate time and this time can vary, depending upon the actual piece of meat. This "approximate total time" gives you a general idea of how long the meat should be in the Radarange Oven. Notice that there are two total times given for each meat: a time for cooking from the refrigerator temperature, and a time for cooking from the frozen temperature. The "refrigerator temperature time" refers to the time required to cook non-frozen meats. The "frozen time" refers to the total amount of time required to defrost, hold, and cook frozen meats. When programming your Radarange Oven for defrosting, and then cooking, you will also be using the "Roast Defrosting Chart", on page 167. You will first program the defrost time, according to the "Roast Defrosting Chart", and then program the cooking time, according to the cooking method recommended on the beef, pork, lamb, or veal charts. See the examples, on pages 169, 170, and 171.

There are some meats which are exceptions, and do not "fit" into the categories for the three major methods. Therefore, these meats have separate charts of cooking instructions. Most of the meats which don't use one of the three major methods are items which are smaller meat cuts, pre-cooked, or require the use of a browning skillet.

RECOMMENDED END TEMPERATURE CHART

MEAT TYPE	COOKED DEGREE	END TEMPERATURE
Beef	Rare	140°F
	Medium	160°F
	Well-Done	170°F
Lamb	Well-Done	170°F
Pork	Well-Done	170°F
Pre-Cooked Ham	Heated Through	130°F
Veal	Well-Done	170°F

BEEF COOKING CHART

SECTION	CUT	WEIGHT	COOKING METHOD	APPROXIMATE TOTAL TIME ** (Not Including Holding)
Rib	Standing	Under 3 lbs.	#1	Refrig. Temp. 20 to 40 min. / Frozen* 1 to 1-1/2 hrs.
		3 to 6 lbs.	#1	Refrig. Temp. 40 to 65 min. / Frozen* 2 to 2-3/4 hrs.
		Over 6 lbs.	#1	Refrig. Temp. 1-1/4 to 2 hrs. / Frozen* 2-3/4 to 3 hrs.
Rib	Rolled	Under 3 lbs.	#1	Refrig. Temp. 20 to 45 min. / Frozen* 45 to 75 min.
		3 to 6 lbs.	#1	Refrig. Temp. 45 to 70 min. / Frozen* 2 to 2-1/2 hrs.
		Over 6 lbs.	#1	Refrig. Temp. 1-1/2 to 2 hrs. / Frozen* 3 hrs. or more
Sirloin	Tip Roast	Under 3 lbs.	#1	Refrig. Temp. 20 to 45 min. / Frozen* 45 min. to 1-1/2 hrs.
		3 to 6 lbs.	#1	Refrig. Temp. 45 to 75 min. / Frozen* 1-3/4 to 2-1/2 hrs.
		Over 6 lbs.	#1	Refrig. Temp. 1-1/2 to 2 hrs. / Frozen* 3 hrs. or more
Round	Rump Roast (Rolled)	Under 3 lbs.	#2	Refrig. Temp. 25 to 45 min. / Frozen* 1 to 1-1/2 hrs.
		3 to 6 lbs.	#2	Refrig. Temp. 45 to 75 min. / Frozen* 2 to 2-1/2 hrs.
		Over 6 lbs.	#2	Refrig. Temp. 1-1/2 to 2 hrs. / Frozen* 3 hrs. or more
Round	Pot Roast (Arm)	Under 3 lbs.	#3	Refrig. Temp. 25 to 45 min. / Frozen* 1 to 1-3/4 hrs.
		3 to 6 lbs.	#3	Refrig. Temp. 45 min. to 1-1/2 hrs. / Frozen* 2 to 2-1/2 hrs.
Chuck	Blade Steak or Roast	2 to 3 lbs.	#3	Refrig. Temp. 30 to 60 min. / Frozen* 1-1/2 to 2 hrs.
		3 to 6 lbs.	#3	Refrig. Temp. 1 to 1-1/2 hrs. / Frozen* 2 to 2-1/2 hrs.

*See the "Roast Defrosting Chart," page 167, when preparing frozen meat. Before programming the cooking instructions for the recommended cooking method, program the defrost time.

**See the "Recommended End Temperature Chart," page 173.

LAMB COOKING CHART

SECTION	CUT	WEIGHT	COOKING METHOD	APPROXIMATE TOTAL TIME ** (Not Including Holding)
Shoulder	Shoulder Roast	2 to 5 lbs.	#2 or #3	Refrig. Temp. 1 to 1-1/2 hrs. Frozen* 1-1/2 to 2-1/2 hrs.
Leg	Leg	3 to 5 lbs.	#1	Refrig. Temp. 45 min. to 1 hr. Frozen* 1-1/4 to 1-3/4 hrs.
		5 to 8 lbs.	#1	Refrig. Temp. 1 to 1-1/2 hrs. Frozen* 2-1/2 hrs.

*See the "Roast Defrosting Chart," page 167, when preparing frozen meat. Before programming the cooking instructions for the recommended cooking method, program the defrost time.

**See the "Recommended End Temperature Chart," page 173.

PORK COOKING CHART

SECTION	CUT	WEIGHT	COOKING METHOD	APPROXIMATE TOTAL TIME ** (Not Including Holding)
Loin	Loin Roast	2 to 5 lbs.	#1	Refrig. Temp. 40 to 60 min. Frozen* 1-1/4 to 2 hrs.
		5 to 8 lbs.	#1	Refrig. Temp. 1 to 1-1/2 hrs. Frozen* 2-1/2 to 3 hrs.
Boston Butt	Butt Roast	2 to 5 lbs.	#2	Refrig. Temp. 50 min. to 1-1/4 hrs. Frozen* 1-1/4 hrs.
		5 to 8 lbs.	#2	Refrig. Temp. 1-1/4 to 2 hrs. Frozen* 2-1/2 hrs.

*See the "Roast Defrosting Chart," page 167, when preparing frozen meat. Before programming the cooking instructions for the recommended cooking method, program the defrost time.

**See the "Recommended End Temperature Chart," page 173.

VEAL COOKING CHART

SECTION	CUT	WEIGHT	COOKING METHOD	APPROXIMATE TOTAL TIME ** (Not Including Holding)
Breast (stuffed & rolled)	Brisket	1 to 3 lbs.	#3	Refrig. Temp. 25 to 40 min. Frozen* 40 to 60 min.
Shoulder	Roast	2 to 5 lbs.	#2	Refrig. Temp. 35 to 60 min. Frozen* 1-1/2 to 2-1/4 hrs.

*See the "Roast Defrosting Chart," page 167, when preparing frozen meat. Before programming the cooking instructions for the recommended cooking method, program the defrost time.

**See the "Recommended End Temperature Chart," page 173.

PRE-COOKED HAM CHART

SECTION	CUT	WEIGHT	COOKMATIC LEVEL	APPROXIMATE TOTAL COOKING TIME*
Boneless	Ham	2 to 5 lbs.	Cookmatic Level 5 (SLO COOK)	30 to 60 min.
		5 to 8 lbs.	Cookmatic Level 5 (SLO COOK)	1-1/2 to 2 hrs.
Ham w/Bone	Ham	2 to 5 lbs.	Cookmatic Level 5 (SLO COOK)	45 min. to 1-1/4 hrs.
		5 to 8 lbs.	Cookmatic Level 5 (SLO COOK)	1-1/4 to 1-3/4 hrs.
Picnic	Ham	2 to 5 lbs.	Cookmatic Level 5 (SLO COOK)	25 to 40 min.
		5 to 8 lbs.	Cookmatic Level 5 (SLO COOK)	40 to 90 min.
		8 to 12 lbs.	Cookmatic Level 5 (SLO COOK)	1-3/4 to 2-1/2 hrs.
Canned	Ham	2 to 5 lbs.	Cookmatic Level 5 (SLO COOK)	30 to 45 min.

*Insert the temperature probe, and use the Temperature-Control to stop the Radarange Oven at 130°F, the serving temperature for pre-cooked ham.

PRE-COOKED HAM

General Instructions for Cooking Pre-Cooked Ham

Pre-cooked ham should be cooked by the following method, instead of by one of the three major cooking methods previously described.

1. Place the ham fat-side-down on a cooking grill. Cover the ham with heavy-duty plastic wrap.

2. Cook in Radarange Oven on Cookmatic Level 5 (SLO COOK), until the temperature of 130°F is reached. Consult the "Pre-Cooked Ham Chart" for an estimate of the total cooking time required. For the best results, you may wish to turn the ham over halfway through the cooking time. (You may want to turn larger hams over 2 to 3 times during cooking time.) A basting sauce may be used as desired.

Suggested Basting Sauces

a. Fruit Glaze
   1 cup brown sugar, firmly packed
   1/2 cup fruit juice
   (Ham may be decorated with fruit such as pineapple or oranges. The fruit should be added to the ham during the last 1/2 hour of cooking time.)

b. Sweet-Sour Mustard Sauce
   1/2 cup vinegar
   1/2 cup water
   2 teaspoons prepared mustard
   1/4 cup brown sugar, firmly packed
   Whole cloves (insert directly into ham)

c. Cranberry Sauce
   1-1/2 cups raw cranberries, halved
   1 cup honey
   1/2 teaspoon ground cloves

SAUSAGE COOKING CHART

SAUSAGE TYPE	WEIGHT	COOKING TIME ON FULL POWER
Bratwurst	16 ozs.	3 to 4 min.
Fresh Sausage Patties***	4 ozs.	1-1/2 to 2 min.
	8 ozs.	2-1/2 to 3 min.
	12 ozs.	3 to 3-1/2 min.
	16 ozs.	4-1/2 to 5-1/2 min.
Polish Sausage	16 ozs.	3-1/2 to 5 min.
Pre-Cooked Sausage Links	8 ozs.*	1-1/2 to 2-1/2 min.
	8 ozs.**	2-1/2 to 4 min.
	2 links*	1 to 1-1/2 min.
	2 links**	1 to 2 min.

*Refrigerator Temperature
**Frozen
***Cook fresh sausage until it is no longer pink in the center of each patty.

CURED BREAKFAST MEATS COOKING CHART

(Canadian Bacon, Ham Slices, Smoked Pork Chops)

WEIGHT	COOKING TIME ON FULL POWER
2 ozs.	15 to 30 sec.
4 ozs.	40 sec.
8 ozs.	1 min.

General Instructions for Cooking Sausage or Cured Breakfast Meats

1. Preheat a browning skillet for the maximum amount of time, according to the manufacturer's instructions. Pierce the sausage before cooking if in a casing, using tines of a fork or a knife. Place the sausage or meat in the skillet. Press the meat firmly against the skillet for good heat contact.

2. Cook on FULL POWER. Do not cook, covered, with the glass lid, since meat will develop a "steamed" flavor. A paper towel may be used to prevent spattering. Do not allow a paper towel to touch the hot skillet bottom. Turn the meat over after 45 to 60 seconds of cooking.

BACON COOKING CHART

NO. OF SLICES	COOKING TIME ON FULL POWER
2	1 min., 30 sec.
4	2 min., 45 sec. to 3 min.
12	6 to 7 min.

BACON

Bacon should be cooked by the following method, instead of by one of the three major cooking methods previously described.

General Instructions for Cooking Bacon

1. Arrange bacon slices on a cooking grill. Cover the bacon with a paper towel.

OR

Arrange bacon slices on a paper towel, cover with another paper towel, and repeat the process of layering the bacon slices between paper towels.

2. Cook in the Radarange Oven, until browned and crisp, according to the directions on the chart.

FRANKFURTER COOKING CHART

NO. OF FRANKFURTERS	COOKING TIME ON FULL POWER
2	45 sec.
4	1 min., 15 sec. to 1 min., 30 sec.
6	1 min., 45 sec. to 2 min., 15 sec.

FRANKFURTERS

Frankfurters should be cooked by the following method, instead of by one of the three major cooking methods previously described.

General Instructions for Cooking Frankfurters

1. Place the frankfurters on a cooking grill. Pierce the skins with a fork or a knife. Cover with a paper towel, if desired, to catch spatters.

2. Cook in the Radarange Oven, covered, on FULL POWER until steaming hot.

MICRO-TIP: Frankfurters can also be heated in buns. Wrap in a paper towel, and heat for approximately the same amount of time on the chart.

PORK, LAMB, AND VEAL CHOPS — LAMB AND VEAL SHOULDER STEAKS

Pork, lamb, and veal chops, as well as lamb and veal shoulder steaks should be cooked by the following method, instead of by one of the three major cooking methods previously described.

1. Preheat a browning skillet or grill for the maximum amount of time, according to the manufacturer's instructions. Add chops or steaks. Cook in Radarange Oven on FULL POWER for 1 minute per side.
2. Add a sauce. Select from one of the 5 sauces suggested on page 172. One tablespoon of wine, vermouth, or water may be substituted for the sauce. Season to taste, omitting salt until just before serving.
3. Cook in Radarange Oven, covered, on Cookmatic Level 5 (SLO COOK) for 8 to 12 minutes per pound, or until meat is tender.

TENDER BEEF STEAK COOKING CHART*

SIZE AND COOKED DEGREE	COOKING TIME ON FULL POWER
14 to 16 oz. (.88 to 1.0 lb.) (approx. 3/4" thick)**	
Rare	2 min., 15 sec. to 2 min., 45 sec.
Medium	3 min. to 3 min., 30 sec.
Well-Done	3 min., 45 sec. to 4 min., 45 sec.
12 to 14 oz. (.75 to .87 lb.) (approx. 3/4" thick)**	
Rare	2 min. to 2 min., 45 sec.
Medium	3 min. to 3 min., 15 sec.
Well-Done	3 min., 30 sec. to 4 min.
10 to 12 oz. (.63 to .74 lb.) (approx. 3/4" thick)**	
Rare	1 min., 45 sec. to 2 min., 15 sec.
Medium	2 min., 30 sec. to 3 min.
Well-Done	3 min., 15 sec. to 3 min., 45 sec.
8 to 10 oz. (.50 to .62 lb.) (approx. 3/4" thick)**	
Rare	1 min., 15 sec. to 1 min., 45 sec.
Medium	2 min. to 2 min., 30 sec.
Well-Done	2 min., 45 sec. to 3 min., 15 sec.

*Follow this procedure to cook rib, rib eye (Delmonico), club, sirloin, porterhouse, filet, tenderloin, cube steak, minute steak, T-bone, strip steak, filet mignon.
**Thicker steaks may require slightly longer cooking times; thinner steaks may require slightly shorter cooking times.

BEEF STEAKS

Because of their relatively small size and short cooking times, steaks do not brown when cooked in a microwave oven. Therefore, it is recommended that steaks be cooked in a browning skillet.

General Instructions for Cooking Beef Steaks

1. Preheat the browning skillet or grill for the maximum amount of time, according to the manufacturer's instructions. Add the steak(s). Press the steak(s) firmly against the bottom of the skillet for good heat contact. See "Browning," page 17.

2. Cook the steak(s), according to the directions on the chart. Turn the steak(s) over after 45 to 60 seconds of cooking.

3. Do not cook steak(s) which is (are) not completely thawed. See the "Small Size Meats Defrosting Chart" on page 166.

GROUND MEAT PATTY COOKING CHART

TYPE OF MEAT AND WEIGHT	COOKING TIME ON FULL POWER FOR COOKED DEGREE		
	RARE	MEDIUM	WELL
Beef			
1/4 lb.	45 sec. to 1 min.	1 to 1-1/2 min.	1-1/2 to 2 min.
1/2 lb.	1-1/2 to 2 min.	2 to 2-1/2 min.	2-1/2 to 3 min.
1 lb.	2-1/2 to 3 min.	3 to 3-1/2 min.	3-1/2 to 4 min.
Lamb or Veal			
1/4 lb.	—	—	1 min., 45 sec. to 2 min., 15 sec.
1/2 lb.	—	—	2 min., 45 sec. to 3 min.
1 lb.	—	—	3 min., 15 sec. to 3 min., 45 sec.

GROUND MEAT PATTIES

Because of their relatively small size, and short cooking times, ground meat patties will not brown when cooked in a microwave oven. Therefore, it is recommended that ground meat patties be cooked in a browning skillet, unless they will be used in sandwiches where a lack of browning is not noticed.

General Instructions for Cooking Ground Meat Patties

1. Preheat the browning skillet or grill for the maximum amount of time, according to the manufacturer's instructions. Add patties. Press patties firmly against the bottom of the skillet for good heat contact. See "Browning", page 17.

2. Cover patties with a paper towel or waxed paper to reduce spattering inside the Radarange Oven. If covered with the glass lid, patties will develop a "steamed" flavor.

3. Cook in the Radarange Oven on FULL POWER, according to the directions on the chart. Turn the patties over after 45 to 60 seconds of cooking.

4. Do not cook patties which are not completely thawed. See "Small Size Meats Defrosting Chart" on page 166.

5. Ground beef which has been "extended" with soy or another vegetable protein cooks more quickly than 100% ground meat. To cook ground meat with an "extender" reduce the cooking time by approximately 1/3.

BULK GROUND MEAT

To prepare ground meat cooked "loosely", place in a 1-1/2-quart casserole. Break meat apart with a fork. Cover with waxed paper or a paper towel, if desired, to prevent spattering. Cook in the Radarange Oven on FULL POWER for 3 to 4 minutes per lb., or until meat is no longer pink. Stir halfway through cooking time. Drain.

General Hints for Cooking Meat Main Dishes

1. Prepare ingredients, such as chopped meat and vegetables, in uniform sizes and shapes whenever possible. Main dishes will cook more evenly when the ingredients have similar sizes and shapes.
2. Since casseroles cook more rapidly in the Radarange Oven than in a conventional oven, you may wish to use less liquid in your own favorite recipes. Liquid will not evaporate to the extent that it does in conventional cooking.
3. When preparing purchased frozen convenience main dishes, remove all metal parts, including containers, before cooking in the Radarange Oven.
4. Cover main dishes as recommended in the recipes. Use a glass lid or heavy-duty plastic wrap, since these coverings are the most water-vapor-proof. Usually, by covering a main dish, the cooking time is shortened.
5. Most main dishes are cooked on FULL POWER. However, main dishes containing "delicate" or "special" ingredients may require a lower Cookmatic Level or setting. When melting shredded cheese on top of a main dish during the last 1 to 1-1/2 minutes of cooking, use Cookmatic Level 5 (SLO COOK).
6. Casseroles may require occasional stirring during cooking.
7. Most main dishes should be served at a temperature of 150°F. Use the Temperature-Control to stop the Radarange Oven at one of these temperatures. Use the Temperature-Hold feature to maintain 150°F until ready to serve, if desired.
8. Main dishes will not have "crisp" exteriors as they often do when conventionally cooked. The amount of cooking time in a microwave oven is not long enough for crisping to occur.
9. Whenever possible, stir main dishes before serving to equalize the food temperature. Keep casseroles covered before serving to keep them hot, and to equalize temperatures.
10. By making main dishes, you can save on your food budget. Extenders, such as rice, pasta, potatoes or vegetables may be used with meat. Other main dishes in addition to the ones in this chapter can be found in the "Rice, Cereals, and Pastas," "Fish and Seafood," and "Poultry" chapters.
11. You can prepare frozen main dishes ahead and later defrost and reheat them quickly in the Radarange Oven. See the instructions on page 184. If you don't wish to use the automatic temperature control system, you can estimate the total amount of Radarange Oven time. See the "Approximate Total Time" column on the "Start Time for Frozen Main Dishes Chart," page 187.
12. Many of the main dishes in this chapter give you the opportunity to use leftover meats. Leftovers can become "planned-overs." Prepare extra meat, use the extra to make a casserole, and freeze the casserole for future use.
13. When cooking your own favorite main dishes, (or freezing your own favorite dishes for later use) use a similar recipe in this cookbook as a guide. Use the same setting and same approximate amount of cooking time. Use a similar food on the "Start Time for Frozen Main Dishes Chart," page 187, as a guide when defrosting and heating your own casseroles. Make a note of the Radarange Oven timings on your recipe card for future use.

FROZEN CONVENIENCE MEAT AND MAIN DISH CHART**

FROZEN FOOD	QUANTITY OR PKG. SIZE	PROGRAMMING INSTRUCTIONS				SPECIAL INSTRUCTIONS
Buffet Supper	32 ozs.	1	COOKING PROGRAM	8:00	DEFROST	Remove from metal container. Place in 2-quart utility dish. Cover with plastic wrap.
		2	COOKING PROGRAM	4:00	HOLD	
		3	COOKING PROGRAM	12:00 to 17:00	COOK	
Cholesterol-Free Breakfast Links	8 ozs.	1	COOKING PROGRAM	1:30	DEFROST	Place on plastic rack, paper towels or paper plate. Cover with paper towel.
		2	COOKING PROGRAM	:30	HOLD	
		3	COOKING PROGRAM	:45 to 1:30	COOK	
Cholesterol-Free Breakfast Patties	8 ozs.	1	COOKING PROGRAM	1:30	DEFROST	Place on plastic rack, paper towels or paper plate. Cover with paper towel.
		2	COOKING PROGRAM	:45	HOLD	
		3	COOKING PROGRAM	1:15 to 1:30	COOK	
Cholesterol-Free Breakfast Slices	1/2 lb. (8 ozs.)	1	COOKING PROGRAM	1:00	DEFROST	Place on plastic rack, paper towels or paper plates. Cover with paper towel.
		2	COOKING PROGRAM	:30	HOLD	
		3	COOKING PROGRAM	:30 to 1:00	COOK	
Cholesterol-Free Breakfast Strips	4 slices			1:30 to 2:30	COOK	Place on plastic rack, paper towels or paper plate. Cover with paper towel.
Dinners	7 to 9 ozs.	1	COOKING PROGRAM	3:00	DEFROST	Remove from metal container. Place on dish.* Cover with plastic wrap.
		2	COOKING PROGRAM	1:30	HOLD	
		3	COOKING PROGRAM	2:30 to 3:30	COOK	

*Sectioned paper plates also work well.
**Frozen Convenience Meat and Main Dish Chart continues on the following page.

FROZEN FOOD	QUANTITY OR PKG. SIZE	PROGRAMMING INSTRUCTIONS				SPECIAL INSTRUCTIONS
Dinners	9 to 12 ozs.	1	COOKING PROGRAM	3:00	DEFROST	Remove from metal container. Place on dish.* Cover with plastic wrap.
		2	COOKING PROGRAM	2:00	HOLD	
		3	COOKING PROGRAM	2:30 to 4:00	COOK	
Dinners	12 to 15 ozs.	1	COOKING PROGRAM	3:00	DEFROST	Remove from metal container. Place on dish.* Cover with plastic wrap.
		2	COOKING PROGRAM	2:00	HOLD	
		3	COOKING PROGRAM	4:00 to 6:00	COOK	
Dinners	15 to 18 ozs.	1	COOKING PROGRAM	5:00	DEFROST	Remove from metal container. Place on dish.* Cover with plastic wrap.
		2	COOKING PROGRAM	3:00	HOLD	
		3	COOKING PROGRAM	5:00 to 6:00	COOK	
Dinners in Cooking Bags	5 to 6-1/2 ozs.			3:00 to 4:00	COOK	Slit bag before cooking.
Entrees	5 to 7 ozs.	1	COOKING PROGRAM	3:00	DEFROST	Remove from metal container. Place on dish. Cover with plastic wrap.
		2	COOKING PROGRAM	1:30	HOLD	
		3	COOKING PROGRAM	2:30 to 3:30	COOK	
Pot Pies	8 ozs.	1	COOKING PROGRAM	3:00	DEFROST	Remove from metal container. Place in dish of same approximate size and shape.
		2	COOKING PROGRAM	1:30	HOLD	
		3	COOKING PROGRAM	2:30 to 3:30	COOK	

*Sectioned paper plates also work well.

General Instructions for Frozen Convenience Meats and Main Dishes
1. Read the Special Instructions on the chart. Then, DEFROST, HOLD and COOK, according to the instructions.
2. The 2nd setting is always HOLD. This allows for the food to equalize in temperature and finish defrosting.
3. The 3rd setting is COOK. This provides FULL POWER for heating quickly. However, if a dinner or entree includes a food which has a "delicate" ingredient, a lower Cookmatic Level may be used, if desired. If a lower Cookmatic Level is used, slightly increase the amount of cooking time.

CONVENIENCE MAIN DISH MIX COOKING CHART

CONVENIENCE MIX TYPE AND PKG. SIZE	AMOUNT OF GROUND BEEF	1ST COOKING TIME ON FULL POWER	AMOUNT OF HOT WATER	2ND COOKING TIME ON FULL POWER
Chili-Tomato Mix (7.25 oz.)	1 lb.	4 to 5 min.	4 cups	12 to 14 min.
Hamburger Hash Mix (6 oz.)	1 lb.	4 to 5 min.	3 cups	14 to 15 min.
Hamburger Stew Mix (5.5 oz.)	1 lb.	4 to 5 min.	4 cups	14 to 15 min.

General Instructions for Cooking Convenience Main Dish Mixes

1. Crumble the ground beef in a 3-quart casserole. Cook in the Radarange Oven on FULL POWER, according to the 1st cooking time on the chart. Stir halfway through the cooking time. Drain.

2. Stir in the mix and the hot water. Cook in the Radarange Oven on FULL POWER, according to the 2nd cooking time on the chart, or until all ingredients are tender and the sauce is thickened.

START TIME FEATURE

The START TIME feature is especially recommended for frozen casseroles or main dishes, solidly frozen meats, and non-frozen soups or casseroles which don't contain meat, milk, or eggs. There are some general hints you should follow when using the START TIME feature with these different foods.

General Hints for Using the START TIME Feature with Frozen Main Dishes

1. Hints for Foods
   Baked beans, lima bean casseroles and cooked vegetables in sauces will all freeze well.

   Eggs in casseroles freeze well, but only use eggs that have been finely chopped.

   Rice, macaroni and noodles will freeze very well in casseroles. Be sure to undercook casseroles slightly for freezing, because as the food is reheated, it will continue to cook.

   Season prepared foods lightly. Add any additional seasonings, if needed, during reheating or at serving time. Some seasonings increase in strength during a long freezing time.

2. Hints for Freezing
   Freeze the food directly in the cooking dish, or line the dish intended for reheating with freezer cellophane or paper. Allow the paper to overlap the dish, enough to finish wrapping later. Pour in the cooked and cooled food. Cut a plastic drinking straw the depth of the food. Insert the straw slightly off-center in the middle of the food. Avoid touching the bottom of the dish. Trim the straw with scissors, so that only 1/4-inch to 1/2-inch of the straw extends above the surface of the food. (This process is similar to the process for freezing meats. See pages 165 and 166.) Freeze. When frozen, lift out the frozen food block and finish wrapping. Label the food, and store it in the freezer. For reheating, remove the wrapping and place the frozen food in the same dish used for freezing. Insert the temperature probe in the straw. Cover the dish with a glass lid or heavy-duty plastic wrap. Be sure to insert the probe jack in the oven receptacle. Program the Defrost—Hold—Cook time, according to the directions on the chart.

3. Using the Chart
   There are two sets of timings given on the chart. One timing is for frozen food left out at room temperature

for 4 hours, and the other timing is for food left out for 9 to 11 hours.

Example: (4 Hours Out) You might take a casserole out of the freezer at 7:00 A.M. You might be leaving the house and want defrosting and cooking to begin at 11:00 A.M. You will put the food in the Radarange Oven and program the start time. In this example, you will actually "touch in" these START TIME instructions:

11:00 represents eleven o'clock. You will actually "touch in" the digits  to set

eleven o'clock, or 11:00.

Next, you will touch the START TIME pad: **START TIME**.

Then, program the defrosting and cooking instructions. Remember to insert the temperature probe in the straw. Be sure to insert the probe jack in the oven receptacle. Finally, you will press the **START** switch.

The Radarange Oven won't begin to operate at the programmed start time if the **START**

switch is not pressed.

The food will stand for 4 hours before the Radarange Oven begins to operate. For a casserole cooked in this way, the "4 Hours Out" time is used since there are 4 hours of time elapsing between 7:00 A.M. and 11:00 A.M. A 2-quart casserole cooked this way will be done by noon, or shortly after, just in time for lunch. (See the "Start Time for Frozen Main Dishes Chart", on page 186.) Or, take a food out of the freezer during your lunch break at 12:30 P.M., and set the START TIME for 4:30 P.M. Your supper, or dinner will be ready at 5:30 or 6:00 P.M.

Example: (9 to 11 Hours Out) You might take a casserole out of the freezer at 7:00 A.M. You might be leaving the house and want defrosting and cooking to begin at 4:00 to 6:00 P.M. You will put the food in the Radarange Oven and program the start time. Then, program the defrosting and cooking instructions. Remember to insert the temperature probe in the straw. Be sure to insert the probe jack in the oven receptacle. Finally, press the **START** switch.

The food will stand for 9 to 11 hours before the Radarange Oven begins to operate. For a casserole cooked in this way, the "9 to 11 Hours Out" time is used since there are 9 to 11 hours elapsed between 7:00 A.M. and 4:00 or 6:00 P.M. A 2-quart casserole cooked in this way will require 30 to 50 minutes of defrosting and cooking time. (See the "Start Time for Frozen Main Dishes Chart", on page 186.) The casserole will be done by 5:00 or 5:20 if the Radarange Oven begins to operate at 4:30 P.M. If you want to serve dinner at 6:30, set the START TIME between 5:40 and 6:00.

Always remember to consider the total approximate amount of Radarange Oven time when setting the START TIME.

The approximate amount of Radarange Oven time is given in the "Start Time for Frozen Main Dishes Chart," pages 186 and 187.

A good formula to remember is: serving time − approximate oven time = start time.

If the food requires 1 hour of total Radarange Oven time, for example, and you want to serve at 5:00 P.M., set the START TIME to 4:00. The Radarange Oven will start at 4:00 and be finished by 5:00. The Automatic Temperature Control should be used to indicate when the food reaches the serving temperature of 140°F. Hold the food on Cookmatic Level 8 (MEDIUM HIGH), as indicated in the chart.

4. Casserole Examples

Here are some examples of recipes which can be prepared in the following dish size categories:

1-1/2-quart dish size: Goulash
　　　　　　　　　　　Beef Corkscrew Bake

2-quart dish size: 　Chili Con Carne
　　　　　　　　　　Tetrazzini Bake
　　　　　　　　　　Tater Tot® Casserole

3-quart dish size: 　Western Beef 'N' Beans

4-quart dish size: 　Italian Spaghetti

You can prepare other casseroles in this cookbook, as well as your own favorites. Consult the chart, and use the amount of cooking time recommended for your dish size.

START TIME FOR FROZEN MAIN DISHES CHART

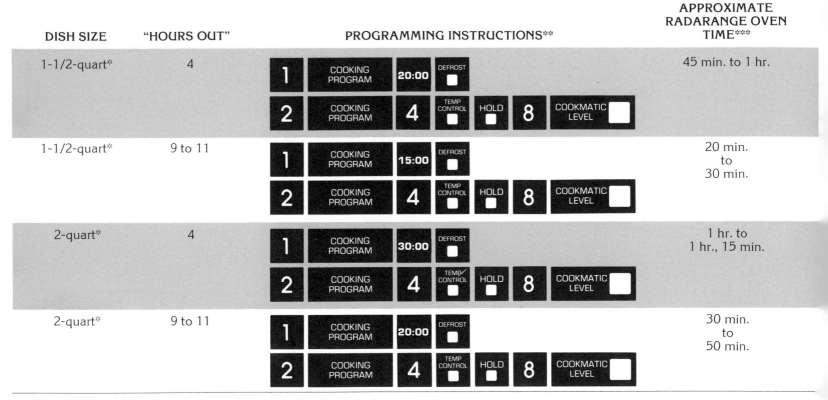

DISH SIZE	"HOURS OUT"	PROGRAMMING INSTRUCTIONS**	APPROXIMATE RADARANGE OVEN TIME***
1-1/2-quart*	4	**1** COOKING PROGRAM 20:00 DEFROST ☐ / **2** COOKING PROGRAM 4 TEMP CONTROL ☐ HOLD ☐ 8 COOKMATIC LEVEL ☐	45 min. to 1 hr.
1-1/2-quart*	9 to 11	**1** COOKING PROGRAM 15:00 DEFROST ☐ / **2** COOKING PROGRAM 4 TEMP CONTROL ☐ HOLD ☐ 8 COOKMATIC LEVEL ☐	20 min. to 30 min.
2-quart*	4	**1** COOKING PROGRAM 30:00 DEFROST ☐ / **2** COOKING PROGRAM 4 TEMP CONTROL ☐ HOLD ☐ 8 COOKMATIC LEVEL ☐	1 hr. to 1 hr., 15 min.
2-quart*	9 to 11	**1** COOKING PROGRAM 20:00 DEFROST ☐ / **2** COOKING PROGRAM 4 TEMP CONTROL ☐ HOLD ☐ 8 COOKMATIC LEVEL ☐	30 min. to 50 min.

*If a food has a high liquid content and less than 1-inch of space at top of dish (such as Chili Con Carne) use Cookmatic Level 6 (ROAST) rather than Cookmatic Level 8 (MEDIUM HIGH) and allow for a slightly longer heating time. Use the Temperature-Hold feature to maintain the food temperature at 140°F for at least 10 to 15 minutes if you don't stir during the cooking time.

**Remember to set 00:00 START TIME ☐ before programming the defrosting and cooking instructions. See the instructions on page 188.

Remember to press the  switch.

***Includes both the defrosting and cooking time.

START TIME FOR FROZEN MAIN DISHES CHART (Continued)

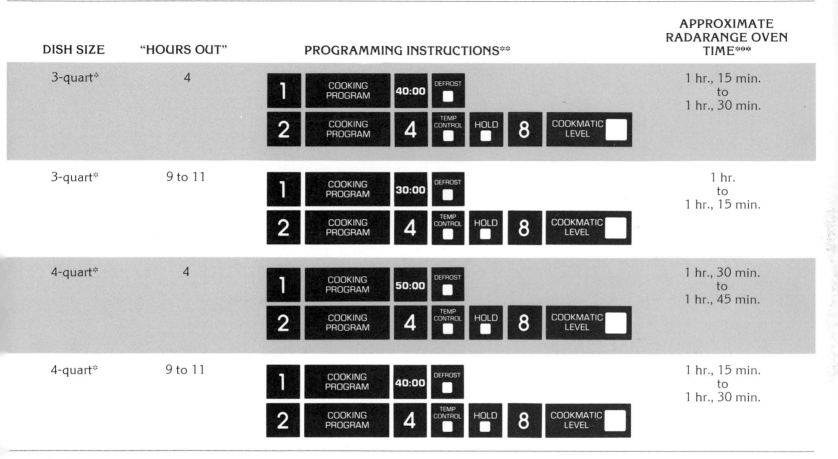

DISH SIZE	"HOURS OUT"	PROGRAMMING INSTRUCTIONS**	APPROXIMATE RADARANGE OVEN TIME***
3-quart*	4	**1** COOKING PROGRAM · 40:00 · DEFROST □ **2** COOKING PROGRAM · 4 · TEMP CONTROL □ · HOLD □ · 8 · COOKMATIC LEVEL □	1 hr., 15 min. to 1 hr., 30 min.
3-quart*	9 to 11	**1** COOKING PROGRAM · 30:00 · DEFROST □ **2** COOKING PROGRAM · 4 · TEMP CONTROL □ · HOLD □ · 8 · COOKMATIC LEVEL □	1 hr. to 1 hr., 15 min.
4-quart*	4	**1** COOKING PROGRAM · 50:00 · DEFROST □ **2** COOKING PROGRAM · 4 · TEMP CONTROL □ · HOLD □ · 8 · COOKMATIC LEVEL □	1 hr., 30 min. to 1 hr., 45 min.
4-quart*	9 to 11	**1** COOKING PROGRAM · 40:00 · DEFROST □ **2** COOKING PROGRAM · 4 · TEMP CONTROL □ · HOLD □ · 8 · COOKMATIC LEVEL □	1 hr., 15 min. to 1 hr., 30 min.

*If a food has a high liquid content and less than 1-inch of space at top of dish (such as Chili Con Carne) use Cookmatic Level 6 (ROAST) rather than Cookmatic Level 8 (MEDIUM HIGH) and allow for a slightly longer heating time. Use the Temperature-Hold feature to maintain the food temperature at 140°F for at least 10 to 15 minutes if you don't stir during the cooking time.

**Remember to set before programming the defrosting and cooking instructions. See the instructions on page 188.

Remember to press the  switch.

***Includes both the defrosting and cooking time.

General Instructions for Defrosting and Cooking Frozen Main Dishes

1. Prepare the main dish, according to the general hints on pages 184 and 185. Place the main dish in the proper size utensil for the food. Cover with plastic wrap.

2. Before programming the defrosting and cooking times, set the START TIME in the following way:

   The 00:00 represents any time of day you wish for the Radarange Oven to begin cooking. For 4 o'clock, you would set:

   4:00

   You will actually "touch in" the digits

   to set four o'clock or 4:00.

   Next, touch the START TIME pad. For the entire process you will touch

.

3. Program the cooking and defrosting instructions, according to the programmed cooking instructions on the chart. Remember to insert the temperature probe in the straw. Be sure to insert the probe jack in the oven receptacle.

4. Finally, press the **START** switch. The Radarange Oven won't begin to operate at the programmed start time if the **START** switch is not pressed.

General Hints for Using the START TIME Feature with Frozen Meats

1. Hints for Preparing Meats

   Prepare meats for defrosting and cooking, in exactly the same way as you do when preparing them for defrosting and cooking without using the START TIME Feature. Use the same 3 major cooking methods, described on pages 168 to 172. Use the utensils and coverings recommended.

2. Using the Charts

   Use the "Start Time for Frozen Meats Charts" on pages 190 to 195 for all defrosting and cooking times. You will notice that defrosting times on these charts are different from the times on the "Roast Defrosting Chart", on page 167. These meats will be sitting in the Radarange Oven for a period of time before the Radarange Oven begins to operate, and some defrosting will occur during this "hours out" time. Therefore, the defrosting times in these charts have been adjusted accordingly.

   There are two sets of timings given on the charts. One timing is for frozen meat left out at room temperature for 4 hours, and the other timing is for meat left out for 8 to 10 hours.

   Example: (4 Hours Out) You might take a meat out of the freezer at 7:00 A.M. You might be leaving the house and want defrosting and cooking to begin at 11:00 A.M. You will put the frozen meat in the Radarange Oven and program the start time. In this example you will actually "touch in" these START TIME instructions:

   11:00 represents eleven o'clock. You will actually "touch in" the digits **1 1 0 0** to set

   eleven o'clock, or 11:00.

Next, you will touch the START TIME pad:

Then, program the defrosting and cooking instructions. Remember to insert the temperature probe in the straw. Be sure to insert the probe jack in the oven receptacle. Finally, you will press the

 switch.

The Radarange Oven won't begin to operate at the programmed start time if the

switch is not pressed.

The meat will stand for 4 hours before the Radarange Oven begins to operate. For a meat cooked in this way, the "4 Hours Out" time is used since there are 4 hours of time elapsing between 7:00 A.M. and 11:00 A.M. A tender meat weighing less than 3 lbs. cooked this way will be done by 11:45 to 12:15, just in time for lunch. (See the "Start Time for Frozen Meats Chart: Tender Meats", on page 190.) Or, take a food out of the freezer during your lunch break at 12:30 P.M., and set the START TIME for 4:30 P.M. Your supper, or dinner will be ready at about 5:15 to 5:45 P.M.

Example: (8 to 10 Hours Out) You might take a meat out of the freezer at 7:00 A.M. You might be leaving the house and want defrosting and cooking to begin at 3:00 to 5:00 P.M. You will put the food in the Radarange Oven and program the start time. Then, program the defrosting and cooking instructions. Remember to insert the temperature probe in the straw. Be sure to insert the probe jack in the oven receptacle. Finally, press the  switch.

The food will stand for 8 to 10 hours before the Radarange Oven begins to operate. For a meat cooked in this way, the "8 to 10 Hours Out" time is used since there are 8 to 10 hours elapsed between 7:00 A.M. and 3:00 or 5:00 P.M. A 3 to 6 lb. medium tender meat cooked in this way will require 1 hour and 30 minutes to 2 hours of defrosting and cooking time. (See the "Start Time for Frozen Meats Chart: Tender Meats", on page 191.) The meat will be done by 5:00 or 5:30 if the Radarange Oven begins to operate at 3:30 P.M. If you want to serve dinner at 6:30, set the START TIME between 4:30 and 5:00.

Always remember to consider the total approximate amount of Radarange Oven time when setting the START TIME.

The approximate amount of Radarange Oven time is given in the "Start Time for Frozen Meats Charts", on pages 190 to 195.

A good formula to remember is: serving time − approximate oven time = start time.

The meat requires 1 hour of total Radarange Oven time, for example, and you want to serve at 5:00 P.M., set the START TIME to 4:00. The Radarange Oven will start defrosting and cooking at 4:00 and be finished by 5:00. The Automatic Temperature Control should be used to indicate when the food reaches the desired temperature of 140°F, 150°F, 160°F, or 170°F. See the "Recommended End Temperature Chart", on page 173. Hold the meat as recommended for tender, medium tender and less tender meats, according to the 3 major cooking methods described on pages 168 to 172.

START TIME FOR FROZEN MEATS CHART: TENDER MEATS

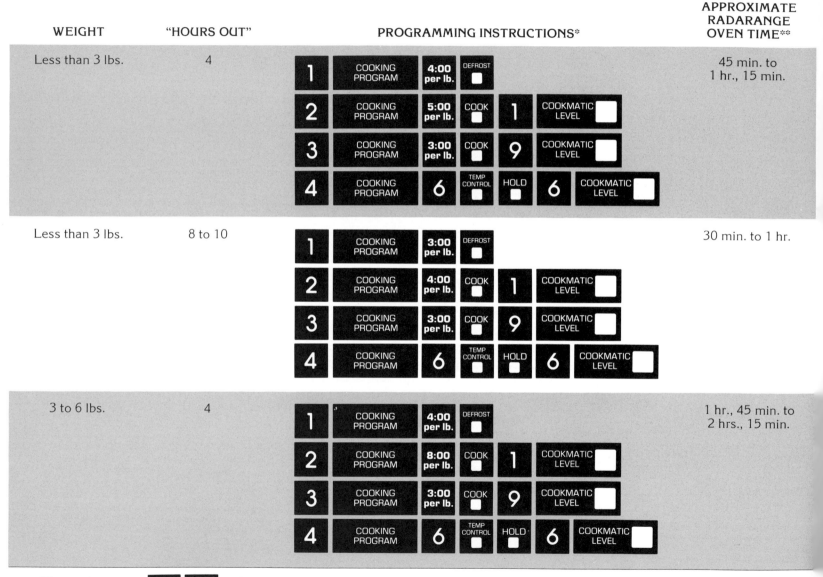

WEIGHT	"HOURS OUT"	PROGRAMMING INSTRUCTIONS*	APPROXIMATE RADARANGE OVEN TIME**
Less than 3 lbs.	4	**1** COOKING PROGRAM / 4:00 per lb. / DEFROST **2** COOKING PROGRAM / 5:00 per lb. / COOK / 1 / COOKMATIC LEVEL **3** COOKING PROGRAM / 3:00 per lb. / COOK / 9 / COOKMATIC LEVEL **4** COOKING PROGRAM / 6 / TEMP CONTROL / HOLD / 6 / COOKMATIC LEVEL	45 min. to 1 hr., 15 min.
Less than 3 lbs.	8 to 10	**1** COOKING PROGRAM / 3:00 per lb. / DEFROST **2** COOKING PROGRAM / 4:00 per lb. / COOK / 1 / COOKMATIC LEVEL **3** COOKING PROGRAM / 3:00 per lb. / COOK / 9 / COOKMATIC LEVEL **4** COOKING PROGRAM / 6 / TEMP CONTROL / HOLD / 6 / COOKMATIC LEVEL	30 min. to 1 hr.
3 to 6 lbs.	4	**1** COOKING PROGRAM / 4:00 per lb. / DEFROST **2** COOKING PROGRAM / 8:00 per lb. / COOK / 1 / COOKMATIC LEVEL **3** COOKING PROGRAM / 3:00 per lb. / COOK / 9 / COOKMATIC LEVEL **4** COOKING PROGRAM / 6 / TEMP CONTROL / HOLD / 6 / COOKMATIC LEVEL	1 hr., 45 min. to 2 hrs., 15 min.

*Remember to set **00:00** **START TIME** before programming the defrosting and cooking instructions. See the instructions on pages 188 and 189. Remember to press the **START** switch.

**This total includes both the defrosting and cooking times, but does not include the holding time. See the 3 major cooking methods on pages 168 to 172 for recommended holding times.

START TIME FOR FROZEN MEATS CHART: TENDER MEATS (Continued)

WEIGHT	"HOURS OUT"	PROGRAMMING INSTRUCTIONS*	APPROXIMATE RADARANGE OVEN TIME**
3 to 6 lbs.	8 to 10		1 hr., 15 min. to 1 hr., 45 min.
Over 6 lbs.	4		2-1/2 hrs. or more
Over 6 lbs.	8 to 10		2 hrs. or more

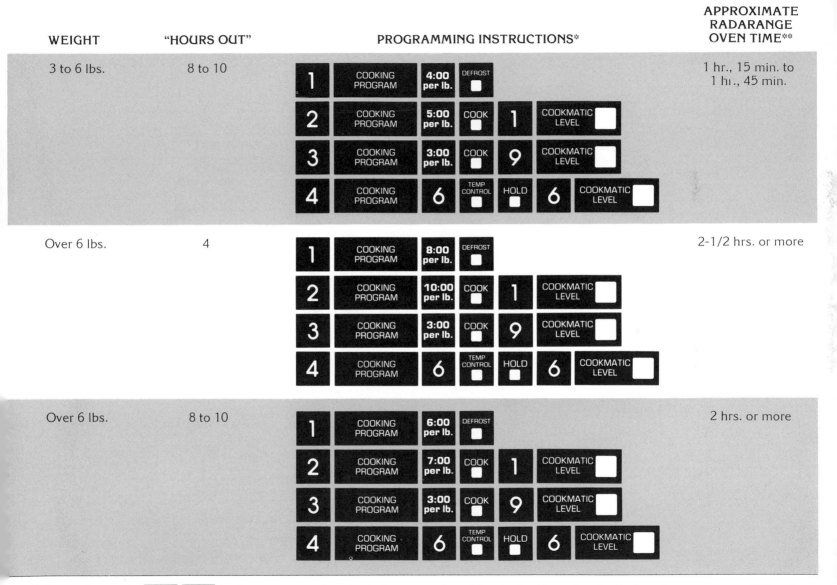

*Remember to set **00:00** **START TIME** before programming the defrosting and cooking instructions. See the instructions on pages 188 and 189. Remember to press the **START** switch.

**This total includes both the defrosting and cooking times, but does not include the holding time. See the 3 major cooking methods on pages 168 to 172 for recommended holding times.

START TIME FOR FROZEN MEATS CHART: MEDIUM TENDER MEATS*

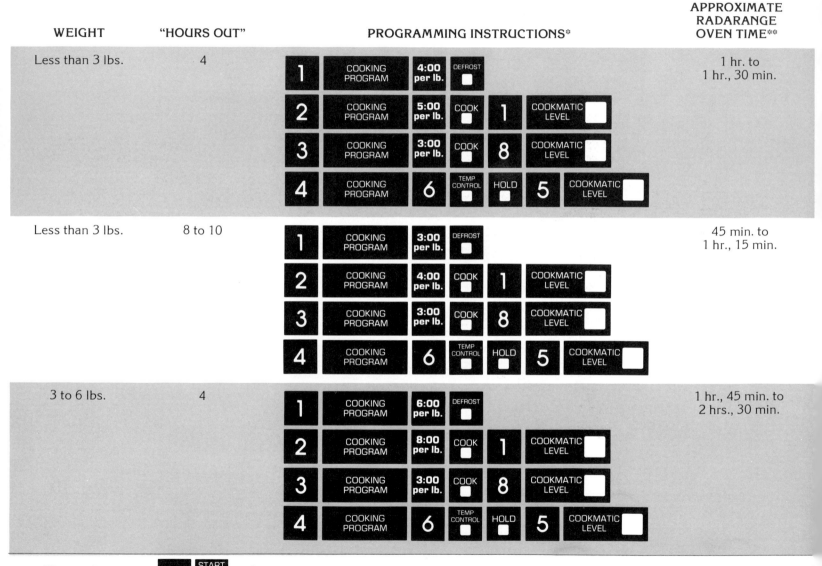

WEIGHT	"HOURS OUT"	PROGRAMMING INSTRUCTIONS*	APPROXIMATE RADARANGE OVEN TIME**
Less than 3 lbs.	4	**1** COOKING PROGRAM · 4:00 per lb. · DEFROST **2** COOKING PROGRAM · 5:00 per lb. · COOK · 1 · COOKMATIC LEVEL **3** COOKING PROGRAM · 3:00 per lb. · COOK · 8 · COOKMATIC LEVEL **4** COOKING PROGRAM · 6 · TEMP CONTROL · HOLD · 5 · COOKMATIC LEVEL	1 hr. to 1 hr., 30 min.
Less than 3 lbs.	8 to 10	**1** COOKING PROGRAM · 3:00 per lb. · DEFROST **2** COOKING PROGRAM · 4:00 per lb. · COOK · 1 · COOKMATIC LEVEL **3** COOKING PROGRAM · 3:00 per lb. · COOK · 8 · COOKMATIC LEVEL **4** COOKING PROGRAM · 6 · TEMP CONTROL · HOLD · 5 · COOKMATIC LEVEL	45 min. to 1 hr., 15 min.
3 to 6 lbs.	4	**1** COOKING PROGRAM · 6:00 per lb. · DEFROST **2** COOKING PROGRAM · 8:00 per lb. · COOK · 1 · COOKMATIC LEVEL **3** COOKING PROGRAM · 3:00 per lb. · COOK · 8 · COOKMATIC LEVEL **4** COOKING PROGRAM · 6 · TEMP CONTROL · HOLD · 5 · COOKMATIC LEVEL	1 hr., 45 min. to 2 hrs., 30 min.

*Remember to set [00:00 START TIME] before programming the defrosting and cooking instructions. See the instructions on pages 188 and 189. Remember to press the **START** switch.

**This total includes both the defrosting and cooking times, but does not include the holding time. See the 3 major cooking methods on pages 168 to 172 for recommended holding times.

START TIME FOR FROZEN MEATS CHART: MEDIUM TENDER MEATS (Continued)

WEIGHT	"HOURS OUT"	PROGRAMMING INSTRUCTIONS*	APPROXIMATE RADARANGE OVEN TIME**
3 to 6 lbs.	8 to 10		1 hr., 30 min. to 2 hrs.
Over 6 lbs.	4		2 hrs., 45 min. or more
Over 6 lbs.	8 to 10		2 hrs. or more

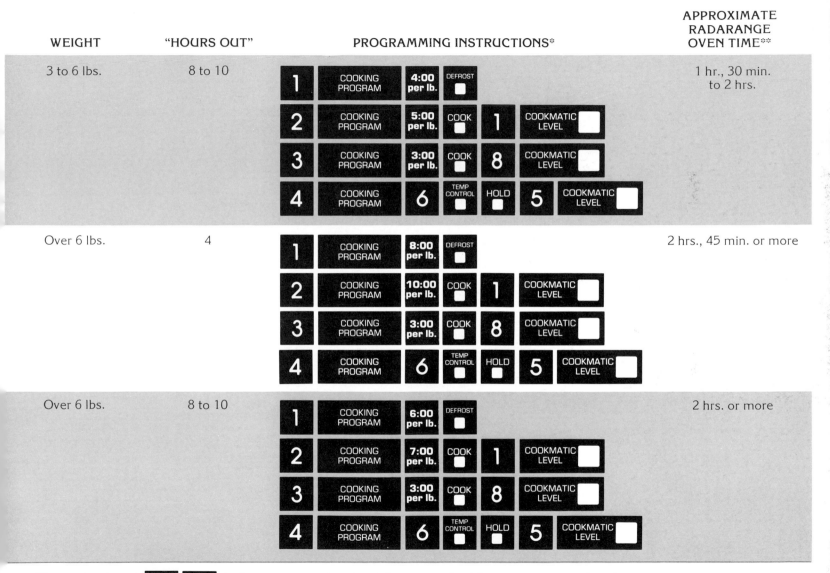

*Remember to set [00:00] [START TIME] before programming the defrosting and cooking instructions. See the instructions on pages 188 and 189. Remember to press the **START** switch.

**This total includes both the defrosting and cooking times, but does not include the holding time. See the 3 major cooking methods on pages 168 to 172 for recommended holding times.

START TIME FOR FROZEN MEATS CHART: LESS TENDER MEATS

WEIGHT	"HOURS OUT"	PROGRAMMING INSTRUCTIONS*	APPROXIMATE RADARANGE OVEN TIME**
Least Tender: Less than 3 lbs.	4		1 hr. to 1 hr., 30 min.
Less than 3 lbs.	8 to 10		1 hr. to 1 hr., 15 min.
3 to 6 lbs.	4		2 hrs. to 2 hrs., 30 min.

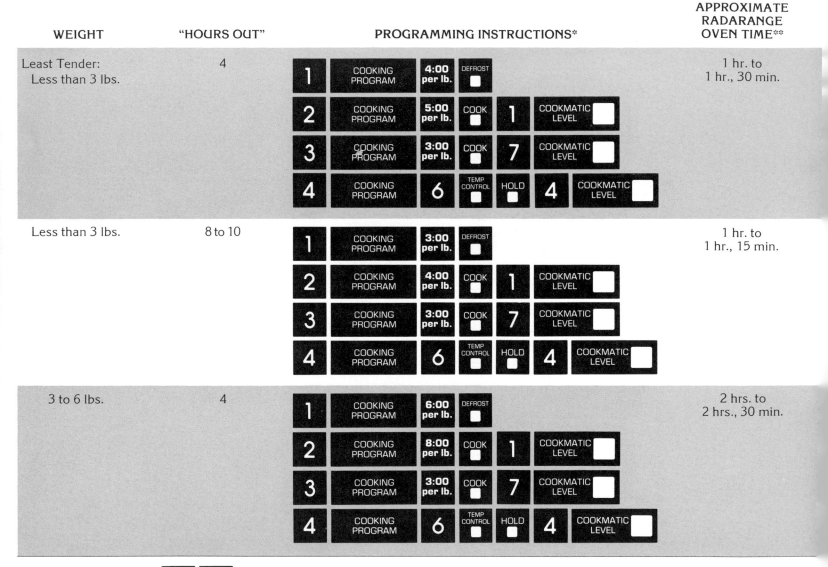

*Remember to set [00:00] [START TIME] before programming the defrosting and cooking instructions. See the instructions on pages 188 and 189. Remember to press the **START** switch.

**This total includes both the defrosting and cooking times, but does not include the holding time. See the 3 major cooking methods on pages 168 to 172 for recommended holding times.

START TIME FOR FROZEN MEATS CHART: LESS TENDER MEATS (Continued)

WEIGHT	"HOURS OUT"	PROGRAMMING INSTRUCTIONS*	APPROXIMATE RADARANGE OVEN TIME**

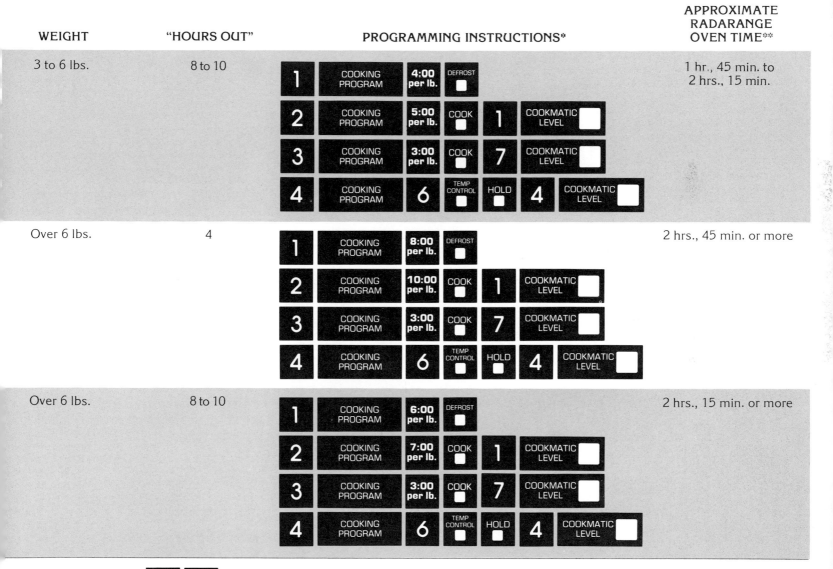

WEIGHT	"HOURS OUT"	PROGRAMMING INSTRUCTIONS	APPROXIMATE RADARANGE OVEN TIME
3 to 6 lbs.	8 to 10	**1** COOKING PROGRAM · 4:00 per lb. · DEFROST **2** COOKING PROGRAM · 5:00 per lb. · COOK · 1 · COOKMATIC LEVEL **3** COOKING PROGRAM · 3:00 per lb. · COOK · 7 · COOKMATIC LEVEL **4** COOKING PROGRAM · 6 · TEMP CONTROL · HOLD · 4 · COOKMATIC LEVEL	1 hr., 45 min. to 2 hrs., 15 min.
Over 6 lbs.	4	**1** COOKING PROGRAM · 8:00 per lb. · DEFROST **2** COOKING PROGRAM · 10:00 per lb. · COOK · 1 · COOKMATIC LEVEL **3** COOKING PROGRAM · 3:00 per lb. · COOK · 7 · COOKMATIC LEVEL **4** COOKING PROGRAM · 6 · TEMP CONTROL · HOLD · 4 · COOKMATIC LEVEL	2 hrs., 45 min. or more
Over 6 lbs.	8 to 10	**1** COOKING PROGRAM · 6:00 per lb. · DEFROST **2** COOKING PROGRAM · 7:00 per lb. · COOK · 1 · COOKMATIC LEVEL **3** COOKING PROGRAM · 3:00 per lb. · COOK · 7 · COOKMATIC LEVEL **4** COOKING PROGRAM · 6 · TEMP CONTROL · HOLD · 4 · COOKMATIC LEVEL	2 hrs., 15 min. or more

*Remember to set  before programming the defrosting and cooking instructions. See the instructions on pages 188 and 189. Remember to press the **START** switch.

**This total includes both the defrosting and cooking times, but does not include the holding time. See the 3 major cooking methods on pages 168 to 172 for recommended holding times.

General Instructions for Defrosting and Cooking Frozen Meats

1. Prepare the meat, according to one of the 3 major cooking methods. Determine whether the cut of meat is tender, medium tender, or less tender, according to the titles on the "Start Times for Frozen Meats Charts", pages 190 to 195.

Use the cooking methods recommended, for the following cuts of meat:

TENDER MEATS: COOKING METHOD #1
MEDIUM TENDER MEATS: COOKING METHOD #2
LESS TENDER MEATS: COOKING METHOD #3

Instructions for these cooking methods are found on pages 168 to 172. Use the same utensil, type of covering and other general instructions as recommended in the cooking methods when preparing the meat for actual defrosting and cooking. For instructions about how to prepare meats for the freezer (which will later be defrosted and cooked in one process) see the instructions on pages 165 and 166.

2. Set the START TIME in the following way:

The 00:00 represents any time of day you wish for the Radarange Oven to begin cooking. For 4 o'clock, you would set:

You will actually "touch in" the digits

to set four o'clock or 4:00.

Next, touch the START TIME pad. For the entire process you will touch:

3. Program the cooking and defrosting instructions, according to the programmed cooking instructions on the chart. Use the Temperature-Hold feature to maintain the meat temperature as long as is recommended, according to the 3 major cooking methods, depending on whether the meat is tender, medium tender, and less tender. Temperature holding times can differ due to the variances in meat sizes and shapes. Remember to insert the temperature probe in the straw. Be sure to insert the probe jack in the oven receptacle.

4. Finally, press the 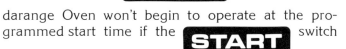 switch. The Radarange Oven won't begin to operate at the programmed start time if the **START** switch is not pressed.

General Hints for Using the Start Time Feature with Non-Frozen Foods

1. Soups or casseroles which don't contain meat, milk, or eggs are good to use with the Automatic Start Time Feature. Vegetable soups or casseroles work especially well. Prepare the soup or casserole, following the recipe instructions. Then, place the food in the Radarange Oven and set the START TIME, as when setting the Start Time for frozen main dishes or meats. Program the cooking instructions. Insert the temperature probe, if the recipe requires it. If used, be sure to insert the probe jack in the oven receptacle. Finally, press the **START** switch.

The Radarange Oven won't begin to operate at the programmed start time if the **START** switch is not pressed.

2. Avoid using non-frozen foods such as meats or dishes containing meat, milk, or eggs with the Automatic Start Time Feature.

Beef Stroganoff

Yield: 4 servings

1 lb. sirloin steak, 1/2-inch thick
2 tablespoons all-purpose flour
1 teaspoon salt
1/4 teaspoon pepper

2 tablespoons butter or margarine

1/3 cup onion, finely chopped
1 clove garlic, minced

1 (10-3/4 oz.) can cream of mushroom soup or cream of chicken soup
1 (4 oz.) can sliced mushrooms, drained
1/4 cup water
2 tablespoons tomato paste

1 cup dairy sour cream

1. Trim excess fat from meat. Combine flour, salt and pepper. Pound into both sides of meat. Cut beef into thin strips.

2. Place butter in 2-quart casserole. Cook in Radarange Oven on FULL POWER for 30 seconds, or until melted. Add meat. Cook in Radarange Oven, on FULL POWER for 5 to 6 minutes, or until no longer pink.

3. Stir in onion and garlic. Cook in Radarange Oven on FULL POWER for 2 to 3 minutes, or until onion and garlic are tender.

4. Stir in soup, mushrooms, water and tomato paste. Cook in Radarange Oven on FULL POWER for 8 to 10 minutes, or until meat is tender.

5. Stir in sour cream. Heat in Radarange Oven on FULL POWER for 1 minute.

MICRO-TIP: May be served over cooked noodles or rice.

Shish Kabobs

Yield: 2 to 3 servings

1 lb. sirloin steak, cut into 1-inch cubes (about 20)
1 (8 oz.) bottle French dressing (vinegar kind)

1 large green pepper, cut in squares (about 8)
12 fresh or canned mushrooms
12 small canned or frozen whole onions
12 cherry tomatoes (optional)

1. Marinate meat in dressing for about 1 hour in refrigerator.

2. Thread meat and vegetables alternately on 4 wooden skewers. Lay kabobs on cooking grill. Brush with French dressing marinade.

3. Cook in Radarange Oven on FULL POWER for 5-1/2 to 7 minutes, or until meat is cooked to desired degree. Turn kabobs over halfway through cooking time, and baste.

MICRO-TIP: Double this recipe for 4 servings. Allow 2 shish kabobs per person.

Roast Beef Hash

Yield: 8 to 10 patties, or 9 x 5 x 2-inch loaf

4 cups cooked beef, cubed
4 medium potatoes, peeled and cubed
1 small onion, quartered

1/4 cup catsup
2 tablespoons butter or margarine, melted
2 tablespoons evaporated milk
1 teaspoon salt
1/4 teaspoon pepper

Spray-on vegetable coating

1. Grind together beef, potatoes and onion.

2. Stir in remaining ingredients. Mix well. Shape into patties or loaf.*

3. Preheat large browning skillet or grill for maximum amount of time, according to manufacturer's instructions. Spray with non-stick vegetable coating. Add 4 patties. Cook in Radarange Oven on FULL POWER for 2 minutes. Turn patties over halfway through cooking time.

   *MICRO-TIP: To make a loaf, add an egg and press hash into a 9 x 5 x 2-inch loaf dish. Cook in Radarange Oven, covered, on FULL POWER for 5 to 7 minutes, or until temperature of 140°F is reached. Use the Temperature-Control to stop the Radarange Oven at 140°F.

Hamburger Stroganoff

Yield: 4 to 6 servings

1/2 cup onion, chopped
1 tablespoon vegetable oil

1 lb. ground beef

1 (4 oz.) can mushrooms, drained
2 tablespoons all-purpose flour
1 teaspoon salt
1/2 teaspoon paprika
1 (10-3/4 oz.) can cream of chicken soup

1 cup dairy sour cream

1. Place onion and oil in 2-quart casserole. Cook in Radarange Oven on FULL POWER for 2 minutes, or until onion is tender.

2. Add meat. Cook in Radarange Oven on FULL POWER for 3 to 4 minutes, or until beef is no longer pink. Stir halfway through cooking time. Drain.

3. Add mushrooms, flour, salt and paprika. Blend well. Stir in soup.

4. Cook in Radarange Oven, covered, on FULL POWER for 5 minutes. Stir halfway through cooking time.

5. Blend in sour cream. Cook in Radarange Oven on Cookmatic Level 8 (MEDIUM HIGH) for 2 minutes, or until heated through. Stir halfway through cooking time.

   MICRO-TIP: May be served over cooked noodles or rice.

Liver and Onions

Yield: 4 to 6 servings

1 lb. beef liver
1/4 cup all-purpose flour
1 teaspoon salt
Dash pepper

6 slices bacon
1 cup onion, chopped

1. Coat liver with mixture of flour, salt and pepper.

2. Place bacon and onion in 2-quart casserole. Cook in Radarange Oven, covered, on FULL POWER for 8 to 10 minutes, or until bacon is almost crisp.

3. Remove bacon and onion. Add liver to bacon grease. Cook in Radarange Oven on FULL POWER for 5 to 7 minutes, or until liver is no longer pink. Turn liver over halfway through cooking time.

4. Put onions and bacon on top of liver. Cook in Radarange Oven on FULL POWER for 1 minute, or until heated through.

Sauerbraten

Yield: 6 to 8 servings

1-1/2 cups water
1/2 cup red wine vinegar
1 teaspoon salt
1/2 teaspoon whole cloves
1/4 teaspoon pepper
6 to 8 gingersnaps, crushed
2 tablespoons brown sugar

2-1/2 to 3 lb. beef pot roast, or heel of round
1 large onion, sliced

1. Combine liquids, spices, gingersnaps and brown sugar in 1-quart glass measure.

2. Cut meat into serving-size pieces and place in 2-1/2 to 3-quart casserole. Add onion. Pour liquid over meat.

3. Cook in Radarange Oven, covered, on Cookmatic Level 4 (MEDIUM) for 45 to 60 minutes, or until meat is tender, and temperature of 170°F is reached. Turn meat over halfway through cooking time.

London Broil

Yield: 4 to 6 servings

1 to 1-1/2 lb. flank steak
2 tablespoons sherry
2 tablespoons soy sauce
1 tablespoon honey
1 clove garlic, minced
1 tablespoon sugar
1 teaspoon salt
1/8 teaspoon pepper
2 tablespoons vegetable oil

1. Combine sherry, soy sauce, honey, garlic, sugar, salt and pepper. Spread over steak. Marinate for 10 to 12 hours in refrigerator. Preheat large browning skillet or grill for maximum amount of time, according to manufacturer's instructions. Add 1 tablespoon oil. Cut steak in half, diagonally across grain. Add to skillet.

2. Cook in Radarange Oven on FULL POWER for 3 to 4 minutes. Turn steak over halfway through cooking time. Wipe out skillet or grill with paper towel. Re-preheat browning skillet or grill, according to manufacturer's instructions. Repeat cooking time with remaining oil and steak.

Chinese Pepper Beef

Yield: 4 servings

1 tablespoon butter or margarine
1 clove garlic, minced
1 lb. round or sirloin steak,
    thinly sliced

1 cup beef bouillon

2 tablespoons cornstarch
2 tablespoons water
4 teaspoons soy sauce
1/8 teaspoon ginger
1 green pepper, finely sliced

1. Place butter and garlic in 2-quart casserole. Cook in Radarange Oven on FULL POWER for 30 to 40 seconds or until butter is melted. Add beef. Cook in Radarange Oven on FULL POWER for 5 to 6 minutes, or until meat is no longer pink.

2. Pour bouillon over meat. Cook in Radarange Oven on FULL POWER for 1 minute, or until heated through.

3. Mix together cornstarch, water, soy sauce and ginger to make smooth paste. Stir into bouillon. Blend in green pepper. Cook in Radarange Oven on FULL POWER for 3-1/2 to 5 minutes, or until sauce is thickened. Stir halfway through cooking time.

Beef Strips with Tomatoes

Yield: 5 servings

1 (1 lb.) flank steak
1/3 cup soy sauce
1/3 cup dry white wine
1 teaspoon sugar

2 tablespoons cornstarch
1 medium onion, sliced
2 cups fresh mushrooms, sliced
1/2 green pepper, sliced

1 pint cherry tomatoes

1. Slice steak very thin, diagonally across grain. Place in 2-quart casserole. Combine soy sauce, wine and sugar. Pour over meat. Mix lightly to coat evenly. Marinate for 1 to 2 hours, in refrigerator.

2. Stir in cornstarch, onion, mushrooms and green pepper.

3. Cook in Radarange Oven, covered, on FULL POWER for 7 to 9 minutes, or until sauce is thickened. Stir halfway through cooking time. Add tomatoes. Pierce skin slightly.

4. Cook in Radarange Oven, covered, on FULL POWER for 1 minute, or until tomatoes are heated.

MICRO-TIP: This recipe is excellent for calorie watchers. There are only 232 calories per serving.

Steak Teriyaki

Yield: 2 servings

1/2 cup soy sauce
1/4 cup dry white wine
1 clove garlic, minced
2 tablespoons sugar
1/2 teaspoon ginger

1-1/2 lb. sirloin steak or rib steak

1. Combine soy sauce, wine, garlic, sugar and ginger in small bowl or glass measure. Let stand for 5 minutes to dissolve sugar.

2. Place steak in heavy duty plastic bag. Pour marinade over steak. Secure bag, making sure marinade surrounds meat. Refrigerate for 4 to 24 hours.

3. Preheat large browning skillet or grill for maximum amount of time, according to manufacturer's instructions. Remove steak from marinade and place in skillet. Cook in Radarange Oven on FULL POWER for 6 to 8 minutes, or until steak is cooked to desired degree. Turn steak over after first minute of cooking.

Sukiyaki

Yield: 4 servings

1 lb. round or sirloin steak
1 tablespoon vegetable oil

1 (8 oz.) can bamboo shoots,
  drained
1 (8 oz.) can water chestnuts,
  drained
1 (16 oz.) can bean sprouts, drained
1/2 lb. fresh mushrooms, sliced
1 medium onion, sliced
3 stalks celery, sliced diagonally
  in 1/2-inch pieces
3 tablespoons sugar
1/3 cup soy sauce
1/2 cup beef bouillon

1. Slice steak very thin, diagonally across grain. Place beef and oil in 2-quart casserole. Cook in Radarange Oven on FULL POWER for 5 to 6 minutes, or until meat is no longer pink.

2. Add vegetables to skillet. Combine sugar, soy sauce and bouillon. Pour over vegetables.

3. Cook in Radarange Oven, covered, on FULL POWER for 6 to 8 minutes. Do not overcook. Vegetables should be quite crisp.

   MICRO-TIP: If desired, thicken sauce with mixture of 1 tablespoon cornstarch and 2 tablespoons water. Cook in Radarange Oven, uncovered, for 1 minute, or until thickened.

Peppered Tenderloin

Yield: 6 to 8 servings

2 tablespoons butter or margarine
2 lb. boneless beef tenderloin
  or sirloin

1/2 teaspoon salt
1/4 teaspoon pepper
Dash ground sage
Dash ground cumin

1 lb. fresh mushrooms, sliced

1 medium onion, cut in eighths
2 medium green peppers, cut in
  1-inch pieces
2 cloves garlic, minced
2 medium tomatoes, each cut into
  8 wedges

1/2 cup soy sauce
2 tablespoons vinegar
2 tablespoons tomato paste

1. Place butter in 2-quart casserole. Cook in Radarange Oven on FULL POWER for 30 to 40 seconds, or until melted. Slice beef into thin strips. Add to butter. Cook in Radarange Oven on FULL POWER for 7 to 9 minutes, or until meat is no longer pink. Reserve drippings.

2. Remove meat with slotted spoon to 3-quart casserole. Sprinkle with salt, pepper, sage and cumin. Toss lightly to mix.

3. Add mushrooms to drippings in casserole. Cook in Radarange Oven on FULL POWER for 1-1/2 minutes, or until mushrooms are warmed. Stir mushrooms into meat. Reserve drippings.

4. Blend onion, peppers and garlic with drippings in casserole. Cook in Radarange Oven on FULL POWER for 3 minutes, or until vegetables are heated. Stir into entire meat mixture. Stir tomatoes into meat.

5. Combine soy sauce, vinegar and tomato paste in casserole. Heat in Radarange Oven on FULL POWER for 1-1/2 minutes, or until heated. Stir halfway through cooking time. Pour over meat. Toss lightly to mix.

6. Cook in Radarange Oven, covered, on FULL POWER for 8 to 10 minutes, or until vegetables are tender. Stir halfway through cooking time.

Quick Chop Suey

Yield: 6 servings

1-1/2 lbs. ground beef
1 cup onion, coarsely chopped

1 teaspoon instant beef bouillon
1 cup boiling water
2 tablespoons cornstarch
1/4 cup soy sauce
1/4 teaspoon ginger

1 (4 oz.) can sliced mushrooms, with liquid
1 (8 oz.) can bamboo shoots, drained
1 (8 oz.) can water chestnuts, drained and halved
1 (1 lb.) can bean sprouts, drained

1. Place beef and onion in 2-quart casserole. Cook in Radarange Oven on FULL POWER for 4 to 5 minutes, or until beef is no longer pink. Stir halfway through cooking time. Drain.

2. Combine bouillon and boiling water. Gradually stir into cornstarch. Add soy sauce and ginger. Pour over meat. Cook in Radarange Oven on FULL POWER for 6 to 7 minutes, or until thickened. Stir twice during cooking time.

3. Add remaining ingredients. Cook in Radarange Oven, covered, on FULL POWER for 3 to 4 minutes, or until heated through. Stir halfway through cooking time.

MICRO-TIP: May be served over cooked rice or chow mein noodles.

Stuffed Peppers

Yield: 4 servings

4 medium green peppers
3 cups boiling water

1 cup cooked roast beef, finely diced
1 (7-1/2 to 8 oz.) can tomato sauce
1 cup cooked rice
1/4 cup celery, finely chopped
1 tablespoon instant, minced onion
1/2 teaspoon seasoned salt

1. Cut off tops of each pepper. Remove seeds and inner membrane from each. Place peppers in water. Cook in Radarange Oven on FULL POWER for 4 to 5 minutes, or until partially cooked. Drain.

2. Combine remaining ingredients and fill peppers. Place peppers in 9 x 2-inch round dish. Bake in Radarange Oven on FULL POWER for 8 to 10 minutes, or until filling is heated through.

MICRO-TIP: Peppers may be prepared ahead and refrigerated. Increase cooking time slightly if peppers are of refrigerator temperature.

Swiss Cubed Steak

Yield: 5 to 6 servings

1/4 lb. bacon
1 medium onion, chopped
1 green pepper, chopped
2 lbs. cubed steaks

1/2 (10-3/4 oz.) can golden cream of mushroom soup
1 (14-1/2 oz.) can tomatoes
Salt
Pepper

1. Cut bacon into small pieces. Place bacon, onion and green pepper in 2-1/2 to 3-quart casserole. Cook in Radarange Oven on FULL POWER for 8 to 10 minutes, or until onion and green pepper are tender. Drain off fat. Add cubed steaks.

2. Combine soup and tomatoes. Pour over meat. Mix all ingredients gently. Season with salt and pepper, as desired.

3. Cook in Radarange Oven, covered, on Cookmatic Level 5 (SLO COOK) for 20 to 25 minutes, or until meat is tender. Turn meat over halfway through cooking time.

Swiss Steak

Yield: 6 servings

3 lb. pot roast
Half clove garlic
1/4 to 1/3 cup all-purpose flour

3 to 4 tablespoons butter or margarine

1 (14-1/2 oz.) can tomatoes
1 cup carrots, chopped
1 cup celery, chopped
1/2 cup onion, chopped
1 teaspoon salt

1. Rub meat with garlic. Pound flour into it.

2. Place butter in 3-quart casserole. Heat in Radarange Oven on FULL POWER for 45 seconds to 1 minute, or until melted. Place meat in dish. Heat in Radarange Oven on FULL POWER for 5 minutes. Turn meat over halfway through cooking time.

3. Place vegetables around edge of dish and salt. Insert temperature probe in meat. Cook in Radarange Oven, covered. 60 to 65 minutes will be necessary for the meat to reach 170°F.

| 1 | COOKING PROGRAM | 7 | TEMP CONTROL | HOLD | 4 | COOKMATIC LEVEL |

After temperature of 170°F is reached, use the Temperature-Hold to keep the meat at 170°F for 30 minutes, or until tender.

MICRO-TIP: To thicken sauce, mix 1 tablespoon cornstarch with 1 tablespoon water. Add to meat juices. Cook in Radarange Oven on FULL POWER for 1 minute, or until thickened.

Salisbury Steak

Yield: 6 servings

1/2 cup onion, chopped
1 teaspoon vegetable oil

1-1/2 lbs. ground beef
1 (10-3/4 oz.) can golden cream of mushroom soup
1/2 cup bread crumbs
1 egg, slightly-beaten
Dash pepper

1/4 cup water

1. Place onion and oil in 1-1/2-quart casserole. Cook in Radarange Oven on FULL POWER for 1-1/2 to 2 minutes, or until onion is tender.

2. Add ground beef, 1/4 cup soup, bread crumbs, egg and pepper. Mix well, and shape into 6 patties. Arrange in 2-quart utility dish. Cover with waxed paper. Cook in Radarange Oven, covered, on FULL POWER for 6 to 7 minutes. Turn patties over halfway through cooking time. Drain.

3. Blend remaining soup with water. Pour over meat. Cook in Radarange Oven, covered, on FULL POWER for 2 to 4 minutes, or until meat is cooked as desired.

MICRO-TIP: For a zestier flavor, use Italian seasoned bread crumbs.

Fancy Meat Loaf

Yield: 4 to 6 servings

1 lb. ground beef
2/3 cup quick-cooking, rolled oats
1/4 cup onion, minced
1/4 cup green pepper, chopped
1/4 cup celery, chopped
1 egg, beaten
1 clove garlic, minced
1 tablespoon parsley, minced
1/2 cup tomato juice
3/4 teaspoon salt
1/4 teaspoon pepper

1/4 cup catsup

1. Combine all ingredients, except catsup, in large mixing bowl. Pat mixture evenly into 1-1/2-quart utility dish. Cook in Radarange Oven on FULL POWER for 6 minutes.

2. Drizzle catsup over top of loaf. Cook in Radarange Oven on FULL POWER for 5 minutes, or until temperature of 160°F is reached.*

*MICRO-TIP: Use the Temperature-Control to stop the Radarange Oven at 160°F.

Beef 'N' Tater Casserole

Yield: 6 servings

1 lb. ground beef

1 (1 lb.) pkg. frozen Tater Tots®
2 teaspoons instant, minced onion
1 (10-3/4 oz.) can cream of
  celery soup
1 (10-3/4 oz.) can golden cream
  of mushroom soup

1. Crumble meat in 2-quart casserole. Cook in Radarange Oven on FULL POWER for 3 to 4 minutes, or until beef is no longer pink. Stir halfway through cooking time. Drain.

2. Top with Tater Tots® and onion. Mix soups together and pour over Tater Tots®.

3. Bake in Radarange Oven on FULL POWER for 12 to 14 minutes, or until heated through, and temperature of 150°F is reached.

Western Beef and Beans

Yield: 8 servings

1-1/2 lbs. ground beef
1 medium onion, chopped (about
  3/4 cup)
1/2 cup celery, chopped

1 teaspoon instant beef bouillon
1/3 cup boiling water
1 (31 oz.) can pork and beans
3/4 cup catsup
1/4 cup dark brown sugar,
  firmly packed
3 tablespoons dark molasses
1 tablespoon prepared mustard
1 teaspoon salt
1/4 teaspoon pepper
1/8 teaspoon instant, minced
  garlic
Dash cayenne pepper

1. Place beef, onion and celery in 3-quart casserole. Heat in Radarange Oven on FULL POWER for 6 to 7 minutes, or until beef is no longer pink and onion and celery are tender. Stir halfway through cooking time. Drain.

2. Dissolve bouillon in water. Add to meat mixture. Combine remaining ingredients. Add to meat mixture.

3. Cook in Radarange Oven, covered, on FULL POWER for 15 minutes, or until temperature of 150°F is reached.* Stir halfway through cooking time.

MICRO-TIPS:

•The celery provides a crisp surprise in this dish. If you prefer more tender celery, precook it with the onion before adding the beef, in 1 tablespoon oil in Radarange Oven on FULL POWER for about 3 minutes, or until tender.

*Use the Temperature-Control to stop the Radarange Oven at 150°F.

Mexi-Tot Casserole

Yield: 4 to 5 servings

1/2 cup onion, chopped
1 tablespoon vegetable oil
1 lb. ground beef

1. Place onion and oil in 1-1/2-quart casserole. Cook in Radarange Oven on FULL POWER for 2 minutes, or until onion is tender. Add beef. Cook in Radarange Oven on FULL POWER for 3 to 4 minutes, or until beef is no longer pink. Stir halfway through cooking time. Drain.

1 (8 oz.) can tomato sauce
1/2 teaspoon chili powder*
1/2 teaspoon salt
1/8 teaspoon garlic powder
1/2 lb. frozen Tater Tots®

2. Add tomato sauce and spices. Top with Tater Tots®. Cook in Radarange Oven on FULL POWER for 5 minutes, or until heated through and temperature of 150°F is reached.**

1/4 cup Cheddar cheese, shredded

3. Sprinkle cheese over top. Heat in Radarange Oven on Cookmatic Level 5 (SLO COOK) for 1 minute, or until cheese is melted.

MICRO-TIPS:

*This makes quite a hot casserole, but add more chili powder if you like it really hot.

**Use the Temperature-Control to stop the Radarange Oven at 150°F.

Taco Casserole

Yield: 4 to 6 servings

1 lb. ground beef

1. Place meat in 1-1/2-quart casserole. Cook in Radarange Oven on FULL POWER for 3 to 4 minutes, or until beef is no longer pink. Stir halfway through cooking time. Drain.

1 (15 oz.) can tomato sauce
1 (1-3/4 oz.) envelope taco seasoning mix
1 (16 oz.) can refried beans
1/4 cup pimento-stuffed olives, chopped

2. Combine with remaining ingredients, except corn chips and cheese.

2-1/2 cups corn chips
1/2 cup Cheddar cheese, shredded

3. Spoon meat mixture over 2 cups of corn chips in 1-1/2-quart casserole. Cook in Radarange Oven on FULL POWER for 5 minutes, or until heated through.

4. Crush remaining corn chips. Sprinkle casserole with corn chips and cheese. Heat in Radarange Oven on Cookmatic Level 5 (SLO COOK) for 1 minute, or until cheese is melted.

Creamed Dried Beef

Yield: 2 servings

3 tablespoons butter or margarine

3 tablespoons all-purpose flour
1-1/2 cups milk

1 (4 oz.) pkg. dried beef
1 teaspoon instant, minced onion
Pepper

1. Place butter in 1-quart casserole. Heat in Radarange Oven on FULL POWER for 30 to 45 seconds, or until melted.

2. Blend in flour to form smooth paste. Gradually stir in milk. Cook in Radarange Oven on Cookmatic Level 8 (MEDIUM HIGH) for 3 to 4 minutes, or until thickened. Stir occasionally during cooking time.

3. Tear beef into bite-size pieces. Stir beef and onion into sauce. Season with pepper, as desired. Cook in Radarange Oven on Cookmatic Level 8 (MEDIUM HIGH) for about 1 minute, or until beef is warmed and temperature of 150°F is reached.*

MICRO-TIPS:

- May be served over toast, toasted English muffins, or mashed potatoes.

- Rinse dried beef in boiling water before adding to recipe to decrease saltiness.

*Use the Temperature-Control to stop the Radarange Oven at 150°F.

Dried Beef Casserole

Yield: 10 to 12 servings

4 cups cooked macaroni
2 (10-3/4 oz. each) cans cream of mushroom soup
1/2 cup milk
4 hard-cooked eggs, chopped*
1/4 cup onion, chopped
1/2 lb. longhorn cheese, cubed
1/4 lb. dried beef, chopped

1. Combine all ingredients in 3-quart casserole.

2. Cook in Radarange Oven on Cookmatic Level 8 (MEDIUM HIGH) for 20 to 25 minutes, or until temperature of 140°F to 150°F is reached.**

MICRO-TIPS:

*Remember, do not hard-cook eggs in the Radarange Oven.

- Rinse dried beef in boiling water before adding to casserole to decrease saltiness.

**Use the Temperature-Control to stop the Radarange Oven at 140°F or 150°F.

Beef and Snow Peas Casserole

Yield: 4 to 6 servings

1 lb. lean ground beef

1 (7 oz.) pkg. frozen Chinese pea pods

1/2 cup green onion, diagonally sliced

1 (10-3/4 oz.) can cream of mushroom soup
1 tablespoon soy sauce
1/8 teaspoon pepper

1 (3 oz.) can chow mein noodles

1. Crumble meat into 1-1/2-quart casserole. Cook in Radarange Oven on FULL POWER for 3 to 4 minutes, or until beef is no longer pink. Stir halfway through cooking time. Drain.

2. Place pea pods in small casserole or loosen package. Cook in Radarange Oven on FULL POWER for 45 seconds, or until partially thawed.

3. Mix onion into meat mixture. Layer pea pods over meat mixture.

4. Blend together soup, soy sauce and pepper. Spoon over meat mixture. Cook in Radarange Oven on FULL POWER for 10 to 15 minutes, or until temperature of 150°F is reached.

5. Place noodles on paper plate. Heat in Radarange Oven on FULL POWER for 1-1/2 minutes, or until just warmed. Stir halfway through heating time. Sprinkle over casserole.

Wiener Delight

Yield: 6 servings

12 ozs. frankfurters, cut in thin slices
1 (5.3 oz.) can evaporated milk
1 (10-3/4 oz.) can cream of chicken soup
1 (10-3/4 oz.) can cream of celery soup
1 (5-1/2 oz.) can chow mein noodles

1. Combine all ingredients, except 1/2 cup chow mein noodles. Pour into 2-quart casserole. Top with reserved chow mein noodles.

2. Heat in Radarange Oven on FULL POWER for 10 to 12 minutes, or until temperature of 150°F is reached.

Classic Meat Loaf

1-1/2 lbs. ground beef
1 (8 oz.) can tomato sauce
1 egg, slightly-beaten
1 cup quick-cooking, rolled oats
1 tablespoon instant, minced onion
1/8 teaspoon instant, minced garlic
1-1/2 teaspoons salt
1/4 teaspoon pepper

SAUCE (Optional)

1/3 cup catsup
1 teaspoon Worcestershire sauce
1 tablespoon dark brown sugar
1 tablespoon prepared mustard

1. Combine all ingredients. Pat into 9 x 5 x 2-inch loaf dish.

2. Cook in Radarange Oven on FULL POWER for 8 to 10 minutes, or until temperature of 160°F is reached.*

3. For sauce, blend ingredients well. Pour over meat loaf halfway through cooking time.

MICRO-TIPS:

•For a firmer meat loaf, decrease tomato sauce to 3/4 cup.

*Use the Temperature-Control to stop the Radarange Oven at 160°F.

Bacon-Topped Meat Loaf

Yield: 5 to 6 servings

1 lb. ground beef
1 (8 oz.) can tomato sauce
1 (5.3 oz.) can evaporated milk
1 egg
1 cup bread crumbs
1 medium onion, finely chopped
1 teaspoon salt
1/4 teaspoon pepper
3 slices bacon

1. Mix together all ingredients, except bacon. Pat into 9 x 5 x 2-inch loaf dish. Top with bacon slices.

2. Cook in Radarange Oven on FULL POWER for 14 to 15 minutes, or until temperature of 160°F is reached.*

MICRO-TIPS:

• This meat loaf makes a good sandwich filling when chilled.

*Use the Temperature-Control to stop the Radarange Oven at 160°F.

Deep Dish Pizza

Yield: 1, 8 x 12-inch pizza

3/4 lb. ground beef or Italian sausage

1 (6 oz.) can tomato paste
1/2 cup water
2 teaspoons instant, minced onion
2 teaspoons sugar
1/2 teaspoon salt
1/4 teaspoon oregano
1/4 teaspoon basil
1/4 teaspoon garlic powder
1/8 teaspoon pepper

2 tablespoons cornmeal

1 cup water
1 (13-3/4 oz.) pkg. hot roll mix

1-1/2 teaspoons bottled browning sauce

1 (4 oz.) can mushrooms, drained
1/4 cup grated Parmesan cheese
1 cup (4 oz.) Mozzarella cheese, shredded

1. Crumble meat in 1-quart casserole. Cook in Radarange Oven on FULL POWER for 3 to 4 minutes, or until beef is no longer pink. Stir halfway through cooking time. Drain.

2. Combine tomato paste, water and seasonings in 1-quart glass measure or casserole. Cook in Radarange Oven on FULL POWER for 2 to 3 minutes, or until mixture boils.

3. Grease bottom of 2-quart utility dish. Sprinkle with cornmeal.

4. Place water in 2-quart casserole. Heat in Radarange Oven on FULL POWER for 45 seconds to 1 minute, or until temperature of 110°F to 115°F is reached.* Dissolve yeast from roll mix in warm water.

5. Blend in browning sauce, and then flour from mix until dough is smooth. Spread dough over bottom and sides of utility dish. Prick dough with toothpick or tines of fork.

6. Bake in Radarange Oven on Cookmatic Level 7 (BAKE) for 5 to 6 minutes, or until center feels firm. Spread sauce over dough. Arrange meat and then mushrooms over sauce. Sprinkle Parmesan cheese and Mozzarella cheese over all.

7. Bake in Radarange Oven on Cookmatic Level 5 (SLO COOK) for 6 to 8 minutes, or until cheese is melted.

*MICRO-TIP: Use the Temperature-Control to stop the Radarange Oven at 110° F.

Pizza Meat Loaf

Yield: 4 to 6 servings

SAUCE

1 (6 oz.) can tomato paste
1 cup water
2 tablespoons instant, minced onion
1-1/2 teaspoons sugar
1/4 teaspoon salt
1/4 teaspoon oregano
Dash garlic powder
Dash cayenne pepper

1-1/2 lbs. ground chuck
1 cup fine bread crumbs
1 egg

1-1/2 teaspoons salt
3/4 teaspoon oregano
1/2 teaspoon basil
1/4 teaspoon pepper
1/8 teaspoon instant, minced garlic

1 cup Mozzarella cheese, shredded
1 tablespoon grated Parmesan cheese

1. Combine first 8 ingredients in 1-quart casserole. Cook in Radarange Oven on FULL POWER for 5 minutes. Stir twice during cooking. Reserve.

2. Mix 1/2 cup of reserved sauce together with remaining ingredients, except cheeses. Form into loaf in 1-1/2-quart utility dish. Cook in Radarange Oven on FULL POWER for 8 minutes, or until temperature of 160°F is reached.*

3. Top with remaining sauce and cheeses. Cook in Radarange Oven on Cookmatic Level 5 (SLO COOK) for 1 to 2 minutes, or until cheese is melted.

   *MICRO-TIP: Use the Temperature-Control to stop the Radarange Oven at 160°F.

Beefy Green Bean Bake

Yield: 6 servings

1 cup onion, chopped
1 tablespoon vegetable oil

1 lb. ground beef

1 (16 oz.) can green beans, drained
1 (10-3/4 oz.) can tomato soup
1 teaspoon salt
1/2 lb. frozen Tater Tots® or hash browns

1. Place onion and oil in 1-1/2-quart casserole. Cook in Radarange Oven on FULL POWER for 2 to 2-1/2 minutes, or until onion is tender.

2. Add meat. Cook in Radarange Oven on FULL POWER for 3 to 4 minutes, or until beef is no longer pink. Stir halfway through cooking time. Drain.

3. Blend green beans, soup and salt into meat mixture. Spread Tater Tots® over top.

4. Cook in Radarange Oven on FULL POWER for 10 to 12 minutes, or until heated through, and temperature of 150°F is reached.*

   *MICRO-TIP: Use the Temperature-Control to stop the Radarange Oven at 150°F.

Frank 'N' Green Bean Casserole

Yield: 4 servings

1/4 cup butter or margarine
3 tablespoons all-purpose flour
2 cups milk

1 lb. frankfurters, cut in 1-inch pieces
1 (16 oz.) can green beans, drained
1/2 teaspoon Worcestershire sauce
1/2 teaspoon salt
Dash pepper
1/2 cup Cheddar cheese, shredded
1 tablespoon cornflake crumbs

1. Place butter in 1-1/2-quart casserole. Heat in Radarange Oven on FULL POWER for 45 seconds to 1 minute, or until melted. Stir in flour until smooth. Gradually blend in milk. Cook in Radarange Oven on Cookmatic Level 8 (MEDIUM HIGH) for 5 to 7 minutes, or until thickened. Stir occasionally during cooking.

2. Stir in frankfurters, green beans, Worcestershire sauce, salt and pepper. Top with cheese and crumbs. Cook in Radarange Oven on Cookmatic Level 5 (SLO COOK) for 5 minutes, or until heated through, cheese is melted, and temperature of 150°F is reached.*

MICRO-TIPS:

•Serve over toasted bread or English muffins.

*Use the Temperature-Control to stop the Radarange Oven at 150°F.

Meatza Pie

Yield: 4 to 5 servings

1 lb. ground beef
2/3 cup evaporated milk
1/2 cup bread crumbs
1 teaspoon instant, minced onion
1/2 teaspoon garlic salt

1/3 cup tomato paste
1/8 teaspoon oregano
1/8 teaspoon basil
1/4 teaspoon salt
1/8 teaspoon pepper

1 (4 oz.) can mushrooms, drained

1/2 cup Mozzarella cheese, shredded
Grated Parmesan cheese

1. Combine beef, milk, crumbs, onion and garlic salt. Mix well. Press into 9 or 10-inch glass pie plate.

2. Combine tomato paste, oregano, basil, salt and pepper. Spread over meat.

3. Sprinkle mushrooms over tomato paste and seasonings. Cook in Radarange Oven on FULL POWER for 8 minutes, or until meat is fully cooked.

4. Sprinkle Mozzarella cheese over all. Cook in Radarange Oven on Cookmatic Level 5 (SLO COOK) for 1 minute, or until cheese is melted. Sprinkle with Parmesan cheese, as desired.

Cantonese Ribs (page 215)

Hamburger Pie

Yield: 5 to 6 servings

1 lb. ground beef
1 (8 oz.) can green beans or
    corn, drained
1 egg
1 small onion, chopped
1 cup bread crumbs
1/2 cup catsup
1/2 cup evaporated milk
1 teaspoon salt
1/8 teaspoon pepper

2 cups hot mashed potatoes
1/2 cup sharp Cheddar cheese,
    shredded

1. Mix together beef, green beans, egg, onion, bread crumbs, catsup, milk, salt and pepper. Press mixture into 9-inch glass pie plate. Bake in Radarange Oven on FULL POWER for 8 to 10 minutes, or until meat is cooked as desired.

2. Top meat with mashed potatoes. Sprinkle with cheese. Bake in Radarange Oven on Cookmatic Level 5 (SLO COOK) for 1 minute, or until cheese is melted.

MICRO-TIPS:

•Instant mashed potatoes may be used, if desired. Prepare 4 servings as directed on package. See instructions on page 260.

•This dish may be served with hot catsup, if desired.

Swedish Meat Balls

Yield: 4 servings

1 cup milk
1 cup bread crumbs

1/2 lb. ground round steak
1/2 lb. ground lean pork
1 egg
1 tablespoon steak sauce
1 tablespoon instant, minced onion
1 teaspoon salt
1/4 teaspoon pepper

3 tablespoons butter or margarine

1/4 cup all-purpose flour
1 cup water
2 teaspoons instant beef bouillon

1. Pour milk over crumbs. Let stand for 15 minutes.

2. Lightly mix in meats, and then egg and seasonings. Shape into 12 meat balls. Place meat balls on rack in 2-quart utility dish. Cover with waxed paper. Cook in Radarange Oven, covered, on FULL POWER for 5 to 7 minutes, or until no longer pink.

3. Remove meat balls and reserve. Drain grease from 2-quart utility dish. Add butter. Heat in Radarange Oven on FULL POWER for 30 to 40 seconds, or until melted.

4. Sprinkle flour into hot butter in dish. Stir until smooth. Gradually blend in water and bouillon, stirring constantly. Cook in Radarange Oven on FULL POWER for 2 to 3 minutes, or until thickened. Stir 2 to 3 times during cooking.

5. Place meat balls in gravy. Cook in Radarange Oven, covered, on FULL POWER for 5 to 7 minutes, or until meat is cooked as desired.

Basic Meat Balls

Yield: 4 servings

1 lb. ground beef
1 small onion, finely chopped
1/3 cup dry bread crumbs
1/4 cup milk
1 egg
3/4 teaspoon salt
1/8 teaspoon pepper

1. Combine all ingredients in large mixing bowl. Mix well. Form into about 18 meat balls, 1-1/2 inches each in diameter. Arrange in 8 x 2-inch round dish. Cover with waxed paper.

2. Cook in Radarange Oven, covered, on FULL POWER for 4 to 6 minutes, or until meat is cooked as desired. Drain.

   MICRO-TIP: May be served with "Sweet-Sour Sauce," page 268, or "Mornay Sauce," page 271.

Oriental Meat Ball Supper

Yield: 4 to 6 servings

1 lb. ground beef
1/4 cup fine bread crumbs
1 egg
1 teaspoon instant, minced onion
1/8 teaspoon garlic powder

1 (10-3/4 oz.) can golden cream of mushroom soup
1 tablespoon cornstarch
1 cup canned tomatoes, chopped and drained
1 cup cooked rice
2 tablespoons brown sugar
1 tablespoon vinegar
1 tablespoon soy sauce
Dash pepper

Chow mein noodles (optional)

1. Combine beef, bread crumbs, egg, onion and garlic powder. Form into meat balls, 1-1/2 inches each in diameter. Place in 2-quart casserole. Cook in Radarange Oven on FULL POWER for 4 to 5 minutes, or until beef is no longer pink. Drain.

2. Blend together soup and cornstarch. Stir in remaining ingredients, except chow mein noodles. Pour over meat balls.

3. Cook in Radarange Oven on FULL POWER for 8 to 10 minutes, or until temperature of 150°F is reached. Stir halfway through cooking time. Top with chow mein noodles before serving, if desired.

Porcupine Meat Balls

Yield: 6 to 8 servings

1-1/2 lbs. ground beef
1 cup cooked rice
1 egg
1/2 cup bread crumbs, or quick-cooking, rolled oats
1 small onion, minced
2 tablespoons tomato paste
1 teaspoon salt
1/2 teaspoon pepper

1 (15 oz.) can tomato sauce
1 teaspoon sugar
1/8 teaspoon oregano
1/8 teaspoon instant, minced garlic

1. Combine first 8 ingredients and form into 8 large meat balls. Place in 2-quart utility dish. Cook in Radarange Oven on FULL POWER for 8 minutes, or until beef is no longer pink. Drain.

2. Mix together tomato sauce, sugar, oregano, and garlic. Pour over meat balls. Cook in Radarange Oven on FULL POWER for 4 to 5 minutes, or until bubbling.

   MICRO-TIP: Sprinkle with grated Parmesan cheese before serving, if desired.

Veal Parmigiana

Yield: 4 servings

1 egg, slightly-beaten
2 tablespoons milk
1 teaspoon salt
3/4 to 1 lb. veal cutlets
1/2 cup dry bread crumbs
1/4 cup grated Parmesan cheese

1. Combine egg, milk and salt in small bowl. Dip veal first in egg mixture, and then in mixture of bread crumbs and cheese.

2 tablespoons butter or margarine

2. Preheat large browning skillet for maximum amount of time, according to manufacturer's instructions. Add half of butter and half of meat. Cook in Radarange Oven on FULL POWER for 2 to 2-1/2 minutes, or until cooked. Turn meat over after 1 minute of cooking. Wipe out skillet with paper towel. Re-preheat browning skillet, according to manufacturer's instructions. Repeat cooking time with remaining butter and meat. Return all meat to skillet.

1 (8 oz.) can tomato sauce
1/4 teaspoon Italian seasoning
1/8 teaspoon instant, minced garlic

3. Combine tomato sauce, seasoning and garlic. Pour over meat. Cook in Radarange Oven, covered, on FULL POWER for 6 minutes, or until meat is tender.

4 ozs. Mozzarella cheese, sliced

4. Top with cheese. Cook in Radarange Oven, covered, on Cookmatic Level 5 (SLO COOK) for 1-1/2 to 2 minutes, or until cheese is melted.

Veal Scallopini

Yield: 4 servings

1/4 cup vegetable oil
1 lb. veal, thinly sliced
1 clove garlic, minced

1. Preheat large browning skillet for maximum amount of time, according to manufacturer's instructions. Add oil, veal and garlic. Cook in Radarange Oven on FULL POWER for 2 minutes, or until browned. Turn meat over halfway through cooking time. Remove garlic and veal from skillet.

3/4 cup onion, sliced
1 (4 oz.) can mushrooms, drained
2 tablespoons all-purpose flour
1 teaspoon salt
1/8 teaspoon pepper
1 (8 oz.) can tomato sauce
1/2 cup water

2. Stir onion and mushrooms into hot oil. Cook in Radarange Oven on FULL POWER for 3 minutes. Stir in flour, salt and pepper until well-blended. Gradually stir in tomato sauce and water. Cook in Radarange Oven on FULL POWER for 5 minutes. Stir halfway through cooking time.

3. Arrange veal in skillet. Cook in Radarange Oven, covered, on FULL POWER for 5 to 6 minutes, or until veal is tender.

Veal Cordon Bleu

Yield: 6 to 8 servings

2 lbs. veal cutlets, thinly sliced
1 (6 oz.) pkg. sliced ham or prosiutto
1 (6 oz.) pkg. sliced Mozzarella cheese, halved

1. Pound cutlets to 1/8-inch thickness, if necessary. Top each cutlet with slice of ham and cheese. Roll each up, starting from narrow ends. Secure with toothpicks.

1 egg, slightly-beaten
1/2 cup seasoned bread crumbs
1 (10-3/4 oz.) can golden cream of mushroom soup

2. Dip rolls in egg, and then in crumbs. Place seam-side-down in 2-quart utility dish. Pour soup over rolls.

3. Bake in Radarange Oven, covered, on Cookmatic Level 8 (MEDIUM HIGH) for 12 to 15 minutes, or until veal is tender.*

*MICRO-TIP: You may want to turn dish halfway through cooking time.

Tangy Pork Ribs

Yield: 2 to 3 servings

2 lbs. pork ribs

1 cup onion, chopped
2 tablespoons brown sugar
2 tablespoons vinegar
1 teaspoon prepared mustard
1 (15 oz.) can tomato sauce

Salt
Pepper

1. Place ribs in 2-quart utility dish.
2. Combine remaining ingredients, except salt and pepper. Pour over ribs.
3. Cook in Radarange Oven, covered, on Cookmatic Level 5 (SLO COOK) for 25 to 30 minutes, or until meat is tender, and temperature of 170°F is reached. Turn ribs over halfway through cooking time. Season with salt and pepper, as desired.

Cantonese Ribs

Yield: 6 servings

4 lbs. country style pork ribs

1/2 cup soy sauce
1/2 cup dry sherry
1/2 cup lemon juice
1-1/2 tablespoons brown sugar
1 teaspoon lemon peel, grated
1/2 teaspoon garlic powder
1/4 teaspoon ginger

1 cup orange marmalade

1. Separate ribs. Place in 2-quart utility dish.
2. Combine remaining ingredients, except orange marmalade, in 2-cup glass measure. Pour over ribs. Cover with plastic wrap. Let stand at room temperature for 2 hours. Baste frequently. Drain, reserving 1/3 cup marinade.
3. Cook in Radarange Oven, covered, on Cookmatic Level 5 (SLO COOK) for 25 minutes. Turn ribs over halfway through cooking time.
4. Mix together marmalade and reserved marinade. Pour over ribs. Cook in Radarange Oven, covered, on Cookmatic Level 5 (SLO COOK) for 20 to 25 minutes, or until meat is tender and temperature of 170°F is reached.

Breaded Pork Chops

Yield: 6 servings

2 to 2-1/2 lbs. pork chops
1 (2-1/4 oz.) pkg. seasoned coating mix for pork

1. Coat pork chops with seasoned mix, according to package directions. Place pork chops in 2-quart utility dish.
2. Cook in Radarange Oven on Cookmatic Level 5 (SLO COOK) for 30 to 40 minutes, or until chops are tender.

MICRO-TIP: Breaded pork chops will not be crisp when prepared in the Radarange Oven.

Chili Chops

Yield: 4 servings

4 pork chops (about 1-1/2 lbs.)

1/3 cup chili sauce
1 (4 oz.) can sliced mushrooms, drained (optional)
1 tablespoon Worcestershire sauce
1 tablespoon vinegar
1/2 teaspoon salt

1. Preheat large browning skillet for maximum amount of time, according to manufacturer's instructions. Place chops in skillet. Cook in Radarange Oven on FULL POWER for 2 minutes. Turn chops over, halfway through cooking time. Drain, if necessary.
2. Combine remaining ingredients. Pour over chops.
3. Cook in Radarange Oven, covered, on Cookmatic Level 5 (SLO COOK) for 15 to 20 minutes, or until chops are tender. Turn chops over halfway through cooking time.

Pork Chops Maui

Yield: 4 servings

4 pork chops (about 1-1/2 lbs.)

1/2 cup canned, crushed pineapple, drained
1/4 cup onion, chopped
1/4 cup brown sugar, firmly packed
3 tablespoons cider vinegar
1 clove garlic, minced
1 teaspoon salt
1/2 teaspoon orange peel, grated (optional)
1/2 teaspoon ground ginger
1/4 teaspoon seasoned pepper
Dash Tabasco sauce

1. Preheat large browning skillet for maximum amount of time, according to manufacturer's instructions. Place chops in skillet. Cook in Radarange Oven on Cookmatic Level 5 (SLO COOK) for 5 minutes. Turn chops over halfway through cooking time. Drain.

2. Combine remaining ingredients. Pour over chops.

3. Cook in Radarange Oven, covered, on Cookmatic Level 5 (SLO COOK) for 14 to 16 minutes, or until chops are tender. Turn chops over halfway through cooking time.

Stuffed Pork Chops

Yield: 4 servings

4 pork chops, 1-inch thick

1 cup stuffing croutons
2 tablespoons butter or margarine, melted
1 tablespoon instant, minced onion
1 teaspoon parsley flakes
1/4 teaspoon salt
Dash pepper
Dash poultry seasoning
1 tablespoon hot water

Spray-on vegetable coating

4 slices apple
1/4 cup honey
Nutmeg

1. Cut large gash or pocket in side of each chop.

2. Mix together stuffing croutons, butter, onion and seasonings in large mixing bowl. Gradually add hot water, until stuffing is just moistened.

3. Divide stuffing, fill each chop.

4. Preheat large browning skillet for maximum amount of time, according to manufacturer's instructions. Spray with vegetable coating. Place chops in skillet. Cook in Radarange Oven on Cookmatic Level 5 (SLO COOK) for 5 minutes. Turn chops over after 1 minute of cooking time.

5. Place apple slice on each chop. Brush generously with honey. Sprinkle with nutmeg, as desired.

6. Bake in Radarange Oven, covered, on Cookmatic Level 5 (SLO COOK) for 17 to 20 minutes, or until chops are tender.

Oriental Pork

Yield: 4 to 6 servings

1 (1 lb.) pork tenderloin
3 tablespoons soy sauce
1 tablespoon cornstarch
1 teaspoon instant chicken
   bouillon

1 (6 oz.) pkg. frozen pea pods
1 (8 oz.) can bamboo shoots,
   drained
1 (8 oz.) can water chestnuts,
   drained and sliced
1/2 cup green onions, sliced
1/2 cup onion, sliced
1/2 cup water

1. Trim fat from pork. Cut pork into bite-size pieces. Combine pork, soy sauce, cornstarch, and bouillon in 2-quart casserole.

2. Cook in Radarange Oven, covered, on Cookmatic Level 5 (SLO COOK) for 7 to 9 minutes, or until pork is no longer pink. Add remaining ingredients.

3. Cook in Radarange Oven, covered, on Cookmatic Level 5 (SLO COOK) for 10 to 12 minutes, or until meat and vegetables are cooked as desired. Stir halfway through cooking time.

   MICRO-TIP: This dish may be served over cooked rice, if desired.

Sweet-Sour Pork

Yield: 4 servings

2 tablespoons vegetable oil
1-1/2 lbs. boneless pork
   loin, cubed

1 (1 lb., 4 oz.) can pineapple
   chunks, with liquid
1/2 cup water
1/4 cup brown sugar, firmly packed
3 tablespoons vinegar
2 tablespoons cornstarch
1 tablespoon soy sauce
1/2 teaspoon salt

1. Place pork in 1-1/2-quart casserole. Cook in Radarange Oven, covered, on FULL POWER for 3 to 4 minutes, or until meat is fully cooked and tender. Stir halfway through cooking time.

2. Combine liquid from pineapple, water, brown sugar, vinegar, cornstarch, soy sauce and salt in 2-cup glass measure or small bowl. Cook in Radarange Oven on FULL POWER for 3 to 4 minutes, or until thickened. Stir halfway through cooking time.

3. Pour sauce over pork. Add pineapple. Cook in Radarange Oven on FULL POWER for 2 to 3 minutes, or until heated through.

Shepherd's Pie

Yield: 4 servings

2 cups cooked pork or
   lamb, cubed
1 (10-1/4 oz.) can beef gravy
1 (8 oz.) can whole mushrooms,
   drained*
1 (8 oz.) can sliced carrots,
   drained*
1 (8 oz.) can green peas, drained*
1/2 teaspoon salt
1/2 teaspoon pepper
3 cups hot, mashed potatoes

1. Combine meat, gravy, mushrooms, carrots and peas in 9-inch glass pie plate. Season with salt and pepper. Mix lightly to combine ingredients. Spread potatoes over top.

2. Heat in Radarange Oven on FULL POWER for 8 to 10 minutes, or until temperature of 140°F is reached.***

   MICRO-TIPS:

   *Frozen vegetables may be used. First, cook and drain.

   •This is a good way to use leftover meat.

   ***Use the Temperature-Control to stop the Radarange Oven at 140°F.

Pork Mushroom Bake

Yield: 4 to 6 servings

1-1/2 to 2 lbs. pork chops or steaks
1 cup onion, sliced
1 teaspoon salt
1/4 teaspoon pepper
1 (10-3/4 oz.) can golden cream
   of mushroom soup

1. Place pork chops in a 2-1/2 to 3-quart casserole. Top with onion, salt, pepper and soup.

2. Cook in Radarange Oven, covered, on Cookmatic Level 5 (SLO COOK) for 30 to 45 minutes, or until pork is tender. Turn pork chops over halfway through cooking time.

Baked Canadian Bacon

Yield: 8 servings

2 lbs. Canadian bacon

1/2 cup brown sugar, firmly packed
1/2 cup unsweetened pineapple
   juice
1/2 teaspoon dry mustard

1. Place Canadian bacon in 1-1/2-quart casserole.

2. Combine brown sugar, pineapple juice and mustard. Pour over Canadian bacon.

3. Cook in Radarange Oven, covered, on Cookmatic Level 5 (SLO COOK) for 25 to 30 minutes, or until temperature of 130°F is reached.* Turn meat over halfway through cooking time.

   *MICRO-TIP: Use the Temperature-Control to stop the Radarange Oven at 130°F.

Pork-Vegetable Roast

Yield: 6 to 8 servings

2-1/2 to 3 lb. pork roast
Garlic salt
Pepper
3 medium potatoes, peeled and
   cut in eighths
1 medium onion, sliced
1/2 teaspoon oregano
1 (14-1/2 oz.) can tomatoes

1. Place pork roast in 3-quart casserole. Sprinkle with garlic salt and pepper, as desired. Add remaining ingredients.

2. Cook in Radarange Oven, covered, on Cookmatic Level 5 (SLO COOK) for 1 to 1-1/2 hours, or until temperature of 170°F is reached.*

   *MICRO-TIP: Use the Temperature-Control to stop the Radarange Oven at 170°F.

Roast Pork and Sauerkraut

Yield: 4 servings

1 (1 lb., 4 oz.) can sauerkraut,
   with liquid
1 teaspoon caraway seed
4 large (3 to 4 ozs. each) slices
   cooked roast pork

Salt
Pepper

1. Drain kraut. Reserve 1/2 cup juice. Turn kraut into 1-1/2-quart casserole. Add kraut juice and caraway seed. Arrange meat slices on top of kraut mixture.

2. Heat in Radarange Oven on FULL POWER for 4 minutes, or until heated through. Season with salt and pepper, as desired.

Spiced Cider Baked Ham

Yield: 4 to 6 servings

2 slices (2-1/2 to 3 lbs.)
  ham steak, center cut
1 large onion, thinly sliced
1 cup sweet cider or apple juice
3 tablespoons brown sugar
1 teaspoon cloves (optional)

SAUCE

1/2 cup seedless raisins
2 tablespoons cornstarch
2 tablespoons water
1/4 teaspoon cinnamon
1/8 teaspoon nutmeg

1. Place both steaks in 2-quart utility dish. Arrange onion over steaks. Mix together cider and sugar. Pour over onion. Place cloves in fat along edges of ham, if desired. Cook in Radarange Oven, covered, on FULL POWER for 8 to 10 minutes. Turn ham over halfway through cooking time.

2. Remove ham from juice. Add raisins to juice. Combine cornstarch, water, cinnamon and nutmeg. Add to juice.

3. Cook in Radarange Oven on FULL POWER for 3 to 4 minutes, or until thickened. Stir occasionally. Serve sauce over ham.

Old-Fashioned German Supper

Yield: 6 servings

4 strips bacon
1-1/2 tablespoons all-purpose flour

1 (2 lb.) can sauerkraut
3 apples, cubed
1/4 cup brown sugar, firmly packed
1-1/2 teaspoons caraway seeds

1-1/2 to 2 lbs. bratwurst or pork
  sausage
2 tablespoons bottled browning
  sauce (optional)

1. Cut bacon in small pieces. Place in 3-quart casserole. Cook in Radarange Oven on FULL POWER for 3 to 4 minutes, or until crisp. Remove bacon pieces and add flour to drippings.

2. In separate dish, combine bacon pieces, sauerkraut, apples, brown sugar and caraway seeds. Mix well.

3. Place half of sauerkraut mixture in casserole. Stir well to blend in flour mixture.

4. Brush bratwurst with bottled browning sauce and arrange on top of sauerkraut mixture. Pierce skin of bratwurst with knife or tines of fork. Add rest of sauerkraut mixture to cover bratwurst.

5. Cook in Radarange Oven, covered, on Cookmatic Level 5 (SLO COOK) for 35 to 45 minutes, or until heated through.

Fancy Ham and Beef Loaf

Yield: 8 to 10 servings

1 lb. ground ham
1/2 lb. ground chuck
1 cup milk
2 eggs, slightly-beaten
1 cup bread crumbs
1 teaspoon dry mustard
1/2 teaspoon Worcestershire sauce
1/2 teaspoon salt
1/4 teaspoon pepper

1/3 cup dark brown sugar, firmly packed
1 (8 oz.) can crushed pineapple

1. Combine meats, milk, eggs, crumbs, mustard, Worcestershire sauce, salt and pepper. Pat into 9 x 5 x 2-inch loaf dish.

2. Combine brown sugar and pineapple. Pour over meat loaf.

3. Cook in Radarange Oven on FULL POWER for 10 to 12 minutes, or until temperature of 160°F is reached.*

   *MICRO-TIP: Use the Temperature-Control to stop the Radarange Oven at 160°F.

Tangy Ham Loaf

Yield: 4 to 5 servings

1 lb. ground ham
1/3 cup milk
1 egg, slightly-beaten
1/2 cup graham cracker crumbs
1/4 cup onion, finely chopped
Dash pepper

1/2 cup dark brown sugar, firmly packed
1/4 cup tomato juice
1 teaspoon dry mustard
1 teaspoon vinegar

1. Blend together ham, milk, egg, crumbs, onion and pepper. Pat into 9 x 5 x 2-inch loaf dish.

2. Combine sugar, tomato juice, mustard and vinegar. Pour over meat loaf.

3. Cook in Radarange Oven on FULL POWER for 9 to 11 minutes, or until temperature of 160°F is reached.*

   *MICRO-TIP: Use the Temperature-Control to stop the Radarange Oven at 160°F.

Spanish Lamb Chops

Yield: 4 servings

4 (1/2 lb. each) shoulder lamb chops
1 tablespoon vegetable oil

1 (16 oz.) can stewed tomatoes
1 small green pepper, sliced
1/2 cup onion, chopped
4 slices lemon
1 teaspoon salt
1/4 teaspoon pepper

1. Preheat large browning skillet for maximum amount of time, according to manufacturer's instructions. Place oil, and then chops in skillet. Cook in Radarange Oven on FULL POWER for 4 minutes. Turn meat over halfway through cooking time.

2. Mix in tomatoes, green pepper, onion, lemon, salt and pepper. Cook in Radarange Oven, covered, on Cookmatic Level 5 (SLO COOK) for 25 to 35 minutes, or until meat is tender.

Ham Tetrazzini

Yield: 6 to 8 servings

1 (4 oz.) can sliced mushrooms
Water

1/2 cup onion, chopped
1/2 cup celery, chopped
6 tablespoons butter or margarine

6 tablespoons all-purpose flour
1/4 teaspoon pepper
1 cup light cream
2 teaspoons instant chicken
  bouillon

3 cups ham, cubed
1 (7 oz.) pkg. spaghetti, cooked
1/4 cup grated Parmesan cheese

1. Drain mushrooms. Reserve liquid. Add enough water to measure 2 cups.

2. Place onion, celery, and butter in 2-quart casserole. Cook in Radarange Oven on FULL POWER for 4 minutes, or until onion and celery are tender. Stir halfway through cooking time.

3. Mix in flour, pepper and reserved liquid. Stir until smooth. Cook in Radarange Oven on FULL POWER for 5 minutes. Blend in light cream, and dissolve bouillon in mixture.

4. Lightly stir in mushrooms and ham. Blend spaghetti into mixture. Sprinkle with Parmesan cheese.

5. Bake in Radarange Oven on FULL POWER for 13 to 15 minutes, or until temperature of 150°F is reached,* and center of casserole is hot and slightly bubbly.

MICRO-TIPS:

•For extra flavor, add 3 tablespoons dry sherry in Step #4.

*Use the Temperature-Control to stop the Radarange Oven at 150°F.

Quick Cassoulet

Yield: 6 servings

1/2 lb. sausage links, halved
1 cup onion, chopped
1 clove garlic, minced

1-1/2 cups boiling water
1 tablespoon parsley, minced
1/2 teaspoon thyme, crushed
2 cups cooked lamb, cubed*
2 (16 ozs. each) cans Boston-style
  baked beans
1 (8 oz.) can tomato sauce

1/4 cup dried bread crumbs**
  (optional)

1. Place sausage, onion and garlic in e-quart casserole. Cook in Radarange Oven on FULL POWER for 3-1/2 to 4 minutes, or until onion and garlic are tender, and sausage is no longer pink. Stir halfway through cooking time. Drain.

2. Add remaining ingredients, except bread crumbs, to sausage mixture. Cook in Radarange Oven on FULL POWER for 8 to 10 minutes, or until heated through, and temperature of 150°F is reached.****

3. Sprinkle toasted bread crumbs over top before serving, if desired.

MICRO-TIPS:

*Pork may be substituted for lamb.

**See page 362 for instructions on preparing dried bread crumbs in the Radarange Oven.

****Use the Temperature-Control to stop the Radarange Oven at 150°F.

In this chapter, you will find poultry prepared in a variety of ways in the Radarange Oven. You'll find that poultry will be more moist when prepared in the Radarange Oven, than when prepared in a conventional oven.

Herbs such as tarragon, curry, saffron and sage complement poultry. The next time you have leftover chicken, or make a chicken salad, look for an appropriate recipe in this chapter. Many recipes are well-suited to using leftover chicken or turkey, and the poultry will taste freshly cooked when reheated in the Radarange Oven.

Before preparing poultry, read the general defrosting and cooking hints.

General Hints for Defrosting Poultry

1. Poultry may remain in its original wrappings for defrosting. Pierce the plastic wrap or bag before defrosting. Remove metal clamps from poultry as soon as possible, during or after defrosting.
2. Poultry may be placed directly on the Radarange Oven glass tray for defrosting.
3. When defrosting whole poultry, large poultry may need to be turned over occasionally for even defrosting. Remove loosened giblets as soon as possible, and set them aside for gravy, soup or dressing.
4. When defrosting poultry pieces, turn the pieces over, separate, and rearrange them during defrosting. Cover pieces with heavy-duty plastic wrap to hasten defrosting.
5. If poultry begins to feel warm or starts to cook during defrosting, remove it from the Radarange Oven and let it stand, covered, or place it in cold water to finish defrosting.
6. Since poultry is such an irregularly-shaped food, it may need to be defrosted partially on Cookmatic Level 1 (WARM) to prevent cooking around the leg and wing areas. Large poultry weighing over 5 pounds requires a soaking period in cold water to complete the defrosting process.

General Hints for Cooking Poultry

1. Remove metal clamps from poultry and tie the legs and wings with string, if desired, before cooking.
2. Small poultry items can be cooked on the cooking grill. The 2-quart utility dish will catch the drippings.
3. The Radarange Oven glass tray can be used as a "roasting platter." You may place large poultry directly on the glass tray for cooking. The fluted edge will catch juices, until they can be "basted off."
4. The Radarange Oven will hold a family-size turkey. You may prefer to cook your turkey in a roasting bag. Choose a heavy-duty roasting bag. Pierce the bag before cooking. Secure the bag with string. Do not secure the bag with a metal twist.
5. Poultry weighing 3 pounds or more will brown by itself "naturally" in the Radarange Oven. For some poultry items, you may wish to add additional color. Seasoned coating mixes and paprika will improve the color of poultry. Try making a paste of 1 tablespoon of paprika and 2 tablespoons of shortening. Rub this paste over poultry for a nice reddish-brown color.
6. A non-salted vegetable oil is best for basting poultry. Do not salt poultry until just before serving, since salt will dehydrate the surface of poultry, making it tough. Salt may be added before cooking to a sauce that covers the poultry.
7. Begin cooking chicken pieces skin-side-down. Turn the pieces over halfway through the cooking time in most recipes.
8. When cooking whole poultry, begin by cooking breast-side-down. When the poultry is turned over, cooking can be completed breast-side-up for a nicer, browned, finished appearance.
9. Pierce the skin of poultry before placing it in the Radarange Oven, to prevent popping.
10. Cook poultry, covered. Use a glass lid or heavy-duty plastic wrap since they are more water-vapor-proof than other types of coverings. Poultry pieces cooked in a sauce should be cooked, covered, to blend flavors.

uckling Bordeaux (page 236)

11. When browning chicken in a browning skillet, do not cover the skillet with the glass lid, since a "steamed" flavor will develop. A paper towel covering may be used to prevent spattering. Do not allow a paper towel to touch the bottom of the hot browning skillet.

12. Poultry should be cooked on FULL POWER for approximately 5 to 6 minutes per pound. Since poultry is a tender food, a lower Cookmatic Cycle or setting is not necessary for cooking. Poultry pieces will cook slightly faster per pound than whole poultry. Poultry cooked in a sauce which includes a "special" or "delicate" ingredient may be cooked at a lower Cookmatic Level or setting.

13. You may wish to stuff poultry with a dressing. The addition of dressing should not alter the cooking time.

14. After the poultry has started to brown, you may wish to cover the wing tips, the narrow part of the legs and the high point of the breast bone with small, thin strips of foil. This process is called shielding. The small amount of foil will slow the cooking of these areas, and prevent them from dehydrating and over-cooking.

15. Large poultry items, such as large turkeys may need to be turned over several times during cooking, for more even cooking.

16. When cooking large poultry items, you may wish to "baste off" the juices as they accumulate. The microwaves will be attracted to the liquid, thus keeping the energy away from the poultry and resulting in a longer cooking time. By "basting off," spattering is also reduced.

17. Poultry is done when it is fork tender, and the thickest part of the thigh or "dark meat" has a temperature of 170°F. Also, the flesh and juices should no longer be pink. Juices should be clear. Slice the poultry between the leg and body to see if it is done. On whole poultry, the joints of the legs should move easily when done. The thick meat on the leg should feel soft. The "white meat" pieces, such as the breast should register 180° F when done. Since poultry contains many bones, and since large poultry items need to be turned over 2 to 3 times during cooking for good results, cook poultry for the 5 to 6 minutes per pound, rather than using the Automatic Temperature Control for cooking. The Automatic Temperature Control may be used, however, when the cooking process is finished. Check the temperature of both the "dark" and "white" meat areas, before serving.

18. A 10 to 15 minute standing time before carving will help the juices to set in the meat, keep the meat more moist, and make the poultry easier to carve. The poultry will continue to cook if it stands, covered. Poultry should be completely defrosted before cooking.

19. When preparing your own favorite poultry recipes, use a recipe in this chapter as a guide. Use FULL POWER for most poultry cooking, unless the dish includes a "delicate" ingredient. Then, select a lower Cookmatic Level or setting.

Shake and Bake Chicken

Yield: 6 servings

2 lb. broiler-fryer, cut-up
1 (1-1/4 oz.) pkg. seasoned coating mix for chicken*
Spray-on vegetable coating

1. Coat chicken with seasoned mix by shaking in bag, according to directions on package.

2. Preheat large browning skillet or grill for maximum amount of time, according to manufacturer's instructions. Spray skillet with vegetable coating.

3. Arrange chicken with larger pieces, such as thighs and breasts, at corners, skin-side-down. Place small pieces such as legs and wings at center.

4. Bake in Radarange Oven on FULL POWER for 8 to 10 minutes, or until chicken is tender. Turn chicken pieces over after 1 minute of cooking. Turn chicken pieces over again halfway through cooking time.

*MICRO-TIP: You may use your own favorite coating for the chicken in this recipe.

POULTRY DEFROSTING CHART*

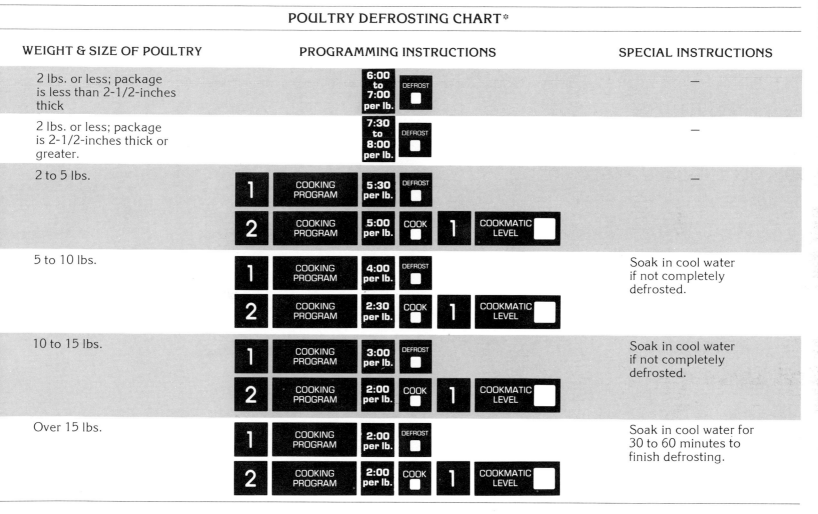

WEIGHT & SIZE OF POULTRY	PROGRAMMING INSTRUCTIONS	SPECIAL INSTRUCTIONS
2 lbs. or less; package is less than 2-1/2-inches thick	6:00 to 7:00 per lb. — DEFROST	—
2 lbs. or less; package is 2-1/2-inches thick or greater.	7:30 to 8:00 per lb. — DEFROST	—
2 to 5 lbs.	1 — COOKING PROGRAM — 5:30 per lb. — DEFROST 2 — COOKING PROGRAM — 5:00 per lb. — COOK — 1 — COOKMATIC LEVEL	—
5 to 10 lbs.	1 — COOKING PROGRAM — 4:00 per lb. — DEFROST 2 — COOKING PROGRAM — 2:30 per lb. — COOK — 1 — COOKMATIC LEVEL	Soak in cool water if not completely defrosted.
10 to 15 lbs.	1 — COOKING PROGRAM — 3:00 per lb. — DEFROST 2 — COOKING PROGRAM — 2:00 per lb. — COOK — 1 — COOKMATIC LEVEL	Soak in cool water if not completely defrosted.
Over 15 lbs.	1 — COOKING PROGRAM — 2:00 per lb. — DEFROST 2 — COOKING PROGRAM — 2:00 per lb. — COOK — 1 — COOKMATIC LEVEL	Soak in cool water for 30 to 60 minutes to finish defrosting.

*The "Poultry Defrosting Chart" lists defrosting times for all types of poultry, in terms of minutes-per-pound. The chart applies to Cornish hens, capon, duck and individual poultry pieces, as well as to whole chicken and turkey. For best results when defrosting, be sure to consider the general hints.

General Instructions for Defrosting Poultry

1. Place the frozen poultry on a plate or cooking grill. Cover with plastic wrap. Remove all metal pieces, if possible.

2. Defrost, according to the instructions on the chart. Turn large poultry over halfway through the defrosting time for best results. Soak large poultry in cool water, if necessary, to finish defrosting.

FROZEN FRIED CHICKEN COOKING CHART

PACKAGE SIZE	PROGRAMMING INSTRUCTIONS

PACKAGE SIZE	PROGRAMMING INSTRUCTIONS			
16 oz.	1 COOKING PROGRAM	6:00	DEFROST ☐	
	2 COOKING PROGRAM	3:00	HOLD ☐	
	3 COOKING PROGRAM	3:00 to 4:00	COOK ☐	
28 oz.	1 COOKING PROGRAM	7:00	DEFROST ☐	
	2 COOKING PROGRAM	3:30	HOLD ☐	
	3 COOKING PROGRAM	4:00 to 6:00	COOK ☐	
32 oz.	1 COOKING PROGRAM	8:00	DEFROST ☐	
	2 COOKING PROGRAM	4:00	HOLD ☐	
	3 COOKING PROGRAM	5:00 to 7:00	COOK ☐	

General Instructions for Defrosting and Cooking Frozen Fried Chicken

1. Spread chicken pieces in 2-quart utility dish. Arrange the chicken pieces with the large, thicker pieces, such as thighs and breasts, at the corners of the dish. Place the smaller pieces, such as legs and wings, at the center of the dish.

2. DEFROST, HOLD, and COOK, according to the directions on the chart.

FROZEN TURKEY ROAST COOKING CHART

ROAST SIZE	UTENSIL	1ST SETTING	1ST COOKING TIME	2ND SETTING	2ND COOKING TIME	3RD SETTING	FINAL TEMPERATURE	APPROXIMATE TOTAL COOKING TIME
2 lb.	9 x 5 x 2-inch	DEFROST	15 min.	Cookmatic Level 1 (WARM)	20 min.	FULL POWER	170°F	50 min. to 1 hour
3 lb.	2-quart utility dish	DEFROST	25 min.	Cookmatic Level 1 (WARM)	25 min.	FULL POWER	170°F	1 hour, 10 min. to 1 hour, 20 min.

General Instructions for Defrosting and Cooking Frozen Turkey Roasts

1. Remove the frozen roast from the metal container. Place it in the glass utensil listed on chart. Cover loosely with plastic wrap. Cook in Radarange Oven, covered, on DEFROST and Cookmatic Level 1 (WARM), according to the times on the chart.

2. Insert the temperature probe into the center of the roast through the plastic wrap, thereby piercing the plastic wrap. Cook in the Radarange Oven on FULL POWER to the final temperature of 170°F, as indicated on the chart. Turn roast over halfway through cooking time.

Chicken 'N' Dumplings

Yield: 4 to 6 servings

3 lb. broiler-fryer, cut-up
3 small onions, quartered
4 medium carrots, cut in 1-inch pieces, and then halved
4 parsley sprigs
1 (13-3/4 oz.) can chicken broth
2 cups water
2 bay leaves
2-1/2 teaspoons salt
1/4 teaspoon thyme
1/4 teaspoon poultry seasoning
1/8 teaspoon pepper

3 tablespoons cornstarch
1/3 cup water

DUMPLINGS

1 cup biscuit baking mix
1/3 cup milk
1/4 teaspoon poultry seasoning

1. Combine chicken, vegetables, parsley, broth, water and seasonings in 4-quart casserole. Cook in Radarange Oven, covered, on FULL POWER for 25 minutes, or until vegetables are tender.

2. Remove chicken. Add mixture of cornstarch and 1/3 cup water. Blend well. Cook in Radarange Oven on FULL POWER for 3 minutes, or until thickened. Return chicken to casserole.

3. Mix together biscuit mix, milk and seasoning until moistened. Spoon mixture over casserole. Cook in Radarange Oven, covered, on FULL POWER for 3 to 4-1/2 minutes, or until dumplings are done.

Roasting Directions for Whole Poultry
(Including: Chicken, Turkey, Duckling or Cornish Hens)

1. Wash body cavity of poultry with water, after removing giblets and neck from poultry.* Pat dry with paper towels.
2. Sprinkle poultry cavity with salt. If dressing is used, stuff just before roasting. Allow 3/4 cup stuffing per pound of ready-to-cook weight. Fill main cavity and neck cavity with dressing. Close neck and body cavity openings with wooden picks or skewers. Pierce skin of poultry with tines of fork to prevent popping.
3. Tie legs together and wings to body, loosely, with string. Place poultry in 2-quart utility dish or directly on Radarange Oven glass tray, breast-side-down. Brush exterior with melted butter or margarine, or use 2 to 1 ratio mixture of melted butter or margarine and paprika. Cover with heavy-duty plastic wrap. (Poultry may also be cooked in heavy-duty plastic roasting bag, if desired.)
4. Cook in Radarange Oven, covered, on FULL POWER for 5 to 6 minutes per pound, or until temperature of 165°F to 170°F is reached in thigh and 175°F is reached in breast meat. (Use the Automatic Temperature Control System to check the temperatures in these areas, after cooking.) Turn poultry over 2 to 3 times during roasting to ensure even cooking of entire poultry. For large poultry items, baste off excess accumulated juices when turning. Baste the poultry, if desired. If tips of legs, wings or other areas become too brown, use thin strips of aluminum foil to cover these areas. Finish cooking breast-side-up.
5. Let stand, covered, with aluminum foil, for 10 to 15 minutes before serving. Temperature will increase 10°F to 15°F during this time.

Other tests for determining when whole poultry is fully cooked are:

Pierce inside thigh muscle deeply with tines of fork. If juices are clear without tinge of pink, poultry is done.

Press thickest part of drumstick between fingers. It should feel very soft when done. Move drumstick. Leg joint should move freely or break when poultry is done.

*MICRO-TIP: Use giblets for dressing, if desired. The "Poultry Dressing" recipe, page 229, or your own favorite dressing recipe, may be used. Save drippings to use for gravy.

Chicken and Zucchini Delish
Yield: 4 servings

2 chicken breasts, halved*

4 to 6 cups zucchini, sliced
1 small onion, sliced
1 clove garlic, minced
2 tablespoons all-purpose flour
2 teaspoons instant chicken bouillon
1/2 teaspoon salt
1/4 teaspoon leaf thyme

2 medium tomatoes, cut in wedges
1 cup seasoned salad croutons

1. Remove and discard skin and bone. Cut chicken into bite-size pieces. Place in 2-quart casserole.
2. Add zucchini, onion, garlic, flour, bouillon, salt and thyme. Mix well. Cook in Radarange Oven, covered, on FULL POWER for 8 to 10 minutes, or until vegetables are just about tender. Stir mixture once or twice during cooking time.
3. Add tomatoes. Cook in Radarange Oven, covered, on FULL POWER for about 2 minutes, or until tomatoes are heated through. Garnish with croutons.

*MICRO-TIP: Cubed, cooked chicken or turkey can be substituted chicken breasts and added in step 3. Use about 3 cups. The skin bones can be boiled to prepare soup stock.

Poultry Dressing

Yield: Stuffing for a 12 to 16 lb. turkey

1 lb. pork sausage

1/2 cup butter or margarine

1 cup onion, chopped
1 cup celery, chopped
1 medium apple, chopped

1 tablespoon parsley flakes
1 teaspoon poultry seasoning
1 teaspoon ground sage
1/2 teaspoon salt
1/2 teaspoon pepper
1 egg, slightly-beaten

10 cups dry whole wheat or white bread cubes (about 1, 1 lb. loaf)
3/4 cup chicken broth or bouillon

1. Crumble sausage in 1-1/2-quart casserole. Cook in Radarange Oven on FULL POWER for 3 to 4 minutes, or until sausage is no longer pink. Stir halfway through cooking time. Drain.

2. Place butter in 3 to 4-quart casserole. Heat in Radarange Oven on FULL POWER for 1 minute, or until melted.

3. Add onion, celery and apple. Stir to coat with butter. Cook in Radarange Oven, covered, on FULL POWER for 5 to 7 minutes, or until tender.

4. Stir in sausage and seasonings. When slightly cooled, stir in egg.

5. Gradually stir in bread cubes. Pour chicken broth over all and toss to moisten. Stuff bird.

Variations: Add: 1 to 2 cups cooked neck and giblets, chopped or 2 (6 oz. each) cans sliced mushrooms, drained.

MICRO-TIPS:

• To dry the bread in the Radarange Oven, spread half of the slices, one or two deep, on a plastic rack. Heat in Radarange Oven on FULL POWER for 1 to 3 minutes, or until hot. Spread out on paper towels to cool. Repeat with remaining bread. Allow to stand 30 to 60 minutes.

• To cook dressing separately, add 1/4 to 1/2 cup more broth. Cook in Radarange Oven, covered, on FULL POWER for 6 to 8 minutes, or until heated through. Let stand, covered, for 5 to 10 minutes.

Barbecued Chicken Deluxe

Yield: 4 to 6 servings

1/2 cup onion, chopped
1/2 cup green pepper, chopped
1-1/2 tablespoons butter or margarine

1 (8 oz.) can tomato sauce with onions
2 tablespoons soy sauce
1 tablespoon brown sugar
1 tablespoon lemon juice
1 tablespoon vinegar
1 teaspoon prepared mustard
1 teaspoon Worcestershire sauce
1/8 teaspoon salt
1/8 teaspoon pepper

3 lb. broiler-fryer, cut-up

1. Place onion, green pepper and butter in 1-quart casserole. Cook in Radarange Oven on FULL POWER for 2-1/2 to 3-1/2 minutes, or until onion and green pepper are tender.

2. Add remaining ingredients, except chicken. Cook in Radarange Oven on FULL POWER for 1-1/2 minutes.

3. Arrange chicken pieces in 10-inch ceramic skillet or 2-quart utility dish with larger pieces, such as thighs and breasts, at corners, skin-side-down. Place small pieces such as legs and wings towards center. Pour sauce over chicken. Cook in Radarange Oven, covered, on FULL POWER for 18 to 20 minutes, or until chicken is tender. Turn chicken pieces over halfway through cooking time. Baste with sauce.

Cranberry Chicken

Yield: 4 to 6 servings

3 lb. broiler-fryer, cut-up
1 tablespoon vegetable oil

1. Preheat large browning skillet for maximum amount of time, according to manufacturer's instructions. Add oil. Arrange chicken with larger pieces, such as thighs and breasts, at corners, skin-side-down. Place small pieces such as legs and wings at center. Cook in Radarange Oven on FULL POWER for 1-1/2 minutes, or until chicken is lightly browned. Turn chicken pieces over halfway through cooking time.

1 cup whole cranberry sauce
1 tablespoon water
1/4 teaspoon cinnamon
1/8 teaspoon ground cloves
Salt
Pepper

2. Combine cranberry sauce, water, cinnamon and cloves. Add salt and pepper, as desired. Pour over chicken. Cook in Radarange Oven, covered, on FULL POWER for 12 to 15 minutes, or until chicken is tender. Turn chicken pieces over halfway through cooking time.

MICRO-TIP: May be served with additional cranberry sauce, if desired.

Speedy Baked Chicken

Yield: 4 servings

2 tablespoons butter or margarine
3 lb. broiler-fryer, cut-up
Pepper
Paprika

1. Preheat large browning skillet for maximum amount of time, according to manufacturer's instructions. Add butter. Arrange chicken with larger pieces, such as thighs and breasts, at corners, skin-side-down. Place small pieces such as legs and wings at center. Season with pepper and paprika, as desired. Cover with waxed paper or plastic wrap.

Salt

2. Cook in Radarange Oven, covered, on FULL POWER for 12 to 15 minutes, or until chicken is tender. Turn chicken pieces over halfway through cooking time. Drain. Salt before serving, as desired.

MICRO-TIP: Gravy may be made from drippings, if desired.

Apricot-Baked Chicken

Yield: 4 to 6 servings

2-1/2 lb. broiler-fryer, cut-up

1. Arrange chicken in 2-quart utility dish with larger pieces, such as thighs and breasts, at corners, skin-side-down. Place small pieces such as legs and wings at center.

2 tablespoons mayonnaise
1/2 (1-1/2 oz.) pkg. dry onion soup mix
1/4 cup bottled Russian salad dressing
1 cup apricot preserves

2. Combine remaining ingredients. Spread over chicken. Cover with waxed paper or plastic wrap.

3. Bake in Radarange Oven, covered, on FULL POWER for 12 to 14 minutes, or until chicken is tender. Turn chicken pieces over halfway through cooking time.

Barbecued Chicken Thighs

Yield: 6 to 8 servings

2 lbs. chicken thighs (about 8)
  or 2 lb. broiler-fryer, cut-up
3/4 cup cola

Salt
1 cup catsup

1. When using broiler-fryer, cut up, arrange chicken in ceramic skillet with larger pieces, such as thighs and breasts, at corners, skin-side-down. Place smaller pieces, such as legs and wings at center. Pour cola over chicken. Cook in Radarange Oven, covered, on FULL POWER for 10 minutes. Turn chicken pieces over halfway through cooking time.

2. Drain off about 1/4 cup cola. Sprinkle chicken with salt, as desired. Pour catsup over chicken. Cook in Radarange Oven on FULL POWER for 5 to 7 minutes, or until chicken is tender. Turn chicken pieces over halfway through cooking time.

Easy Barbecued Chicken

Yield: 4 to 6 servings

3 lb. broiler-fryer, cut-up
3/4 cup bottled barbecue sauce
1 teaspoon liquid smoke (optional)
1 teaspoon instant, minced onion
  (optional)

1. Arrange chicken in 2-quart utility dish with larger pieces, such as thighs and breasts, at corners, skin-side-down. Place small pieces such as legs and wings at center. Mix sauce, liquid smoke, and onion together. Pour over chicken. Cover with waxed paper or plastic wrap.

2. Cook in Radarange Oven, covered, on FULL POWER for 12 to 15 minutes, or until chicken is tender. Turn chicken pieces over halfway through cooking time.

MICRO-TIP: Try using hickory smoke flavor barbecue sauce or barbecue sauce with onion bits.

Chicken Teriyaki

Yield: 4 to 6 servings

1/2 cup soy sauce
1/4 cup dry white wine
1 clove garlic, minced
2 tablespoons sugar
1/2 teaspoon ginger

3 lb. broiler-fryer, cut-up

1. Combine soy sauce, wine, garlic, sugar and ginger. Stir well.

2. Place chicken in heavy-duty plastic bag. Pour marinade sauce over chicken. Tie securely with string. Refrigerate for 1 to 2 hours.

3. Arrange chicken pieces in 10-inch ceramic skillet or 2-quart utility dish with larger pieces, such as thighs and breasts, at corners, skin-side-down. Place small pieces such as legs and wings towards center. Cover with waxed paper, plastic wrap or glass lid. Cook in Radarange Oven, covered, on FULL POWER for 12 to 15 minutes, or until chicken is tender. Turn chicken pieces over halfway through cooking time.

MICRO-TIP: For "Quick Chicken Teriyaki", blend 1 (1-1/2 oz.) pkg. instant teriyaki sauce mix for chicken with 1/2 cup water, or use bottled teriyaki sauce. Omit ingredients in step 1. Proceed with cooking procedures for steps #2 and #3.

Chicken Cacciatore

Yield: 4 to 6 servings

3 lb. broiler-fryer, cut-up
1/4 cup all-purpose flour
1 teaspoon salt
1/2 teaspoon pepper

1/3 cup vegetable oil

4 parsley sprigs
2 medium onions, sliced
2 cloves garlic, minced
1 bay leaf
1/4 teaspoon leaf basil
1/4 teaspoon oregano
1/4 teaspoon saffron (optional)
2 pimentos, diced (optional)

1 (20 oz.) can Italian tomatoes, drained
1 teaspoon salt

1. Combine flour, salt and pepper. Coat chicken pieces with seasoned mixture.

2. Preheat large browning skillet for maximum amount of time, according to manufacturer's instructions. Place oil and chicken in skillet. Cook in Radarange Oven on FULL POWER for 1-1/2 minutes, or until chicken is lightly browned. Turn chicken pieces over after 45 seconds of cooking.

3. Remove chicken. Combine remaining ingredients, except tomatoes and salt, in browning skillet. Cook in Radarange Oven, covered, on FULL POWER for 5 minutes.

4. Return chicken to skillet. Pour tomatoes over chicken. Blend in salt. Cook in Radarange Oven, covered, on FULL POWER for 20 to 24 minutes, or until chicken is tender. Turn chicken pieces over halfway through cooking time. Remove bay leaf before serving.

Chicken 'N' Rice

Yield: 2 to 4 servings

1 (10-3/4 oz.) can golden cream of mushroom soup
1 (5.3 oz.) can evaporated milk
1/2 cup milk

3/4 cup quick-cooking rice
1 (2-1/2 oz.) can mushrooms, with liquid
1/2 (1-1/2 oz.) pkg. onion soup mix
2 tablespoons pimentos, chopped (optional)

2 chicken breasts, halved

1. Mix together soup and milks. Reserve 1/2 cup of mixture.

2. Mix remaining soup mixture with rice, mushrooms, 1/4 pkg. of onion soup mix, and pimento. Pour into 8 x 8 x 2-inch glass dish. Cover with waxed paper or plastic wrap. Cook in Radarange Oven, covered, on FULL POWER for 4 minutes.

3. Place chicken breasts on rice mixture. Pour reserved soup mixture over chicken. Sprinkle with remaining 1/4 pkg. onion soup mix. Cover with waxed paper or plastic wrap. Cook in Radarange Oven, covered, on FULL POWER for 15 to 18 minutes, or until chicken is tender. Turn chicken over 1 to 2 times during cooking time.

Hawaiian Chicken

Yield: 4 to 6 servings

1/4 cup onion, chopped
1/2 cup green pepper, chopped
1 tablespoon butter or margarine

1/3 cup water
1/2 cup dark brown sugar, firmly packed
1/4 cup apple cider vinegar
2 tablespoons cornstarch
1-1/2 teaspoons soy sauce
1/4 teaspoon salt
1/8 teaspoon instant, minced garlic

3 cups cooked chicken, cubed
1 (15-1/2 oz.) can pineapple chunks, with liquid
1 (7 oz.) pkg. frozen pea pods

1. Place onion, green pepper and butter in 1-1/2-quart casserole. Cook in Radarange Oven on FULL POWER for 2 to 3 minutes, or until onion and green pepper are tender.

2. Blend in all of remaining ingredients, except chicken, pineapple and pea pods. Cook in Radarange Oven, covered, on FULL POWER for 4 to 5 minutes, or until thickened. Stir halfway through cooking time.

3. Add chicken, pineapple and pea pods. Cook in Radarange Oven, covered, on FULL POWER for 4 to 6 minutes, or until pea pods are almost tender. Stir halfway through cooking time.

MICRO-TIP: May be served over rice with additional soy sauce.

Chicken Curry

Yield: 4 to 6 servings

1/4 cup onion, chopped
1 green pepper, cut into 1/2-inch strips (about 1/2 cup)
1 clove garlic, minced
2 tablespoons butter or margarine

1-1/2 cups water
1/3 cup catsup
1 (4 oz.) can mushrooms, stems and pieces, drained
1 teaspoon instant chicken bouillon
1 teaspoon curry powder
1 teaspoon ginger
1/2 teaspoon salt
1/2 teaspoon pepper
2 cups cooked chicken, cubed

2 tablespoons cornstarch
1/4 cup water

1. Place onion, green pepper, garlic and butter in 2-quart casserole. Cook in Radarange Oven on FULL POWER for 2-1/2 to 3-1/2 minutes, or until onion and green pepper are tender.

2. Blend in remaining ingredients, except cornstarch and water. Cook in Radarange Oven, covered, on FULL POWER for 5 minutes, or until heated through.

3. Blend together cornstarch and water. Stir into curry mixture. Cook in Radarange Oven on FULL POWER for 2 to 3 minutes, or until thickened. Stir halfway through cooking time.

MICRO-TIP: May be served over rice or noodles. Garnish with toasted slivered almonds, if desired.

Chicken Supreme

Yield: 6 servings

3 chicken breasts, halved
3/4 teaspoon seasoned salt
1 teaspoon paprika

1 teaspoon instant chicken bouillon
1 (4 oz.) can sliced mushrooms,
  with liquid
1/2 cup white wine*
1/4 cup hot water
1 teaspoon instant, minced onion
1/2 teaspoon curry powder
1/4 teaspoon leaf tarragon or
  parsley flakes

1 tablespoon cornstarch
2 tablespoons water

1. Sprinkle seasoned salt and paprika generously over chicken breasts in 10-inch ceramic skillet or 2-quart utility dish. Cook in Radarange Oven, uncovered, on FULL POWER for 10 minutes.

2. Combine instant bouillon, mushrooms, wine, water, onion, curry powder, and tarragon. Pour over chicken. Cook in Radarange Oven, covered, on FULL POWER for 5 to 10 minutes, or until chicken is tender. Turn chicken pieces over halfway through cooking time.

3. Remove chicken and stir mixture of cornstarch and water into wine sauce. Cook in Radarange Oven on FULL POWER for 2 to 3 minutes, or until thickened. Stir halfway through cooking time. Return chicken to skillet and coat with sauce. Reheat, if desired, in Radarange Oven, covered, on FULL POWER for 1-1/2 to 2 minutes.

*MICRO-TIP: If using salted cooking wine, decrease amount of seasoned salt.

Sausage-Stuffed Chicken Rolls

Yield: 2 to 4 servings

2 chicken breasts, halved

4 brown and serve sausages
1 egg, beaten
1/2 cup cornflake crumbs
Spray-on vegetable coating

1 cup water
1 teaspoon instant chicken bouillon
2 teaspoons cornstarch

1. Remove bone and skin from chicken breasts. Pound each chicken-breast-half between 2 sheets of waxed paper with flat side of meat mallet to 1/4-inch thickness.

2. Roll each chicken-breast around a sausage and secure each roll with wooden picks. Dip chicken rolls in egg, and then roll in cornflake crumbs. Coat thoroughly.

3. Preheat large browning skillet for maximum amount of time, according to manufacturer's instructions. Spray with non-stick vegetable coating. Place chicken in browning skillet. Cook in Radarange Oven on FULL POWER for 2 minutes, or until chicken is lightly browned. Turn rolls over halfway through cooking time.

4. Remove rolls. Add water and instant bouillon. Heat in Radarange Oven on FULL POWER for 1 minute, or until instant bouillon is dissolved. Stir in cornstarch with wire whip. Heat in Radarange Oven on FULL POWER for 1 minute, or until thickened.

5. Add chicken rolls to gravy. Cook in Radarange Oven, covered, on FULL POWER for 5 to 6 minutes, or until chicken is tender.

MICRO-TIP: You can roll chicken with a slice of boiled ham and mozzarella cheese for a quick Cordon Bleu.

Hot Chicken Salad

Yield: 3 to 3-1/2 cups

2 cups cooked chicken, cubed
1 cup celery, chopped
3/4 cup mayonnaise
1/3 cup green pepper
2 tablespoons onion, chopped
2 tablespoons pimento, chopped
2 teaspoons lemon juice
1/2 teaspoon salt

3/4 cup Cheddar cheese, cubed
1/2 cup potato chips, crushed

1. Combine all ingredients, except cheese and potato chips, in 1-quart casserole. Cook in Radarange Oven on FULL POWER for 4 to 5 minutes, or until heated through, and temperature of 150°F is reached.

2. Stir in cheese. Top with potato chips. Cook in Radarange Oven on Cookmatic Level 5 (SLO COOK) for 2 minutes, or until cheese is softened.

Chicken Livers Chablis

Yield: 4 to 6 servings

2 tablespoons butter or margarine

1-1/2 lbs. chicken livers
   (about 16 to 20)
2-1/2 tablespoons all-purpose flour

3/4 cup white wine
1/4 cup onion, minced
2 tablespoons catsup
Salt
Pepper

1. Place butter in 10-inch ceramic skillet or 2-quart casserole. Heat in Radarange Oven on FULL POWER for 30 to 45 seconds, or until melted.

2. Dredge livers in flour. Arrange in melted butter. Cook in Radarange Oven on FULL POWER for 5-1/2 to 6-1/2 minutes, or until no longer pink. Turn livers over halfway through cooking time.

3. Lightly stir in wine, onion and catsup. Cook in Radarange Oven on FULL POWER for 2 to 3 minutes, or until heated through. Season with salt and pepper, as desired.

MICRO-TIP: May be served over rice or noodles.

Chicken Parmesan

Yield: 4 to 6 servings

3 lb. broiler-fryer, cut-up
1 egg, beaten
1/2 cup cornflake crumbs
1/2 cup grated Parmesan cheese
1/4 teaspoon ground oregano
Dash ground thyme
Dash garlic salt
Dash pepper

1 (10-3/4 oz.) can golden cream
   of mushroom soup
1/3 cup milk
2 tablespoons parsley, snipped

1. Dip chicken in egg. Roll in mixture of crumbs, cheese, and spices. Coat thoroughly.

2. Arrange chicken in 10-inch ceramic skillet or 2-quart utility dish with larger pieces, such as thighs and breasts, at corners, skin-side-down. Place small pieces such as legs and wings at center. Cook in Radarange Oven, covered, on FULL POWER for 10 minutes. Turn chicken pieces over halfway through cooking time.

3. Combine soup and milk. Pour over chicken. Cook in Radarange Oven, covered, on FULL POWER for 4 to 6 minutes, or until chicken is tender. Garnish with any remaining cheese mixture and parsley.

Chicken Liver Stroganoff

Yield: 4 servings

2 tablespoons butter or margarine
1 medium onion, sliced

3/4 lb. chicken livers (about 8)
1-1/2 cups fresh mushrooms, sliced*
1 teaspoon paprika
1/2 teaspoon salt
Dash pepper

1 tablespoon all-purpose flour
3/4 cup dairy sour cream

1. Place butter and onion in 10-inch ceramic skillet or 2-quart utility dish. Cook in Radarange Oven on FULL POWER for 2 to 3 minutes, or until onion is tender.

2. Cut each chicken liver in half. Add livers and mushrooms to onion mixture. Sprinkle with paprika, salt and pepper. Cook in Radarange Oven, covered, on FULL POWER for 8 to 9 minutes, or until livers are cooked. Stir halfway through cooking time.

3. Stir flour into sour cream. Spoon over chicken livers. Cook in Radarange Oven on FULL POWER for 1 minute, or until heated through.

MICRO-TIPS:

*1 (4 oz.) can sliced mushrooms, drained, may be substituted for fresh mushrooms.

•This dish may be served over rice or noodles.

Duckling Bordeaux

Yield: 4 servings

4 to 5 lb. duckling
2 tablespoons vegetable oil

1/2 cup marmalade
1 tablespoon soy sauce

SAUCE

1 tablespoon butter or margarine
1 tablespoon all-purpose flour
3/4 cup white wine
1/3 cup chicken broth
1 tablespoon vinegar
1/4 teaspoon pepper

1. Quarter duckling. Preheat large browning skillet for maximum amount of time, according to manufacturer's instructions. Add 1 tablespoon of oil. Place two pieces of duckling skin-side-down in skillet. Cook in Radarange Oven on FULL POWER for 5 minutes. Turn duckling halfway through cooking time. Drain.

2. Wipe out skillet with paper towel. Re-preheat browning skillet, according to manufacturer's instructions. Add 1 tablespoon of oil. Repeat cooking time with remaining duckling.

3. Mix together marmalade and soy sauce. Reserve 1/4 cup of mixture. Use remainder to baste duckling. Arrange all duckling quarters in skillet with thicker portions toward outside. Cook, in Radarange Oven, covered, on FULL POWER for 8 to 10 minutes. Turn duckling pieces over halfway through cooking time. Cover, and let stand while preparing sauce.

4. Place butter in 1-quart mixing bowl. Heat in Radarange Oven on FULL POWER for 20 to 30 seconds, or until melted. Stir in flour. Add remaining ingredients.

5. Cook in Radarange Oven on FULL POWER for 1 minute. Add reserved marmalade mixture. Cook in Radarange Oven on FULL POWER for 1 to 1-1/2 minutes, or until smooth. Spoon over duckling.

Stuffed Duckling L'Orange

Yield: 4 to 6 servings

4 to 5 lb. duckling with giblets
1 cup water

12 ozs. pork sausage
1/2 cup celery, chopped
1/2 cup onion, chopped

2 cups apples, peeled and chopped
2 cups croutons
1/2 cup walnuts, chopped
1 teaspoon salt
1/2 teaspoon thyme
1/2 teaspoon poultry seasoning
1/4 teaspoon pepper

1/2 cup marmalade
2 tablespoons white wine
1 tablespoon butter or margarine, melted
1 tablespoon soy sauce
1/2 teaspoon thyme
1/8 teaspoon dry mustard
1/8 teaspoon salt

1. Place giblets and water in 1-quart casserole. Cook in Radarange Oven, covered, on FULL POWER for 10 to 15 minutes, or until tender. Chop giblets.

2. Place sausage in 1-quart casserole. Cook in Radarange Oven on FULL POWER for 3 to 4 minutes, or until meat is no longer pink. Remove sausage. Add celery and onion. Cook in Radarange Oven on FULL POWER for 3 to 4 minutes, or until celery and onion are almost tender.

3. Combine sausage, celery, onion, giblets, apples, croutons, walnuts and seasonings. Stuff cleaned duckling. Secure openings with wooden picks and tie with string, if desired. Pierce skin of duckling near thighs.

4. Combine remaining ingredients. Baste duckling. Cook in Radarange Oven, covered, on FULL POWER for 20 to 25 minutes. Turn duckling over and baste 3 to 4 times during cooking time.

Swiss Turkey and Ham Bake

Yield: 6 servings

2 tablespoons butter or margarine
1/2 cup cornflake, cracker or bread crumbs

2 cups cooked turkey, cubed
1 cup cooked ham, cubed
1 (8 oz.) can water chestnuts, drained and sliced
1 (4 oz.) can sliced mushrooms, drained
1-1/2 teaspoons parsley flakes
1 (10-3/4 oz.) can cream of onion soup
1/4 teaspoon salt
1/8 teaspoon pepper

1/2 cup Swiss cheese, shredded
Paprika

1. Place butter in small bowl. Heat in Radarange Oven on FULL POWER for 20 to 30 seconds, or until melted. Mix in crumbs. Set aside.

2. Combine turkey, ham, water chestnuts, mushrooms, parsley, soup and seasonings in 2-quart casserole. Cook in Radarange Oven on FULL POWER for 7 to 9 minutes, or until heated through, and temperature of 150°F is reached. Stir halfway through cooking time.

3. Top with cheese, and sprinkle with buttered crumbs. Sprinkle with paprika, as desired. Cook in Radarange Oven on Cookmatic Level 5 (SLO COOK) for 1-1/2 minutes, or until cheese is melted.

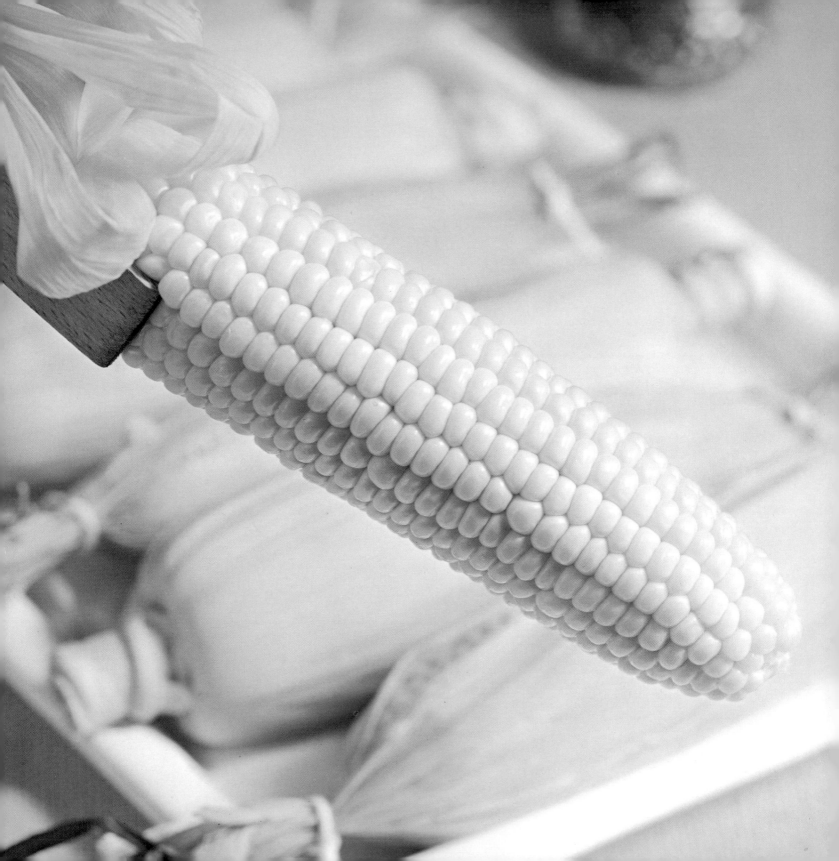

You'll be "cooking in color" when you prepare vegetables in the Radarange Oven. Vegetables require very little liquid to cook, and thus they retain their bright colors as well as good texture. Vitamin retention is another plus when cooking vegetables in the Radarange Oven, due to the small amount of liquid used, and the short amount of cooking time.

Be sure to read the general hints before cooking vegetables.

General Hints for Cooking Vegetables
1. Vegetables can vary in the amount of cooking time they require. The age, freshness, size, shape, temperature, and variety can all affect cooking times. You may need to adjust cooking times slightly.
2. Prepare vegetables for cooking as you normally would for conventional cooking, but don't add salt until just before serving. Salt will dehydrate vegetables, making them tough, if added before cooking.
3. For preparing fresh, canned or frozen vegetables, see the individual charts for cooking instructions.
4. Many vegetable recipes in this chapter can use fresh, frozen or canned vegetables. For recipes requiring canned vegetables, either cooked fresh vegetables, or thawed frozen vegetables may be used. When substituting a canned vegetable for frozen, the cooking time may have to be decreased slightly.
5. Arrange the "toughest", thickest parts of a vegetable toward the outside of the dish where they will cook faster. Broccoli stalks, for example, should be placed toward the dish edge and the more delicate heads placed toward the dish center.
6. Pierce the skins of vegetables such as squash, potatoes, or sweet potatoes before cooking. Piercing will allow steam to escape during cooking, and will avoid bursting.
7. Always cook vegetables, especially fresh vegetables, covered. Use a glass lid or heavy-duty plastic wrap since these coverings are the most water-vapor-proof. By covering vegetables, they will cook faster and more evenly. Pierce plastic wrap coverings before cooking. Unwrap plastic wrap and remove glass lids carefully after cooking to avoid steam burns.
8. When cooking vegetables such as baked potatoes, or individual squashes, arrange them in a circle. Leave a space of about 1-inch between each. You may want to turn individual vegetables over halfway through the cooking time.
9. Fresh vegetables should be eaten soon after they are harvested or purchased for maximum retention of vitamins. Fresh vegetables should be cooked covered. Between 2 to 4 tablespoons water should be added for steaming. Some of the water may be substituted with butter or oil, if desired. Calorie-watchers will prefer to use water.
10. When cooking a quantity of vegetables, note that as with any food cooked in the Radarange Oven, the amount of cooking time will increase almost proportionately to a weight change. Use **slightly less** than double the amount of cooking time when doubling a quantity.
11. Cook vegetables on FULL POWER, unless they are cooked with a sauce which contains a "delicate" or "special" ingredient.
12. Whole vegetables will require a slightly longer cooking time than vegetables cut in pieces. For fast, even cooking, cut vegetables into small, uniformly-shaped pieces.
13. You may want to stir some vegetables halfway through the cooking time to redistribute heat and moisture.
14. Recipes in this cookbook give cooking times for vegetables to be cooked to the "barely tender" stage. If a softer vegetable texture is desired, add slightly more liquid, cook covered, and slightly increase the amount of cooking time.
15. Be careful not to overcook vegetables. Vegetables will continue to cook slightly after removed from the Radarange Oven. If vegetables will be standing for several minutes before serving, slightly undercook them and they will finish cooking by themselves. Keep vegetables covered to retain heat, before serving. Baked potatoes can be wrapped in aluminum foil **after** cooking to keep them "piping" hot, until served.
16. Home canning should not be done in a microwave oven. Home canning is generally done with metal

lids. Since metal lids reflect microwaves, you cannot be assured that the food product will be heated uniformly to 212°F or above, and there is a probability of deterioration of the food product. Vegetables may be blanched in the Radarange Oven with good results. See the chart on page 247.

17. Grated or shredded cheese may be added to vegetables. Top vegetables with cheese just before serving. Heat in Radarange Oven on Cookmatic Level 5 (SLO COOK) for 1 to 1-1/2 minutes, or until cheese is melted.

18. Fresh vegetable dishes can be prepared in "planned-over" quantities. Prepare a large quantity, and freeze the extra or planned-over for future use.

19. For vegetable sauces and salad dressings, see the "Sauces, Jams and Relishes" chapter, on page 265.

20. Fruits are prepared similarly to vegetables. Information about fruits is found in the "Desserts" chapter, on page 283.

21. When preparing your own vegetable recipes, select a recipe in this chapter as a guide. Then, use about the same amount of time and cook, covered, on FULL POWER.

FROZEN VEGETABLE COOKING CHART

FROZEN VEGETABLE	PACKAGE SIZE OR AMOUNT	AMOUNT OF WATER, BUTTER OR MARGARINE	COOKING TIME ON FULL POWER
Artichoke Hearts	9 oz.	1 tablespoon water	4 to 5 min.
Asparagus Cuts	10 oz.	2 tablespoons water	5 to 6 min.
Asparagus Spears	10 oz.	2 tablespoons water	6 to 8 min.
Baked Potato	12 oz.	—	4 to 5 min.
Broccoli Cuts	10 oz.	2 tablespoons water	5 to 7 min.
Broccoli Spears	8 oz.	2 tablespoons water	5 to 7 min.
Broccoli in Cheese Sauce	10 oz.	—	6-1/2 to 7-1/2 min.
Brussel Sprouts	8 oz.	1 tablespoon water	5 to 6 min.
Carrots	10 oz.	2 tablespoons water	5 to 7 min.
Cauliflower	10 oz.	2 tablespoons water	4 to 5 min.
Cauliflower in Cheese Sauce	10 oz.	—	6 to 7 min.
Corn, Cream Style	10 oz.	—	4-1/2 to 5-1/2 min.
Corn on the Cob	1 ear 2 ears 4 ears	— — —	3-1/2 to 4-1/2 min. 5 to 6 min. 10 to 11 min.
Corn, Whole Kernel	10 oz.	2 tablespoons water	4 to 5 min.
Green Beans, Cut	10 oz.	2 tablespoons water	5 to 7 min.
Green Beans, French Cut	9 oz.	1 tablespoon water	5-1/2 to 6-1/2 min.
Green Beans, French Cut with Almonds	9 oz.	1 tablespoon water	5-1/2 to 6-1/2 min.
Green Beans, Italian	10 oz.	2 tablespoons water	5 to 7 min.
Green Beans, Whole	9 oz.	1 tablespoon water	6 to 7 min.
Lima Beans, Baby	10 oz.	2 tablespoons water	4-1/2 to 6 min.
Lima Beans, Fordhook	10 oz.	2 tablespoons water	7-1/2 to 8-1/2 min.

FROZEN VEGETABLE	PACKAGE SIZE OR AMOUNT	AMOUNT OF WATER, BUTTER OR MARGARINE	COOKING TIME ON FULL POWER
Mixed Vegetables	10 oz.	2 tablespoons water	4-1/2 to 5-1/2 min.
Onion Rings, Fried**	7 oz.	—	2 to 2-1/2 min.
	9 oz.	—	2-1/2 to 3 min.
Pea Pods	6 oz.	1 tablespoon water	2 to 3 min.
Peas	10 oz.	2 tablespoons water	5 to 6 min.
Peas, Baby Early	10 oz.	2 tablespoons water	3 to 3-1/2 min.
Peas and Carrots	10 oz.	2 tablespoons water	4 to 5 min.
Peas, Green with Cream Sauce	8 oz.	2/3 cup water	5 to 6 min.
Peas, Green and Pearl Onions	10 oz.	1 teaspoon water	3 to 4 min.
Peas, Green and Potatoes	8 oz.	3/4 cup water	5 to 6 min.
Spinach, Chopped	10 oz.	1 tablespoon water	4-1/2 to 5-1/2 min.
Spinach, Leaf	10 oz.	2 tablespoons water	4-1/2 to 5-1/2 min.
Squash	12 oz.	2 tablespoons butter or margarine	3-1/2 to 4-1/2 min.
Succotash	10 oz.	1 tablespoon water	4 to 5 min.
Sweet Potatoes, Candied	12 oz.	1 tablespoon butter or margarine	4 to 4-1/2 min.
Tater Tots***	16 oz.	—	3-1/2 to 4-1/2 min.
Vegetable Combinations (Green Beans and Spaetzle, etc.)	10 oz.	2 tablespoons water	4 to 5 min.

*Place in covered casserole or wrap in plastic wrap or waxed paper.
**Place on paper plate or towels. Cover with paper towels. These will not be crisp when cooked in a microwave oven.
***Place on plastic rack or paper plate. Cover with paper towels. These will not be crisp when cooked in a microwave oven.

General Instructions for Cooking Frozen Vegetables

1. Place the frozen vegetable in a 1 to 1-1/2-quart casserole, unless another utensil is recommended. Add water or butter as needed. Cook in Radarange Oven, covered, on FULL POWER for the amount of time given for the specific vegetable on the chart.

2. When cooking a vegetable frozen in a plastic cooking pouch, make one or two 1-inch slits on the top of the pouch to allow for steam to escape. Place the pouch directly on the Radarange Oven glass tray to cook.

3. There is no need to defrost frozen vegetables, before cooking.

4. Always keep vegetable covered to hold in steam after cooking.

5. With vegetables frozen in a solid block, stir to break them apart halfway through the cooking time.

6. If the amount or package size is doubled, the cooking time will be slightly less than two times as long.

Vegetables

FRESH VEGETABLE COOKING CHART

VEGETABLE	AMOUNT	UTENSIL	COOKING TIME ON FULL POWER
Asparagus	1 lb.	1-1/2-quart casserole	6 min.
Beans, Green (Pole Beans)	3 cups	1-1/2-quart casserole	10 to 12 min.
Beans, Green	1 lb.	2-quart casserole	10 to 12 min.
Beans, Yellow Wax	1 lb.	2-quart casserole	10 to 12 min.
Beets	1 lb., thinly sliced	1-1/2-quart casserole	8 min.
Broccoli	1-1/2 lbs.	3-quart casserole	10 to 11 min.
Brussels Sprouts	1-1/2 lbs.	1-1/2-quart casserole	7 to 8 min.
Cabbage, Red or Green	2-1/2 to 3 lbs., quartered (medium head)	3-quart casserole	13 to 15 min.
Cabbage, Chinese Celery	1 lb.	1-1/2-quart casserole	8 min.
Carrots	1 lb. whole, sliced in 1/2-inch pieces.	2-quart casserole	6 to 8 min.
Cauliflower _with water_	1-1/2 lbs. whole — 1 lb. flowerets	1-1/2 to 2-quart casserole 1-1/2-quart casserole	8 to 10 min. 8 min.
Celery	4 cups, diced	1-1/2-quart casserole	7 to 8 min.
Corn on the Cob	4 ears	2-quart utility dish, waxed paper or the husk	6 to 8 min.
Eggplant	4 cups, diced	10-inch ceramic skillet	3 to 4 min.
Mushrooms	1/2 lb.	1-1/2-quart casserole	2-1/2 to 3-1/2 min.
Okra	1 lb.	1-1/2-quart casserole	5 min.
Parsnips	1 lb., sliced in 1/2-inch pieces.	2-quart casserole	6 to 8 min.
Peas, Green	2 lbs. (2 cups) 4 lbs. (4 cups)	1-1/2-quart casserole	6 min. 9 to 10 min.
Pea Pods (Chinese)	1 lb.	2-quart casserole	10 min.
Potatoes, Baked	2 medium	paper towels	5 to 6 min.

FRESH VEGETABLE COOKING CHART (Continued)

VEGETABLE	AMOUNT	UTENSIL	COOKING TIME ON FULL POWER
Potatoes, Red Boiled	2 lbs. (4 large) in 1/4-cup water	2-quart casserole	10 to 12 min.
Potatoes, New Boiled in Jackets	6, 2-inch diameter, in 1/4-cup water	2-quart casserole	8 to 10 min.
Potatoes, Sweet	2 medium 4 medium	paper towels paper towels	4-1/2 to 5-1/2 min. 7 to 9 min.
Rutabaga	3 cups, cubed	1-1/2-quart casserole	8 to 10 min.
Spinach	10 ozs.	3-quart casserole	3 to 4 min.
Squash, Acorn	1-1/2 lbs., split and remove seeds	Shallow baking dish	6 to 8 min.
Squash, Butternut	3 lbs., pared and cut into 1-inch slices	2-quart casserole	8 to 10 min.
Squash, Summer Yellow Crookneck	1 lb. (5 small)	Shallow baking dish	4 to 6 min.
Swiss Chard	3/4 lb., with 1/4 cup water	1-1/2-quart casserole	6 to 7 min.
Tomatoes, Baked	1 lb. (2 medium)	1-1/2-quart casserole	3 to 4 min.
Turnips	3 cups, cubed	1-1/2-quart casserole	7 to 9 min.
Zucchini	2 medium (3 cups) sliced in 1/4-inch slices	1-1/2-quart casserole	4 to 6 min.

[handwritten note across Spinach row: "turnover to keep top from drying out"]

General Instructions for Cooking Fresh Vegetables

1. Place the prepared vegetable in the utensil recommended on the chart.

2. Add 2 to 4 tablespoons of water when cooking most vegetables. Cream, melted butter, or oil may also be used for moisture, if desired. Use a larger quantity of liquid for larger quantities of vegetables and for fibrous vegetables, such as green beans and broccoli.

3. The cooking times in the chart are only guidelines. Cook vegetables until tender, as desired. To prepare a smaller quantity of vegetables than the amount on the chart, decrease the cooking time. See page 18 for instructions on increasing or decreasing a recipe size.

4. Cook in the Radarange Oven, covered, on FULL POWER, according to the time on the chart. Stir or rearrange the vegetable halfway through the cooking time, if necessary. Keep the vegetable covered, until ready to serve.

DRIED LEGUME COOKING CHART

LEGUME TYPE	PROGRAMMING INSTRUCTIONS
Baby Lima Beans	**1** COOKING PROGRAM · 8:00 · COOK ☐ **2** COOKING PROGRAM · 12:00 to 15:00 · COOK ☐ · **4** · COOKMATIC LEVEL ☐
Black-Eyed Beans	**1** COOKING PROGRAM · 9:00 · COOK ☐ **2** COOKING PROGRAM · 8:00 to 12:00 · COOK ☐ · **5** · COOKMATIC LEVEL ☐
Black Turtle Beans	**1** COOKING PROGRAM · 9:00 · COOK ☐ **2** COOKING PROGRAM · 17:00 to 19:00 · COOK ☐ · **4** · COOKMATIC LEVEL ☐
Garbanzos (Chick Peas)	**1** COOKING PROGRAM · 9:00 · COOK ☐ **2** COOKING PROGRAM · 10:00 to 15:00 · COOK ☐ · **3** · COOKMATIC LEVEL ☐
Lentils	**1** COOKING PROGRAM · 9:00 · COOK ☐ **2** COOKING PROGRAM · 5:00 to 7:00 · COOK ☐ · **5** · COOKMATIC LEVEL ☐
Lima Beans	**1** COOKING PROGRAM · 7:00 · COOK ☐ **2** COOKING PROGRAM · 14:00 to 18:00 · COOK ☐ · **4** · COOKMATIC LEVEL ☐

Vegetables

DRIED LEGUME COOKING CHART (Continued)

LEGUME TYPE	PROGRAMMING INSTRUCTIONS

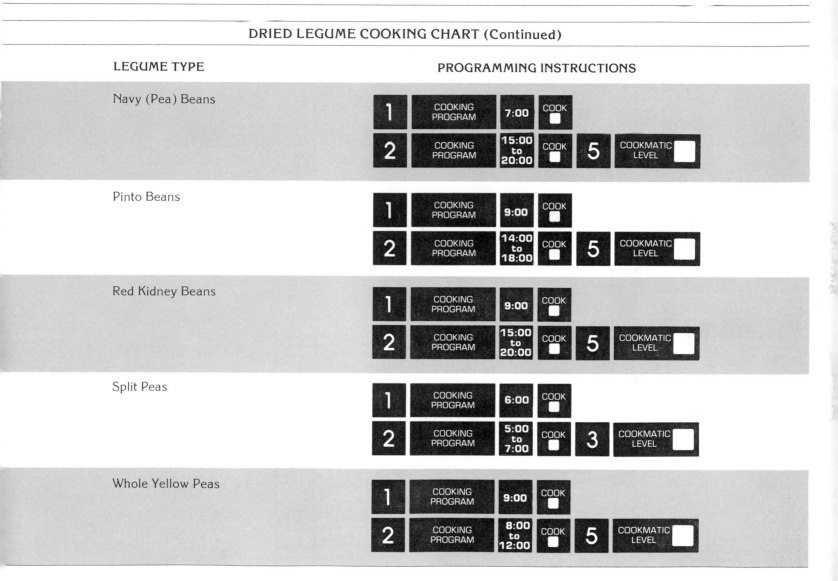

Navy (Pea) Beans

1 | COOKING PROGRAM | 7:00 | COOK ☐

2 | COOKING PROGRAM | 15:00 to 20:00 | COOK ☐ | 5 | COOKMATIC LEVEL ☐

Pinto Beans

1 | COOKING PROGRAM | 9:00 | COOK ☐

2 | COOKING PROGRAM | 14:00 to 18:00 | COOK ☐ | 5 | COOKMATIC LEVEL ☐

Red Kidney Beans

1 | COOKING PROGRAM | 9:00 | COOK ☐

2 | COOKING PROGRAM | 15:00 to 20:00 | COOK ☐ | 5 | COOKMATIC LEVEL ☐

Split Peas

1 | COOKING PROGRAM | 6:00 | COOK ☐

2 | COOKING PROGRAM | 5:00 to 7:00 | COOK ☐ | 3 | COOKMATIC LEVEL ☐

Whole Yellow Peas

1 | COOKING PROGRAM | 9:00 | COOK ☐

2 | COOKING PROGRAM | 8:00 to 12:00 | COOK ☐ | 5 | COOKMATIC LEVEL ☐

General Instructions for Cooking Dried Legumes

1 cup dried legumes
3 cups water

1 teaspoon salt
1/8 teaspoon baking soda
2 tablespoons vegetable oil

1. Soak legumes in water overnight in 3 to 4-quart casserole.

2. Add salt, baking soda and oil. Cover. Cook in Radarange Oven, covered, according to directions on chart, or until legumes are tender, as desired. Stir occasionally during cooking time.

Blanching and Freezing Vegetables

Select only the best vegetables for freezing. They should be slightly immature by table or canning standards. Use vegetables which are the most brightly colored and have the best texture.

To preserve their fresh qualities, almost all vegetables should be blanched before freezing. Blanching slows and checks the plant enzyme activity responsible for losses in quality. Blanching maintains color, making vegetables more attractive. It softens vegetables, making packaging easier. Blanching also cleans the vegetable and destroys harmful and undesirable bacteria.

Blanching may be done more easily and quickly in the Radarange Oven than conventionally. Follow the special instructions and timings on the "Blanching Vegetables Chart" for each specific vegetable. For any vegetable not listed, a general rule to follow is: blanching time is approximately equal to half of the regular microwave cooking time. See the "Fresh Vegetable Cooking Chart," on pages 242 to 243 for cooking times. Always blanch on FULL POWER. Stir or rearrange the vegetables halfway through blanching to assure even distribution of heat.

General Instructions for Blanching Vegetables

1. Prepare the vegetables, according to the "Preparation" described in the chart. Use only the amount of vegetables recommended and use the size of utensil stated in the chart. When increasing or decreasing the amounts of vegetables listed, adjust the blanching time accordingly.
2. Add the amount of water suggested in the chart. Do not salt the vegetables.
3. Heat in the Radarange Oven, covered, on FULL POWER. Stir and rearrange the vegetables halfway through the cooking time, if necessary.
4. Plunge the vegetables into ice water immediately after blanching so cooking will cease. Remove excess moisture from vegetables with paper towels.
5. Package the vegetables for the freezer in airtight containers, using proper freezing methods. Label the vegetable with its name and the date.

BLANCHING VEGETABLES CHART

VEGETABLE	PREPARATION	AMOUNT OF VEGETABLE	CASSEROLE SIZE	AMOUNT OF WATER	BLANCHING TIME ON FULL POWER
Asparagus	Wash and trim as for table use (do not use woody portions). Cut in 1-inch pieces. (Less desirable pieces may be completely cooked and frozen for use in soups.)	1 lb.	2-quart	1/4 cup	2-1/2 to 3-1/2 min.
Beans, Yellow, Snap Green	Select tender pods, with beans slightly under-mature. Wash thoroughly. Remove ends and cut into desired lengths, leave whole, or French cut.	1 lb. or 3 cups	1-1/2-quart	1/3 cup	4 to 5 min.
Broccoli	Use compact heads of uniform green color. (Soak first in salt solution for 1/2 hour to remove insects.) Rinse. Remove woody portions, cut into pieces not more than 1" across and 5-6" long.	1 lb.	2-quart	1/3 cup	3-1/2 to 4-1/2 min.
Carrots	Select young, tender carrots. Remove tops, wash and scrape. Small carrots may be frozen whole. Others may be sliced, diced or Frenched.	1 lb.	1-1/2-quart	1/4 cup	3-1/2 to 4-1/2 min.
Cauliflower	Use compact, tender white heads. Wash. Break into flowerets. (Soak in salt solution if desired—see Broccoli.)	1 head	2-quart	1/3 cup	4 to 5 min.
Corn on the Cob	Select tender, ripe ears, in full milk stage. Remove husks and silk. Wash and trim ears.	4 ears	2-quart	none	3-1/2 to 4-1/2 min.
Corn, Whole Kernel	Same as corn-on-the-cob.	4 cups	1-1/2-quart	none	3-1/2 to 4-1/2 min.
Peas	Select tender peas, not fully mature. Shell. (If hard to shell, plunge pods in boiling water for 1 min. Cool quickly.) Do not wash after shelling.	4 cups	1-1/2-quart	1/4 cup	4 to 5 min.
Spinach	Pick young, tender leaves. Discard tough, large stems. Wash very thoroughly. Blanch only a small amount at one time.	1/2 lb.	2-quart	none	1-1/2 to 2 min.
Squash, Summer, Zucchini	Pick squash while rind is still tender and seeds small. Wash, then peel, if desired, or leave unpeeled. Cut in 1/4-inch slices.	1 lb.	1-1/2-quart	1/4 cup	2 to 3 min.

CANNED VEGETABLE HEATING CHART

CAN SIZE OR QUANTITY	HEATING TIME ON FULL POWER
7 to 8 oz.	1 to 2 min.
12 oz.	1-1/2 to 2-1/2 min.
16 oz.	2 to 3 min.
27 oz.	3 to 4 min.

General Instructions for Reheating Canned Vegetables

1. Drain most of the liquid, if desired, and place the vegetable in a 1-quart casserole, or in a smaller casserole or bowl.

2. Most canned vegetables require about the same amount of heating time. Heat on FULL POWER, according to the quantities on the chart.

3. Stir halfway through the cooking time.

CANNED PORK AND BEANS HEATING CHART

CAN SIZE OR QUANTITY	HEATING TIME ON FULL POWER
8 oz.	1 to 1-1/2 min.
16 oz.	1-1/2 to 2-1/2 min.
25 oz.	3 to 4-1/2 min.
31 oz.	4-1/2 to 5-1/2 min.

General Instructions for Heating Canned Pork and Beans

1. Place the pork and beans in a 1-quart casserole, or in a smaller glass dish or bowl.

2. Heat on FULL POWER for the times listed on the chart, or use the Temperature-Control to stop the Radarange Oven at 150° F.

3. Stir halfway through the cooking time.

Acorn Squash

Yield: 2 servings

1 acorn squash
1 tablespoon brown sugar
1/4 teaspoon cinnamon
1 tablespoon butter or margarine

1. Cut squash in half, lengthwise. Remove seeds. Combine brown sugar and cinnamon. Sprinkle half of mixture in each squash half. Dot with butter. Place in shallow dish. Cover loosely with plastic wrap.

2. Cook in Radarange Oven, covered, on FULL POWER for 6 to 8 minutes, or until tender.

Acorn Squash Marmalade

Yield: 2 servings

1 acorn squash
3 tablespoons butter or margarine, softened
3 tablespoons orange marmalade
Cinnamon

1. Cut squash in half, lengthwise. Remove seeds. Place in shallow dish. Cover loosely with plastic wrap. Cook in Radarange Oven, covered, on FULL POWER for 4 minutes. Combine butter and marmalade. Blend well. Spoon mixture into each half. Sprinkle with cinnamon, as desired. Cover loosely with plastic wrap.

2. Cook in Radarange Oven, covered, on FULL POWER for 3 to 5 min minutes, or until tender.

Apple-Filled Acorn Squash

Yield: 2 servings

1 acorn squash
1 medium apple, peeled and chopped
1 tablespoon brown sugar
1/4 teaspoon cinnamon
1 tablespoon butter or margarine

1. Cut squash in half, lengthwise. Remove seeds. Combine apple, brown sugar and cinnamon. Sprinkle half of mixture in each squash half. Dot with butter. Place in shallow dish. Cover loosely with plastic wrap.

2. Cook in Radarange Oven, covered, on FULL POWER for 7 to 9 minutes, or until tender.

Cranberry Squash

Yield: 2 servings

1 acorn squash
1/4 cup cranberries
1/4 cup brown sugar, firmly packed
1/4 teaspoon cinnamon
1 tablespoon butter or margarine

1. Cut squash in half, lengthwise. Remove seeds. Combine cranberries, brown sugar and cinnamon. Sprinkle half of mixture in each squash half. Dot with butter. Place in shallow dish. Cover loosely with plastic wrap.

2. Cook in Radarange Oven, covered, on FULL POWER for 7 to 9 minutes, or until tender.

Au Gratin Carrots

Yield: 4 servings

3 cups carrots, thinly sliced
2 tablespoons water
1 cup (4 oz.) Cheddar cheese, shredded
1 (10-3/4 oz.) can cream of mushroom soup

1 tablespoon butter or margarine
1/4 cup cornflake crumbs

1. Place carrots and water in 2-quart casserole. Cook in Radarange Oven, covered, on FULL POWER for 3 to 4 minutes, or until tender. Drain. Stir in cheese and soup.

2. Place butter in small dish. Heat in Radarange Oven on FULL POWER for 30 to 45 seconds, or until melted. Toss crumbs in butter to coat. Sprinkle over carrots.

3. Cook in Radarange Oven on FULL POWER for 2 to 3 minutes, or until heated through.

Artichoke

Yield: 1 artichoke

2 tablespoons water
1 teaspoon vinegar
4 drops olive oil
1 medium artichoke

1. Combine water, vinegar and olive oil in 4-cup glass measure. Trim sharp ends of artichoke leaves with kitchen shears. Invert artichoke in measure. Cover with waxed paper.

2. Cook in Radarange Oven, covered, on FULL POWER for 4 to 6 minutes, or until barely tender.

Asparagus Royale

Yield: 6 servings

1/2 small onion, chopped
1/3 cup green pepper, chopped
2 tablespoons water

2 (10 oz. each) pkgs. frozen asparagus spears
1 tablespoon pimento, diced
1 tablespoon parsley flakes
Salt
Pepper

1. Combine onion, green pepper and water in 2-quart casserole. Cook in Radarange Oven, covered, on FULL POWER for 2 to 3 minutes, or until onion and green pepper are tender.

2. Add remaining ingredients. Season with salt and pepper, as desired. Mix well. Cover with plastic wrap. Cook in Radarange Oven, covered, on FULL POWER for 8 to 10 minutes, or until asparagus is tender. Stir halfway through cooking time.

MICRO-TIP: This is a colorful recipe for weight watchers.

Asparagus Sea Shore Style

Yield: 6 servings

2 (10 oz. each) pkgs. frozen asparagus pieces
1/4 cup water

1 (10-3/4 oz.) can cream of shrimp soup
1 (3 oz.) pkg. cream cheese, softened
Dash cayenne pepper
1 (4-1/2 oz.) can small shrimp, drained
1/2 cup buttered bread crumbs
Paprika

1. Place asparagus and water in 2-quart glass casserole. Cook in Radarange Oven, covered, on FULL POWER for 8 to 10 minutes. Drain.

2. Blend together soup, cream cheese and pepper. Stir in shrimp. Pour over asparagus. Top with buttered crumbs. Sprinkle with paprika, as desired.

3. Cook in Radarange Oven on FULL POWER for 4 to 5 minutes, or until tender.

Boston-Style Baked Corn

Yield: 6 servings

1 cup catsup
2 tablespoons brown sugar
1 teaspoon dry mustard
1/2 teaspoon salt
1/4 cup onion, chopped
2 (12 oz. each) cans whole kernel corn, drained

3 slices bacon, cooked and crumbled

1. Combine catsup, brown sugar, mustard and salt in 1-1/2-quart casserole. Stir in onion and corn. Cook in Radarange Oven, covered, on FULL POWER for 5 minutes, or until warmed. Stir halfway through cooking time.

2. Sprinkle bacon pieces over top. Cook in Radarange Oven on FULL POWER for 5 minutes, or until heated through and temperature of 150°F is reached.

MICRO-TIP: Use the Temperature-Control to stop the Radarange Oven at 150°F.

Snappy Baked Beans

Yield: 6 servings

4 slices bacon, cut in small pieces

2 (1 lb. each) cans pork and beans
1/4 cup dark corn syrup
1/4 cup catsup
2 tablespoons onion, chopped
3/4 cup gingersnaps, finely crushed

1. Place bacon in 1-1/2-quart casserole or bean pot. Cook in Radarange Oven on FULL POWER for 3-1/2 to 4-1/2 minutes, or until crisp. Stir halfway through cooking time. Drain.

2. Stir in remaining ingredients. Cook in Radarange Oven on FULL POWER for 10 minutes, or until temperature of 150° F is reached. Stir halfway through cooking time.

MICRO-TIP: Use the Temperature-Control to stop the Radarange Oven at 150°F.

Toll House Baked Beans

Yield: 6 to 8 servings

2 (1 lb. 2 oz. each) cans New England style baked beans
1 (1 lb.) can solid pack tomatoes
1/4 lb. bacon, cooked and crumbled
1/2 cup onion, minced
2 tablespoons dark molasses
1 tablespoon sugar
2 teaspoons dry mustard

1. Pour beans into 3-quart casserole or bean pot. Break up tomatoes and combine with remaining ingredients. Mix into beans.

2. Cook in Radarange Oven, covered, on FULL POWER for 10 to 12 minutes, or until a temperature of 150° F is reached. Stir halfway through cooking time.

MICRO-TIP: Use the Temperature-Hold to maintain 150°F until ready to serve.

Calico Bean Pot

Yield: 12 servings

8 slices bacon, cut in small pieces

1 cup onion, chopped

1 (1 lb.) can green beans, drained
1 (1 lb.) can lima beans, drained
1 (1 lb. 15 oz.) can pork and beans
1 (1 lb.) can kidney beans, drained
3/4 cup brown sugar, firmly packed
1/2 cup vinegar
1/2 teaspoon garlic salt
1/2 teaspoon dry mustard
1/8 teaspoon pepper

1. Place bacon in 4-quart casserole. Cook in Radarange Oven on FULL POWER for 6 to 7 minutes, or until crisp. Remove bacon and reserve.

2. Place onion in bacon fat. Cook in Radarange Oven on FULL POWER for 2 to 3 minutes, or until onion is tender.

3. Add remaining ingredients and bacon. Mix lightly. Cook in Radarange Oven on FULL POWER for 12 to 15 minutes, or until heated through, and temperature of 150°F is reached. Stir halfway through cooking time.

MICRO-TIP: For extra rich flavor, use the Temperature-Control to cook to 150°F on Cookmatic Level 5 (SLO COOK). This method should take about twice as long, but will slow cook for maximum blending of flavors.

Honeyed Beets
Yield: 6 servings

1 tablespoon cornstarch
1/2 teaspoon salt
1 tablespoon water or beet juice
2 tablespoons vinegar
1/4 cup honey
1 tablespoon butter or margarine

2 cups cooked beets, diced or sliced

1. Combine cornstarch and salt in small glass bowl or measure. Blend in water. Stir in vinegar, honey and butter. Cook in Radarange Oven on FULL POWER for 45 seconds to 1 minute, or until thickened. Stir occasionally during cooking time.

2. Place beets in 1-1/2-quart casserole. Pour sauce over beets. Heat in Radarange Oven, covered, on FULL POWER for 1 to 1-1/2 minutes, or until heated through.

   MICRO-TIP: For maximum blending of flavors, let stand 10 minutes, covered. Reheat in Radarange Oven on FULL POWER for 1 minute.

Herbed Broccoli
Yield: 3 to 4 servings

3 tablespoons water
1 teaspoon instant chicken bouillon
1 teaspoon Italian seasoning
1/4 teaspoon onion powder
1 (10 oz.) pkg. frozen broccoli

1. Combine water and instant bouillon in 1-1/2-quart casserole. Cook in Radarange Oven on FULL POWER for 30 seconds, or until boiling. Stir in seasonings. Add broccoli.

2. Cook in Radarange Oven, covered, on FULL POWER for 5 to 7 minutes, or until tender. Break apart and stir halfway through cooking time.

Broccoli-Onion Casserole
Yield: 6 to 8 servings

2 (10 oz. each) pkgs. frozen broccoli cuts
2 tablespoons water
1 (8 oz.) can pearl onions, drained
1 (10-3/4 oz.) can cream of celery or cream of mushroom soup
1/4 cup cracker crumbs

1/2 cup Cheddar cheese, shredded

1. Place frozen broccoli and water in 2-quart casserole. Cook in Radarange Oven, covered, on FULL POWER for 10 to 11 minutes, or until tender. Drain. Stir to break up. Stir in onions and soup. Top with cracker crumbs.

2. Cook in Radarange Oven on FULL POWER for 5 to 7 minutes, or until heated through. Sprinkle with cheese. Cook in Radarange Oven on Cookmatic Level 5 (SLO COOK) for 1 to 1-1/2 minutes, or until cheese is melted.

Broccoli-Rice Casserole
Yield: 6 to 8 servings

2 (10 oz. each) pkgs. frozen broccoli, cuts
2 cups cooked rice
1 (10-3/4 oz.) can cream of mushroom soup
1 (8 oz.) jar cheese spread
3 tablespoons bread crumbs

1. Place broccoli in 2-quart utility dish. Cover with plastic wrap. Cook in Radarange Oven, covered, on FULL POWER for 10 to 11 minutes, or until tender. Drain. Stir to break up. Stir in rice, soup and cheese spread. Top with bread crumbs.

2. Cook in Radarange Oven on FULL POWER for 6 to 8 minutes, or until heated through and temperature of 150° F is reached.*

   *MICRO-TIP: Use the Temperature-Control to stop the Radarange Oven at 150°F.

Broccoli-Corn Casserole

Yield: 6 servings

1 (10 oz.) pkg. frozen broccoli cuts
1 tablespoon water
1 (1 lb.) can cream style corn
2 tablespoons butter or margarine, melted
1 egg, slightly-beaten
1 teaspoon instant, minced onion
2 strips bacon, cooked and crumbled
1 cup croutons, herb-seasoned

1. Place broccoli and water in 1-quart casserole. Cook in Radarange Oven, covered, on FULL POWER for 5 to 7 minutes, or until tender. Drain. Stir to break up. Blend in corn, butter, egg and onion. Top with bacon and croutons.

2. Cook in Radarange Oven on FULL POWER for 5 minutes, or until heated through and temperature of 150°F is reached.*

MICRO-TIPS:

*Use the Temperature-Control to stop the Radarange Oven at 150°F.

•Herb seasoned stuffing mix may be used for the topping.

Sweet-Sour Red Cabbage

Yield: 6 servings

1 medium red cabbage, shredded
2 tart apples, peeled and chopped
1 cup boiling water
1/2 cup apple cider vinegar
3 tablespoons butter or margarine
3 tablespoons sugar
1/2 teaspoon salt
1 stick cinnamon

1. Combine all ingredients in 3-quart casserole.

2. Cook in Radarange Oven, covered, on FULL POWER for 10 to 12 minutes, or until cabbage is barely tender. Stir halfway through cooking time.

Parsley Buttered Carrots

Yield: 3 to 4 servings

2 cups carrots, sliced into 1/3 to 1/2-inch pieces
2 tablespoons butter or margarine
1 tablespoon parsley flakes

1. Place butter in 1-quart casserole. Heat in Radarange Oven on FULL POWER for 20 to 30 seconds, or until melted. Stir in carrots and parsley flakes. Mix well.

2. Cook in Radarange Oven, covered, on FULL POWER for 4 to 5 minutes, or until tender.

MICRO-TIP: Calorie watchers may substitute 2 tablespoons of water for butter.

Marmalade Carrots

Yield: 6 to 8 servings

4 cups carrots, thinly sliced
1/3 cup orange juice
1/2 teaspoon salt
1/4 teaspoon ginger
1/3 cup marmalade
1 tablespoon butter or margarine

1. Combine carrots, orange juice, salt, ginger and marmalade in 2-quart casserole. Mix well. Dot with butter.

2. Cook in Radarange Oven, covered, on FULL POWER for 7 to 9 minutes, or until tender. Stir halfway through cooking time.

Mandarin Carrots

Yield: 6 servings

4 cups carrots, cut into 2-inch slices
2 tablespoons butter or margarine
1 (11 oz.) can mandarin orange sections, drained
1/2 teaspoon salt
1/8 teaspoon ginger

1. Place carrots and butter in 1-1/2-quart casserole. Cook in Radarange Oven, covered, on FULL POWER for 7 to 9 minutes, or until tender. Stir halfway through cooking time. Add mandarin oranges, salt and ginger.

2. Cook in Radarange Oven, covered, on FULL POWER for 2 minutes, or until heated through.

Cauliflower Oriental

Yield: 6 servings

1 medium head cauliflower, broken into pieces
2 tablespoons water

1/2 cup onion, chopped
1/2 cup celery, diced
1 tablespoon parsley, chopped
1 tablespoon butter or margarine

1 teaspoon instant chicken bouillon
1 cup boiling water
1 tablespoon cornstarch
1 tablespoon soy sauce
Dash pepper

1. Place cauliflower and water in 2-quart casserole. Cook in Radarange Oven, covered, on FULL POWER for 8 to 10 minutes, or until tender. Let stand, covered.

2. Combine onion, celery, parsley and butter in 1-quart casserole. Cook in Radarange Oven on FULL POWER for 3 to 4 minutes, or until vegetables are tender. Stir halfway through cooking time.

3. Dissolve bouillon in water. Blend in cornstarch, soy sauce and pepper. Pour into onion mixture. Cook in Radarange Oven on FULL POWER for 2 minutes, or until thickened. Stir halfway through cooking time.

4. Drain cauliflower. Place in serving dish if other than casserole. Spoon sauce over.

MICRO-TIP: 2 (10 oz. each) pkgs. frozen cauliflower may be used instead of fresh.

Corn-in-the-Husk

Yield: 3 to 5 servings

5 ears corn
Butter or margarine (optional)

1. Remove outer husks, but leave inner husk on corn. Carefully remove silk. Spread butter on corn, if desired. Replace husks and fasten with string or rubber band. Place corn on plastic rack or directly on Radarange Oven glass tray.

2. Cook in Radarange Oven on FULL POWER for 8 to 9 minutes, or until steaming hot. Turn corn over halfway through cooking time.

MICRO-TIPS:

•If husks are removed, wrap corn in waxed paper.

•To cook a smaller quantity of corn, cook 1 ear in Radarange Oven on FULL POWER for 1-1/2 to 2 minutes, or until steaming hot.

Scalloped Corn

Yield: 4 to 6 servings

1 (17 oz.) can cream-style corn
1/2 cup milk
1 egg
1/2 teaspoon onion salt
1/4 cup cornflake crumbs
1/4 cup Cheddar cheese, shredded

1. Combine corn, milk, egg and onion salt in 1-quart casserole. Combine cornflake crumbs and cheese. Spread over corn mixture.

2. Bake in Radarange Oven on Cookmatic Level 5 (SLO COOK) for 15 to 18 minutes, or until knife inserted near center comes out clean.*

   *MICRO-TIP: You may want to turn dish halfway through cooking time.

Onion Lovers' Corn On The Cob

Yield: 4 servings

2 tablespoons dry onion soup mix
1 tablespoon water
4 ears frozen corn on the cob

1. Combine soup and water. Spread on frozen corn. Place in 8 x 8 x 2-inch dish or on cooking grill. Cover with waxed paper.

2. Cook in Radarange Oven, covered, on FULL POWER for 10 to 11 minutes, or until heated through and tender.

   MICRO-TIPS:

   • This is a low calorie corn recipe, with about 85 calories per ear of corn.

   • Fresh corn can be substituted by cooking on FULL POWER for 2 minutes per ear of corn.

Grecian Eggplant

Yield: 4 servings

1 medium eggplant

2 slices bacon

1 cup onion, chopped
1 large green pepper, chopped
1 (1 lb.) can stewed tomatoes, partially drained
1 teaspoon leaf oregano
1 teaspoon leaf basil
1/8 teaspoon instant, minced garlic
1/8 teaspoon pepper

1 tablespoon pimento, chopped
1 tablespoon capers (optional)

1. Cut eggplant in half lengthwise. Score surface crosswise, leaving shell intact. Remove and cube pulp of eggplant. Set aside.

2. Place bacon in 10-inch ceramic skillet or 2-quart casserole. Cook in Radarange Oven on FULL POWER for 1-1/2 to 2 minutes, or until crisp. Remove bacon and reserve.

3. Place onion and green pepper in bacon fat. Cook in Radarange Oven on FULL POWER for 3 minutes, or until onion and green pepper are tender. Add eggplant, tomatoes and seasonings.

4. Cook in Radarange Oven on FULL POWER for 5 to 6 minutes, or until eggplant is tender. Stir halfway through cooking time. Drain juices. Fill eggplant shells with vegetable mixture. Garnish with crumbled bacon, pimento and capers.

   MICRO-TIPS:

   • Grecian Eggplant can be prepared ahead, refrigerated, and then reheated in the Radarange Oven on FULL POWER for 3 minutes.

   • This is a low calorie vegetable, with only 96 calories per serving.

Eggplant-Tomato Bake

Yield: 4 servings

1 medium eggplant (about 1-1/2 lbs.), pared and sliced into 3/4-inch thick slices
1/2 teaspoon salt
1/4 teaspoon pepper
1/2 teaspoon oregano
1 medium onion, thinly sliced
1 (14-1/2 oz.) can stewed tomatoes

3/4 cup Mozzarella cheese, shredded

1. Place eggplant in 2-quart utility dish. Season with salt, pepper and oregano. Top with onion and tomatoes. Cover loosely with plastic wrap.

2. Cook in Radarange Oven, covered, on FULL POWER for 7 to 9 minutes, or until eggplant is tender. Top with cheese. Cook in Radarange Oven on Cookmatic Level 5 (SLO COOK) for 30 seconds to 1 minute, or until cheese is melted.

Ratatouille

Yield: 4 to 6 servings

1-1/2 cups eggplant, peeled and diced
1/2 cup onion, thinly sliced
1 clove garlic, minced
3 tablespoons olive oil or vegetable oil

1 medium green pepper, cut in 1/2-inch strips
1-1/2 cups zucchini, sliced
1 (16 oz.) can stewed tomatoes
1 teaspoon salt
1/4 teaspoon Italian seasoning
Dash pepper

1. Place eggplant, onion, garlic and oil in 2-quart casserole. Cook in Radarange Oven on FULL POWER for 5 minutes. Stir halfway through cooking time.

2. Layer peppers and zucchini over eggplant mixture. Add seasonings to tomatoes. Pour over vegetables.

3. Cook in Radarange Oven, covered, on FULL POWER for 8 to 10 minutes, or until vegetables are tender. Let stand 5 minutes, covered, before serving.

Snappy Green Beans

Yield: 6 servings

2 (9 oz. each) pkgs. frozen French-cut green beans
1/4 cup plain yogurt
1 teaspoon salt
1/2 teaspoon prepared mustard
1/4 teaspoon Worcestershire sauce

1. Place beans in 1-1/2-quart casserole. Cook in Radarange Oven, covered, on FULL POWER for 10 to 12 minutes, or until tender. Drain. Combine remaining ingredients. Mix lightly with beans.

2. Cook in Radarange Oven on FULL POWER for 1 minute, or until heated through.

MICRO-TIP: Make your own yogurt in the Radarange Oven. See page 364.

Sweet-Sour Green Beans

Yield: 4 servings

2 strips bacon

1 cup onion, chopped

2 tablespoons all-purpose flour
2 tablespoons brown sugar
1/4 cup vinegar
1/2 cup tomatoes, chopped
1 (1 lb.) can green beans, with
   liquid
1/2 teaspoon salt
1/4 teaspoon pepper

1. Place bacon in 1-1/2-quart casserole. Cook in Radarange Oven on FULL POWER for 2 minutes, or until crisp. Remove bacon and reserve.

2. Place onion in bacon grease. Cook in Radarange Oven on FULL POWER for 2 to 3 minutes, or until onion is tender.

3. Blend in flour, brown sugar, vinegar, tomatoes, liquid from green beans and seasonings. Cook in Radarange Oven on FULL POWER for 2 minutes, or until mixture boils.

4. Add green beans. Cook in Radarange Oven on FULL POWER for 1 minute, or until heated through. Sprinkle with crumbled bacon.

Classic Green Bean Treat

Yield: 4 to 6 servings

2 (10 oz. each) pkgs. frozen green
   beans, regular or French-cut
1/2 teaspoon salt
1 (10-3/4 oz.) can cream of
   celery soup
1 (2 oz.) can sliced mushrooms,
   drained (optional)

1 (3 oz.) can French fried onion
   rings**

1. Place beans in 1-1/2-quart casserole. Sprinkle with salt. Spread soup and mushrooms over beans.

2. Cook in Radarange Oven, covered, on FULL POWER for 7 to 10 minutes, or until warmed. Stir.

3. Sprinkle onion rings over top. Cook in Radarange Oven on FULL POWER for 6 to 7 minutes, or until heated through and temperature of 150°F is reached.*

MICRO-TIPS:

*Use the Temperature-Control to stop the Radarange Oven at 150°F.

•Other cream soups, such as cream of mushroom soup, may be substituted for the cream of celery soup.

•2 (1 lb. each) cans of green beans may be substituted for the frozen green beans. Combine all ingredients and cook in Radarange Oven on FULL POWER for 5 to 7 minutes, or until temperature of 150°F is reached.

**Reserve a few onion rings to put on top just before serving, for extra crunch.

French Green Bean-Mushroom Bake

Yield: 4 servings

1-1/2 teaspoons vegetable oil
2 tablespoons green onion, chopped

1 (2-1/2 oz.) can sliced mushrooms, drained
1 teaspoon lemon juice
1 teaspoon paprika
1/2 teaspoon cornstarch
2 tablespoons water

1 (10 oz.) pkg. frozen French-cut green beans

1. Place oil and onion in 1-1/2-quart casserole. Cook in Radarange Oven, covered, on FULL POWER for 1 minute, or until onion is tender.

2. Add mushrooms, lemon juice, paprika, cornstarch and water. Cook in Radarange Oven, covered, on FULL POWER for 2 to 3 minutes, or until slightly thickened.

3. Add green beans. Cook in Radarange Oven, covered, on FULL POWER for 5-1/2 to 6-1/2 minutes, or until heated through. Stir halfway through cooking to separate and mix frozen beans.

French Onion Casserole

Yield: 4 to 6 servings

4 medium onions, sliced
3 tablespoons butter or margarine

2 tablespoons all-purpose flour
Dash pepper
3/4 cup beef bouillon
1/4 cup dry sherry

1-1/2 cups plain croutons
2 tablespoons butter or margarine, melted
1/2 cup process Swiss cheese, shredded
3 tablespoons grated Parmesan cheese
Paprika

1. Place onion and butter in 1-1/2-quart casserole. Cook in Radarange Oven, covered, on FULL POWER for 7 to 9 minutes, or until onion is tender. Stir halfway through cooking time.

2. Blend in flour and pepper. Add bouillon and sherry. Cook in Radarange Oven on FULL POWER for 2 minutes, or until thickened. Stir halfway through cooking time.

3. Toss croutons with butter. Spoon over onion mixture. Sprinkle with cheeses. Season with paprika, as desired. Cook in Radarange Oven on Cookmatic Level 5 (SLO COOK) for 2 minutes, or until cheese is melted.

Creamy Corn and Mushrooms

Yield: 4 servings

1 (2-1/2 oz.) jar sliced mushrooms, drained
1/4 cup onion, chopped
2 tablespoons butter or margarine

1 (16 oz.) can corn, drained
1/3 cup evaporated milk
1 tablespoon parsley, snipped
Salt
Pepper

1. Combine mushrooms, onion and butter in 1-quart casserole. Cook in Radarange Oven on FULL POWER for 4 minutes, or until onion is tender. Stir halfway through cooking time.

2. Stir in corn. Cook in Radarange Oven on FULL POWER for 2 minutes, or until hot. Blend in milk. Garnish with parsley. Season with salt and pepper, as desired.

CONVENIENCE POTATO CHART

TYPE AND AMOUNT	UTENSIL	EXTRA INGREDIENTS*	COOKING TIME ON FULL POWER	SPECIAL INSTRUCTIONS
Au Gratin Potato Mix (5.5 oz.)	3-quart casserole	2 tablespoons butter or margarine 2-1/4 cups boiling water	12 to 14 min.	Combine all ingredients in casserole. Cook, until potatoes are tender. Stir halfway through cooking time.
Scalloped Potato Mix (5.5 oz.)	3-quart casserole	2 tablespoons butter or margarine 2-1/2 cups boiling water 2/3 cup milk	13 to 15 min.	Combine all ingredients in casserole. Cook until potatoes are tender. Stir halfway through cooking time.
Instant Mashed Potatoes (2 servings)**	2-cup glass measure	3/4 cup water 1 tablespoon butter or margarine 1/4 teaspoon salt 1/4 cup milk 3/4 cup instant mashed potatoes	2 to 3 min.	Combine water, butter and salt in glass measure. Cook in Radarange Oven until boiling. Blend in milk and instant potatoes. Let stand until moisture is absorbed. Stir and serve.

*May vary among different brands. Add extra ingredients as listed on the package.

**For more servings, increase amounts of ingredients and cooking time proportionately.

General Instructions for Cooking Convenience Potatoes

1. Read the "Special Instructions" on the chart before cooking the potatoes.

2. Cook in the Radarange Oven, covered, on FULL POWER, according to the time on the chart.

Cheesy Potato Bake
Yield: 6 to 8 servings

1 (10-3/4 oz.) can Cheddar cheese soup
1/2 cup milk

5 cups potatoes, sliced
2 cups onion, sliced
Paprika

1. Mix together soup and milk.

2. Place half of potatoes in 2-quart casserole. Top with half of onion and half of soup mixture. Repeat process. Sprinkle with paprika, as desired.

3. Bake in Radarange Oven, covered, on Cookmatic Level 8 (MEDIUM HIGH) for 20 to 25 minutes, or until potatoes are tender.

Party Potatoes
Yield: 8 servings

8 to 10 medium potatoes, peeled and cut into eighths
1/2 cup water

1 (8 oz.) pkg. cream cheese
1 (8 oz.) carton French onion dip
1/2 teaspoon salt
1/8 teaspoon pepper
1/2 teaspoon garlic salt (optional)
Butter or margarine

Paprika

1. Place potatoes in 3-quart casserole. Add water. Cook in Radarange Oven, covered, on FULL POWER for 12 to 14 minutes, or until potatoes are tender. Stir halfway through cooking time. Drain.

2. Beat together cream cheese, onion dip, salt, pepper and garlic salt in large mixing bowl, until well-blended. Add hot potatoes, one at a time, beating until light and fluffy. Spoon into 2-quart casserole. Dot with butter, as desired.

3. Cook in Radarange Oven, covered, on Cookmatic Level 8 (MEDIUM HIGH) for 5 to 7 minutes, or until heated through, and temperature of 150° F is reached. Sprinkle with paprika, as desired, before serving.

Scalloped Tomato Potatoes

Yield: 6 to 8 servings

1/2 cup onion, chopped
2 tablespoons butter or margarine

2 tablespoons all-purpose flour
1/2 teaspoon salt
1/8 teaspoon pepper
1 cup water
1 (8 oz.) can stewed tomatoes
2 teaspoons instant chicken
   bouillon

5 cups potatoes, peeled and
   thinly sliced
Grated Parmesan cheese

1. Place onion and butter in 1-1/2-quart casserole. Cook in Radarange Oven on FULL POWER for 1-1/2 minutes, or until onion is tender.

2. Blend in flour, seasonings, water, tomatoes and bouillon. Cook in Radarange Oven on FULL POWER for 4 minutes, or until thickened. Stir halfway through cooking time.

3. Add potatoes. Stir lightly to coat. Cook in Radarange Oven, covered, on FULL POWER for 13 to 15 minutes, or until potatoes are tender. Sprinkle with Parmesan cheese, as desired.

Baked Potatoes

Select uniform, medium-size baking potatoes, about 7-ozs. each. Scrub potatoes well. Prick each potato through the skin with the tines of a fork in several places. Arrange potatoes on a paper towel in the Radarange Oven. Leave about 1-inch space between potatoes and avoid placing one potato in the center surrounded by other potatoes. Arrange the potatoes in a circle. Bake in Radarange Oven on FULL POWER for the times indicated below. These times are approximate and will vary, according to the size and variety of the potatoes being cooked. Turn the potatoes over halfway through the cooking time.

QUANTITY	TIME	SETTING
1 potato	3 to 5 min.	FULL POWER
2 potatoes	5 to 6 min.	FULL POWER
4 potatoes	9 to 11 min.	FULL POWER

MICRO-TIP: If the potatoes are still slightly undercooked, or if you want to keep them warm for several minutes before serving, wrap the potatoes in foil **after** their removal from the Radarange Oven.

Twice-Baked Potatoes

Yield: 4 servings

4 medium (7 oz. each) baking
   potatoes

1/2 cup dairy sour cream
1 (3 oz.) pkg. cream cheese,
   softened
2 tablespoons butter or margarine
1 teaspoon onion salt
1 teaspoon frozen chives
1/8 teaspoon pepper
Paprika
Parsley flakes

1. Pierce skins of potatoes with tines of fork. Arrange potatoes in circle on Radarange Oven glass tray. Bake in Radarange Oven on FULL POWER for 9 to 11 minutes, or until potatoes are done.

2. Cut slice from top of each potato and scoop out insides into mixing bowl. Add remaining ingredients, except paprika and parsley flakes. Beat until smooth. Spoon back into potato shells. Garnish with paprika and parsley flakes, as desired.

3. Heat in Radarange Oven on FULL POWER for 2-1/2 to 3 minutes, or until heated through.

MICRO-TIP: Potatoes may be topped with shredded Cheddar cheese. Heat in Radarange Oven on Cookmatic Level 5 (SLO COOK) for 1 minute, or until cheese is melted.

French Fry Casserole

Yield: 6 to 8 servings

1/2 cup onion, chopped
1/2 cup green pepper, chopped
1 tablespoon vegetable oil

1/2 (10-3/4 oz.) can Cheddar cheese soup (about 1/2 cup)
1 (10-3/4 oz.) can cream of celery soup
1/2 cup mayonnaise
1 teaspoon salt
1/4 teaspoon pepper

1 (20 oz.) pkg. frozen French fried potatoes
1 (10 oz.) pkg. frozen cut green beans

1. Place onion, green pepper and oil in 1-1/2-quart casserole. Cook in Radarange Oven on FULL POWER for 3 to 4 minutes, or until onion and green pepper are tender.

2. Combine soups, mayonnaise and seasonings with onion mixture. Blend well.

3. Mix together potatoes and green beans. Spread in 2-quart utility dish. Pour sauce over potatoes and green beans. Cover loosely with plastic wrap.

4. Cook in Radarange Oven, covered, on FULL POWER for 20 to 25 minutes, or until heated through and temperature of 150°F is reached.

Tomato Casserole

Yield: 6 to 8 servings

1/4 cup butter or margarine
4 cups bread cubes

1 tablespoon butter or margarine
1 cup onion, chopped
2 (1 lb. each) cans tomato wedges
1 tablespoon sugar
1 teaspoon salt
1/4 teaspoon ground oregano
Dash cayenne pepper

1 cup Cheddar cheese, shredded

1. Preheat large browning skillet, according to manufacturer's instructions for bread. Melt half of butter in skillet. Add half of bread cubes. Toss to brown. Cook in Radarange Oven on FULL POWER for 2 minutes. Wipe out skillet with paper towel. Re-preheat browning skillet, according to manufacturer's instructions. Repeat cooking time with remaining butter and bread cubes. Set aside.

2. Place butter and onion in 1-1/2-quart casserole. Cook in Radarange Oven, covered, on FULL POWER for 2 minutes, or until onion is tender. Stir in remaining ingredients, except cheese and bread cubes.

3. Layer bread cubes, tomato mixture and cheese to form two layers in 1-1/2-quart casserole. Top with remaining cheese.

4. Cook in Radarange Oven, covered, on FULL POWER for 8 to 10 minutes, or until temperature of 140°F is reached.*

    *MICRO-TIP: Use the Temperature-Control to stop the Radarange Oven at 140°F.

Wax Bean Casserole

Yield: 4 to 6 servings

1 cup dry bread cubes
1 tablespoon butter or margarine, melted
1 (16 oz.) can wax beans, drained
1 (8 oz.) can stewed tomatoes
1/2 teaspoon instant, minced onion
1/2 teaspoon salt
1/8 teaspoon pepper
1/2 cup Cheddar cheese, shredded

1. Toss bread cubes and butter lightly in 1-1/2-quart casserole. Add beans, tomatoes, onion and seasonings. Stir to blend. Sprinkle cheese over top.

2. Cook in Radarange Oven on Cookmatic Level 5 (SLO COOK) for 6 to 7 minutes, or until heated through and cheese is melted.

Italian-Style Zucchini

Yield: 4 servings

1 lb. small fresh zucchini, thinly sliced
1 cup celery, thinly sliced

1 (8 oz.) can tomato sauce
1/2 teaspoon salt
1/8 teaspoon pepper
1/8 teaspoon thyme
1/8 teaspoon basil
Dash garlic powder

1. Combine zucchini and celery in 1-1/2-quart casserole.

2. Combine remaining ingredients. Pour over vegetables.

3. Cook in Radarange Oven, covered, on FULL POWER for 8 to 10 minutes, or until heated through, and vegetables are tender. Stir halfway through cooking time.

MICRO-TIPS:

•Substitute tomato sauce with cheese for plain tomato sauce.

•After cooking, sprinkle with 1/2 cup shredded Mozzarella cheese. Cook in Radarange Oven, covered, on Cookmatic Level 5 (SLO COOK) for 30 seconds, or until cheese is melted.

Quick Scalloped Potatoes For Two

Yield: 2 servings

6 ozs. frozen hash brown potatoes
1 teaspoon instant, minced onion
1 tablespoon butter or margarine
1/2 cup milk
1/4 teaspoon salt
Dash pepper
Paprika

1. Place frozen potatoes in 1-quart casserole. Cook in Radarange Oven, covered, on FULL POWER for 3 to 4 minutes, or until hot. Mix in onion, butter, milk, salt and pepper. Sprinkle with paprika, as desired.

2. Cook in Radarange Oven, covered, on FULL POWER for 3 to 4 minutes, or until liquid is absorbed and potatoes are tender.

You will find sauces a real joy to make in your Radarange Oven. The double boiler, which often causes steam-burned hands, is gone forever. Scorching is also eliminated. In this chapter, you will find some basic French sauces, as well as dessert and meat sauces. Sauces can be made very easily in glass measuring cups, and require only minimum amounts of stirring. Use the sauces in this chapter to accompany main dishes or desserts found in other chapters. Special sauces can be used to "dress up" otherwise plain foods. Make your own Radarange Oven salad dressings to complement fresh salads.

Jams and jellies are a delightful addition to any table! The Radarange Oven simplifies the usual long, drawn-out process of jelly making. Surprise your family with flavorful jellies and jams made in your Radarange Oven. Original-gift-givers love these recipes. They are unique, yet always appreciated presents.

Pickles and other relishes can be easily made in the Radarange Oven. Make relishes ahead, and refrigerate them for future use.

Before preparing sauces, jams, and relishes in the Radarange Oven, be sure to read the general hints.

General Hints for Cooking Sauces, Jams and Relishes

1. Be sure to use the size container that is recommended in recipes to avoid boil-overs.
2. Sauces can be cooked directly in glass measures, for convenience. A glass measure should not be more than about half-filled to avoid boil-overs.
3. Cover sauces, jams or relishes as recommended in the recipes. Use a glass lid or heavy-duty plastic wrap. Remove these coverings away from you to avoid steam burns. You may wish to keep hot pads handy. Sugar mixtures can become quite hot during cooking.
4. Stir sauces during cooking, as recommended in the recipes. Stirring will prevent lumping. Less stirring is required in the microwave cooking of sauces than in conventional cooking.
5. When adding an ingredient such as pectin to a hot mixture, stir it in gradually.
6. Jams, jellies or preserves should be poured into sterilized jars and sealed with paraffin. If jars are not sterilized, the jams, jellies or preserves may be stored in airtight containers in the refrigerator.
7. Purchased syrups and ice cream toppings may be heated quickly and easily in the Radarange Oven. When syrups and toppings have been refrigerated, they can be quickly warmed or softened. Remove the syrups or toppings from glass jars. Pour syrups or toppings into glass dishes before heating. Heat for only a few seconds since syrups and toppings quickly become quite hot. Some of the jams and jellies in this chapter make good ice cream toppings when warmed in the Radarange Oven.
8. Many sauces, jams and relishes are cooked on FULL POWER. Items containing "special" or "delicate" ingredients, however, are cooked on lower Cook-matic Levels or settings. When preparing your own favorite recipes in the Radarange Oven, select a similar recipe in this chapter as a guide. Be sure to use a large enough utensil to avoid boil-overs. Use the same setting and approximately the same cooking time as the "guide" recipe. Make a note of the microwave cooking time on your recipe for future use.

Clockwise starting at left: Simple Strawberry Preserves (page 273), Grape Jelly (page 273), and Peach-Cherry Conserve (page 274)

CONVENIENCE SAUCE MIX COOKING CHART

TYPE	PKG. SIZE	ADDITIONAL INGREDIENTS*	SETTING	COOKING TIME
Au Jus Mix	3/4 oz.	2 cups water	FULL POWER	3 to 4 min.
Burgundy Wine Sauce Mix	1 oz.	1 cup water 1 tablespoon butter or margarine	FULL POWER	3 to 4 min.
Cheese Sauce Mix	1-1/4 oz.	1 cup milk	Cookmatic Level 8 (MEDIUM HIGH)	2-1/2 to 3 min.
Gravy Mix (Chicken, Beef or Pork)	3/4 oz.	1 cup water	FULL POWER	3 to 4 min.
Hollandaise Sauce Mix	1-1/8 oz.	2/3 cup water	FULL POWER	1 to 1-1/2 min.
Sherry Wine Sauce Mix	1 oz.	1 cup milk 1 tablespoon butter or margarine	Cookmatic Level 8 (MEDIUM HIGH)	3 to 4 min.
Spaghetti Sauce Mix	1-1/2 oz.	2 to 3 tablespoons butter or margarine 1-3/4 cups water 1 (6 oz.) can tomato paste	FULL POWER	7-1/2 to 8-1/2 min.

*May vary among different brands. Add extra ingredients as listed on the package.

General Instructions for Cooking Convenience Sauce Mixes

1. Combine mix and additional ingredients in 1 or 1-1/2-quart casserole.

2. Cook in the Radarange Oven, according to the setting and cooking time on the chart, or until the sauce is boiling or thickened as recommended on the package instructions. Stir occasionally during the cooking time.

CANNED SAUCE HEATING CHART

SAUCE TYPE	CAN SIZE	UTENSIL	COOKING TIME ON FULL POWER
Gravy (Beef or Chicken)	10-1/2 oz.	2-cup glass measure or 1-quart casserole	1 to 2 min.
Spaghetti Sauce	15 oz.	1-quart casserole	2 to 3 min.

General Instructions for Heating Canned Sauces

1. Pour the sauce into the utensil listed on the chart.

2. Heat in the Radarange Oven on FULL POWER, according to the time on the chart. Stir before serving.

Sauces, Jams, and Relishes

White Sauce and Variations
Yield: 1 cup

2 tablespoons butter or margarine

2 tablespoons all-purpose flour
1/2 teaspoon salt
1 cup milk

1. Place butter in 1-quart casserole. Heat in Radarange Oven on FULL POWER for 30 to 45 seconds, or until melted.
2. Stir in flour and salt. Blend to smooth paste. Blend in milk gradually, stirring constantly.
3. Cook in Radarange Oven on Cookmatic Level 8 (MEDIUM HIGH) for 2-1/2 to 3 minutes, or until thickened. Stir 3 to 4 times during cooking.

MICRO-TIP: This recipe makes a medium sauce.

VARIATIONS

Thin White Sauce
1 tablespoon butter or margarine
1 tablespoon all-purpose flour

Omit these amounts of butter and flour from original recipe.

Thick White Sauce
2 tablespoons butter or margarine
2 tablespoons all-purpose flour

Add these additional amounts with butter and flour in original recipe.

Cheese Sauce
3/4 cup sharp Cheddar cheese, shredded
Dash cayenne pepper

Stir cheese into cooked sauce in original recipe. Cook in Radarange Oven on Cookmatic Level 8 (MEDIUM HIGH) for 1 to 1-1/2 minutes, or until cheese is melted. Add cayenne pepper.

Dill Sauce
1/2 teaspoon dill weed

Add to flour in original recipe.

Mustard Sauce
1-1/2 to 2 tablespoons prepared mustard

Add to cooked sauce in original recipe.

Newburg Sauce
1 egg yolk
1/4 cup heavy cream
1 tablespoon dry sherry
Dash cayenne pepper

Add cooked sauce from original recipe gradually to egg yolk. Stir in cream, sherry, and cayenne pepper. Cook in Radarange Oven on Cookmatic Level 8 (MEDIUM HIGH) for 2 minutes, or until heated through.

Quick Curry Sauce
1/2 teaspoon curry powder

Add to flour in original recipe.

Clam Sauce
Yield: about 1-1/2 cups

3 tablespoons butter or margarine
1 small onion, chopped
1 clove garlic, minced

2 tablespoons all-purpose flour
1/4 teaspoon salt
1/8 teaspoon pepper

1 (8 oz.) bottle clam juice
1/4 cup milk or cream
1 tablespoon parsley flakes
1/8 teaspoon thyme
1/8 teaspoon tumeric

1 (6-1/2 oz.) can minced clams, drained
2 tablespoons grated Parmesan cheese

1. Place butter, onion and garlic in 1-1/2-quart casserole. Cook in Radarange Oven on FULL POWER for 3 minutes.
2. Stir in flour, salt and pepper. Heat in Radarange Oven on FULL POWER for about 30 seconds, or until mixture boils.
3. Stir in clam juice gradually. Add milk, parsley, thyme and tumeric. Cook in Radarange Oven on Cookmatic Level 8 (MEDIUM HIGH) for 3 to 4 minutes, or until mixture boils and is thickened. Stir once during cooking.
4. Stir in clams and cheese. Heat in Radarange Oven on Cookmatic Level 8 (MEDIUM HIGH) for 1 to 2 minutes, or until mixture boils.

MICRO-TIP: May be served over cooked spaghetti or rice.

Basic Tomato Sauce

Yield: 2 to 2-1/2 quarts

1 cup onion, chopped
2 cloves garlic, minced
2 stalks celery, chopped
2 tablespoons vegetable oil

2 (28 oz. each) cans whole
   tomatoes
1 (12 oz.) can tomato paste
1 teaspoon parsley flakes
1 tablespoon sugar
2 to 3 teaspoons salt
1/2 teaspoon leaf basil
1/2 teaspoon leaf oregano
1/4 teaspoon pepper
1 bay leaf
1/2 cup red wine (optional)

1. Combine onion, garlic, celery and oil in 3-quart casserole. Cook in Radarange Oven, covered, on FULL POWER for about 5 minutes, or until onion, garlic and celery are tender. Stir halfway through cooking time.

2. Stir in remaining ingredients. Cook in Radarange Oven, covered, on FULL POWER for about 17 to 20 minutes, or until heated through. Stir halfway through cooking time, and break up tomatoes. Cool. Remove bay leaf.

MICRO-TIP: Sauce may be divided among 5, 1-pint freezer containers, covered, and frozen for later use.

Hot Catsup Sauce

Yield: 1/2 cup

1/2 cup catsup
1 teaspoon horseradish
1/8 teaspoon oregano

1. Blend together all ingredients in small bowl or 1-cup glass measure.

2. Cook in Radarange Oven on FULL POWER for 1 minute, or until heated through.

MICRO-TIP: May be used as dip for seafood or appetizers.

Sweet-Sour Sauce

Yield: 1-1/2 cups

1 (8-1/4 oz.) can pineapple chunks,
   with liquid
1-1/2 teaspoons cornstarch
3 tablespoons brown sugar
2 tablespoons vinegar
1 tablespoon soy sauce
1/2 green pepper, chopped

1. Drain pineapple juice into 1-quart glass casserole. Stir in cornstarch, brown sugar, vinegar and soy sauce. Cook in Radarange Oven on FULL POWER for 1 minute, or until mixture boils. Stir halfway through cooking time.

2. Stir in green pepper and pineapple. Cook in Radarange Oven, covered, on FULL POWER for about 2 minutes. Stir halfway through cooking time.

MICRO-TIP: May be served over meat balls, cocktail franks, pea pods or other vegetables.

Honey Dressing

Yield: 1-1/2 cups

1/4 cup butter or margarine, melted
2 tablespoons cornstarch
1 cup milk

1 egg, beaten
1/2 cup vinegar
2 tablespoons honey
1 teaspoon salt
1/2 teaspoon dry mustard
1/2 teaspoon celery seed

1. Combine butter and cornstarch in 2-cup glass measure. Gradually stir in milk. Cook in Radarange Oven on Cookmatic Level 8 (MEDIUM HIGH) for 2 to 3 minutes, or until thickened.

2. Combine remaining ingredients in 1-quart casserole. Gradually stir in hot mixture. Cook in Radarange Oven on Cookmatic Level 8 (MEDIUM HIGH) for 1 to 2 minutes, or until mixture boils. Chill.

MICRO-TIP: May be served on fresh fruit or vegetable salad.

Bordelaise Sauce

Yield: 1-1/4 cups

3 tablespoons butter or margarine
1 tablespoon onion, minced

3 tablespoons all-purpose flour
1 cup beef broth or bouillon
2 tablespoons red wine
1 tablespoon lemon juice
1/2 teaspoon tarragon
1 teaspoon parsley, finely chopped
1/4 teaspoon bottled browning
   sauce

1. Combine butter and onion in 1-quart measure or casserole. Cook in Radarange Oven on FULL POWER for 1 minute, or until onion is tender.

2. Stir in flour. Blend to smooth paste. Pour in broth, wine, lemon juice, tarragon, parsley and browning sauce.

3. Cook in Radarange Oven on Cookmatic Level 8 (MEDIUM HIGH) for 2-1/2 to 3 minutes, or until thickened. Stir halfway through cooking time.

MICRO-TIP: Serve with roast beef or steak.

Bechemel Sauce

Yield: 1 cup

2 tablespoons butter or margarine

2 tablespoons all-purpose flour
1/4 teaspoon salt
1/2 teaspoon onion powder
1/8 teaspoon pepper
Dash thyme
1/2 cup chicken broth
1/4 cup cream

1. Place butter in 1-quart casserole. Heat in Radarange Oven on FULL POWER for 20 to 30 seconds, or until melted.

2. Stir in flour and seasonings. Blend to smooth paste. Mix together chicken broth and cream. Stir in gradually.

3. Cook in Radarange Oven on Cookmatic Level 8 (MEDIUM HIGH) for 2 to 3 minutes, or until bubbling and thickened. Stir occasionally during cooking time.

Curry Sauce

Yield: 3-1/2 cups

1/4 cup butter or margarine
1 cup apples, pared, cored and
   chopped
1/4 cup onion, chopped
1 teaspoon salt
1/2 teaspoon curry powder

1/4 cup all-purpose flour
1 cup chicken broth
1 cup light cream

1. Place butter in 1-quart casserole. Heat in Radarange Oven on FULL POWER for 30 seconds, or until melted. Stir in apples, onion, salt and curry powder. Cook in Radarange Oven, covered, on FULL POWER for 1-1/2 to 2 minutes, or until apples are tender.

2. Combine flour and chicken broth. Stir into apple and onion mixture. Add light cream, stirring thoroughly.

3. Heat in Radarange Oven on Cookmatic Level 8 (MEDIUM HIGH) for 2 minutes, or until hot and thickened. Stir halfway through cooking time.

MICRO-TIP: Serve over chicken or rice.

Lemon Sauce For Fish

Yield: 1-1/2 cups

2 tablespoons butter or margarine
2 tablespoons all-purpose flour
1/2 teaspoon salt

1/2 cup light cream

1 egg yolk
1 cup chicken bouillon
1/4 cup lemon juice
1 tablespoon parsley flakes
Dash Tabasco sauce

1. Place butter in 1-quart casserole. Heat in Radarange Oven on FULL POWER for 20 to 30 seconds, or until melted. Blend in flour and salt.

2. Pour light cream into flour mixture, stirring constantly. Cook in Radarange Oven on Cookmatic Level 8 (MEDIUM HIGH) for 1 minute. Stir halfway through cooking time.

3. Blend egg yolk into bouillon. Stir mixture along with remaining ingredients into light cream mixture. Cook in Radarange Oven on Cookmatic Level 8 (MEDIUM HIGH) for 1-1/2 to 2 minutes, or until heated through.

Shrimp Sauce

Yield: 2 cups

2 tablespoons butter or margarine, melted
2 tablespoons all-purpose flour
1/2 teaspoon salt
1 cup milk

1 cup shrimp, cooked and finely diced
1/2 cup dairy sour cream
1 tablespoon prepared mustard

1. Combine butter, flour and salt in 1-quart casserole. Gradually stir in milk. Cook in Radarange Oven on Cookmatic Level 8 (MEDIUM HIGH) for about 2 minutes, or until bubbling and thickened. Stir with wire whip halfway through cooking time.

2. Stir in remaining ingredients. Cook in Radarange Oven on Cookmatic Level 8 (MEDIUM HIGH) for 1-1/2 minutes, or until heated through.

MICRO-TIP: May be chilled, and served on salad.

Spicy Cheese Sauce

Yield: 1 to 1-1/2 cups

1 (10-3/4 oz.) can Cheddar cheese soup
2 tablespoons milk
1/4 teaspoon onion powder
1/4 teaspoon cayenne pepper

1. Mix together all ingredients in 1-quart casserole.

2. Cook in Radarange Oven on Cookmatic Level 5 (SLO COOK) for 3 to 4 minutes, or until hot. Stir halfway through cooking time.

Orange BBQ Sauce

Yield: 1-1/2 cups

1 tablespoon butter or margarine
1 small onion, chopped

3/4 cup catsup
1/3 cup orange juice
1/2 teaspoon Worcestershire sauce
1/4 cup brown sugar, firmly packed
1-1/2 teaspoons orange peel, grated
1/2 teaspoon dry mustard
1/8 teaspoon cinnamon
Dash nutmeg

1. Place butter and onion in 1-quart casserole. Cook in Radarange Oven on FULL POWER for 1-1/2 to 2 minutes, or until onion is tender.

2. Add remaining ingredients. Cook in Radarange Oven on FULL POWER for 2 to 3 minutes, or until mixture boils and sugar is dissolved. Stir halfway through cooking time.

Mornay Sauce

Yield: 1-3/4 cups

2 tablespoons butter or margarine
2 tablespoons all-purpose flour
1 teaspoon instant chicken bouillon
Dash pepper
1-1/4 cups milk

1/4 cup Swiss cheese, shredded
2 tablespoons grated Parmesan cheese
1 teaspoon parsley flakes

1. Place butter in 1-quart casserole. Heat in Radarange Oven on FULL POWER for 20 to 30 seconds, or until melted. Blend in flour, bouillon, pepper and milk.

2. Cook in Radarange Oven on Cookmatic Level 8 (MEDIUM HIGH) for 2 to 3 minutes, or until mixture boils. Stir occasionally during cooking time. Mix in Swiss cheese. Sprinkle with Parmesan cheese and parsley.

3. Cook in Radarange Oven, covered, on Cookmatic Level 8 (MEDIUM HIGH) for 1 minute, or until heated through.

MICRO-TIP: May be served over meat, vegetables or spaghetti noodles.

Hollandaise Sauce

Yield: 1/2 cup

1/3 cup butter or margarine

1 to 2 tablespoons lemon juice
2 egg yolks
1/4 teaspoon salt
1/4 teaspoon dry mustard
Dash Tabasco sauce

1. Place butter in 1-quart casserole. Heat in Radarange Oven on FULL POWER for 40 to 60 seconds, or until melted.

2. Stir in remaining ingredients. Beat with spoon or whisk until well-mixed. Cook in Radarange Oven on Cookmatic Level 8 (MEDIUM HIGH) for 1 to 1-1/2 minutes, or until thickened. Stir halfway through cooking time.

MICRO-TIP: Serve over vegetables or Eggs Benedict.

Rich Mushroom Sauce

Yield: 1-1/2 cups

3 tablespoons butter or margarine

2 tablespoons all-purpose flour
1 teaspoon soy sauce
3/4 cup light cream
1/4 teaspoon salt
1 (4 oz.) can mushrooms, drained

1. Place butter in 1-quart glass measure or casserole. Heat in Radarange Oven on FULL POWER for 30 to 40 seconds, or until melted.

2. Blend in remaining ingredients. Cook in Radarange Oven on Cookmatic Level 8 (MEDIUM HIGH) for 2 to 3 minutes. Stir halfway through cooking time.

MICRO-TIP: May be served over hamburgers or steak.

Mandarin Sauce

Yield: about 1-1/4 cups

1-1/2 tablespoons cornstarch
1/3 cup brown sugar, firmly packed
1 (11 oz.) can mandarin oranges, drained (reserve syrup)
2 tablespoons lemon juice

2 tablespoons raisins (optional)
1 tablespoon butter or margarine

1. Combine cornstarch, brown sugar, reserved syrup from mandarin oranges and lemon juice in 1-quart casserole. Cook in Radarange Oven on FULL POWER for 2 to 3 minutes, or until mixture boils and is glossy.

2. Stir in raisins, mandarin oranges and butter. Heat in Radarange Oven on FULL POWER for 30 seconds, or until mixture boils. Stir halfway through cooking time.

MICRO-TIP: Serve hot with roast duckling.

Welsh Rarebit

Yield: 4 to 6 servings

1 tablespoon butter or margarine

1/2 cup beer or ale
1 lb. sharp Cheddar cheese, shredded

1 egg, beaten
1 teaspoon salt
1 teaspoon Worcestershire sauce
1/2 teaspoon dry mustard
1/2 teaspoon paprika
Dash cayenne pepper

1. Place butter in 1-1/2-quart casserole. Heat in Radarange Oven on FULL POWER for 20 to 30 seconds, or until melted.
2. Stir in beer and cheese. Cook in Radarange Oven, covered, on Cookmatic Level 8 (MEDIUM HIGH) for 5 to 6 minutes, or until cheese is melted. Stir once or twice during cooking time.
3. Blend egg and seasonings with wire whip. Stir egg mixture into cheese mixture. Stir thoroughly.
4. Cook in Radarange Oven, covered, on Cookmatic Level 8 (MEDIUM HIGH) for 2-1/2 to 3 minutes, or until smooth and creamy.

MICRO-TIP: Stir well before serving over hot, buttered toast. Also makes a great fondue.

Tomato Cheese Rarebit

Yield: 6 servings

1 (10-3/4 oz.) can tomato soup
1 lb. sharp Cheddar cheese, shredded

2 eggs, separated
1 teaspoon brown sugar
1/4 teaspoon paprika
Dash cayenne pepper

1. Pour soup into 2-quart casserole. Blend in cheese. Cook in Radarange Oven, covered, on Cookmatic Level 8 (MEDIUM HIGH) for 6-1/2 to 7 minutes, or until mixture is smooth when stirred.
2. Beat egg yolks in small mixing bowl. Stir in brown sugar, paprika and cayenne pepper. Stir into cheese mixture.
3. Cook in Radarange Oven, covered, on Cookmatic Level 8 (MEDIUM HIGH) for 2 to 2-1/2 minutes, or until very smooth when stirred.
4. Whip egg whites until stiff, and fold into cooked mixture.

MICRO-TIP: Served best over hot toasted French bread or Melba toast. This recipe makes a good luncheon dish.

Bing Cherry Sauce

Yield: 1-1/2 cups

1 (1 lb.) can bing cherries, with liquid
Water

2 tablespoons sugar
1 tablespoon cornstarch
Dash salt

1 teaspoon butter or margarine
1/2 teaspoon lemon juice

1. Measure cherry juice. If necessary, add water to make 3/4 cup total liquid.
2. Combine sugar, cornstarch and salt in 1-quart glass measure or sauce dish. Stir in cherry juice.
3. Cook in Radarange Oven on FULL POWER for 2-1/2 to 4 minutes, or until mixture is thick and clear. Stir 3 to 4 times during cooking time.
4. Stir in butter, lemon juice and cherries. Cook in Radarange Oven on FULL POWER for about 45 seconds. Blend until sauce is smooth.

MICRO-TIP: May be served over cake, pudding or ice cream.

Strawberry-Rhubarb Jam

Yield: 2-1/2 to 3 cups

3 cups rhubarb, cut in 3/4-inch slices
2 cups strawberries, sliced
2-1/2 cups sugar
1/8 teaspoon salt

Combine all ingredients in 3-quart casserole. Cook in Radarange Oven, covered, on FULL POWER for 5 minutes. Remove cover. Cook in Radarange Oven on FULL POWER for 35 to 45 minutes, or until jellying point is reached. Stir once or twice during cooking. Pour into jars and cool. Refrigerate.

Apple Jelly

Yield: 2-1/2 to 3 cups

3-1/2 lbs. apples, washed, cored, and cut into eighths
3-1/2 cups water

3 cups sugar, or 3/4 cup sugar for each 1 cup of juice
2 tablespoons lemon juice

1. Place apples and water in 3-1/2 to 4-quart casserole. Cook in Radarange Oven, covered, on FULL POWER for 15 to 20 minutes, or until apples are tender.

2. Strain apples and liquid through cheesecloth-lined strainer. (There should be 4 cups of juice.) Add sugar and lemon juice. Cook in Radarange Oven on FULL POWER for 30 to 35 minutes, or until jellying point is reached. Pour into jars and let cool. Refrigerate.

Grape Jelly

Yield: 2 to 4 cups

6 cups Concord grapes
2 cups apples, diced
1 cup water

3/4 cup sugar for each 1 cup of juice

1. Combine grapes, apples and water in 4-quart casserole. Cook in Radarange Oven, covered, on FULL POWER for 15 to 20 minutes, or until fruit is tender. Stir two or three times during cooking time.

2. Strain juice, using several thicknesses of cheesecloth or jelly bag. Measure juice, to determine amount of sugar to add. Cook in Radarange Oven on FULL POWER for about 10 minutes, or until juice boils.

3. Add sugar. Stir well. Cook in Radarange Oven on FULL POWER for about 30 minutes, or until jellying point is reached. Stir at 5-minute intervals. Pour into glasses to set. Seal with paraffin.

Simple Strawberry Preserves

Yield: 3 cups

1 (16 oz.) pkg. frozen strawberries

3 tablespoons powdered fruit pectin

2 cups sugar
1 tablespoon lemon juice

1. Place strawberries in 2-quart casserole. Cook in Radarange Oven on FULL POWER for 2 minutes.

2. Stir in powdered fruit pectin. Cook in Radarange Oven on FULL POWER for about 2 minutes, or until few bubbles surface.

3. Stir in sugar and lemon juice. Cook in Radarange Oven on FULL POWER for 6 minutes. Stir 2 or 3 times during cooking time. Pour into glass jars. Cover, and refrigerate.

MICRO-TIP: If sealed with paraffin, jars may be stored in the freezer for use when needed.

Peach-Cherry Conserve

Yield: 1-1/2 quarts

2 cups peaches, chopped
1 (1 lb. 4 oz.) can crushed pineapple, drained
1 (8 oz.) bottle maraschino cherries, chopped, with liquid
7-1/2 cups sugar

1 (6 oz.) bottle liquid fruit pectin

1. Combine peaches, pineapple, cherries and cherry liquid in 4 to 5-quart casserole. Cook in Radarange Oven, covered, on FULL POWER for 10 minutes, or until peaches are tender.

2. Stir in sugar. Cook in Radarange Oven, uncovered, on FULL POWER for 15 minutes, or until mixture boils. Stir twice during cooking time.

3. Stir in liquid fruit pectin. Cook in Radarange Oven on FULL POWER for 10 to 15 minutes, or until jelling point is reached. Stir frequently during cooking time to avoid boiling over.

4. Allow to cool for 5 minutes. Stir occasionally during cooling time. Pour into jars or glasses. Seal with paraffin.

Cranberry Jelly

Yield: 4 cups

1 lb. cranberries, washed and drained
2 sticks cinnamon
6 whole cloves
1/4 cup water

2 cups sugar
1-3/4 cups water

1. Combine cranberries, cinnamon, cloves and 1/4 cup water in 2-quart casserole. Cook in Radarange Oven, covered, on FULL POWER for 6 to 7 minutes, or until cranberry skins open. Strain or put cranberries through food mill. Return to casserole.

2. Add sugar and 1-3/4 cups water. Blend well. Cook in Radarange Oven on FULL POWER for 10 to 12 minutes, or until mixture has boiled for 3 to 4 minutes. Stir occasionally during cooking time. Chill until firm.

MICRO-TIP: May be poured directly into jars or into serving dish to be used as cranberry sauce.

Ruby-Strawberry Sauce

Yield: 4 to 5 cups

4 cups frozen rhubarb, sliced
3/4 cup sugar
2 tablespoons cornstarch
1 (10 oz.) pkg. frozen, sweetened, strawberries, sliced

1. Combine all ingredients in 1-1/2-quart casserole.

2. Cook in Radarange Oven, covered, on FULL POWER for 14 minutes, or until mixture boils. Stir 3 to 4 times during cooking time.

MICRO-TIP: Fresh rhubarb and strawberries may be substituted for frozen. Decrease cooking time slightly.

Spiced Apples

Yield: 4 to 6 servings

1-1/2 cups sugar
1 cup vinegar
1 cup water
1/2 cup red cinnamon hots candy
2 sticks cinnamon
1-1/2 teaspoons whole cloves
1-1/2 teaspoons whole allspice

1 lb. apples, cored and sliced into 1/4-inch slices

1. Combine all ingredients, except apples, in 2-quart casserole. Cook in Radarange Oven, covered, on FULL POWER for 10 minutes, or until mixture boils and candies are dissolved.

2. Add apples. Cook in Radarange Oven, covered, on FULL POWER for 3 minutes, or until apples are tender. Place apples in separate container. Remove spices from syrup. Pour syrup over apples and refrigerate.

Bread and Butter Pickles

Yield: 1-1/2 quarts

2 lbs. cucumbers, sliced
Cold water

1 cup vinegar
1 cup water
1 cup sugar
1 teaspoon salt
1 teaspoon celery seed
1 teaspoon mustard seed
1/2 teaspoon dill seed

1. Place cucumbers in 3-quart casserole. Cover with cold water. Soak until crisp. Cook in Radarange Oven, covered, on FULL POWER for 5 to 7 minutes, or until temperature of 110°F is reached.* Drain. Pack in jars.

2. Mix together remaining ingredients in 1-1/2-quart casserole. Cook in Radarange Oven, covered, on FULL POWER for 7 to 8 minutes, or until mixture boils. Pour over cucumbers in jars. Seal.

*MICRO-TIP: Use the Temperature-Control to stop the Radarange Oven at 110°F.

Sweet Dilled Cucumbers

Yield: 1 quart

2 large cucumbers, thinly sliced

1 cup sugar
1-1/2 teaspoons salt
1-1/2 cups white vinegar
1 cup water
2 to 3 teaspoons dill seed

1. Place cucumbers in 1-1/2-quart casserole.

2. Combine remaining ingredients in 1-quart casserole. Add dill seed, as desired. Cook in Radarange Oven, covered, on FULL POWER for 6 to 9 minutes, or until mixture boils and sugar is dissolved. Stir and pour over cucumbers. Cover, and chill.

Zucchini Pickles

Yield: 2 quarts

2 lbs. small zucchini, thinly sliced
2 medium onions, thinly sliced
Water
1/4 cup salt

3 cups white vinegar
1 cup water
1 cup sugar
1 teaspoon celery seed
1 teaspoon tumeric
1/2 teaspoon dry mustard
1 teaspoon mustard seed

1. Place zucchini and onion in 4-quart casserole. Cover with water and add salt. Let stand 1 hour. Drain.

2. Combine remaining ingredients in 1-1/2-quart casserole. Cook in Radarange Oven on FULL POWER for 8 to 10 minutes, or until mixture boils. Pour over zucchini and onion. Let stand, covered, 1 hour.

3. Cook in Radarange Oven, covered, on FULL POWER for 15 minutes, or until mixture has boiled minimum of 3 minutes. Pack in hot sterilized jars and seal.

Fall Relish

Yield: Approximately 2 cups

1-1/2 cups celery, finely chopped
1 cup onion, finely chopped
3/4 cup carrots, finely chopped
3/4 cup green peppers, finely chopped
3/4 cup vinegar
1/2 cup sugar
1 teaspoon mustard seed
1 teaspoon salt

1. Combine all ingredients in 1-1/2-quart casserole.

2. Cook in Radarange Oven, covered, on FULL POWER for 15 to 20 minutes, or until vegetables are tender, as desired. Ladle into containers and seal.

Picnic Relish

Yield: 2 cups

1 cup onion, finely chopped
1 tablespoon water

1 cup cucumber, chopped
2 medium tomatoes, peeled and chopped
2 tablespoons vinegar
2 teaspoons mustard seed
1 teaspoon salt
1/2 teaspoon sugar
1/8 teaspoon pepper

1. Place onion and water in 1-quart casserole. Cook in Radarange Oven, covered, on FULL POWER for 2 minutes.

2. Stir in remaining ingredients. Cook in Radarange Oven, covered, on FULL POWER for about 5 minutes, or until mixture boils. Pour into jar. Refrigerate.

Pickled Beet Relish

Yield: 2-1/2 cups

1 medium onion, chopped
1 tablespoon water

1 (1 lb.) can diced beets, drained
3/4 cup vinegar
1 cup sugar
1 cinnamon stick

1. Place the onion and water in 1-quart casserole. Cook in Radarange Oven, covered, on FULL POWER for 2 minutes.

2. Add remaining ingredients. Cook in Radarange Oven, covered, on FULL POWER for about 4 to 5 minutes, or until mixture boils. Pour into jar. Refrigerate.

Spiced Pears

Yield: 1-1/2 quarts

2 cups water
2/3 cup white vinegar
2 cups sugar

2 (1 lb. 13 oz. each) cans Bartlett pears
Cinnamon sticks

1. Combine water, vinegar and sugar in 1 to 1-1/2-quart casserole. Cook in Radarange Oven, covered, on FULL POWER for 7 to 9 minutes, or until mixture boils and sugar is dissolved.

2. Place pears in 1-1/2-quart casserole. Heat in Radarange Oven on FULL POWER for 2 minutes, or until warmed. Pack into jars. Add one stick cinnamon to each jar. Pour syrup over pears. Refrigerate one week before using.

MICRO-TIP: Add red or green food coloring to syrup before pouring over fruit, if desired.

Cooked Salad Dressing

Yield: Approx. 1-1/2 cups

2 tablespoons all-purpose flour
1 tablespoon sugar
1/2 teaspoon salt
1/2 teaspoon dry mustard

1 egg yolk
3/4 cup light cream

2 tablespoons vinegar
1 tablespoon butter or margarine

1. Stir together flour, sugar, salt and mustard in 1-quart casserole.

2. Combine egg yolk and light cream. Stir into flour mixture gradually. Cook in Radarange Oven on Cookmatic Level 8 (MEDIUM HIGH) for 1-1/2 to 2 minutes, or until mixture boils and is thickened. Stir halfway through cooking time.

3. Stir in vinegar and butter with wire whip, until smooth. Cool and serve on salads.

VARIATIONS

Creamy French
1/2 teaspoon paprika
Dash cayenne pepper

Add to cooked dressing with vinegar and butter in step #3.

Creamy Italian
1/2 teaspoon celery salt
1/8 teaspoon garlic powder
Dash cayenne pepper

Add to cooked dressing with vinegar and butter in step #3.

Creamy Blue Cheese
1/3 cup blue cheese, crumbled
Dash cayenne pepper

Add to cooked dressing, after cooling.

Hard Sauce

Yield: 1/2 cup

1/3 cup butter or margarine

1 cup confectioners' sugar
1/2 teaspoon vanilla
1/4 teaspoon cinnamon (optional)

1. Place butter in 1-quart casserole. Heat in Radarange Oven on Cookmatic Level 3 (SIMMER) for 45 seconds to 1 minute, or until softened.

2. Mix in remaining ingredients, until smooth.

Fruit Dressing

Yield: 3 cups

1/2 cup sugar
1 tablespoon cornstarch
1 egg yolk
2 tablespoons lemon juice
3/4 cup unsweetened pineapple juice

2 cups whipped cream

1. Combine sugar, cornstarch and egg yolk in 1-quart casserole. Add juices.

2. Cook in Radarange Oven on Cookmatic Level 8 (MEDIUM HIGH) for 3 to 4 minutes, or until thickened. Stir halfway through cooking time. Cool, and fold in whipped cream.

MICRO-TIP: Serve over fresh fruit.

Fruit Sauce

Yield: 2 cups

1 (10 oz.) pkg. frozen strawberries, sliced

1/4 cup sugar
1 tablespoon cornstarch

1/2 cup white rosé or fruit flavor wine

1. Place strawberries in 1-quart casserole. Heat in Radarange Oven on DEFROST for 3-1/2 to 4-1/2 minutes, or until strawberries are thawed.

2. Combine sugar and cornstarch. Stir into strawberries. Cook in Radarange Oven on FULL POWER for about 2 minutes, or until thickened. Stir halfway through cooking time.

3. Stir in wine. Cook in Radarange Oven on FULL POWER for about 1 minute, or until warmed. Stir halfway through cooking time. Chill.

Custard Sauce

Yield: 2-1/4 cups

4 egg yolks, beaten
1/3 cup sugar
1/4 teaspoon salt

1-1/2 cups milk
1/2 cup evaporated milk
1 teaspoon vanilla

1. Place eggs, sugar, and salt in 4-cup glass measure. Mix until well-blended.

2. Stir in milks and vanilla.

3. Cook in Radarange Oven on Cookmatic Level 8 (MEDIUM HIGH) for 5 to 7 minutes, or until back of spoon is coated. Stir once or twice during cooking time. Chill before serving.

VARIATIONS

Rum Custard Sauce

1/2 teaspoon vanilla
1 teaspoon rum flavor

Follow original recipe. Reduce vanilla to 1/2 teaspoon. Stir in rum flavor.

Sherry Custard Sauce

1/2 teaspoon vanilla
1 teaspoon sherry flavor

Follow original recipe. Reduce vanilla to 1/2 teaspoon. Stir in sherry flavor.

Lemon Custard Sauce

1 teaspoon lemon flavor
1/2 teaspoon lemon peel, grated

Follow original recipe. Stir in lemon flavor and lemon peel.

Sour Cream Dressing

Yield: 2 cups

1/2 cup sugar
3 tablespoons all-purpose flour
1 teaspoon dry mustard
1 teaspoon salt

1 cup milk
1 egg

1/2 cup vinegar
1 tablespoon butter or margarine
1 cup dairy sour cream

1. Combine sugar, flour, mustard and salt in 1-quart casserole.

2. Combine milk and egg. Stir into dry ingredients. Cook in Radarange Oven on Cookmatic Level 8 (MEDIUM HIGH) for 2 to 3 minutes, or until thickened.

3. Stir in vinegar and butter. Cook in Radarange Oven on Cookmatic Level 8 (MEDIUM HIGH) for 1-1/2 minutes, or until heated through. Stir well, and chill. When mixture is cold, fold in sour cream.

MICRO-TIP: May be served over fruit or vegetable salads.

Marshmallow-Caramel Sauce

Yield: 2 cups

1-1/2 cups brown sugar, firmly packed
2/3 cup light corn syrup
1/3 cup water

1/3 cup butter or margarine
1/2 cup milk
6 large marshmallows, diced

1. Combine sugar, corn syrup and water in 1-quart casserole. Cook in Radarange Oven on FULL POWER for 7 to 9 minutes, or until soft ball stage is reached.* Stir occasionally during cooking.

2. Beat in remaining ingredients. Chill.

MICRO-TIPS:

•This sauce tastes great when served over ice cream.

*The soft ball stage is described on page 352.

Hot Fudge Sauce

Yield: 1 cup

1/2 cup sugar
3 tablespoons cocoa
1-1/2 tablespoons cornstarch
Dash salt
1/2 cup water, room temperature

2 tablespoons butter or margarine
1 teaspoon vanilla

1. Mix together dry ingredients in 1-quart casserole or 2-cup glass measure. Stir in water.

2. Cook in Radarange Oven on FULL POWER for about 1-1/2 minutes. Stir 2 or 3 times during cooking time. Blend in butter. Cook in Radarange Oven on FULL POWER for 30 seconds, or until butter is melted. Stir halfway through cooking time. Blend in vanilla. Stir thoroughly.

Vanilla Sauce

Yield: 1 cup

3 tablespoons butter or margarine, softened
1/2 cup sugar

2 egg yolks, slightly-beaten
1/2 cup boiling water
Dash salt
1 teaspoon vanilla

1. Cream butter and sugar in 1-quart casserole.

2. Combine egg yolks with creamed mixture. Beat in water and salt. Heat in Radarange Oven on FULL POWER for about 2 minutes, or until sauce is smooth. Stir well 2 or 3 times during cooking time. Be careful not to overcook. Stir in vanilla. Serve sauce hot.

Dessert Lemon Sauce

Yield: 1 cup

1/2 cup sugar
1 tablespoon cornstarch
1 cup water

2 tablespoons butter or margarine
1/2 teaspoon lemon peel, grated
1-1/2 tablespoons lemon juice
Dash salt

1. Combine sugar and cornstarch in 1-quart casserole. Stir in water.

2. Heat in Radarange Oven on FULL POWER for 1-1/2 to 2 minutes, or until thickened. Stir 2 or 3 times during cooking.

3. Blend in butter, lemon peel, lemon juice and salt. Blend until smooth.

MICRO-TIP: May be served warm or cold.

Cashew Caramel Sauce

Yield: 1 cup

1/2 cup dark brown sugar, firmly packed
1 tablespoon cornstarch
1/2 cup water

1 tablespoon butter or margarine
1/4 cup evaporated milk
1/3 cup cashews, halved

1. Blend together brown sugar, cornstarch and water in 1-quart casserole. Cook in Radarange Oven on FULL POWER for 2 to 3 minutes, or until thick and bubbly.

2. Add butter, and stir until melted. Blend in milk and cashews.

MICRO-TIP: May be served warm over ice cream.

Golden Pancake Syrup

Yield: 2 cups

1 cup water

2-1/3 cups brown sugar, firmly packed
1/2 teaspoon maple flavor (optional)

1. Place water in 2-quart casserole. Heat in Radarange Oven on FULL POWER for 1 to 2 minutes, or until boiling.
2. Stir in brown sugar. Heat in Radarange Oven on FULL POWER for 1 to 2 minutes, or until sugar is dissolved. Add maple flavor.

MICRO-TIP: Pour into syrup pitcher and serve warm. May be stored in refrigerator in covered jar.

Bottled Pancake Syrup

Yield: 2 cups

1 (16 oz.) bottle pancake syrup, or 2 cups pancake syrup

1. Remove cap from syrup bottle. If bottle is too tall, pour into shorter glass pitcher before heating.
2. Heat in Radarange Oven on FULL POWER for 1-1/2 to 2 minutes, or until warm.

Blueberry Syrup

Yield: 1-3/4 cups

1/2 cup sugar
1 tablespoon cornstarch
1/4 cup water
1/4 cup light corn syrup
2 teaspoons lemon juice
2 cups blueberries

1. Combine sugar and cornstarch in 1-quart casserole. Add water, syrup and lemon juice. Stir in blueberries.

2. Cook in Radarange Oven on FULL POWER for 4-1/2 to 5 minutes, or until thickened.

MICRO-TIP: For a thicker sauce, add 1 additional teaspoon of cornstarch.

Heating Ice Cream Topping

Remove ice cream topping from glass jar. Pour ice cream topping into glass dish or short glass pitcher before heating. Heat in Radarange Oven on FULL POWER for 30 to 60 seconds, or until warm, depending upon the quantity being heated. Decrease heating time if quantity is small.

Chocolate Sauce

Yield: 1-1/2 cups

3 (1 oz. each) squares unsweetened chocolate
1 tablespoon butter or margarine

1 cup sugar
1/2 cup light cream
1/3 cup corn syrup
1 teaspoon vanilla
1/8 teaspoon salt

1. Place chocolate and butter in 1-cup glass measure. Heat in Radarange Oven on Cookmatic Level 6 (ROAST) for 1-1/2 to 2 minutes, or until melted.
2. Combine sugar, light cream and corn syrup in 1-quart casserole. Heat in Radarange Oven on Cookmatic Level 8 (MEDIUM HIGH) for about 2 to 3 minutes, or until mixture boils. Stir halfway through cooking time. Add melted chocolate to sugar mixture. Stir in vanilla and salt.

Melba Sauce

Yield: 2 cups

1 (10 oz.) pkg. frozen raspberries

1/2 cup sugar
2 tablespoons cornstarch
1/2 cup currant or apple jelly

1. Place frozen raspberries in 1-quart casserole. Heat in Radarange Oven on DEFROST for 3-1/2 to 4-1/2 minutes, or until raspberries are thawed.

2. Combine sugar and cornstarch. Stir into raspberries. Fold in jelly.

3. Cook in Radarange Oven on FULL POWER for 3 minutes. Stir halfway through cooking time. Strain, if desired. Allow to cool.

MICRO-TIP: Especially good when served over ice cream.

Applesauce

Yield: 3 to 4 cups

6 cups apples, pared, cored and coarsely chopped (about 6 to 7 medium size apples)
2 tablespoons water
1 tablespoon lemon juice
1/2 cup brown sugar, firmly packed
1/4 cup sugar
1 teaspoon cinnamon
1/2 teaspoon nutmeg
1/2 teaspoon salt

1. Combine all ingredients in 1-1/2-quart casserole.

2. Cook in Radarange Oven, covered, on FULL POWER for 4 to 6 minutes, or until apples are tender. Mash, or put through sieve, if desired.

MICRO-TIP: Lemon juice, brown sugar, cinnamon, nutmeg, and salt can be omitted to make a simple sauce

Baked Rhubarb Sauce

Yield: 2 cups

2 cups rhubarb, chopped
2 tablespoons water
Dash salt

1/2 cup sugar

1. Combine rhubarb and water in 2-quart glass casserole. Stir in salt. Cook in Radarange Oven, covered, on FULL POWER for about 3 to 4 minutes, or until rhubarb is tender. Stir halfway through cooking time.

2. Mix in sugar. Cook in Radarange Oven on FULL POWER for 1 minute, or until sugar is dissolved. Cool, covered.

MICRO-TIP: May be served warm or cold. Add few drops of red food coloring to sauce before cooking, if desired.

Apple-Raisin Sauce

Yield: 1-1/2 cups

2 tablespoons brown sugar
1 tablespoon cornstarch
1/8 teaspoon salt
1/8 teaspoon allspice
1 cup apple juice

1/4 cup seedless raisins
1/2 cup apples, diced

1. Combine brown sugar, cornstarch, salt and allspice in 1-quart casserole. Blend in apple juice. Cook in Radarange Oven on FULL POWER for about 2 minutes, or until thickened. Stir halfway through cooking time.

2. Mix in raisins. Cook in Radarange Oven on FULL POWER for about 1 minute, or until warmed. Stir halfway through cooking. Add apples just before serving.

The Radarange Oven is a "natural" for the preparation of many desserts, ranging from simple puddings to fruit crisps and custards.

Puddings will become popular desserts after you try them in the Radarange Oven. You'll find that they are fun to prepare in your glass measuring cups. Also, there is no scorching!

Custards can also be made with ease. Just remember not to overcook them. If overcooked, they will curdle and separate.

Fruits and fruit desserts are easily made in the Radarange Oven. Due to the short amount of cooking time, fruits retain their fresh flavor.

In this chapter, you'll find recipes for the above mentioned desserts, as well as others, such as impressive cheesecakes. Many desserts can be prepared and cooked in minutes in the Radarange Oven! Cakes, cookies, candies and pies can be found in separate chapters in this cookbook. The "Radarange Oven Extras" chapter includes directions for rehydrating dried fruits, as well as for toasting nuts that can be used for dessert toppings.

Be sure to read the general hints before cooking desserts in the Radarange Oven.

General Hints for Cooking Desserts

1. Fruits
Fruits are generally cooked, covered. Follow the recipe instructions for the types of utensils and coverings recommended. Pierce the skins of fresh fruits, or peel them before cooking. Cooking times are approximations, since the age, size and shape of fruits can affect the amount of cooking time. The amount of sugar and spices in fruit recipes can be adjusted, as desired.

Canned fruits can be warmed in the Radarange Oven, if desired. Fruits can also be rehydrated easily in the Radarange Oven. For directions on how to rehydrate dried fruits, see the "Radarange Oven Extras" chapter, on page 383.

2. Puddings
Puddings are easily prepared in the Radarange Oven. Avoid using non-fat-dry milk in the preparation of puddings. Puddings will not "set" properly if non-fat-dry milk is used. Skim milk can be used for making puddings, and is often preferred by calorie-watchers. Stirring is required during cooking to avoid lumping.

Puddings can be prepared directly in glass measures, for convenience. Be sure to use a large enough utensil when preparing puddings to avoid spill-overs. A general rule to follow is: use a utensil which is about twice as large as the amount of pudding to be cooked. Prepare commercially packaged puddings, according to the directions on page 290. Canned puddings can be warmed on FULL POWER for a few seconds to give them a "freshly-made" taste.

3. Other Desserts
Commercial ice cream can be softened in the Radarange Oven, if it is frozen too solidly to easily scoop. It should be softened at a lower Cookmatic Level to avoid melting. Place the loosened carton (1/2 gallon) in the Radarange Oven and heat on Cookmatic Level 2 (LOW) for 4 to 6 minutes, or until softened. Be careful not to melt.

Frozen, unbaked pastry-type desserts do not bake with good results in a microwave oven. The pastry tends to become soggy.

Cheerleader Cheesecake (page 286)

Frozen Cheese-cake

Yield: 6 servings

1 (17 oz.) frozen cheesecake

1. Remove cheesecake from metal pan. Place on plate.
2. Heat in Radarange Oven on DEFROST for 4 to 5 minutes, or until thawed. Turn plate halfway through defrosting time. Be careful not to melt.

FROZEN FRUIT DEFROSTING CHART

PACKAGE SIZE	UTENSIL	SETTING	DEFROSTING TIME
10 oz.	1-quart casserole	DEFROST	3-1/2 to 4-1/2 min.
20 oz.	1-1/2-quart casserole	DEFROST	8 to 10 min.

General Instructions for Defrosting Fruit

1. Place the fruit in the utensil recommended on the chart. Cover the fruit with a glass lid or plastic wrap.
2. Defrost, according to the amount of time recommended on the chart. Stir the fruit halfway through the cooking time to break the fruit apart and rearrange.

Meringue Shells

Yield: 8 meringues

3 egg whites
1 teaspoon vanilla
1/4 teaspoon cream of tartar
Dash salt
3/4 cup sugar

1. Combine egg whites, vanilla, cream of tartar and salt in small mixing bowl. Beat on medium speed until soft peaks form. Gradually add sugar, beating at high speed until stiff peaks form and sugar is dissolved.
2. Cover Radarange Oven glass tray with brown paper.* Draw 4, 3-1/2-inch diameter circles on paper. Spread about 1/2 cup meringue on each of circles. Shape into shells with back of spoon.
3. Bake in Radarange Oven on Cookmatic Level 2 (LOW) for 20 to 23 minutes, or until almost dry and firm. Cool and remove from paper. Repeat with remaining meringue.

   MICRO-TIPS:
   *A brown paper bag may be used.

   •Meringue shells may be filled with fresh fruit or pudding.

Marvelous Marble Cheese-cake

Yield: 6 to 8 servings

1/4 cup butter or margarine
1 cup vanilla wafer crumbs
1/4 cup sugar

1. Place butter in 9 x 2-inch glass pie plate. Cook in Radarange Oven on FULL POWER for 30 to 40 seconds, or until melted. Stir in crumbs and 1/4 cup sugar. Blend well.

2. Press crumb mixture firmly against bottom and sides of pie plate. Bake in Radarange Oven on FULL POWER for 1 minute, or until bubbling near edges.

4 (3 oz. each) pkgs. cream cheese
2 eggs
1/2 cup sugar
1 teaspoon vanilla

3. Beat cream cheese until smooth. Beat in eggs, one at a time. Beat in sugar and vanilla, until smooth and creamy. Pour over crust.

1/3 cup semi-sweet chocolate morsels*
1 tablespoon milk

4. Place chocolate morsels in 1-cup glass measure or small dish. Heat in Radarange Oven on Cookmatic Level 6 (ROAST) for 1-1/2 to 2 minutes, or until melted. Stir halfway through cooking time. Stir in milk until well-blended. Spoon mixture over cream cheese filling. Use fork, and lightly swirl chocolate into filling, using minimum number of strokes.

5. Bake in Radarange Oven on Cookmatic Level 8 (MEDIUM HIGH) for 3 to 4 minutes, or until outer edge is set.** Chill.

MICRO-TIPS:

* 1/3 cup butterscotch morsels may be substituted for chocolate morsels.

** You may want to turn dish halfway through cooking time.

Peachy Cheese Torte

Yield: 12 servings

1/2 cup butter or margarine, softened
1/3 cup brown sugar, firmly packed
1/2 teaspoon vanilla
3/4 cup all-purpose flour
2/3 cup pecans, finely chopped

1. Beat butter, sugar and vanilla until well-blended. Gradually add flour and beat until well-blended. Stir in pecans. Press mixture firmly against bottom and sides of 2-quart utility dish. Bake in Radarange Oven on Cookmatic Level 7 (BAKE) for 3 to 4 minutes, or until firm.

2 (8 oz. each) pkgs. cream cheese
2 eggs
1/2 cup sugar
1 teaspoon vanilla
1 teaspoon cinnamon
1 (29 oz.) can peach slices, drained
1 tablespoon brown sugar
1/2 teaspoon cinnamon

2. Beat cream cheese until smooth. Beat in eggs, one at a time. Mix in sugar, vanilla and cinnamon until smooth and creamy. Pour over crust. Arrange peach slices on top of cheese mixture. Sprinkle with brown sugar and cinnamon.

3. Bake in Radarange Oven on Cookmatic Level 8 (MEDIUM HIGH) for 8 to 10 minutes, or until outer edge is set. Chill.

Cheerleader Cheese-cake

Yield: 12 to 15 servings

1/2 cup butter or margarine
2 cups graham cracker crumbs
1/2 cup sugar
1/2 teaspoon cinnamon

3 (8 oz. each) pkgs. cream cheese
5 eggs
1 cup sugar
1/2 teaspoon vanilla

2-1/2 cups dairy sour cream
1/3 cup sugar
1-1/2 teaspoons vanilla

1. Place butter in 2-quart utility dish. Heat in Radarange Oven on FULL POWER for 1 minute, or until melted. Blend in crumbs, sugar and cinnamon.

2. Press crumb mixture firmly against bottom and sides of dish. Bake in Radarange Oven on FULL POWER for 1-1/2 minutes, or until firm.

3. Beat cream cheese until smooth. Beat in eggs, one at a time. Mix in sugar and vanilla, until smooth and creamy. Pour over crust. Bake in Radarange Oven on Cookmatic Level 8 (MEDIUM HIGH) for 12 to 15 minutes, or until knife inserted near center comes out clean.*

4. Combine sour cream, sugar and vanilla. Blend well. Pour mixture over cheese cake. Bake in Radarange Oven on Cookmatic Level 8 (MEDIUM HIGH) for 1-1/2 to 2-1/2 minutes, or until outer edge is set. Chill.

MICRO-TIPS:

• Glazed fresh fruit, or fruit pie fillings such as strawberry, cherry or blueberry may be spread over top after chilled.

* You may want to turn dish halfway through cooking time.

Vanilla Custard Ice Milk

1-1/2 quarts
Yield: 1-1/4 to

1 tablespoon unflavored gelatin
1 quart, plus 2/3 cup milk

1 cup sugar
1 teaspoon salt
2 egg yolks

1-1/2 teaspoons vanilla

2 egg whites
1/4 teaspoon cream of tartar

1. Dissolve gelatin in 1 cup of cold milk.

2. Place remaining milk in 2-quart casserole. Heat in Radarange Oven on Cookmatic Level 8 (MEDIUM HIGH) for 6 to 7 minutes, or until scalded.

3. Gradually stir sugar and salt into egg yolks in 4-quart casserole. Gradually blend in hot milk, stirring constantly. Cook in Radarange Oven on Cookmatic Level 8 (MEDIUM HIGH) for 5 to 7 minutes, or until mixture begins to thicken and coats spoon. Do not overcook, since mixture will curdle.

4. Add gelatin and milk mixture to hot custard, stirring until dissolved. Cool. When cooled, add vanilla.

5. Beat egg whites with cream of tartar until stiff peaks form. Fold into cooled custard mixture. Freeze.*

*MICRO-TIP: You may want to use an ice cream freezer for best results.

Ice Cream Sundae Dessert

Yield: 12 to 15 servings

1/3 cup butter or margarine
1 (15 oz.) pkg. chocolate
  sandwich cookies, crushed

1/2 gallon ice cream, any flavor

1 (12 oz.) jar chocolate fudge
  topping

1. Place butter in large mixing bowl. Cook in Radarange Oven on FULL POWER for 40 to 60 seconds, or until melted. Blend together cookie crumbs and butter. Press 3/4 of crumb mixture in bottom of 9 x 13 x 2-inch conventional metal pan.

2. Allow ice cream to soften at room temperature, until soft enough to spread.* Spread evenly over crumbs.

3. Pour topping into small bowl or glass measure. Heat in Radarange Oven on FULL POWER for 30 to 60 seconds, or until topping has thinned. Drizzle over ice cream. Sprinkle top with remaining crumbs. Freeze.

MICRO-TIPS:

• Chocolate mint and peppermint ice cream are especially good flavors to use.

*For very hard ice cream, place loosened container in Radarange Oven. Heat in Radarange Oven on Cookmatic Level 2 (LOW) for 7 to 9 minutes, or until softened. Do not completely melt.

Frozen Lemon Dessert

Yield: 9 to 12 servings

3 eggs, separated
1/2 cup sugar
Dash salt
1/4 cup fresh lemon juice
1/2 teaspoon lemon peel, grated

1 cup whipped cream

3/4 to 1 cup vanilla wafer crumbs

1. Set egg whites aside. Combine egg yolks, sugar and salt in 1-quart casserole. Blend well. Stir in lemon juice and lemon peel. Cook in Radarange Oven on Cookmatic Level 8 (MEDIUM HIGH) for 2 to 3 minutes, or until mixture is thickened and coats spoon. Stir mixture once or twice during cooking time. Chill.

2. Beat egg whites until stiff. Fold in whipped cream, and then lemon mixture.

3. Sprinkle half of crumbs in 8 x 8 x 2-inch dish. Pour in lemon mixture. Sprinkle remaining crumbs over top. Freeze until firm.

Lemon Ice

Yield: Approximately 1-1/2 quarts

4 cups water
2 cups sugar
1/2 cup light corn syrup

2 lemons, juice and peel (or
  about 1/2 cup lemon juice)

1. Combine water, sugar, and corn syrup in 2-quart casserole. Cook in Radarange Oven, covered, on FULL POWER for 20 to 25 minutes, or until mixture boils and temperature of 210°F to 220°F is reached.

2. Add lemon juice and peel. Pour into 2, 9 x 5 x 2-inch glass loaf dishes. Cover with plastic wrap and freeze until slushy.

3. Scrape into chilled bowl. Beat until smooth, but not melted. Pour back into loaf dishes and freeze.

Spiced Fruit Compote

Yield: 4 to 6 servings

1 (1 lb.) can pear halves,*
  with liquid
2 medium apples, pared, cored and
  sliced into eighths (2 cups)

1/2 cup whole cranberry sauce
1/8 teaspoon cinnamon
Dash cloves
Dash allspice

1. Drain pear halves. Reserve 1 tablespoon of liquid. Cut pear halves in half, lengthwise. Layer apples and pears in 1-1/2-quart casserole.

2. Combine reserved pear liquid with cranberry sauce and spices. Spoon over apples and pears. Cook in Radarange Oven, covered, on FULL POWER for 5 to 7 minutes, or until apples are tender. Stir halfway through cooking time. Serve warm or chilled.

*MICRO-TIP: 1 (1 lb.) can of either pineapple chunks or apricot halves may be substituted for the pears.

Pineapple-Banana Sundae

Yield: 6 servings

3 tablespoons butter or margarine
1/4 cup brown sugar, firmly packed

1 (20 oz.) can crushed pineapple in heavy syrup, undrained
1 teaspoon cinnamon
1/2 teaspoon mace
2 tablespoons water
1 tablespoon cornstarch

3 bananas, halved and sliced crosswise
1/4 cup walnuts, chopped
Vanilla ice cream

1. Place butter and brown sugar in 1-1/2-quart dish. Heat in Radarange Oven on FULL POWER for 30 to 40 seconds, or until melted.

2. Add pineapple with syrup and spices to sugar mixture. Add cornstarch mixed with water. Heat in Radarange Oven on FULL POWER for 4 to 5 minutes, or until mixture boils. Stir once or twice during cooking time.

3. Place bananas in pineapple mixture and stir gently. Sprinkle with walnuts. Cook in Radarange Oven on FULL POWER for 2 minutes, or until heated through. Serve over vanilla ice cream, as desired.

MICRO-TIP: Sprinkle with additional nuts, if desired.

Pistachio Ice Cream Dessert

Yield: 8 to 10 servings

1/3 cup butter or margarine

3/4 cup butter flavor cracker crumbs

1 (3-3/4 oz.) pkg. instant pistachio pudding mix
3/4 cup milk
1 pint vanilla ice cream, softened

1 (4-1/2 oz.) container frozen non-dairy whipped topping
2 (1-1/4 oz. each) chocolate-covered English toffee bars, crushed*

1. Place butter in 8 x 8 x 2-inch dish. Heat in Radarange Oven on FULL POWER for 40 to 60 seconds, or until melted.

2. Blend in cracker crumbs. Press crumb mixture evenly against bottom of dish. Cook in Radarange Oven on FULL POWER for 2-1/2 minutes, or until bubbling over surface.

3. Combine pudding mix and milk in large mixing bowl. Beat at high speed with electric mixer until thick. Blend in ice cream. Pour over crust. Freeze for 2 hours.

4. Top with whipped topping and candy bars. Freeze 1 additional hour.

*MICRO-TIP: Toffee bars crush more easily when cold or frozen.

Cranberry Whip Dessert

Yield: 8 servings

1 cup sugar
1 cup water

2 cups fresh cranberries

1 (3 oz.) pkg. orange flavor gelatin
1 cup boiling water

1/2 cup evaporated milk
1 teaspoon lemon juice

1. Combine sugar and 1 cup water in 3-quart casserole. Heat in Radarange Oven on FULL POWER for 3 to 4 minutes, or until mixture boils. Stir halfway through cooking time.

2. Stir in cranberries. Cook in Radarange Oven on FULL POWER for 3 to 4 minutes, or until mixture boils, and cranberries open.

3. Dissolve gelatin in water. Add to cranberries. Chill until thickened.

4. Chill evaporated milk in freezer until ice crystals form. Whip milk until frothy. Stir in lemon juice. Beat until stiff.

5. Fold whipped milk mixture into thickened gelatin mixture. Pour into 10 x 10 x 2-inch dish. Chill until firm.

Pineapple Bridge Dessert

Yield: 8 to 10 servings

2/3 cup butter or margarine
1-1/2 cups vanilla wafer crumbs

2-1/2 cups crushed pineapple, with liquid
1 (3 oz.) pkg. lemon flavor gelatin

1/2 cup sugar
3 eggs, separated
1/2 cups nuts, chopped

1/4 cup sugar

1. Place half of butter in 8 x 8 x 2-inch dish. Heat in Radarange Oven on FULL POWER for 40 to 60 seconds, or until melted. Stir in crumbs. Blend well. Press 1 cup crumb mixture firmly against bottom of dish. Reserve remaining crumbs for topping.

2. Place pineapple syrup in 1-1/2-quart glass casserole. Heat in Radarange Oven on FULL POWER for 2 minutes, or until boiling. Stir in gelatin until dissolved. Cool to room temperature.

3. Cream remaining butter with 1/2 cup sugar. Mix in egg yolks, one at a time, beating well. Add cooled gelatin mixture, pineapple and nuts.

4. Beat egg whites until they form soft peaks. Gradually mix in 1/4 cup sugar and continue to beat until stiff. Fold egg whites into pineapple mixture. Pour into crumb-lined dish. Top with reserved crumbs. Chill until firm.

New England Carrot Pudding

Yield: 8 servings

1/2 cup butter or margarine
1/2 cup brown sugar, firmly packed
1 egg
1 cup carrots, grated and firmly packed
1/2 cup raisins (optional)

1-1/4 cups cake flour, or
   1 cup plus 1 tablespoon all-purpose flour
1 teaspoon baking powder
1/2 teaspoon soda
1/2 teaspoon cinnamon
1/2 teaspoon nutmeg
1/2 teaspoon ginger

1. Cream butter and brown sugar. Beat in egg until well-blended. Stir in carrots and raisins.

2. Sift together flour, baking powder, soda, cinnamon, nutmeg and ginger. Stir into carrot mixture until well-blended. Spread into well-greased, 8 x 8 x 2-inch dish.

3. Bake in Radarange Oven on FULL POWER for 4-1/2 to 5 minutes, or until slightly firm throughout.* Cut pudding into squares while still warm.

MICRO-TIPS:

• May be served with "Hard Sauce", page 277, or "Dessert Lemon Sauce", page 279.

* You may want to turn dish halfway through cooking time.

Some-Mores

Yield: 1 serving

1 graham cracker
1 marshmallow
1/2 milk chocolate candy bar

1. Break graham cracker in half and place one half on paper plate. Top with chocolate, and then marshmallow.

2. Heat in Radarange Oven on FULL POWER for 20 seconds, or until marshmallow and chocolate are melted. Top with second half of graham cracker.

Light 'N' Fruity Tapioca

Yield: 6 servings

2 cups skim milk
1/4 cup sugar
1/4 cup quick-cooking tapioca
1/4 teaspoon salt
2 eggs, separated

2 tablespoons sugar
1 teaspoon vanilla

2 cups fresh or canned fruit,
   sliced

1. Place milk in 1-quart glass measure or casserole. Add 1/4 cup sugar, tapioca, salt and egg yolks. Blend well. Cook in Radarange Oven on Cookmatic Level 8 (MEDIUM HIGH) for 5-1/2 to 6 minutes, or until mixture begins to boil. Stir well after 4 minutes of cooking.

2. Beat egg whites until frothy. Gradually add sugar, beating until mixture forms soft peaks. Beat in vanilla. Fold into pudding mixture. Cool. Chill, if desired.

3. Spoon fruit into 6 serving dishes. Top with pudding.

MICRO-TIPS:

•This pudding has only 100 calories per serving.

•Pudding servings may be topped with mandarin orange slices and maraschino cherries for colorful desserts.

Pudding From Prepared Mix

Yield: 4 servings

1 (3-1/2 oz.) pkg. prepared pudding
   mix
2 cups milk

1. Place pudding in 1-quart glass measure or casserole. Stir in enough milk to dissolve pudding. Stir in remaining milk.

2. Cook in Radarange Oven on Cookmatic Level 8 (MEDIUM HIGH) for 5-1/2 to 7 minutes, or until smooth or thickened. Stir 2 or 3 times during cooking.

Apple Tapioca

Yield: 8 servings

1/3 cup quick-cooking tapioca
1 cup brown sugar, firmly packed
4 cups tart apples, pared and
   thinly sliced
1 cup water
1 cup milk
2 tablespoons lemon juice
2 tablespoons butter or margarine,
   melted
1/2 teaspoon cinnamon
1/2 teaspoon salt

1. Combine all ingredients in 2-quart casserole. Let stand for 5 minutes.

2. Cook in Radarange Oven on Cookmatic Level 8 (MEDIUM HIGH) for 8 to 10 minutes, or until tapioca is thickened. Stir halfway through cooking time. Cover, and let stand until ready to serve.

MICRO-TIP: May be served warm with a sprinkle of nutmeg and a scoop of ice cream.

Minute Tapioca Pudding

Yield: 6 servings

3 tablespoons quick-cooking tapioca
1/3 cup sugar
2 cups milk
1/8 teaspoon salt
1 egg, separated

1/2 teaspoon vanilla

1 tablespoon sugar

1. Mix together tapioca, sugar, milk, salt and egg yolk in 1-1/2-quart casserole. Let stand 5 minutes.

2. Cook in Radarange Oven on Cookmatic Level 8 (MEDIUM HIGH) for 7 to 8 minutes, or until mixture boils and is thickened. Stir in vanilla.

3. Beat egg white until foamy. Gradually add sugar, beating until mixture forms soft peaks. Fold into pudding mixture. Serve warm or chilled.

Easy Rice Pudding

Yield: 4 to 6 servings

1 cup quick-cooking rice
1 (3-3/4 oz.) pkg. vanilla pudding mix
1/2 teaspoon cinnamon (optional)
1/4 teaspoon salt
3 cups milk

1/2 cup raisins (optional)
Nutmeg (optional)

1. Combine rice, pudding mix, cinnamon and salt in 2-1/2 to 3-quart casserole. Stir in milk gradually.

2. Cook in Radarange Oven, covered, on Cookmatic Level 8 (MEDIUM HIGH) for 7 to 9 minutes, or until mixture begins to boil. Stir halfway through cooking time with wire whip.

3. Stir in raisins. Sprinkle with nutmeg, as desired. Serve warm or chilled.

MICRO-TIP: Try French vanilla pudding for a richer flavor.

Fancy Bread Pudding

Yield: 6 to 8 servings

3 eggs, beaten
3/4 cup sugar
1 (13 oz.) can evaporated milk
1 cup milk
1/4 teaspoon nutmeg
1/4 teaspoon cinnamon

6 cups bread cubes
1 (1 lb. 4 oz.) can apple pie filling
1 cup raisins

1. Combine eggs, sugar, milks and spices in 3-quart casserole. Stir until blended.

2. Add bread cubes, apples, raisins. Let mixture stand until bread cubes have become saturated.

3. Cook in Radarange Oven on Cookmatic Level 5 (SLO COOK) for 15 to 20 minutes, or until knife inserted near center comes out clean.

Pot de Creme

Yield: 6 to 8 servings

1-1/4 cups light cream
1 (6 oz.) pkg. semi-sweet
  chocolate morsels
1/4 cup sugar

3 eggs, separated
1 teaspoon vanilla
1/4 teaspoon salt

1/2 teaspoon vanilla
1/4 teaspoon cream of tartar
1/3 cup sugar

1. Combine light cream, chocolate morsels and sugar in 1-quart glass measure or casserole. Heat in Radarange Oven on Cookmatic Level 8 (MEDIUM HIGH) for 3 to 4 minutes, or until chocolate is melted. Mix thoroughly. Stir once or twice during cooking.

2. Beat together egg yolks, vanilla and salt, until thick and lemon-colored. Beat chocolate mixture into egg yolks. Chill.

3. Beat egg whites, vanilla and cream of tartar until frothy. Gradually add sugar, beating until mixture forms stiff peaks. Fold into chocolate mixture. Chill in custard cups or dessert dishes.

MICRO-TIP: 2 to 3 teaspoons of orange liqueur may be added to chocolate mixture, if desired.

Vanilla Cream Pudding

Yield: 4 servings

2 cups milk

1/4 cup cornstarch
2/3 cup sugar
1/2 teaspoon salt

2 eggs, slightly-beaten

2 tablespoons butter or margarine
1 teaspoon vanilla

1. Place milk in 2-cup glass measure. Heat in Radarange Oven on Cookmatic Level 8 (MEDIUM HIGH) for 2-1/2 to 3 minutes, or until heated through.

2. Blend together cornstarch, sugar and salt in 1-1/2-quart casserole. Gradually stir milk into cornstarch mixture with wire whip. Cook in Radarange Oven on Cookmatic Level 8 (MEDIUM HIGH) for 3 minutes or until thickened and glossy. Stir halfway through cooking time.

3. Beat half of hot mixture into eggs. Return to hot mixture. Cook in Radarange Oven on Cookmatic Level 8 (MEDIUM HIGH) for 1 to 2 minutes, or until mixture begins to boil.

4. Mix well with wire whip, stirring in butter and vanilla. Pour into 4, 6 oz. custard cups or dessert dishes.

Chocolate Fondue

Yield: 3/4 to 1 cup

1 (6 oz.) pkg. semi-sweet chocolate
  morsels

1/4 cup light cream
1/4 cup corn syrup
1 teaspoon vanilla
Dash salt

1. Place chocolate morsels in 1-quart casserole. Heat in Radarange Oven on Cookmatic Level 6 (ROAST) for 2-1/2 to 3 minutes, or until melted.

2. Stir in remaining ingredients. Heat in Radarange Oven on Cookmatic Level 6 (ROAST) for 3 to 4 minutes, or until heated through. Stir once or twice with wire whip, until smooth.

Egg Custard Mix

Yield: 6, 1/2-cup servings

2-3/4 cups milk
1 (4-1/2 oz.) pkg. egg custard mix

Nutmeg

1. Mix milk and custard mix in 1-quart glass measure or casserole.

2. Cook in Radarange Oven on Cookmatic Level 8 (MEDIUM HIGH) for about 6 to 8 minutes, or until boiling. Stir frequently during cooking. Pour into dessert dishes and sprinkle with nutmeg, as desired.

Baked Custard

Yield: 4 servings

1-3/4 cups milk

1/4 cup sugar
1/8 teaspoon salt
3 eggs, slightly-beaten
1 teaspoon vanilla

1. Place milk in 2-cup glass measure. Heat in Radarange Oven on Cookmatic Level 8 (MEDIUM HIGH) for 4 minutes, or until hot.
2. Stir sugar and salt into eggs. Blend well. Gradually stir in hot milk and vanilla, stirring constantly. Pour mixture into 4, 6-oz. custard cups or dessert dishes. Arrange custard cups in circle in Radarange Oven.
3. Bake in Radarange Oven on Cookmatic Level 4 (MEDIUM) for 9 to 10 minutes, or until custards are set but still quivery.* Cool at room temperature. Chill, if desired.

   MICRO-TIPS:

   • Custards may be topped with fruit, if desired.

   * You may want to rearrange custard cups halfway through cooking time.

Mocha Bread Custard

Yield: 6 servings

1/2 cup semi-sweet chocolate morsels

1/2 cup strong coffee
1-1/2 cups milk
1 tablespoon butter or margarine, melted

3 eggs, beaten
6 tablespoons sugar
1/4 teaspoon salt
1/2 teaspoon vanilla

2 cups white bread cubes
1/4 teaspoon cinnamon (optional)

1. Place chocolate morsels in 1-quart casserole. Heat in Radarange Oven on Cookmatic Level 6 (ROAST) for 2 to 3 minutes, or until chocolate softens.
2. Add coffee, milk, and butter. Heat in Radarange Oven on Cookmatic Level 8 (MEDIUM HIGH) for 3 to 4 minutes, or until mixture can be well-blended.
3. Mix together eggs, sugar, salt and vanilla in large mixing bowl. Stir chocolate mixture into egg mixture.
4. Place bread cubes in 1-1/2-quart casserole. Pour chocolate-egg mixture on cubes. Sprinkle with cinnamon, as desired.
5. Cook in Radarange Oven on Cookmatic Level 4 (MEDIUM) for 10 to 11 minutes, or until knife inserted near center comes out clean.

   MICRO-TIP: May be served warm or cold with whipped cream.

Chocolate Custard

Yield: 8 custards

1/2 cup semi-sweet chocolate morsels
1 (13 oz.) can evaporated milk
1 cup water

4 eggs
1/2 cup sugar
1/2 teaspoon salt
1/2 teaspoon vanilla

1. Combine chocolate morsels, evaporated milk and water in 1-quart casserole. Cook in Radarange Oven on Cookmatic Level 8 (MEDIUM HIGH) for 3 to 4 minutes, or until chocolate is melted. Stir halfway through cooking time.
2. Beat together eggs, sugar, salt and vanilla with rotary beater until well-blended. Pour in chocolate mixture, stirring constantly. Beat until well-blended. Pour into 8, 6-oz. custard cups. Arrange 4 custards in circle in Radarange Oven.
3. Bake in Radarange Oven on Cookmatic Level 4 (MEDIUM) for 9 to 10 minutes, or until custards are barely set. Be careful not to overcook.* Repeat procedure with remaining custards.

   *MICRO-TIP: You may want to rearrange custard cups halfway through cooking time.

Indian Pudding

Yield: 8 to 10 servings

4 cups milk

1 cup yellow cornmeal

1/2 cup brown sugar, firmly packed
1/2 cup molasses
2 eggs, slightly-beaten
2 tablespoons butter or margarine, melted
1 teaspoon salt
1/2 teaspoon cinnamon
1/2 teaspoon ginger
Dash nutmeg

1. Place milk in 1-quart glass measure or casserole. Heat in Radarange Oven on Cookmatic Level 8 (MEDIUM HIGH) for 5 minutes.

2. Stir in cornmeal. Cook in Radarange Oven on Cookmatic Level 8 (MEDIUM HIGH) for 4 to 5 minutes, or until smooth and thickened. Stir once during cooking time.

3. Combine remaining ingredients in large bowl. Stir hot milk mixture into egg mixture. Pour into greased, 2-quart casserole.

4. Bake in Radarange Oven on Cookmatic Level 5 (SLO COOK) for 15 to 17 minutes, or until set but still quivery on top.

Butterscotch Pudding Parfait

Yield: 4 servings

3/4 cup brown sugar, firmly packed
2 tablespoons cornstarch
1/4 teaspoon salt
1 cup milk
1 cup evaporated milk

1 egg, slightly-beaten

2 tablespoons butter or margarine
1 teaspoon vanilla
3/4 cup macaroons, crumbled

1. Combine sugar, cornstarch and salt in 1-quart glass measure or casserole. Gradually stir in milks. Cook in Radarange Oven on Cookmatic Level 8 (MEDIUM HIGH) for 5 to 6 minutes, or until thickened and bubbly.

2. Stir half of hot mixture into egg, stirring constantly. Return to hot mixture. Cook in Radarange Oven on Cookmatic Level 8 (MEDIUM HIGH) for 30 to 60 seconds, or until mixture begins to boil.

3. Stir in butter and vanilla. In 4 dessert dishes, alternate pudding and crumbled macaroons to make parfaits.

Heavenly Tarts

Yield: Filling for 6 tarts

6 (1-1/2 oz. each) filled, chocolate almond bars, cut into small pieces
1/4 cup butter or margarine
1/4 cup milk

1 cup coconut, shredded
6 tart shells, baked
Whipped cream (optional)
Almonds (optional)

1. Place chocolate bars in 1-quart casserole. Add butter and milk. Heat in Radarange Oven, covered, on Cookmatic Level 6 (ROAST) for 4 to 5 minutes, or until chocolate bars are melted. Stir once during cooking time.

2. Add coconut. Mix well, and spoon into tart shells. Chill before serving. Top each with whipped cream and almonds, if desired.

Desserts

Mocha Mousse

Yield: 5 to 6 servings

2 tablespoons water
1-1/2 teaspoons unflavored gelatin

1/2 cup evaporated milk
1/2 cup milk
2 (1 oz. each) squares unsweetened chocolate

3/4 cup sugar
1 teaspoon instant coffee
1/2 teaspoon salt
1 teaspoon vanilla

2 cups heavy cream

1. Soften gelatin in water.

2. Place milks and chocolate in 2-cup glass measure. Heat in Radarange Oven on Cookmatic Level 8 (MEDIUM HIGH) for 3 to 4 minutes, or until chocolate is melted. Blend in gelatin mixture, stirring until dissolved.

3. Blend in sugar, instant coffee and salt, with wire whip, stirring until dissolved and smooth. Stir in vanilla. Cool.

4. Beat cream until it piles softly. Fold chocolate mixture into whipped cream. Pour mixture into freezer tray or mold. Freeze until firm, about 3 to 4 hours. Before serving, allow to soften slightly in refrigerator.

Cinnamon Apples

Yield: 6 servings

1 cup sugar
1 cup water
2 tablespoons red cinnamon hots candy

Whole cloves
6 medium tart apples, cored and pared

1. Combine sugar, water and cinnamon hots candy in 2-quart utility dish. Cook in Radarange Oven on FULL POWER for 3 to 5 minutes, or until cinnamon hots candy is dissolved.

2. Put 3 or 4 whole cloves into each apple. Place apples in cinnamon syrup.

3. Cook in Radarange Oven, covered, on FULL POWER for 5 to 7 minutes, or until apples are tender. Cool apples in syrup before serving.

Hot Frosted Gingerbread

Yield: 6 to 8 servings

1/2 cup butter or margarine
1/2 cup hot, strong coffee

2 eggs, beaten
1/2 cup sugar
1/2 cup molasses

1-1/2 cups all-purpose flour
2 teaspoons baking powder
1 teaspoon ginger

1 cup confectioners' sugar
2 tablespoons cream
1/2 teaspoon vanilla

1. Stir butter into hot coffee. Stir until butter is melted. If butter is not completely melted, heat in Radarange Oven on FULL POWER for 30 seconds, or until melted.

2. Combine eggs, sugar and molasses in large mixing bowl. Add coffee mixture.

3. Blend together flour, baking powder and ginger. Add to coffee mixture. Mix well. Pour into greased, 8 x 8 x 2-inch dish.

4. Bake in Radarange Oven on FULL POWER for 4 to 5 minutes, or until center springs back when lightly pressed with finger.*

5. Stir remaining ingredients together. Spread on hot gingerbread.

*MICRO-TIP: You may want to turn dish halfway through cooking time.

Baked Apples

Yield: 4 servings

4 medium apples, cored
1/4 cup sugar
Butter or margarine

1. Slice thin circle of peel from top of each apple. Arrange apples in 9 x 2-inch round dish. Spoon 1 tablespoon sugar into each apple cavity. Place small piece of butter on each apple, as desired. Cover with plastic wrap.

2. Cook in Radarange Oven, covered, on FULL POWER for 3 to 4 minutes, or until apples are tender. Let apples stand few minutes before serving.

MICRO-TIP: Apples may be filled with mincemeat, whole cranberry sauce, or raisins and nuts, if desired. Increase cooking time by 1 to 2 minutes.

Baked Grapefruit

Yield: 2 servings

1 grapefruit, cut in half
2 teaspoons brown sugar
1 teaspoon butter or margarine

1. Cut around each grapefruit section with sharp knife. Remove seeds. Sprinkle brown sugar over top. Dot with butter. Place grapefruit halves on paper plate or in 1-quart glass casserole.

2. Bake in Radarange Oven on FULL POWER for 1-1/2 to 2-1/2 minutes, or until heated through. Serve warm.

MICRO-TIP: Maraschino cherries may be placed in centers of grapefruit halves for added color.

Fruit Soup

Yield: 6 to 8 servings

1 (12 oz.) pkg. dried apricots
1/2 lemon, thinly sliced
1/2 cup raisins
2 quarts water
1 cup sugar
2 tablespoons quick-cooking tapioca
1/2 teaspoon salt
3 cinnamon sticks

1. Combine apricots, lemon slices, raisins, and water in 3 to 4-quart casserole. Stir in sugar, tapioca, salt, and cinnamon sticks. Cover with glass lid.

2.

1	COOKING PROGRAM	15:00	COOK		
2	COOKING PROGRAM	25:00	COOK	5	COOKMATIC LEVEL

Cook, covered, on Cookmatic Level 5 (SLO COOK) until fruits are tender. Serve warm or chilled.

Chilled Fruit Cup

Yield: 6 to 8 servings

1 cup water
2 tablespoons sugar
3 tablespoons quick-cooking tapioca
Dash salt

1 (6 oz.) can frozen orange juice concentrate, undiluted
1-1/2 cups water

1 (10 oz.) pkg. frozen raspberries
1 tablespoon lemon juice
3 oranges, peeled and cubed
3 bananas, peeled and sliced

1. Mix together 1 cup water, sugar, tapioca and salt in 2-quart casserole. Cook in Radarange Oven, covered, on FULL POWER for 2 to 3 minutes, or until mixture boils. Stir halfway through cooking time.

2. Blend in orange juice concentrate and water. Chill for 1/2 hour.

3. Blend in raspberries and lemon juice. Refrigerate 6 hours or overnight. Add oranges and bananas when completely chilled.

Fruit Crisp Topping

Yield: Topping for one fruit crisp recipe

2/3 cup all-purpose flour
1/2 cup quick-cooking, rolled oats
1/4 cup nuts, chopped
3 tablespoons brown sugar
1/2 teaspoon cinnamon
1/4 teaspoon nutmeg
1/4 cup butter or margarine

Combine flour, oats, nuts, brown sugar, and spices in mixing bowl. Cut in butter with pastry blender. Bake on fruit crisp desserts, on pages 297 and 298.

Cherry Crisp

Yield: 6 servings

Fruit Crisp Topping*

1 (1 lb. 5 oz.) can prepared cherry pie filling
1/2 teaspoon almond extract

1. Press half of topping mixture into bottom of 8 x 8 x 2-inch dish.

2. Combine pie filling and almond extract. Spread evenly over crumb layer. Sprinkle remaining topping mixture over filling.

3. Bake in Radarange Oven on FULL POWER for 5 to 7 minutes, or until bubbling.

   *MICRO-TIP: See the "Fruit Crisp Topping" recipe on this page.

Peach Crisp

Yield: 6 to 8 servings

1 (18 oz.) pkg. oatmeal cookie mix
1/2 cup coconut, shredded
1/2 cup butter or margarine

6 medium peaches, peeled and sliced (4 cups)*
1 cup brown sugar, firmly packed
2 teaspoons lemon juice
2 tablespoons all-purpose flour
1/2 teaspoon cinnamon
2 tablespoons butter or margarine

1. Combine cookie mix and coconut in mixing bowl. Cut in butter with pastry blender. Press half of topping mixture into bottom of 2-quart utility dish. Set aside remaining topping mixture.

2. Combine peaches, brown sugar, lemon juice, flour and cinnamon in a mixing bowl. Spread peach mixture over crust. Dot with butter. Sprinkle remaining topping mixture over filling.

3. Bake in Radarange Oven on FULL POWER for 6 to 8 minutes, or until peaches are tender.

   MICRO-TIP: To make an "Easy Peach or Apple Crisp," 2 (21 oz. each) cans peach or apple pie filling can be substituted for the fresh peaches. Dot with only cinnamon and butter in step #2. Use "Fruit Crisp Topping," on page 297 instead of topping in step #1. Bake in Radarange Oven on FULL POWER for 4 to 6 minutes, or until bubbling.

Strawberry-Rhubarb Crisp

Yield: 8 servings

4 cups rhubarb, cut in 1/2-inch pieces
1-1/2 cups strawberries, sliced
1 cup sugar
1 tablespoon lemon juice
1 tablespoon quick-cooking tapioca
Fruit Crisp Topping*

1. Combine rhubarb, strawberries, sugar, lemon juice and tapioca in 8 x 8 x 2-inch dish. Sprinkle topping mixture over fruit.

2. Bake in Radarange Oven on FULL POWER for 10 to 12 minutes, or until rhubarb is tender.

MICRO-TIPS:

• May be served warm or cold with whipped cream or vanilla ice cream

*See the "Fruit Crisp Topping" recipe on page 297.

Peach-Pineapple Cobbler

Yield: 6 to 8 servings

1 (21 oz.) can peach pie filling
1 (8-1/2 oz.) can crushed pineapple, with liquid

1 cup all-purpose flour
2 tablespoons sugar
2 teaspoons baking powder
1/2 teaspoon orange peel, grated
1/4 cup butter or margarine

1/4 cup milk
1 egg, slightly-beaten
Cinnamon

1. Combine pie filling and pineapple with liquid in 8 x 8 x 2-inch dish. Cook in Radarange Oven on FULL POWER for 6 to 8 minutes. Stir halfway through cooking time.

2. Combine flour, sugar, baking powder and orange peel in mixing bowl. Cut in butter with pastry blender.

3. Add milk and egg. Mix lightly with fork until just blended. Drop dough by tablespoons onto fruit. Sprinkle with cinnamon, as desired.

4. Bake in Radarange Oven on FULL POWER for 5 to 7 minutes, or until dough is fully baked.

Gingered Apple Cobbler

Yield: 6 to 8 servings

4 medium apples, pared, cored and sliced (4 cups)
1/2 cup brown sugar, firmly packed
1 tablespoon lemon juice
1 teaspoon cinnamon
2 tablespoons butter or margarine

1 (14.5 oz.) pkg. gingerbread mix
1 cup quick-cooking or old-fashioned, rolled oats
1/2 cup butter or margarine

1. Combine apples, brown sugar, lemon juice and cinnamon in 8 x 8 x 2-inch dish. Dot with butter.

2. Combine gingerbread mix and oats in mixing bowl. Cut in butter with pastry blender. Sprinkle over apples.

3. Bake in Radarange Oven on FULL POWER for 6 to 8 minutes, or until apples are tender.

Apple Brown Betty

Yield: 6 to 8 servings

6 medium apples, pared, cored
  and sliced
1/2 cup raisins
1/2 cup walnuts, chopped
1/3 cup honey
1/4 cup brown sugar, firmly packed
3 tablespoons all-purpose flour
2 tablespoons lemon juice
1 teaspoon cinnamon
1/4 teaspoon nutmeg

1/2 cup quick-cooking, rolled oats
1/2 cup whole wheat flour
1/2 cup wheat germ
1/4 cup brown sugar, firmly packed
1 teaspoon cinnamon
1/4 cup butter or margarine

1. Combine apples, raisins, walnuts, honey, brown sugar, flour, lemon juice, cinnamon and nutmeg in 8 x 8 x 2-inch dish.

2. Combine remaining dry ingredients in mixing bowl. Cut in butter with pastry blender. Sprinkle over top of apple mixture.

3. Bake in Radarange Oven on FULL POWER for 6 to 8 minutes, or until apples are tender.

Strawberry Foam

Yield: 5 servings

2 cups water
1 (3 oz.) pkg. strawberry flavor
  gelatin

1 egg white
1 cup strawberries, sliced

1. Place 1 cup water in 4-cup glass measure. Heat in Radarange Oven on FULL POWER for 2 minutes, or until boiling. Stir in gelatin until dissolved. Blend in 1 cup cold water. Refrigerate until mixture starts to thicken.

2. Beat egg white at high speed until frothy. Gradually beat in thickened gelatin. Divide strawberries among five serving dishes, or put in large serving bowl. Pour gelatin mixture into dishes or bowl. Refrigerate for 3 hours, or until set.

MICRO-TIPS:

• This is a good dessert for calorie watchers, since there are just 71 calories per serving.

• Top with additional strawberries, if desired.

Fruit-Flavor Gelatin

Yield: 4 servings

1 cup water

1 (3 oz.) pkg. fruit flavor
  gelatin
1 cup cold water

1. Place water in 1-quart casserole or glass measure. Heat in Radarange Oven on FULL POWER for 1-1/2 to 2 minutes, or until boiling.

2. Add gelatin. Stir until dissolved. Add cold water. Chill until set.

MICRO-TIP: For a 6 oz. pkg. of gelatin, double the amount of water and heating time.

You will be most pleased with cakes baked in the Radarange Oven because they are very moist, light, and have a full volume. Undercook cakes rather than overcook them, in order to prevent dehydration. The "carry-over" cooking of cakes is greater in microwave cooking than in conventional cooking. After cakes stand for several minutes, they will be ready to serve. Moisture which appears on the tops of cakes after baking, will disappear during the "carry-over cooking" time.

Cakes will not become brown when baked in a microwave oven, due to the short baking time. Since most cakes are frosted or served with a topping, however, this lack of browning is generally not noticed.

Read the baking hints before baking cakes in the Radarange Oven.

General Hints for Baking Cakes
1. **All testing for cakes in this chapter was done using glass utensils. When a plastic or ceramic utensil is used, cooking times may need to be shortened or lengthened, respectively.**
2. Dish shapes can affect cake results. Circular dishes provide best cooking results. Arrange cupcakes in circle, if baking them in custard cups. Use circular-shaped cupcake trays.
3. If you do not have a glass, ceramic or plastic Bundt® dish, you can "create" one by placing a 2 to 3-inch diameter drinking glass in a 3 or 4-quart casserole. Pour the cake batter around the glass.
4. If you want to turn a cake out of the dish and onto a serving platter, grease the dish or, for best results, line it with waxed paper before baking. This will allow easy removal of the cake. Do not use flour when greasing a dish, since it will tend to lump in the bottom of the dish. Avoid using spray-on vegetable coating, as it makes cakes sticky.
5. You may wish to decrease the amount of batter slightly when baking microwave oven cakes. Dishes should be about half-filled with batter. Excess bat-

ter can be used for baking cupcakes. See the chart, on page 302.
6. Bake cake layers separately, one at a time. The same dish may be used, if desired. Use a fresh piece of waxed paper when baking the second layer.
7. Cakes should be baked on FULL POWER for best results. You may want to turn some cakes halfway through the cooking time.
8. You may wish to open the Radarange Oven door and turn some cake dishes. Cakes will not "fall" when the Radarange Oven door is opened, as they will if a conventional oven door is opened. Since microwave cooking is a "cool" type of cooking, there is no heat build-up within the Radarange Oven. The only heat is within the food itself. Since the air surrounding the cake inside the Radarange Oven remains cool, there is no air pressure change when the door is opened, as there is when the door of a conventional oven is opened. Therefore, cakes will not "fall."
9. Cakes are done when a toothpick inserted near the center comes out clean, or when the top springs back when lightly pressed with a finger. Cakes may appear slightly moist after baking. "Moisture" is not "raw" batter. This moisture will disappear when the cake stands for 3 to 5 minutes after baking. Remember to allow for this "carry-over cooking" time.
10. Due to the short amount of baking time, microwave oven-baked cakes will not brown. By using frostings or toppings, however, the lack of browning is not noticed, and cakes look very attractive. Try some of the frosting recipes in this chapter, or one of your own favorites. Confectioners' sugar, a mixture of cinnamon and sugar, nuts or coconut may be sprinkled over the top of a cake. Sauces, fruit toppings, and fresh or frozen fruit may be served over cake. Even pudding can be used as a topping for cake!
11. Cook frosting in a large enough utensil to avoid boil-overs. Glass measures may be used. Frosting will spread more evenly and easily after the cake's "carry-over cooking" time. The cake's surface should be slightly dry. Also, the cake can be cooled for a short time in the refrigerator, before frosting. The cake's surface should be cool enough to prevent

ncy Pistachio Nut Cake (page 309)

the frosting from melting.

12. Fruit cakes will require a longer baking time than most cakes, since the batter is dense.

13. Due to the short baking time, angel food cakes or cakes leavened entirely with egg whites will not bake with good results in a microwave oven.

14. Cake batter from a mix may be stored in the refrigerator, if you wish to bake one layer first, and bake the other later.

15. For coffee cake recipes, see the "Breads" chapter.

16. When baking one of your own favorite cakes in the Radarange Oven, use one of the recipes in this chapter as a guide. You may get better results if the amount of liquid is decreased by about 1/4. Use the same setting and approximately the same amount of baking time. Always slightly undercook a cake, when first experimenting with your own recipe. Then, allow the cake to stand for 3 to 5 minutes. The moisture on the cake top should disappear during this "carry-over cooking" time. If necessary, the cake can be returned to the Radarange Oven for a few additional seconds (or minutes).

FROZEN CONVENIENCE CAKE DEFROSTING CHART

CAKE TYPE	SIZE	SETTING	DEFROSTING TIME
Cake	10 to 11-1/2 oz.	DEFROST	1-1/2 to 2-1/2 min.
	12 to 13 oz.	DEFROST	2 to 3 min.
	16 to 18 oz.	DEFROST	2 to 3-1/2 min.
Pound Cake	10 to 11 oz.	DEFROST	2 to 3 min.

General Instructions for Defrosting Frozen Cakes

1. Remove the cake from the container, if metal. Place the cake on a plastic rack or a paper plate. Cover with a paper towel, if not frosted.

2. Defrost, according to the time on the chart. Do not melt the frosting.

CUPCAKE BAKING CHART*

QUANTITY OF CUPCAKES	BAKING TIME ON FULL POWER
1	10 to 15 sec.
2	20 to 30 sec.
4	35 to 45 sec.
6	50 sec. to 1 min., 10 sec.

*Any flavor or type of cupcake may be baked, according to the times on this chart.

General Instructions for Baking Cupcakes

1. Place the cupcake batter in glass custard cups, or in compartments of a plastic muffin tray. Fill custard cups or tray compartments with 2 level tablespoons of batter. For trays having holes in the bottom, paper liners should be used. When using custard cups, arrange them in a circle, rather than in rows on the Radarange Oven glass tray. If a plastic tray is used, the cooking time may need to be shortened.

2. Bake in the Radarange Oven on FULL POWER, according to the time on the chart. Remove the cupcakes from the custard cups or the plastic tray immediately after baking. If the cupcakes are not removed, a small amount of moisture will collect on the cupcake bottoms, causing the paper liners and cupcake bottoms to become soggy.

3. Be careful not to overcook cupcakes. Cupcakes will appear slightly moist, when done. Allow cupcakes to set on a cooling rack for 2 to 3 minutes, after baking.

CONVENIENCE CAKE MIX BAKING CHART

TYPE OF CAKE MIX	PKG. SIZE	DISH SIZE	COOKING TIME ON FULL POWER
Boston Cream Pie Cake Mix	15 to 16 ozs.	9-inch round	3 to 3-1/2 min.**
Bundt® Cake Mix	22 to 23 ozs.	12-cup Bundt® dish*	6-1/2 to 7-1/2 min.**
	26 to 28 ozs.	12-cup Bundt® dish*	7-1/2 to 8-1/2 min.**
Chocolate Cake Mix	9 ozs.	8 x 8 x 2-inch or 9-inch round	3 to 4 min.**
	18 to 20 ozs.	2 (8 x 8 x 2-inch) or 2 (9-inch round)	3 to 3-1/2 min.** (one layer at a time)
Pineapple Upside Down Cake Mix	21 to 22 ozs.	8 x 8 x 2-inch or 9-inch round	5 to 6 min.**
Pound Cake Mix	16 ozs.	2 (8-1/2 x 4-1/2 x 2-1/2-inch) loaf dishes	2-1/2 to 3 min.** (one loaf at a time)
Pudding Cake Dessert Mix Chocolate	11 ozs.	8 x 8 x 2-inch or 9-inch round	4-1/2 to 5-1/2 min.**
Lemon	11 ozs.	8 x 8 x 2-inch or 9-inch round	4 to 5 min.**
Snack Cake Mix	13 to 15 ozs.	8 x 8 x 2-inch or 9-inch round	3 to 4-1/2 min.**
Stir and Frost	11 to 13-1/2 ozs.	Use paperboard dish provided with mix.	2 to 3 min.**
Streusel Swirl Cake Mix	27 to 28 ozs.	10-cup Bundt® dish*	7-1/2 to 8-1/2 min.**
Yellow, White or Other	9 ozs.	8 x 8 x 2-inch or 9-inch round	3 to 3-1/2 min.**
Flavor Cake Mixes	18 to 20 ozs.	2 (8 x 8 x 2-inch) or 2 (9-inch round)	3 to 3-1/2 min.** (one layer at a time)
	18 to 20 ozs.	10-cup Bundt® dish*	6 to 7 min.**

*3-quart, round casserole with 2-inch diameter glass in center may also be used.

**With some cake mixes and some cake dishes, you may want to turn dish halfway through cooking time.

General Instructions for Baking Convenience Cake Mixes

1. Prepare the cake mix, according to the package instructions. For best results, use 1/4 less liquid than recommended on the package. Grease the dish, but do not flour. Line the bottom of the dish with waxed paper, if desired, for easy removal of the cake after baking.

2. Bake, according to the instructions on the chart. The cake is done when a toothpick inserted in the center comes out clean, or when the top springs back when lightly pressed with a finger.

Coconut-Pecan Frosting

Yield: Frosting for 2-layer or 3-layer cake

1/2 cup butter or margarine

1 cup evaporated milk
1 cup sugar
3 egg yolks
1 teaspoon vanilla

1-1/3 cups coconut, flaked
1 cup pecans, chopped

1. Place butter in 1-1/2-quart casserole. Heat in Radarange Oven on FULL POWER for 1 minute, or until melted.

2. Blend milk, sugar, egg yolks and vanilla into butter. Cook in Radarange Oven on Cookmatic Level 8 (MEDIUM HIGH) for 5 to 8 minutes, or until thickened. Stir occasionally during cooking.

3. Add coconut and pecans. Stir until cooled and of spreading consistency.

MICRO-TIP: This is the traditional frosting for German Chocolate Cake.

Chocolate Icing Deluxe

Yield: Frosting for 3 dozen cupcakes or 1, 2-layer cake

1 large egg
2 cups confectioners' sugar

2 (1 oz. each) squares unsweetened chocolate

1/4 teaspoon salt
1/3 cup butter or margarine, softened
1 teaspoon vanilla

1. Beat egg with electric mixer until fluffy. Continue to beat while adding sugar gradually.

2. Place chocolate in 1-cup glass measure or small custard cup. Heat in Radarange Oven on Cookmatic Level 6 (ROAST) for 2-1/2 to 3 minutes, or until melted.

3. Stir salt, butter and chocolate into egg and sugar mixture. Beat until smooth and creamy. Stir in vanilla.

White Mountain Frosting

Yield: Frosting for 3 dozen cupcakes, or 2-layer cake

1/2 cup sugar
1/4 cup light corn syrup
2 tablespoons water

2 egg whites
1 teaspoon vanilla

1. Combine sugar, corn syrup and water in 1-quart casserole. Cook in Radarange Oven on FULL POWER for about 3 to 4 minutes, or until soft ball stage is reached.*

2. Beat egg whites until stiff peaks form. Pour hot syrup in thin stream, and then vanilla into egg whites, while beating. Beat until stiff peaks form. Spread on cake.

*MICRO-TIP: The soft ball stage is described on page 352.

Chocolate Cream Cheese Frosting

Yield: Frosting for 1, 8 x 12-inch cake

1 (6 oz.) pkg. semi-sweet chocolate morsels
1/4 cup butter or margarine

1 (3 oz.) pkg. cream cheese, softened
1 teaspoon vanilla
1/4 teaspoon salt

2-1/2 to 2-3/4 cups confectioners' sugar, sifted

1. Place chocolate morsels and butter in 2-cup glass measure. Heat in Radarange Oven on Cookmatic Level 6 (ROAST) for 3 to 4 minutes, or until melted. Stir halfway through cooking time.

2. Beat cream cheese in small mixing bowl until smooth. Beat in melted chocolate. Add vanilla and salt.

3. Gradually beat in confectioners' sugar. Beat until frosting is smooth and of spreading consistency.

Lime Gelatin Delight Cake

Yield: 1,
9-inch round cake

1 (9 oz.) pkg. white cake mix
1/2 cup water
1 egg white

1 (3 oz.) pkg. lime flavor gelatin
1 cup water

1 cup whipped topping
Green crystal sugar

1. Prepare cake mix, according to package directions. Pour batter into greased, 9 x 2-inch round dish. Bake in Radarange Oven on FULL POWER for 3 to 3-1/2 minutes, or until top springs back when lightly pressed with finger.*

2. Place water in 2-cup glass measure. Heat in Radarange Oven on FULL POWER for 1-1/2 to 2 minutes, or until boiling. Stir in gelatin to dissolve.

3. Poke holes in cake with toothpick. Pour gelatin over cake. Refrigerate for 1 hour.

4. Spread whipped topping over cake. Sprinkle with green crystal sugar, as desired.

   MICRO-TIPS:

   •Undissolved lime flavor gelatin may be added to topping, or 1 to 2 drops green food coloring may be added to tint green.

   •1 teaspoon reserved, undiluted gelatin may be sprinkled on top.

   •This is a good dessert for St. Patrick's Day, or for other holidays. Use other flavors of gelatin and colors of sugar.

   *You may want to turn dish halfway through cooking time.

Surprise Cupcakes

Yield: 3 dozen

1 (17 to 18 oz.) pkg. chocolate cake mix

1 (8 oz.) pkg. cream cheese
1/3 cup sugar
1 egg
Dash of salt
1 (6 oz.) pkg. semi-sweet chocolate morsels

1. Prepare cake mix, according to package directions, in large mixing bowl.

2. Beat together cream cheese and sugar. Mix in egg. Add salt. Beat until smooth. Fold in chocolate morsels.

3. Line 6 custard cups or plastic cupcake tray with paper cupcake liners. Drop 1 level tablespoon of batter into each. Drop rounded teaspoon cream cheese mixture into center of cake batter. Cover by dropping another level tablespoon of chocolate mixture. Arrange cupcakes in circle in Radarange Oven if using custard cups.

4. Bake half-dozen in Radarange Oven on FULL POWER for 1 minute, 20 seconds, to 1 minute, 40 seconds, or until tops spring back when lightly pressed with finger. Edges may be moist. Remove cupcakes from custard cups or plastic tray immediately. Place on cooking rack. Repeat with remaining cupcakes.

   MICRO-TIP: Frost cupcakes with favorite chocolate icing.

Quick Chocolate Cake

Yield: 1,
8 x 8 x 2-inch cake

1 cup cold, strong coffee
1/2 cup 40% bran cereal

1/4 cup shortening, melted
1 tablespoon vinegar
1 teaspoon vanilla

1-1/2 cups all-purpose flour
1/4 cup cocoa
1 teaspoon baking soda
1 teaspoon cinnamon
1/2 teaspoon salt
1/2 cup sugar
1/2 cup brown sugar, firmly packed

1. Blend together coffee and cereal in 8 x 8 x 2-inch dish. Let stand 1 to 2 minutes, until most of liquid is absorbed.

2. Mix in shortening, vinegar, and vanilla. Stir.

3. Mix in remaining ingredients, stirring until smooth.

4. Bake in Radarange Oven on FULL POWER for 5-1/2 to 6-1/2 minutes, or until toothpick inserted in center comes out clean.*

MICRO-TIPS:

• Chopped nuts may be sprinkled over top before serving, if desired.

* You may want to turn dish halfway through cooking time.

German Chocolate Cake

Yield: 1, 3-layer cake

1 (4 oz.) pkg. German's sweet chocolate
1/2 cup hot water

1 cup butter or margarine
2 cups sugar
4 egg yolks
1 teaspoon vanilla

2-1/2 cups cake flour or 2-1/4 cups all-purpose flour
1 teaspoon baking soda
1/2 teaspoon salt

1 cup buttermilk
4 egg whites, stiffly-beaten

1. Place chocolate in 1-quart casserole. Heat in Radarange Oven on Cookmatic Level 6 (ROAST) for 4-1/2 to 5 minutes, or until melted. Stir in water. Blend well.

2. Cream butter and sugar in large mixing bowl. Add yolks, one at a time. Beat well after each addition. Blend in chocolate, and then vanilla.

3. Sift together flour, soda and salt.

4. Add sifted mixture alternately with buttermilk to chocolate mixture, beating after each addition. Fold in egg whites. Line bottoms of 3, 9 x 2-inch round dishes with waxed paper. Evenly distribute batter among dishes. Bake each layer separately.

5. Bake in Radarange Oven on FULL POWER for 5 to 6 minutes, or until center springs back when lightly pressed with finger.* Repeat with remaining layers.

MICRO-TIPS:

• Use "Coconut-Pecan Frosting," page 304. Frost only top of each layer.

* You may want to turn dish halfway through cooking time.

Fudge Pudding Cake

Yield: 6 to 8 servings

2 tablespoons butter or margarine
1/2 cup sugar
1 teaspoon vanilla

1 cup all-purpose flour
3 tablespoons cocoa
1 teaspoon baking powder
1/2 teaspoon salt
1/2 cup milk
1/2 cup nuts, chopped

1-2/3 cups boiling water
1/2 cup sugar
5 tablespoons cocoa
1/4 teaspoon salt

Confectioners' sugar

1. Place butter in medium-size mixing bowl or 1-1/2-quart casserole. Heat in Radarange Oven on FULL POWER for 20 to 30 seconds, or until melted. Stir in 1/2 cup sugar and vanilla.

2. Mix together flour, 3 tablespoons cocoa, baking powder, and 1/2 teaspoon salt. Stir into sugar mixture, alternately with milk. Stir in nuts.

3. Combine water with 1/2 cup sugar, cocoa and salt in 8 x 8 x 2-inch dish. Drop batter from Step 2 by rounded tablespoons onto this hot mixture.

4. Cook in Radarange Oven on FULL POWER for 4-1/2 to 5-1/2 minutes, or until top springs back when lightly pressed with finger.* Sprinkle with confectioners' sugar, as desired. While still warm, spoon out servings.

MICRO-TIPS:

• May be served with whipped cream or ice cream, if desired.

* You may want to turn dish halfway through cooking time.

Chocolate Layer Cake

Yield: 1, 9-inch layer cake

1/2 cup butter or margarine
2 cups sugar
2 egg yolks
1 teaspoon vanilla

2 cups cake flour
3/4 cup cocoa
3/4 teaspoon salt
1 teaspoon baking soda

1-3/4 cups milk

1. Cream butter and sugar in large mixing bowl. Add egg yolks and vanilla. Beat well.

2. Combine dry ingredients.

3. Alternately add dry ingredients and milk to creamed mixture. Line bottoms of 2, 9 x 2-inch round dishes with waxed paper. Evenly distribute batter between dishes. Bake each layer separately.

4. Bake in Radarange Oven on FULL POWER for 5 to 6 minutes, or until top springs back when lightly pressed with finger.* Repeat with remaining layer.

MICRO-TIPS:

• Frost with "Chocolate Icing Deluxe" or "White Mountain Frosting," page 304.

* You may want to turn dish halfway through cooking time.

Oatmeal Cinnamon Cake

Yield: 1, 8 x 12-inch cake

1-1/2 cups boiling water
1 cup quick-cooking, rolled oats
1/2 cup butter or margarine

1-1/2 cups all-purpose flour
1-1/2 teaspoons cinnamon
1 teaspoon baking soda
1 teaspoon salt

1 cup brown sugar, firmly packed
3/4 cup sugar
2 eggs, beaten

TOPPING

3/4 cup brown sugar, firmly packed
6 tablespoons butter or margarine
2 tablespoons milk

1 cup coconut, shredded
1/2 cup pecans, chopped

1. Pour water over oats in large mixing bowl. Break butter into chunks and drop over oats. Stir mixture until butter is melted.

2. Sift together flour, cinnamon, soda and salt. Stir into oat mixture. Mix well.

3. Stir in brown sugar and sugar. Stir in eggs. Mix thoroughly. Pour into 2-quart utility dish.

4. Bake in Radarange Oven on FULL POWER for 8 to 9 minutes, or until top springs back when lightly pressed with finger.*

5. For topping, combine brown sugar, butter and milk in 1-1/2-quart casserole. Heat in Radarange Oven on FULL POWER for 1 to 1-1/2 minutes, or until mixture boils. Boil for 1 additional minute.

6. Blend in coconut and pecans. Spread on cooled cake.

*MICRO-TIP: You may want to turn dish halfway through cooking time.

Honey Bran Kuchen

Yield: 1, 8 x 8 x 2-inch cake

3/4 cup all-purpose flour
2-1/2 teaspoons baking powder
1/2 teaspoon cinnamon
1/4 teaspoon nutmeg
1/4 teaspoon salt

2 cups bran flakes

1/2 cup milk
1 egg, well-beaten
1/4 cup honey
3 tablespoons shortening, melted

1/4 cup brown sugar, firmly packed
2 tablespoons butter or margarine, melted

1. Sift together flour, baking powder and spices in large mixing bowl.

2. Stir in 1-1/2 cups of bran flakes.

3. Combine milk, egg, honey and shortening. Pour into flour mixture. Mix until moistened. Pour into 8 x 8 x 2-inch dish.

4. Mix together brown sugar, butter and remaining bran flakes. Sprinkle over batter.

5. Bake in Radarange Oven on FULL POWER for 3-1/2 to 4-1/2 minutes or until toothpick inserted in center comes out clean.*

*MICRO-TIP: You may want to turn dish halfway through cooking time.

Fancy Pistachio Nut Cake

Yield: 1 cake

1 cup pecans, finely chopped
3/4 cup sugar
2 tablespoons cinnamon

1 (1 lb., 2 oz.) pkg. yellow cake mix
1 (3-1/2 oz.) pkg. instant pistachio pudding
4 eggs
1 cup dairy sour cream
3/4 cup water or orange juice
1/4 cup vegetable oil
1 teaspoon vanilla

1. Mix together nuts, sugar and cinnamon in small bowl. Sprinkle 1/3 of mixture into generously greased, 10-cup glass Bundt® dish, or place 2-inch diameter glass in center of generously greased 4-quart casserole to form ring mold. Cover sides and bottom of dish.

2. Blend together cake mix, pudding, eggs, sour cream, juice, oil and vanilla in large mixing bowl. Alternate layers of batter with remaining nut mixture in dish. Swirl batter with fork.

3. Bake In Radarange Oven on FULL POWER for 10 to 12 minutes, or until toothpick inserted in center comes out clean.* Let stand 10 minutes. Remove glass, and invert on serving platter.
   *MICRO-TIP: You may want to turn dish halfway through cooking time.

Cinnamon Streusel Cake

Yield: 1 cake

1 (16 oz.) pkg. pound cake mix
1 (3-3/4 oz.) pkg. vanilla instant pudding mix
1/2 cup vegetable oil
4 eggs
1/2 cup water
1/4 cup dark corn syrup

STREUSEL

1/2 cup all-purpose flour
1/2 cup dark brown sugar, firmly packed
2 teaspoons cinnamon
2 tablespoons butter or margarine
3/4 cup nuts, chopped

1. Combine dry ingredients in large mixing bowl.

2. Combine liquid ingredients and add to dry ingredients.

3. For streusel, blend together flour, brown sugar, and cinnamon. Cut in butter with pastry blender. Add nuts. Sprinkle 1/3 of streusel mixture, followed by 1/2 of batter into generously greased, 10-cup glass Bundt® dish, or place 2-inch diameter glass in center of 4-quart casserole to form ring mold. Top with another 1/3 streusel mixture. Add remaining batter and top with last 1/3 of streusel.

4. Bake in Radarange Oven on FULL POWER for 8 to 10 minutes, or until top springs back when lightly pressed with finger.* Let stand 10 minutes. Remove glass, and invert on serving platter.

   *MICRO-TIP: You may want to turn dish halfway through cooking time.

Triple Layer Coconut Cake

Yield: 1, 9-inch
3-layer cake

2-1/4 cups sugar
3/4 cup butter or margarine,
    softened
3 eggs
1-1/2 teaspoons vanilla

3-1/4 cups cake flour
4 teaspoons baking powder
1-1/2 teaspoons salt

1-1/2 cups milk

1 (3 oz.) pkg. lemon pudding mix
1/2 cup sugar
2 egg yolks
2-1/4 cups water

FROSTING

1-1/2 cups sugar
1/2 cup water
1/4 teaspoon cream of tartar

4 egg whites
1 teaspoon vanilla

1 cup coconut, shredded

1. Gradually beat sugar into butter in large mixing bowl. Cream mixture. Mix in eggs and vanilla.

2. Sift together flour, baking powder and salt.

3. Alternately mix dry ingredients and milk into creamed mixture, beginning and ending with flour mixture. Beat after each addition. Line bottoms of 3, 9 x 2-inch round dishes with waxed paper. Evenly distribute batter among dishes. Bake each layer separately.

4. Bake in Radarange Oven on FULL POWER for 4 to 5 minutes, or until center springs back when lightly pressed with finger. Edges may appear slightly moist.** Cool. Repeat with remaining layers.

5. Blend together pudding mix, sugar, egg yolks and water, according to package instructions, in 1-quart casserole. Cook in Radarange Oven on Cookmatic Level 8 (MEDIUM HIGH) for 5-1/2 to 7 minutes, or until mixture boils and is thickened. Stir twice during cooking. Cool slightly. Spread between layers of cake.

6. For frosting, combine sugar, water and cream of tartar in 1-1/2-quart casserole. Cook in Radarange Oven on FULL POWER for 7 to 9 minutes, or until hard ball stage is reached.* Stir occasionally during cooking time.

7. Beat egg whites until stiff, but not dry. Gradually stir hot syrup and then vanilla into egg whites, beating constantly until stiff peaks form.

8. Frost cake. Sprinkle coconut on top and sides of cake.

MICRO-TIPS:

   * The hard ball stage is described on page 352.

   ** You may want to turn dish halfway through cooking time.

Boston Cream Pie

Yield: 1, 9-inch layer cake

1/3 cup butter or margarine, softened
1 cup sugar
2 eggs
1 teaspoon vanilla

1-1/2 cups all-purpose flour
2 teaspoons baking powder
1/2 teaspoon salt
1/2 cup milk

1. Cream butter and sugar in large mixing bowl. Beat in eggs and vanilla.

2. Sift together dry ingredients. Add to creamed mixture, alternately with milk.

3. Pour batter into 2 waxed paper-lined, 9 x 2-inch round dishes. Bake each layer separately.

4. Bake in Radarange Oven on FULL POWER for 4 to 6 minutes, or until toothpick inserted in center comes out clean.* Cool. Repeat with remaining layer.

FILLING

1 cup milk

5. For filling, place milk in 2-cup glass measure. Heat in Radarange Oven on Cookmatic Level 8 (MEDIUM HIGH) for 1-1/2 to 2 minutes, or until warmed.

5 tablespoons sugar
2 tablespoons cornstarch
1/4 teaspoon salt

6. Blend together sugar, cornstarch and salt in 1-1/2-quart casserole. Stir milk into sugar mixture, gradually, with wire whip. Cook in Radarange Oven on Cookmatic Level 8 (MEDIUM HIGH) for 1 to 2 minutes, or until thickened. Stir halfway through cooking time.

1 egg, slightly-beaten

7. Gradually mix 1/2 cup of hot mixture with egg. Return to remaining hot mixture.

1 tablespoon butter or margarine
1/2 teaspoon vanilla

8. Cook in Radarange Oven on Cookmatic Level 8 (MEDIUM HIGH) for 1 to 1-1/2 minutes, or until bubbling. Mix well with wire whip, stirring in butter and vanilla. Cool. Spread filling over cooled bottom layer.

FROSTING

1 (1 oz.) square unsweetened chocolate

9. For frosting, place chocolate in 1-quart casserole. Heat in Radarange Oven on Cookmatic Level 6 (ROAST) for 1-1/2 to 2 minutes, or until melted.

1-1/2 ozs. cream cheese
2 tablespoons butter or margarine, melted
1/2 teaspoon vanilla
1 cup confectioners' sugar
1 tablespoon milk

10. Add cream cheese, butter and vanilla to chocolate. Beat until smooth. Gradually beat in confectioners' sugar and milk. Beat until smooth, and of spreading consistency. Add additional milk, if necessary. Place top layer of cake over bottom layer. Frost top of cake. Refrigerate until ready to serve.

*MICRO-TIP: You may want to turn dish halfway through cooking time.

Carrot Cake

Yield: 1, 8 x 8 x 2-inch cake

1 cup sugar
1 cup all-purpose flour
1-1/4 teaspoons cinnamon
1 teaspoon baking soda
1 teaspoon baking powder
1/2 teaspoon salt
1/4 teaspoon ginger
1/4 teaspoon ground cloves

1/2 cup vegetable oil
2 eggs
1-1/2 cups carrots, grated
1 (8 oz.) can crushed pineapple, drained

CREAM CHEESE FROSTING

1 (3 oz.) pkg. cream cheese
1/4 cup butter or margarine
1 teaspoon vanilla
2 cups confectioners' sugar
Milk (optional)

1. Blend together all dry ingredients in large mixing bowl.

2. Stir in oil. Add eggs, one at a time, mixing well after each addition. Blend in carrots and pineapple. Pour batter into greased, 8 x 8 x 2-inch dish.

3. Bake in Radarange Oven on FULL POWER for 7 to 9 minutes, or until top springs back when lightly pressed with finger.* Cool.

4. For frosting, beat together cream cheese, butter and vanilla. Gradually add confectioners' sugar, beating until smooth. If too thick, add few drops milk, as desired.

*MICRO-TIP: You may want to turn dish halfway through cooking time

Pineapple Upside-Down Cake

Yield: 8 to 9 servings

2 tablespoons butter or margarine
1/2 cup dark brown sugar, firmly packed
1 (15-1/4 oz.) can sliced pineapple, with liquid
1 (9 oz.) pkg. one layer yellow cake mix

1. Place butter in 8 x 8 x 2-inch dish. Heat in Radarange Oven on FULL POWER for 20 to 30 seconds, or until melted. Blend brown suga with butter and pack evenly into bottom of dish.

2. Drain pineapple juice into glass measure. Arrange pineapple slices over butter-brown sugar mixture.

3. Prepare cake mix as directed on package, substituting pineapple juice for water. Pour cake batter into dish, evenly distributing batter over entire surface.

4. Bake in Radarange Oven on FULL POWER for 5 to 7 minutes, or until top springs back when lightly pressed with finger. While hot, invert on serving platter.

MICRO-TIPS:

•Crushed pineapple may be substituted for sliced.

•For added color, place maraschino cherry in center of each pineapple ring.

Fruit Cake

Yield: 2, 9 x 5 x 2-inch loaves

1 lb. mixed candied fruits, chopped
8 ozs. pitted dates, chopped
1 cup golden raisins
2 cups pecan halves
4 eggs
1 cup orange juice
1 cup vegetable oil
3/4 cup brown sugar, firmly packed
1/3 cup sugar
1/4 cup molasses
1 teaspoon vanilla
2 teaspoons cinnamon
1 teaspoon nutmeg
1/2 teaspoon allspice

3 cups all-purpose flour
1 teaspoon baking powder
1 teaspoon salt

1. Combine fruits and pecans in large mixing bowl. Add eggs, juice, oil, sugars, molasses, vanilla and spices.

2. Sift together remaining dry ingredients and add gradually to fruit mixture. Mix thoroughly. Divide batter evenly between 2, greased, 9 x 5 x 2-inch loaf dishes. Bake each loaf separately.

3. Bake in Radarange Oven on FULL POWER for 6 to 9 minutes, or until top springs back when lightly pressed with finger. Cool completely. Invert on serving platter. Repeat with remaining loaf.

MICRO-TIPS:

- Wrap loaves in wine-soaked cheesecloth, if desired, for 1 to 2 weeks.

- An electric knife may be used to slice the fruit cake to assure clean-cut pieces of fruit.

Orange Crumb Cake

Yield: 1, 8 x 12-inch cake

2 cups all-purpose flour
1 cup sugar
1/2 cup butter or margarine
2 teaspoons cinnamon

2 teaspoons baking powder
2 eggs
1 cup orange juice

1. Mix together flour, sugar and butter until mixture is crumbly like cornmeal. Combine 1 cup of crumbled mixture with cinnamon and reserve for topping.

2. Combine baking powder with remainder of crumbled mixture. Beat eggs with orange juice lightly into crumb mixture.

3. Pour batter into lightly greased, 2-quart utility dish. Spread evenly into corners. Sprinkle batter with reserved topping.

4. Bake in Radarange Oven on FULL POWER for 5 to 7 minutes, or until top springs back when lightly pressed with finger.

Applesauce-Blueberry Cake

Yield: 1, 8 x 8 x 2-inch, or 9-inch round cake

1/4 cup butter or margarine
1 cup sugar
1 egg
1/2 cup dairy sour cream
1 (8-1/2 oz.) can applesauce (1 cup)

1-1/4 cups all-purpose flour
3/4 teaspoon baking soda
1/4 teaspoon baking powder
1/2 teaspoon cinnamon
1/4 teaspoon cloves
1/4 teaspoon salt

1 (15 oz.) can blueberries, rinsed and drained*
1/4 cup dark brown sugar, firmly packed
1/4 cup all-purpose flour
1/4 teaspoon cinnamon
2 tablespoons butter or margarine

1. Cream butter and sugar in large mixing bowl. Beat in egg. Add sour cream, and then applesauce. Blend well.

2. Mix together dry ingredients. Add to creamed mixture. Blend completely.

3. Fold in blueberries. Pour batter into greased, 8 x 8 x 2-inch dish or 9 x 2-inch round dish. Combine sugar, flour and cinnamon. Cut in butter until crumbly. Sprinkle over batter.

4. Bake in Radarange Oven on FULL POWER for 7 to 8 minutes, or until toothpick inserted in center comes out clean.

MICRO-TIPS:

*One cup of fresh or frozen blueberries may be used instead of canned blueberries.

•For tube cake, grease a round, 2-quart glass casserole. Place greased, 2-inch diameter glass in casserole. Sprinkle all surfaces with sugar and cinnamon. Sprinkle topping evenly around glass. Pour in batter. Bake, according to directions. Partially cool. Remove glass and invert on serving platter.

Banana Layer Cake

Yield: 1, 9-inch round layer cake

1/2 cup butter or margarine
1-1/2 cups sugar

3 egg yolks, beaten
1 cup bananas, mashed

1 teaspoon baking soda
1 teaspoon vanilla
1/2 cup dairy sour cream
2 cups all-purpose flour

3 egg whites, stiffly-beaten

1. Cream butter. Stir sugar in gradually.

2. Stir egg yolks into sugar mixture. Mix in bananas.

3. Combine baking soda and vanilla with sour cream. Stir sour cream mixture alternately with flour into banana mixture.

4. Fold egg whites into banana mixture. Line bottoms of 2, 9 x 2-inch round dishes with waxed paper. Evenly distribute batter between dishes. Bake each layer separately.

5. Bake in Radarange Oven on FULL POWER for 3 to 4 minutes, or until top springs back when lightly pressed with finger.* Repeat with remaining layer.

MICRO-TIPS:

• Frost with "Chocolate Icing Deluxe", page 304.

* You may want to turn dish halfway through cooking time.

Raspberry Preserves Cake

Yield: 1,
8 x 8 x 2-inch cake

1/2 cup butter or margarine
2/3 cup sugar

1/2 cup raspberry preserves, seedless
1/4 cup dairy sour cream
2 eggs

1-1/2 cups cake flour
1/2 teaspoon baking soda
1/2 teaspoon cinnamon
1/4 teaspoon salt

1/2 cup raspberry preserves, seedless

1. Cream butter and sugar in large mixing bowl.

2. Mix in preserves. Blend well. Add sour cream, and then eggs. Beat well.

3. Blend together flour, baking soda, cinnamon and salt. Add gradually to first mixture, beating well. Pour batter into greased, 8 x 8 x 2-inch dish.

4. Bake in Radarange Oven on FULL POWER for 4 to 5 minutes, or until top springs back when lightly pressed with finger.* Cool. Spread top with preserves.

MICRO-TIPS:

•Good when served with whipped cream, or frosted with "Raspberry Frosting," instead of preserves.

RASPBERRY FROSTING

2 tablespoons butter or margarine, melted
2 cups confectioners' sugar
1 teaspoon vanilla
1/4 cup raspberry preserves, seedless

•For frosting, combine butter, 1 cup sugar, vanilla and preserves. Blend well. Stir in remaining sugar until smooth. Spread on cooled cake.

*MICRO-TIP: You may want to turn dish halfway through cooking time.

Chocolate Kraut Cake

Yield: 8 x 12-inch cake

1/2 cup butter or margarine, softened
1-1/2 cups sugar
3 eggs
1 teaspoon vanilla
2 (1 oz. each) squares unsweetened chocolate, melted*

2 cups all-purpose flour
1 teaspoon baking powder
1 teaspoon baking soda
1/4 teaspoon salt
1 cup water
1 (8 oz.) can sauerkraut, drained, rinsed and finely snipped

1. Cream butter and sugar in large mixing bowl. Beat in eggs, one at a time. Stir in vanilla and chocolate.

2. Sift together dry ingredients, and add alternately to creamed mixture with water. Stir in sauerkraut. Spread batter in greased, 2-quart utility dish.

3. Bake in Radarange Oven on FULL POWER for 9 to 11 minutes, or until toothpick inserted in center comes out clean.

MICRO-TIPS:

*Melt chocolate in Radarange Oven on Cookmatic Level 6 (ROAST) for 2 to 3 minutes.

•Frost with "Chocolate Cream Cheese Frosting," on page 304.

Making pies can be a real art. With little effort, you'll find that pies are a real joy to make in the Radarange Oven. Radarange Oven pie crusts are very light and flaky. You'll enjoy preparing our crust recipes. If crusts are a threat to you, there are many ready-to-bake frozen crusts and ready-to-roll pie crust mixes. Instructions for baking frozen unbaked crusts and crusts made from mixes are included in this chapter. This chapter also contains a wide variety of pie fillings.

Read the general hints for baking pie crusts and pies before baking pies in the Radarange Oven.

General Hints for Baking Pie Crusts

1. When mixing pie crust pastry, remember proper mixing techniques, in order to achieve a tender product. Too much liquid will give a soggy crust, so use water only as needed, according to the recipe. The use of too much flour can result in a tough pie crust. Too much shortening will make a pie crust greasy and too crumbly. For best results, use a pastry blender to cut in shortening. Stir with a fork.
2. Be certain that all pie crusts are rolled to an even thickness (approximately 1/8-inch thickness).
3. Always use a glass pie plate.
4. Pie crusts will not brown in a microwave oven, due to the short amount of baking time. To achieve greater browning in a pie crust:
   a. Add yellow food coloring to the pie crust dough, as desired, when mixing.
   b. Brush the pie crust with vanilla and beaten egg white before baking.
   c. Crumb crusts, such as a graham cracker crust, will have a brown appearance, due to dark-colored ingredients.
5. To minimize pie crust shrinkage during baking:
   a. Allow the pie crust dough to "rest" for 3 to 5 minutes before the final shaping.
   b. Place the pie crust dough gently into a glass pie plate, being careful not to stretch the dough.
   c. Prick the bottom and sides of the pie crust dough, using the tines of a fork.
   d. Cover the pie crust dough with a paper towel.
   e. Place an 8-inch pie plate inside of 9-inch pie plate over the pie crust, if desired, to prevent shrinkage. (This is optional.)
   f. Bake in the Radarange Oven on FULL POWER according to the recipe. (Crumb crusts are also baked on FULL POWER.) Remove the 8-inch pie plate, if used, before the final minute of cooking time to allow the pie crust to dry.
6. Do not overcook pie crusts. Allow pie crusts to stand for a few minutes, after baking. Pie crusts will become crisper as they cool, during this standing time, or "carry-over cooking" time. Allow pie crusts to cool before adding the fillings.

General Hints for Baking Pies

1. Always bake the pie crust before adding the filling and baking the pie. If an unbaked crust is used, the entire crust may not cook, and it will become soggy. Frozen pies with unbaked crusts will not bake in a microwave oven with good results. These pies can be baked conventionally, frozen, and later defrosted and reheated in the Radarange Oven with good results. See the "Frozen Baked Pie Defrosting Chart," on page 318.
2. Bake pies in glass pie plates.
3. Cut slits in top pie crust before baking a 2-crust pie. Remember to pre-bake the bottom crust. When adding the top crust, moisten the edges of the baked bottom crust and tuck the edges of the top crust under to seal.
4. Pies are baked using a variety of settings, depending upon the type of ingredients in the filling. Fruit pies are generally baked on FULL POWER, while pies containing milk, eggs and other "special" or "delicate" ingredients should be baked on a lower Cookmatic Level or setting. Custard pies, for example,

require a lower setting to prevent curdling and separation.

5. Pies should be allowed to cool on cooling racks, or chilled before serving. If desired, baked pies can be reheated. See the "Baked Pie Reheating Chart," on page 319.

6. When baking your own favorite pie or pie crust, use a recipe in this chapter as a guide. Use the same setting and approximately the same amount of cooking time. Make a note of the Radarange Oven time required on your recipe for future use.

FROZEN BAKED PIE DEFROSTING CHART**

SIZE OF PIE	DEFROSTING TIME ON DEFROST*
8-inch (20 to 30 ozs.)	12 to 15 min.
9-inch (30 to 40 ozs.)	18 to 22 min.
10-inch (40 to 50 ozs.)	23 to 25 min.

*To avoid overcooking, it may not be possible to **completely** thaw the center of the pie. Allow 15 to 20 minutes of standing time, after defrosting, if necessary.

**The times on this chart can also be used for defrosting unbaked pies in glass pie plates. Bake the pies conventionally.

General Instructions for Defrosting Frozen Baked Pies

1. Pies need to be baked before freezing. In all recipes, the bottom crust needs to be baked before the filling is added. This is necessary to achieve a completely baked, flaky bottom crust. Purchased frozen pies are usually **unbaked.** For good results, bake these pies conventionally and then freeze. Later the frozen pies can be transferred to glass pie plates and quickly defrosted in the Radarange Oven. When baking pies "from scratch," bake them in glass pie plates, and then freeze. Or, bake two pies, eat one, and freeze the other for later use.

2. Place baked, frozen pie in glass pie plate. Do not cover. Defrost in Radarange Oven on DEFROST, according to the time on the chart. Allow the pie to stand for a few minutes after defrosting, if necessary.

BAKED PIE REHEATING CHART

TYPE OF PIE	AMOUNT OF PIE	COOKMATIC LEVEL	REHEATING TIME*	SPECIAL INSTRUCTIONS
Fruit Pie	1 piece**	Cookmatic Level 8 (MEDIUM HIGH)	30 sec. to 1 min.	
	2 pieces**	Cookmatic Level 8 (MEDIUM HIGH)	1 to 2 min.	———————
	Whole Pie	Cookmatic Level 8 (MEDIUM HIGH)	3 to 4 min.	
Custard Pie	1 piece**	Cookmatic Level 6 (ROAST)	30 sec. to 40 sec.	Turn during reheating to avoid melting.
	2 pieces**	Cookmatic Level 6 (ROAST)	45 sec. to 1 min.	
	Whole Pie	Cookmatic Level 6 (ROAST)	2-1/2 to 3-1/2 min.	

*The reheating time in this chart is based upon reheating pies of room-temperature. Increase the reheating time slightly when reheating refrigerator-temperature pies.

**A tart can be reheated by using the same reheat timings required for one piece of the same type of pie.

General Instructions for Reheating Baked Pies

1. Defrost the baked pie first, if necessary, according to the directions on the "Frozen Baked Pie Defrosting Chart," on page 318.

2. Place the pie or piece of pie on a plate, or heat in the glass pie plate. Cover with a paper towel.

3. Reheat in the Radarange Oven, covered, according to the setting and time recommended on the chart. Do not reheat pies for too long. The fillings become hot very quickly.

Peanut Butter Cream Pie

Yield: 1, 9-inch pie

1, 9-inch pie shell, baked

1-1/2 cups brown sugar, firmly packed
1/3 cup all-purpose flour
1-1/2 cups light cream

1 egg, beaten

1/2 cup peanut butter

1. Bake pie shell, as desired. Set aside.

2. Combine sugar, flour and light cream in 1-1/2-quart casserole. Cook in Radarange Oven on Cookmatic Level 8 (MEDIUM HIGH) for 4 to 5 minutes, or until thickened. Stir twice during cooking time with wire whip.

3. Add egg gradually, stirring with wire whip. Cook in Radarange Oven on Cookmatic Level 8 (MEDIUM HIGH) for 2 to 3 minutes, or until boiling. Stir twice during cooking.

4. Add peanut butter, stirring until smooth. Cool. Turn into pie shell.
   MICRO-TIPS:
   • Top with whipped cream, if desired.
   • Use Peanut Butter Crunch Crust, page 321, for a double peanut butter flavor.

Frozen Pie Crust

Yield: 1, 9-inch pie crust

1, 9-inch pie crust, frozen

1. Remove pie crust from metal tin and put into 9-inch glass pie plate. Let stand 10 minutes, or until softened. Prick well with tines of fork. Cover with paper towel.
2. Bake in Radarange Oven, covered, on FULL POWER for 1-1/2 to 2 minutes, or until dough is cooked and no longer moist. Cool. Fill with desired filling.

Pastry I*

Yield: 1, 8 or 9-inch pie shell

1 cup all-purpose flour
1/2 teaspoon salt
1/3 cup shortening

1-1/2 to 2 tablespoons cold water

1. Sift together flour and salt. Cut in shortening with pastry blender or fork.
2. Stir in water, one tablespoon at a time, with fork, until dough pulls away from sides of bowl.
3. Form into smooth ball and roll out on floured board or waxed paper until 1/8-inch thick. Place in 9-inch glass pie plate. Trim and flute edge. Prick bottom and sides well with tines of fork. Cover with paper towel.
4. Bake in Radarange Oven, covered, on FULL POWER for 3 to 4 minutes, or until dough is cooked and no longer moist. Cool. Fill with desired filling.

   MICRO-TIPS:

   •Shell may be baked without pricking by covering with paper towel and placing an 8-inch pie plate on paper towel to keep crust flat and prevent shrinkage.

   *Double this recipe for pastry enough to bake 1, double-crust pie. Bake the bottom crust, according to the above recipe. Bake the top crust as recommended in the pie recipe you use.

Pastry II

Yield: Pastry for 2, double-crust pies

3 cups all-purpose flour
1/2 teaspoon salt
1 cup shortening

1 egg
2 teaspoons vinegar
5 teaspoons cold water

1. Sift together flour and salt. Cut in shortening with pastry blender or fork.
2. Combine egg and vinegar. Add to flour mixture, stirring with fork. Add water, one teaspoon at a time, with fork, until dough pulls away from sides of bowl.
3. Divide dough into fourths, and use as needed: For bottom crust, roll one of the fourths into smooth ball and roll out on floured board or waxed paper until 1/8-in thick. Place in 9-inch glass pie plate. Trim and flute edge. Prick bottom and sides well with tines of fork. Cover with paper towel.
4. Bake in Radarange Oven, covered, on FULL POWER for 3 to 3-1/2 minutes, or until dough is cooked and no longer moist. Cool. Fill with desired filling. Top with another fourth of remaining pastry, sealing edges and slitting top. Bake pie, according to the amount of time in the recipe. Use remaining pastry as crusts for another pie.

Graham Cracker Crust

Yield: 1, 9-inch pie crust

1-1/4 cups graham cracker crumbs
1/4 cup butter or margarine, melted
1/4 cup sugar

1. Mix together all ingredients until well-blended in 9-inch glass pie plate. Press crumb mixture firmly against bottom and sides of pie plate.

2. Bake in Radarange Oven on FULL POWER for 1 minute, 15 seconds. Cool. Fill with desired filling.

   MICRO-TIP: An easy way to press cracker crumbs against bottom of 9-inch glass pie plate is to press them with an 8-inch glass pie plate.

Chocolate Crumb Crust

Yield: 1, 9-inch pie crust

1-1/4 cups chocolate wafer crumbs
1/4 cup butter or margarine, melted

1. Mix together crumbs and butter in 9-inch glass pie plate. Press crumb mixture firmly against bottom and sides of pie plate.

2. Bake in Radarange Oven on FULL POWER for 1 minute, 15 seconds, to 1 minute, 30 seconds. Cool. Fill with desired filling.

   MICRO-TIP: An easy way to press wafer crumbs against bottom of 9-inch glass pie plate is to press them with an 8-inch glass pie plate.

Gingersnap Crumb Crust

Yield: 1, 9-inch pie crust

1-1/3 cups gingersnap crumbs
6 tablespoons butter or margarine

1. Mix together crumbs and butter in 9-inch glass pie plate. Press crumb mixture firmly against bottom and sides of pie plate.

2. Bake in Radarange Oven on FULL POWER for 1 minute, 15 seconds, to 1 minute, 30 seconds. Cool. Fill with desired filling.

   MICRO-TIP: An easy way to press gingersnap crumbs against bottom of 9-inch glass pie plate is to press them with an 8-inch glass pie plate.

Chocolate-Coconut Pie Shell

Yield: 1, 9-inch pie shell

2/3 cup chocolate stars, or 1/2 cup semi-sweet chocolate morsels
2 tablespoons butter or margarine

2-2/3 cups coconut, flaked
2/3 cup confectioners' sugar
2 tablespoons milk

1. Place chocolate and butter in 1-1/2-quart casserole. Heat in Radarange Oven on Cookmatic Level 6 (ROAST) for 1-1/2 to 2-1/2 minutes, or until mixture is melted. Stir once or twice during melting.

2. Stir in remaining ingredients. Mix well. Press mixture firmly against bottom and sides of greased, 9-inch pie plate. Chill until firm. Fill with desired filling.

Peanut Butter Crunch Crust

Yield: 1, 9-inch crust

Butter or margarine

1/3 cup chunky peanut butter
1/3 cup light corn syrup

2 cups toasted rice cereal

1. Grease 9-inch pie plate with butter, as desired. Set aside.

2. Combine peanut butter and corn syrup in 1-quart casserole. Heat in Radarange Oven on FULL POWER for 1 minute, or until peanut butter is softened.

3. Stir in cereal. Press mixture firmly against bottom and sides of pie plate. Chill.

Baking Powder Crust

Yield: 1, 10-inch pie crust

1 cup all-purpose flour
1-1/2 teaspoons baking powder
1/8 teaspoon salt
1/4 cup solid shortening

4 to 5 tablespoons milk

1. Mix together flour, baking powder and salt in small mixing bowl. Cut in shortening with pastry blender or fork.

2. Stir in milk, one tablespoon at a time, with fork, until dough pulls away from sides of bowl.

3. Form into smooth ball and roll out on floured board or waxed paper until 1/8-inch thick. Place in 10-inch glass pie plate. Trim and flute edge. Prick bottom and sides well with tines of fork. Cover with paper towel.

4. Bake in Radarange Oven, covered, on FULL POWER for 3 to 4 minutes, or until dough is cooked but still moist. Cool. Fill with desired filling.

Rhubarb Custard Pie

Yield: 1, 10-inch pie

1, 10-inch pie shell, baked*

4 egg yolks
3/4 cup milk
1 teaspoon vanilla

1-1/2 cups sugar
3 tablespoons all-purpose flour
Dash salt
Dash nutmeg

3 cups rhubarb, diced

MERINGUE

4 egg whites
1/4 teaspoon cream of tartar
1/2 cup sugar

1. Bake pie shell, as desired. Set aside.*
2. Combine egg yolks, milk, and vanilla.

3. Mix together sugar, flour, salt and nutmeg. Add to egg mixture.

4. Spread rhubarb evenly in pie shell. Pour filling into pie shell.
5. Bake in Radarange Oven on Cookmatic Level 8 (MEDIUM HIGH) for 10 to 12 minutes, or until filling is almost set.

6. For meringue, beat egg whites with cream of tartar, until foamy. Add sugar, 1 tablespoon at a time, beating until egg whites are stiff.

7. Spread meringue over filling. Seal edges. Bake in Radarange Oven on Cookmatic Level 9 (HIGH) for 2 to 3 minutes, or until meringue is set.

*MICRO-TIP: Use the "Baking Powder Crust", on this page.

Apple Pie

Yield: 1, 9-inch pie

Pastry for 2-crust, 9-inch pie

6 to 8 medium apples, pared, cored
  and sliced
1/2 cup sugar
1/2 cup brown sugar, firmly packed
2 tablespoons all-purpose flour
1 tablespoon lemon juice
1 teaspoon cinnamon
Dash nutmeg
2 tablespoons butter or margarine

1. Prepare pastry and bake bottom crust, according to directions on page 320.
2. Combine remaining ingredients, except butter. Pour filling into pie shell. Dot with butter. Top with remaining pastry. Seal edges and slit top.
3. Bake on FULL POWER for 8 to 10 minutes, or until top crust is baked and apples are tender.

MICRO-TIP: For a delicious apple crumb pie, prepare same as above using 5 to 6 apples, and sprinkle crumb topping over top.

CRUMB TOPPING

1/4 cup butter or margarine
1/4 cup all-purpose flour
1/4 cup quick-cooking, rolled oats
1/4 cup brown sugar, firmly packed
1/4 cup nuts, chopped
1/2 teaspoon cinnamon

1. Cut butter into dry ingredients. Sprinkle over apples.
2. Bake in Radarange Oven on FULL POWER for 8 to 10 minutes, or until apples are tender.

1-2-3 Apple Pie

Yield: 1, 9-inch pie

1, 9-inch pie shell, baked

1 (1 lb. 5 oz.) can apple pie filling

1 cup dairy sour cream
3/4 cup milk
1 (3-3/4 or 3-5/8 oz.) pkg. instant
  vanilla pudding mix
2 tablespoons almonds, sliced

1. Bake pie shell, as desired. Set aside.
2. Pour filling into pie shell.
3. Slowly combine sour cream and milk. Mix well. Stir in pudding mix and beat, according to package directions. Pour pudding mixture over pie filling. Top with almonds. Chill.

MICRO-TIP: For toasted almonds, spread almonds on paper plate. Heat in Radarange Oven on FULL POWER for 2 minutes. Stir halfway through cooking time.

Deep Dish Apple Pie

Yield: 8 to 9 servings

Pastry for 1, 9-inch pie

10 medium apples, pared, cored
    and thinly sliced
1/2 cup sugar
1/2 cup brown sugar, firmly packed
1/2 cup maple syrup
1/2 cup all-purpose flour
2 tablespoons lemon juice
1 teaspoon cinnamon
1/2 teaspoon nutmeg
1/4 teaspoon salt
2 tablespoons butter or margarine

1. Prepare pastry, according to directions on page 320. Roll pastry into 10-inch square.

2. Combine remaining ingredients, except butter. Pour filling into 9 x 9 x 2-inch dish. Dot with butter. Top with pastry. Fold edges just inside edge of dish and slit top.

3. Bake on FULL POWER for 12 to 14 minutes, or until top crust is baked and apples are tender.

MICRO-TIP: May be served warm, with a scoop of vanilla ice cream.

Mincemeat-Apple Pie

Yield: 1, 9-inch pie

Pastry for 2-crust, 9-inch pie

1 (28 oz.) jar mincemeat
2 cups apples, pared, cored and
    diced

1. Prepare pastry and bake bottom crust, according to directions on page 320.

2. Combine mincemeat and apples. Pour filling into pie shell. Top with remaining pastry. Seal edges and slit top.

3. Bake on FULL POWER for 7 to 8 minutes, or until top crust is baked and apples are tender.

Hawaiian Cream Pie

Yield: 1, 10-inch pie

1, 10-inch pie shell, baked

1 (1 lb. 4 oz.) can crushed
    pineapple
Water

1 tablespoon gelatin
1/4 cup water

1 (3 oz.) pkg. lemon pudding mix
1 cup sugar
3 egg yolks
1/3 cup coconut, shredded

3 egg whites
1 cup dairy sour cream

1. Bake pie shell, as desired. Set aside.

2. Drain juice from pineapple and reserve. Add water to measure 2 cups.

3. Dissolve gelatin in 1/4 cup water.

4. Place pudding mix, sugar and egg yolks in 2-quart casserole. Gradually add the 2 cups reserved pineapple liquid. Cook in Radarange Oven on Cookmatic Level 8 (MEDIUM HIGH) for 5 to 7 minutes, or until mixture starts to boil. Stir halfway through cooking time. Add gelatin mixture. Blend well. Stir in pineapple and coconut. Chill until thickened.

5. Fold stiffly-beaten egg whites and sour cream into cooled pudding mixture. Pour into pie shell. Chill several hours before serving.

Blueberry Pie

Yield: 1, 9-inch pie

Pastry for 2-crust, 9-inch pie

6 cups (2 lbs.) frozen blueberries,
    thawed and drained*
1-1/4 cups sugar
1/2 cup brown sugar, firmly packed
1/3 cup cornstarch
1 teaspoon lemon juice
1/2 teaspoon cinnamon
1/2 teaspoon salt
Dash nutmeg
2 tablespoons butter or margarine

1. Prepare pastry and bake bottom crust, according to directions on page 320.

2. Combine remaining ingredients, except butter. Pour filling into pie shell. Dot with butter. Top with remaining pastry. Seal edges and slit top.

3. Bake on FULL POWER for 8 to 10 minutes, or until top crust is baked.

   *MICRO-TIP: Fresh blueberries may be used, if desired.

Easy Strawberry Pie

Yield: 1, 9-inch pie

1, 9-inch pie shell, baked*

1 cup water

1 (3 oz.) pkg. strawberry flavor
    gelatin
1 (16 oz.) pkg. sweetened, whole,
    frozen strawberries

1. Bake pie shell, as desired. Set aside.

2. Place water in 4-cup glass measure. Heat in Radarange Oven on FULL POWER for 1-1/2 to 2 minutes, or until boiling.

3. Dissolve gelatin in water. Stir in frozen strawberries, stirring until strawberries are covered. Chill until very thick.

4. Pour filling into pie shell. Chill several hours before serving.

   MICRO-TIPS:

   •May be served topped with whipped cream, if desired.

   *A graham cracker crumb crust may be used with this pie.

Gingered Apple Pie

Yield: 1, 9-inch pie

1, 9-inch gingersnap crumb crust,
    baked

1 (1 lb. 5 oz.) can apple pie filling
1/2 teaspoon cinnamon
Dash nutmeg

1. Prepare crust, according to directions on page 321. Reserve 1/4 cup crumbs for topping.

2. Combine apple pie filling with spices. Pour filling into crust. Sprinkle reserved crumbs on top.

3. Bake in Radarange Oven on FULL POWER for 3 to 4 minutes, or until bubbling.

   MICRO-TIP: May be served with vanilla or coffee ice cream, if desired.

Strawberry Rhubarb Pie

Yield: 1, 9-inch pie

Pastry for 2-crust, 9-inch pie

3 cups rhubarb, sliced in 3/4-inch pieces*
3 cups whole strawberries, sliced*
1 cup sugar
1/2 cup brown sugar, firmly packed
1/4 cup cornstarch
1/2 teaspoon cinnamon
Dash nutmeg
2 tablespoons butter or margarine

1. Prepare pastry and bake bottom crust, according to directions on page 320.
2. Combine remaining ingredients, except butter. Pour filling into pie shell. Dot with butter. Top with remaining pastry. Seal edges and slit top.
3. Bake on FULL POWER for 8 to 12 minutes, or until top crust is baked and fruit is tender.

MICRO-TIPS:

*Frozen rhubarb and frozen whole or sliced strawberries may be used, if desired.

•A lattice design pastry top makes an attractive-looking pie.

Cherry Pie

Yield: 1, 9-inch pie

Pastry for 2-crust, 9-inch pie

2 (16 oz. each) cans pitted, tart cherries, with 1/4 cup liquid
1/2 cup sugar
1/4 cup brown sugar, firmly packed
2 tablespoons cornstarch
1/2 teaspoon almond extract
1/2 teaspoon cinnamon
Dash nutmeg
2 tablespoons butter or margarine

1. Prepare pastry and bake bottom crust, according to directions on page 320.
2. Combine remaining ingredients, except butter. Pour filling into pie shell. Dot with butter. Top with remaining pastry. Seal edges and slit top.*
3. Bake on FULL POWER for 8 to 10 minutes, or until top crust is baked and cherries are tender.

*MICRO-TIP: A lattice design pastry top makes an attractive-looking pie.

Orange Mallow Pie

Yield: 1, 9-inch pie

1, 9-inch pie shell, baked

32 large marshmallows, or 3 cups miniature marshmallows
3/4 cup orange juice
2 tablespoons lemon juice
1 tablespoon orange peel, grated

1-1/2 cups whipping cream*

1. Bake pie shell, as desired. Set aside.

2. Combine marshmallows, juices and orange peel in 1-quart casserole. Cook in Radarange Oven on Cookmatic Level 8 (MEDIUM HIGH) for 45 seconds to 1 minute, or until marshmallows are melted. Stir 2 times during melting. Cool in refrigerator, until mixture begins to thicken.

3. Whip cream, until stiff, in small mixing bowl. Fold into marshmallow mixture. Pour filling into pie shell. Chill several hours before serving.

MICRO-TIPS:

•Chopped, toasted almonds or grated orange peel may be sprinkled on top, if desired.

*Whipped topping mix may be used instead of whipping cream, if desired.

VARIATIONS

Lemon Mallow Pie

1/3 cup lemon juice
1/2 cup water
1 tablespoon lemon peel, grated

Substitute these ingredients for orange juice, lemon juice and orange peel in original recipe.

Pineapple Mallow Pie

1 (8-3/4 oz.) can crushed pineapple
1 tablespoon lemon juice

Substitute these ingredients for orange juice, lemon juice and orange peel in original recipe.

Sour Cream Raisin Pie

Yield: 1, 9-inch pie

1, 9-inch pie shell, baked

1/2 cup sugar
1-1/2 tablespoons all-purpose flour
1 teaspoon cinnamon
1/8 teaspoon salt
2 egg yolks, beaten
1 cup dairy sour cream
1 cup raisins, finely chopped

MERINGUE

2 egg whites
1/8 teaspoon cream of tarter
1/4 cup sugar

1. Bake pie shell, as desired. Set aside.

2. Combine sugar, flour, cinnamon and salt in 1-quart casserole. Stir in egg yolks and sour cream. Stir in raisins. Cook in Radarange Oven on Cookmatic Level 8 (MEDIUM HIGH) for 3 to 4 minutes, or until mixture boils and is thickened. Pour filling into pie shell.

3. For meringue, beat egg whites with cream of tartar, until foamy. Add sugar, 1 tablespoon at a time, beating until egg whites are stiff.

4. Spread meringue over filling. Seal edges. Bake in Radarange Oven on Cookmatic Level 9 (HIGH) for 1 to 1-1/2 minutes, or until meringue is set.

Lemon Meringue Pie

Yield: 1, 9-inch pie

1, 9-inch pie shell, baked

1 cup sugar
1/3 cup cornstarch
1 cup water
2/3 cup milk

4 eggs, separated

1/2 cup lemon juice
1 tablespoon butter or margarine
1 teaspoon lemon peel, grated

MERINGUE

1/4 teaspoon cream of tartar
1/2 cup sugar

1. Bake pie shell, as desired. Set aside.

2. Combine sugar and cornstarch in 1-quart casserole. Slowly stir in water and milk. Cook in Radarange Oven on FULL POWER for 3 to 4 minutes, or until thickened. Stir twice during cooking time.

3. Mix part of hot mixture into slightly-beaten egg yolks. Return all to remaining hot mixture. Cook in Radarange Oven on Cookmatic Level 6 (ROAST) for 3 to 4 minutes, or until mixture begins to boil. Stir once during cooking time.

4. Stir in lemon juice, butter and lemon peel, until butter is melted. Pour filling into pie shell.

5. For meringue, beat egg whites with cream of tartar, until foamy. Add sugar, 1 tablespoon at a time, beating until egg whites are stiff.

6. Spread meringue over filling. Seal edges. Bake in Radarange Oven on Cookmatic Level 9 (HIGH) for 3 to 4 minutes, or until meringue is set.

Lemon Chiffon Pie

Yield: 1, 9-inch pie

1, 9-inch pie shell, baked

1 (3 oz.) pkg. lemon flavor gelatin*
1/2 cup sugar
1/2 teaspoon salt
4 eggs, separated
1 cup water
1 teaspoon lemon peel, grated

1/2 cup whipping cream

1. Bake pie shell, as desired. Set aside.

2. Combine gelatin, sugar and salt in 1-1/2-quart casserole. Beat egg yolks until thick and lemon-colored. Beat water and lemon peel into egg yolks. Stir into gelatin mixture.

3. Cook in Radarange Oven on Cookmatic Level 6 (ROAST) for 3 to 4 minutes, or until mixture boils and gelatin is dissolved. Stir halfway through cooking time. Chill until thickened.

4. Fold stiffly-beaten egg whites into gelatin mixture. Whip cream until stiff in small mixing bowl. Fold into gelatin mixture.

5. Pour filling into pie shell. Chill several hours before serving.

*MICRO-TIP: Other gelatin flavors may be used, if desired.

Cheesy Peach Pie

Yield: 1, 10-inch pie

1, 10-inch pie shell, baked

1 (21 oz.) can peach pie filling*
1 teaspoon vanilla
1/8 teaspoon nutmeg

1 cup dairy sour cream
1 (3 oz.) pkg. cream cheese, softened
2 eggs, slightly-beaten
1/3 cup sugar
1 teaspoon vanilla
1/2 teaspoon cinnamon or nutmeg

1. Bake pie shell, as desired. Set aside.
2. Combine pie filling, vanilla and nutmeg. Turn into baked pie shell.
3. Beat together sour cream and cream cheese in small mixing bowl. Beat in remaining ingredients until smooth. Pour over peach mixture. Sprinkle cinnamon on top.
4. Bake in Radarange Oven on Cookmatic Level 5 (SLO COOK) for 12 to 15 minutes, or until filling is set. Chill before serving.

   *MICRO-TIP: Other fruit pie filling may be used, if desired.

Custard Pie

Yield: 1, 9-inch pie

1, 9-inch pastry shell, baked

2 cups milk

3 eggs, slightly-beaten
1/2 cup sugar
1/4 teaspoon salt
1/2 teaspoon vanilla
Nutmeg

1. Bake pie shell, as desired. Set aside.
2. Place milk in 4-cup glass measure. Heat in Radarange Oven on Cookmatic Level 8 (MEDIUM HIGH) for 5 to 6 minutes, or until almost boiling.
3. Blend together eggs, sugar, salt and vanilla. Gradually stir in hot milk. Pour filling into pie shell. Sprinkle with nutmeg, as desired.
4. Bake in Radarange Oven on Cookmatic Level 4 (MEDIUM) for 15 to 18 minutes, or until knife inserted halfway between center and edge comes out clean and filling is almost set.

   MICRO-TIP: 1/2 cup of shredded coconut may be added to the custard for a delicious coconut-custard pie.

Lemon Buttermilk Pie

Yield: 1, 9-inch pie

1, 9-inch pie shell, baked

1 cup sugar
2 tablespoons all-purpose flour
1/4 teaspoon salt
2 eggs, beaten
2 cups buttermilk
2 tablespoons butter or margarine, melted
1 teaspoon lemon extract
1/2 teaspoon lemon peel, grated

1. Bake pie shell, as desired. Set aside.
2. Combine sugar, flour and salt in 1-1/2-quart casserole. Stir in eggs, buttermilk, butter, lemon extract and lemon peel. Pour into baked crust.
3. Bake in Radarange Oven on Cookmatic Level 4 (MEDIUM) for 20 to 22 minutes, or until set.

Coconut Cream Pie

Yield: 1, 9-inch pie

1, 9-inch pie shell, baked

3 cups milk

3/4 cup sugar
5 tablespoons cornstarch
1/2 teaspoon salt

3 egg yolks, beaten

1-1/2 cups coconut, shredded
2 tablespoons butter or margarine
1-1/2 teaspoons vanilla

1. Bake pie shell, as desired. Set aside.

2. Place milk in 4-cup glass measure. Heat in Radarange Oven on Cookmatic Level 8 (MEDIUM HIGH) for 5 to 6 minutes, or until scalded.

3. Mix together sugar, cornstarch, and salt in 2-quart casserole. Stir hot milk slowly into mixture.

4. Stir about 3/4 cup of hot mixture into egg yolks, stirring constantly. Return egg mixture to 2-quart casserole.

5. Cook in Radarange Oven on Cookmatic Level 8 (MEDIUM HIGH) for 3 to 4 minutes, or until thickened. Stir with wire wisk often during cooking. Add coconut, butter and vanilla. Stir until butter is melted. Pour filling into pie shell. Chill several hours before serving.

MICRO-TIP: May be served topped with whipped cream and coconut, if desired.

Banana Cream Pie

Yield: 1, 9-inch pie

1, 9-inch pie shell, baked*

1 (3-1/4 oz.) pkg. vanilla pudding mix
1-3/4 cups milk

16 large marshmallows, or
   1-1/2 cups miniature marshmallows

1/2 cup whipping cream

2 bananas, sliced

1. Bake pie shell, as desired. Set aside.

2. Place pudding mix in 1-quart casserole. Gradually stir in milk. Cook in Radarange Oven on Cookmatic Level 8 (MEDIUM HIGH) for 5-1/2 to 7 minutes, or until pudding boils and is thickened. Stir 2 to 3 times during cooking.

3. Add marshmallows. Stir until marshmallows are melted. Cover with waxed paper. Chill.

4. Whip cream until stiff in small mixing bowl. Fold into cooled pudding mixture.

5. Slice bananas into pie shell. Pour filling over bananas. Chill several hours before serving.

*MICRO-TIP: This filling is especially good in the Chocolate-Coconut Pie Shell or the Graham Cracker Crust, page 321.

Grasshopper Pie

Yield: 1, 9-inch pie

1, 9-inch chocolate crumb crust pie shell, baked

2/3 cup milk

3 cups miniature marshmallows

1 cup whipping cream
1/4 cup green creme de menthe
2 tablespoons white creme de cacao

1. Prepare crust, according to directions on page 321. Reserve 2 tablespoons of crumbs for topping.

2. Place milk in 1-1/2-quart casserole. Heat in Radarange Oven on Cookmatic Level 8 (MEDIUM HIGH) for 2 to 3 minutes, or until scalded.

3. Place marshmallows in milk. Cook in Radarange Oven on Cookmatic Level 8 (MEDIUM HIGH) for 45 seconds to 1 minute, or until marshmallows are melted. Stir twice during melting. Chill until cooled and thickened.

4. Whip cream until stiff in large bowl. Gradually stir creme de menthe and creme de cacao into marshmallow mixture. Fold into whipped cream. Pour filling into crust. Sprinkle reserved crumbs on top. Freeze at least 2 to 3 hours before serving.

Chocolate Almond Pie

Yield: 1, 9-inch pie

1, 9-inch graham cracker crust, pie shell, baked

1 (3-3/4 oz.) milk chocolate bar with almonds*
16 large marshmallows, or 1-1/2 cups miniature marshmallows
1/2 cup milk

1 cup whipping cream

1. Prepare crust according to directions on page 321.

2. Break chocolate bars into pieces. Combine chocolate bars, marshmallows and milk in 1-quart casserole. Cook in Radarange Oven on Cookmatic Level 8 (MEDIUM HIGH) for 2 to 3 minutes. Stir 2 to 3 times during cooking. Mix until smooth. Cool completely.

3. Whip cream until stiff in small mixing bowl. Fold into marshmallow mixture. Pour filling into crust. Chill several hours before serving.

*MICRO-TIP: 7 (1/2 oz. each) milk chocolate bars with almonds may be substituted.

Marble Cake Pie

Yield: 1, 10-inch pie

1, 10-inch pie shell, baked

1/2 cup sugar
1/4 cup cocoa
1/3 cup hot water
1/4 teaspoon vanilla

1/4 cup butter or margarine
1/2 cup sugar
1 egg
1 cup all-purpose flour
1 teaspoon baking powder
1/4 teaspoon salt
1/2 teaspoon vanilla
1/2 cup milk

1. Bake pie shell, as desired. Set aside.

2. Combine sugar and cocoa in small bowl. Stir in water and vanilla.

3. Cream butter and sugar in small mixing bowl. Add egg. Combine remaining dry ingredients and add to creamed mixture alternately with milk.

4. Pour chocolate mixture into baked pie shell. Pour other batter over top. Swirl chocolate through batter with fork. Bake in Radarange Oven on FULL POWER for 4-1/2 to 5-1/2 minutes, or until toothpick inserted in center comes out clean.*

*MICRO-TIP: You may want to turn dish halfway through cooking time.

Pecan Pie

Yield: 1, 10-inch pie

1, 10-inch pie shell, baked

1-1/4 cups brown sugar, firmly packed
1 cup light corn syrup
1/4 cup water

4 eggs, well-beaten
1/4 cup butter or margarine, softened
1 teaspoon vanilla
1-1/2 cups (5 ozs.) pecan halves

1. Bake pie shell, as desired. Set aside.
2. Mix together sugar, corn syrup and water in 1-1/2-quart casserole. Heat in Radarange Oven on FULL POWER for 3 to 3-1/2 minutes, or until mixture boils. Boil for 2 minutes.
3. Gradually stir hot syrup into eggs. Stir in butter and vanilla. Pour filling into pie shell. Top with pecan halves.
4. Bake in Radarange Oven on Cookmatic Level 8 (MEDIUM HIGH) for 7 to 8 minutes, or until filling is set.

Pumpkin Pie

Yield: 1, 9-inch pie

1, 9-inch pie shell, baked

1 (16 oz.) can pumpkin
3/4 cup brown sugar, firmly packed
1/2 teaspoon cinnamon
1/4 teaspoon ground cloves
1/4 teaspoon ginger
1/4 teaspoon allspice
1/8 teaspoon nutmeg

2 eggs
1 cup evaporated milk

1. Bake pie shell, as desired. Set aside.
2. Mix together pumpkin, sugar and spices in large mixing bowl.
3. Beat eggs and milk together. Stir into pumpkin mixture. Pour filling into pie shell.
4. Bake in Radarange Oven on Cookmatic Level 6 (ROAST) for 18 to 20 minutes, or until filling is set and knife inserted near center comes out clean.

Pumpkin Pie, Mix

Yield: 1, 9-inch pie

1, 9-inch pie shell, baked

1 (30 oz.) can pumpkin pie mix
2 eggs, slightly-beaten
2/3 cup evaporated milk

1. Bake pie shell, as desired. Set aside.
2. Mix together pumpkin pie mix, beaten eggs, and milk. Pour filling into pie shell.
3. Bake in Radarange Oven on Cookmatic Level 6 (ROAST) for 20 to 22 minutes, or until filling is set and knife inserted near center comes out clean.

Coffee Cream Pie

Yield: 1, 9-inch pie

CRUST

3 eggs, separated
1/3 cup sugar
1 cup nuts, finely chopped

1. For crust, beat egg whites until soft peaks form. Gradually beat in sugar until stiff peaks form. Fold in nuts. Spread in greased, 9-inch pie plate. Prick bottom well with tines of fork.

2. Bake in Radarange Oven on Cookmatic Level 6 (ROAST) for 3 to 5 minutes, or until set. Crust will shrink slightly. Set aside.

FILLING

32 large marshmallows, or 3 cups miniature marshmallows
1/4 cup water
1 tablespoon instant coffee

3. Place marshmallows and water in 1-1/2-quart casserole. Cook in Radarange Oven on Cookmatic Level 8 (MEDIUM HIGH for 45 seconds to 1 minute, or until marshmallows are melted. Stir twice during melting. Stir in instant coffee.

4. Stir about 3/4 cup of hot mixture into egg yolks, stirring constantly. Return egg mixture to 1-1/2-quart casserole. Cook in Radarange Oven on Cookmatic Level 6 (ROAST) for 1 to 1-1/2 minutes, or until mixture just begins to boil. Cool in refrigerator until mixture begins to thicken.

1 cup heavy cream

5. Whip cream until stiff in small mixing bowl. Fold into coffee mixture. Pour filling into pie shell. Chill several hours before serving.

MICRO-TIPS:

• Whipped topping mix may be used instead of whipping cream.

• May be served topped with whipped cream, if desired.

Peach Praline Pie

Yield: 1, 9-inch pie

1, 9-inch pie shell, baked

2-1/2 cups canned sliced peaches, drained
1/4 cup sugar
1 tablespoon quick-cooking tapioca
1 tablespoon lemon juice

1/2 cup all-purpose flour, sifted
1/4 cup brown sugar, firmly packed
1/4 cup butter or margarine
1/4 teaspoon salt

1/4 cup nuts, chopped

1. Bake pie shell, as desired. Set aside.

2. Combine peaches, sugar, tapioca and lemon juice.

3. Mix together flour, brown sugar, butter and salt with fork, until mixture is crumbly.

4. Sprinkle 1/3 of flour mixture in bottom of pie shell. Cover with peach mixture. Sprinkle remaining flour mixture over top of peaches. Sprinkle nuts on top. Cover with waxed paper.

5. Bake in Radarange Oven, covered, on FULL POWER for 3 minutes, or until peaches are tender.

Cookies are easily and quickly prepared in the Radarange Oven. Bake a dozen drop-type cookies quickly, when guests arrive unexpectedly. Children will also enjoy baking Radarange Oven cookies.

Cookies can be made ahead and frozen. See the "Frozen Cookie Defrosting Chart", on page 337.

Read the general hints for baking drop cookies or refrigerator cookies and bar cookies, before baking cookies in the Radarange Oven.

General Hints for Baking Drop Cookies or Refrigerator Cookies

1. Cookies will not brown in a microwave oven, since the baking time is so short. Many of the recipes in this chapter use dark colored sugars and spices to give cookies a browned appearance.
2. Cookies bake well on either waxed paper or parchment paper. Place cookies 2 inches apart on the paper. If desired, the entire Radarange Oven glass tray can be removed from the Radarange Oven. The waxed paper or parchment paper will then easily slide off of the tray onto a counter or table.
3. Cookies are done when they are set, but still moist.

Allow cookies to cool slightly, although not completely, before removing them from waxed paper. Cookies will become crisper as they cool.

4. When preparing your own favorite drop or refrigerator cookie recipes in the Radarange Oven, select a similar recipe in this chapter to use as a guide. Also, consider the following guides.

Conventionally prepared drop cookie and refrigerator cookie recipes can be converted to Radarange Oven recipes by following **three basic guidelines.**

1. A stiff dough is needed, so the amount of flour needs to be increased by approximately 20%.
2. The temperature of the cookie dough affects cooking times.
3. Cookies will not brown in a microwave oven like they brown in a conventional oven. Select cookie recipes that:
   a. Do not require browning (example: Sugar Cookies)
   b. Have dark brown sugar, spices, chocolate, or other ingredients which add color. (Cookies may also be frosted or sprinkled with cinnamon and sugar, or colored sugar.)

enter: Peanut Butter and Jelly Cookie-Wiches (page 342)

lockwise starting at top left: Honey Pecan Balls (page 343), Thumbprint Cookies (page 343), Ginger Cream Cookies (page 344), nd Snicker Doodle Cookies (page 341)

CONVENTIONAL DROP COOKIE CONVERSION CHART

QUANTITY OF COOKIES	TEMPERATURE	COOKING TIME ON FULL POWER
*12 cookies on waxed paper	Room Temp.	1 to 2 min.
*12 cookies on waxed paper	Refrig. Temp.	1 to 2 min.

*Times and quantities can be adjusted as needed.

General Instructions for Baking Conventional Drop Cookies in the Radarange Oven

1. Prepare the cookie dough, according to the **3 basic guidelines,** on page 335.
2. Drop cookies on waxed paper on the Radarange Oven glass tray. Bake a dozen at a time.
3. Bake in the Radarange Oven on FULL POWER, according to the time on the chart. Allow the cookies to cool slightly before removing them from the waxed paper.

General Hints for Baking Bar Cookies

1. Bar cookies will not brown in a microwave oven, due to the short cooking time. Use dark-colored sugars and spices to achieve a browned appearance. Many bar cookies can also be frosted so a lack of browning is not noticed.
2. The baking dish for bar cookies may be greased or ungreased, as desired. The dish should not be floured, since the flour will form a layer on the bottom of the cookies.
3. Bar cookies should generally be baked on FULL POWER. Use the setting recommended in the recipe.
4. Bar cookies are done when they are set, and a toothpick inserted near the center comes out clean, or the top springs back when lightly pressed with a finger. Bar cookies may appear moist on top. Allow them to stand for a few minutes after baking. Bar cookies will continue to "carry-over cook" during this time. If bar cookies are hard and tough, they have been overcooked.
5. When preparing your own favorite bar cookie recipe in the Radarange Oven, select a similar recipe in this chapter as a guide. Then use the same setting and approximately the same amount of time. In general, bake bar cookies on FULL POWER for approximately 1/3 of the time required when baked in a conventional oven.

FROZEN COOKIE DEFROSTING CHART

COOKIE TYPE	QUANTITY OR PKG. SIZE	SETTING	DEFROSTING TIME	SPECIAL INSTRUCTIONS
Frosted Brownies	1 (12 to 14 oz.) pkg.	DEFROST	2 to 3 min.	Remove from metal container to paper place. Be careful not to melt frosting.
Cookies, Homemade or Purchased	1 dozen	DEFROST	1-1/2 to 2-1/2 min.	Place on paper plate or plastic rack. Cover with paper towel.

General Instructions for Defrosting Cookies

1. Read the "Special Instructions" in the chart before defrosting cookies.

2. Defrost, according to the recommended time and setting on the chart. If frosted, be careful not to melt the frosting.

REHEATING COOKIES CHART

QUANTITY OF COOKIES	TEMPERATURE	REHEATING TIME ON COOKMATIC LEVEL 8 (MEDIUM HIGH)
1	Room temp.	15 sec.
1	Refrig. temp.	20 sec.

General Instructions for Reheating Cookies

1. Wrap the cookie in a napkin, or place it on a cooking grill or plate. Cover with a paper towel.

2. Reheat in the Radarange Oven, covered, on Cookmatic Level 8 (MEDIUM HIGH) according to the time on the chart. Increase the amount of reheating time when reheating more than 1 cookie. Reheated cookies will give you that "freshly-baked" cookie flavor.

COOKIE MIX BAKING CHART

TYPE OF MIX	PKG. SIZE	UTENSILS AND/OR NUMBER OF COOKIES	EXTRA INGREDIENTS	COOKING TIME ON FULL POWER
Brownie Mix	8 ozs.	9 x 5 x 2-inch loaf dish	—	3 to 4 min.
	22 to 24 ozs.	8 x 8 x 2-inch dish	—	7 to 8 min.
	22 to 24 ozs.	2-quart utility dish	—	7 to 8 min.
Chocolate Chip Cookie Mix	14 to 15 ozs.	12 (3/4-inch diameter) balls on waxed paper	—	1 min., 15 sec. to 1 min., 45 sec.
Date Bar Mix	14 to 15 ozs.	8 x 8 x 2-inch dish	—	4 to 5 min.
Oatmeal Cookie Mix	14 to 18 ozs.	12 (3/4-inch diameter) balls on waxed paper	3 tablespoons all-purpose flour	1 min., 15 sec. to 1 min., 45 sec.
Peanut Butter Cookie Mix	14 to 15 ozs.	12 (3/4-inch diameter) balls on waxed paper	1/4 cup all-purpose flour	1 min., 15 sec. to 1 min., 45 sec.
Sugar Cookie Mix	15 to 17 ozs.	12 (3/4-inch diameter) balls on waxed paper	1/3 cup all-purpose flour	1 min., 15 sec. to 1 min., 45 sec.

General Instructions for Baking Cookies from Mixes

1. Prepare the cookie mix, according to the package instructions. In some cases, additional flour is required as indicated in the chart.

2. Bake the cookies on FULL POWER, according to the time given in the chart, or until the cookies are firm but still moist. When only 12 cookies are baked at one time, repeat the process with the remaining cookies.

3. Brownies should be moist when removed from the Radarange Oven. Brownie mixes may vary in their formulation of ingredients. Because of this, some mixes may require slightly shorter or longer baking times. Check brownies frequently during cooking the first time a particular brand is prepared. Note any variations in timing.

Easy Oatmeal Cookies

Yield: 4 dozen cookies

1 (9 oz.) pkg. spice cake mix
1-1/4 cups quick-cooking or old-fashioned, rolled oats
1/2 cup all-purpose flour
1/4 cup vegetable oil, or 1/4 cup shortening, melted
1/4 cup milk
1 egg
2 tablespoons dark brown sugar

1 cup raisins
1/2 cup nuts, chopped (optional)

1. Mix together all ingredients, except raisins and nuts, in large mixing bowl.

2. Stir in raisins and nuts. Drop by teaspoons onto waxed paper on Radarange Oven glass tray. Bake dozen at a time.

3. Bake dozen in Radarange Oven on FULL POWER for 1 minute, 10 seconds to 1 minute, 20 seconds, or until firm but slightly moist. Allow cookies to cool slightly before removing from waxed paper. Repeat with remaining cookies.

Chocolate Nut Cookies

Yield: 4 to 5 dozen

1/2 cup butter or margarine
3/4 cup semi-sweet chocolate morsels

2 cups sugar
2 teaspoons vanilla
1 egg
1/2 teaspoon salt
2 cups all-purpose flour
1/2 cup walnuts, chopped
Confectioners' sugar

1. Combine butter and chocolate morsels in large mixing bowl. Heat in Radarange Oven on Cookmatic Level 6 (ROAST) for 1-1/2 to 2 minutes, or until mixture is melted. Stir well halfway through cooking time.

2. Beat in sugar, vanilla and egg. Mix in salt and flour until well-blended. Stir in walnuts. Shape dough into 3/4-inch diameter balls. Roll in confectioners' sugar, as desired. Place 12 balls on waxed paper on Radarange Oven glass tray.

3. Bake dozen in Radarange Oven on FULL POWER for 1 minute, 15 seconds to 1 minute, 45 seconds, or until firm but slightly moist. Allow cookies to cool slightly before removing from waxed paper. Repeat with remaining cookies.

Refrigerator Filled Cookies

Yield: 2-1/2 dozen

1/2 cup butter or margarine, softened
1/2 cup brown sugar, firmly packed
1 egg
2 cups all-purpose flour
1/2 teaspoon salt
1/4 teaspoon baking soda

Jam or pie filling

1. Cream butter and brown sugar in large mixing bowl. Add egg. Combine remaining ingredients, except for jam or pie filling. Stir into creamed mixture.

2. Shape dough into 1-1/2-inch diameter rolls. Wrap in waxed paper. Chill 2 to 3 hours.

3. Cut rolls into 1/8-inch slices. Place 12 slices on waxed paper on Radarange Oven glass tray. Top each with 1/4 teaspoon jam or pie filling, as desired. Top each with another cookie slice. Seal edges.

4. Bake dozen in Radarange Oven on FULL POWER for 1 minute, 15 seconds to 1 minute, 45 seconds, or until set. Allow cookies to cool slightly before removing from waxed paper. Repeat with remaining cookies.

Chocolate Chip Cookies

Yield: 3 to 4 dozen cookies

1/2 cup shortening, softened
1/2 cup dark brown sugar, firmly packed
1/4 cup sugar
1 (1 oz. pkg.) instant cocoa mix
1 egg
1/2 teaspoon vanilla

1-1/4 cups all-purpose flour
1/2 teaspoon baking soda
1/2 teaspoon salt
1 (6 oz.) pkg. chocolate morsels
1/2 cup nuts, chopped, or 1/2 cup raisins (optional)

1. Beat together shortening, sugars, cocoa mix, egg and vanilla in large mixing bowl.

2. Combine flour, baking soda, and salt. Stir into creamed mixture. Mix well. Stir in chocolate morsels and nuts. Drop by teaspoons onto waxed paper on Radarange Oven glass tray. Bake dozen at a time.

3. Bake dozen in Radarange Oven on FULL POWER for 1 minute, 10 seconds to 1 minute, 20 seconds, or until firm but slightly moist. Allow cookies to cool slightly before removing from waxed paper. Repeat with remaining cookies.

Chocolate Drops

Yield: 2-1/2 dozen

1/4 cup butter or margarine

1 (9 oz.) pkg. chocolate cake mix
1/3 cup all-purpose flour
1 egg
1/2 cup nuts, chopped, or 1/2 cup coconut, shredded (optional)

Pecan halves

1. Place butter in large mixing bowl. Heat in Radarange Oven on FULL POWER for 30 to 40 seconds, or until melted.

2. Stir cake mix, flour, egg and nuts into butter. Blend well.

3. Shape dough into 3/4-inch diameter balls. Place 12 balls on waxed paper on Radarange Oven glass tray. Top each ball with pecan half.

4. Bake dozen in Radarange Oven on FULL POWER for 1 minute, 45 seconds to 2 minutes, or until firm but slightly moist. Allow cookies to cool slightly before removing from waxed paper. Repeat with remaining cookies.

MICRO-TIPS: Balls may be rolled in additional coconut before baking if desired.

Choco-Chip Oatmeal Drops

Yield: approx. 4 dozen

2/3 cup butter or margarine
1 cup brown sugar, firmly packed
1 egg
1 teaspoon vanilla

1-1/2 cups all-purpose flour
1-1/4 cups quick-cooking or old-fashioned, rolled oats
1/4 teaspoon salt
1 (6 oz.) pkg. semi-sweet chocolate morsels
1 cup walnuts, chopped

1. Cream butter and brown sugar in large mixing bowl. Beat in egg and vanilla.

2. Stir in remaining ingredients. Drop by teaspoon onto waxed paper on Radarange Oven glass tray. Bake dozen at a time.

3. Bake dozen in Radarange Oven on FULL POWER for 1 to 1-1/2 minutes, or until cookies are firm but slightly moist. Allow cookies to cool slightly before removing from waxed paper. Repeat with remaining cookies.

Snicker Doodle Cookies

Yield: 3 dozen

1/2 cup butter or margarine
1/2 cup sugar
1/4 cup dark brown sugar, firmly
  packed
1 egg
1/2 teaspoon vanilla

1-3/4 cups all-purpose flour
1 teaspoon cream of tartar
1/2 teaspoon baking soda
1/4 teaspoon salt

2 tablespoons sugar
1-1/4 teaspoons cinnamon

1. Cream butter and sugars in large mixing bowl. Beat in egg and vanilla.

2. Combine flour, cream of tartar, baking soda and salt. Blend into creamed mixture. Chill.

3. Shape dough into 3/4-inch diameter balls. Roll in mixture of sugar and cinnamon. Place 12 balls on waxed paper on Radarange Oven glass tray.

4. Bake dozen in Radarange Oven on FULL POWER for 1 minute, 30 seconds to 2 minutes, or until cookies are set, but still slightly moist around edges. Allow cookies to cool slightly before removing from waxed paper. Repeat with remaining cookies.

Sugar Cookies

Yield: 2-1/2 to 3 dozen

1/4 cup butter or margarine
1 cup sugar
1 egg
1/2 teaspoon vanilla
1/4 teaspoon almond extract*
1/4 teaspoon lemon extract*

1-3/4 cups all-purpose flour
1/2 teaspoon baking soda
1/2 teaspoon salt
1/2 teaspoon cream of tartar

1. Cream together butter, sugar, egg, vanilla, almond and lemon extract in large mixing bowl.

2. Combine flour, soda, salt and cream of tartar. Blend into creamed mixture. Mix well.

3. Shape dough into 3/4-inch diameter balls. Place 12 balls on waxed paper on Radarange Oven glass tray.

4. Bake dozen in Radarange Oven on FULL POWER for 1-1/2 to 2 minutes, or until set. Allow cookies to cool slightly before removing from waxed paper. Repeat with remaining cookies.

*MICRO-TIP: An additional 1/2 teaspoon of vanilla may be substituted for the almond and lemon extracts. Cookies may be rolled in sugar before baking, or may be sprinkled with cinnamon and sugar mixture or colored sugar.

Peanut Butter Cookies

Yield: 4 dozen

1/2 cup butter or margarine
1/2 cup peanut butter
3/4 cup dark brown sugar, firmly packed
1/4 cup sugar
1 egg
1/2 teaspoon vanilla

1-3/4 cups all-purpose flour
3/4 teaspoon soda
1/4 teaspoon salt

1. Thoroughly cream butter, peanut butter and sugars in large mixing bowl. Beat in egg and vanilla.

2. Stir together flour, soda and salt. Blend into creamed mixture. Cover and chill.

3. Shape dough into 1-inch diameter balls. Place 12 balls on waxed paper on Radarange Oven glass tray. Make "crisscross" pattern on cookies with tines of fork which have been dipped in flour.

4. Bake dozen in Radarange Oven on FULL POWER for 1 minute, 30 seconds to 1 minute, 45 seconds, or until firm but slightly moist. Allow cookies to cool slightly before removing from waxed paper. Repeat with remaining cookies.

MICRO-TIP: If desired, remaining dough may be refrigerated. Baking time should be increased slightly due to refrigerator temperature.

Peanut Butter and Jelly Cookie-Wiches

Yield: 4 to 4-1/2 dozen

1/2 cup butter or margarine
1/2 cup chunky peanut butter
1/2 cup sugar
1/2 cup brown sugar, firmly packed
1 egg
1-1/2 cups all-purpose flour
3/4 teaspoon baking soda
1/2 teaspoon baking powder
1/4 teaspoon salt

Jelly or jam

1. Mix together butter, peanut butter, sugars and egg thoroughly in large mixing bowl. Blend in remaining ingredients, except jelly. Cover and chill.

2. Shape dough into 3/4-inch diameter balls. Place 12 balls on waxed paper on Radarange Oven glass tray.

3. Bake dozen in Radarange Oven on FULL POWER for 1 minute, 30 seconds to 1 minute, 45 seconds, or until set but still slightly moist. Allow cookies to cool slightly before removing from waxed paper. When cool, "sandwich" cookies together with jelly or jam filling, as desired. Repeat with remaining cookies.

MICRO-TIP: Chocolate syrup makes a good filling, too.

Thumbprint Cookies

Yield: 3 dozen

2/3 cup butter or margarine
1/3 cup sugar

2 eggs, separated
1 teaspoon vanilla
1/2 teaspoon salt
1-3/4 cups all-purpose flour, sifted

3/4 cup pecans, finely chopped

1/2 cup preserves

1. Cream butter and sugar until fluffy in large mixing bowl.

2. Stir in egg yolks, vanilla, and salt, beating well. Gradually stir in flour. Mix well.

3. Shape dough into 3/4-inch diameter balls. Dip in slightly-beaten egg whites, and then roll in pecans. Place 12 balls on waxed paper on Radarange Oven glass tray. Make thumbprint in each.

4. Bake dozen in Radarange Oven on FULL POWER for 1 to 1-1/2 minutes, or until firm but slightly moist. Allow cookies to cool slightly before removing from waxed paper. Fill "thumbprints" with preserves just before serving. Repeat with remaining cookies.

MICRO-TIP: Cookies may also be filled with pie filling rather than preserves.

Honey Pecan Balls

Yield: 2-1/2 dozen

1/2 cup butter or margarine, softened
2 tablespoons honey
1 teaspoon vanilla
1-1/2 cups all-purpose flour
1/4 teaspoon salt
1/2 cup pecans, chopped

Confectioners' sugar

1. Cream butter and honey in small mixing bowl. Stir in vanilla. Add remaining ingredients, except confectioners' sugar. Mix thoroughly. Refrigerate dough for at least 2 hours.

2. Shape dough into 1-inch diameter balls. Dough will be crumbly. Place 12 balls on waxed paper on Radarange Oven glass tray.

3. Bake dozen in Radarange Oven on FULL POWER for 1 minute, 15 seconds to 1 minute, 45 seconds, or until no longer moist on outside. Be careful not to overcook. Allow cookies to cool slightly before removing from waxed paper. Roll in confectioners' sugar, as desired, while still warm. Repeat with remaining cookies.

Potato Chip-Nut Cookies

Yield: 3-1/2 dozen

3/4 cup butter or margarine
3/4 cup brown sugar, firmly packed
1 egg
3/4 cup potato chips, crushed
2-1/2 cups all-purpose flour
1/2 cup walnuts, chopped

1. Cream butter and brown sugar in large mixing bowl. Beat in egg.

2. Stir in remaining ingredients.

3. Shape dough into 1-1/2-inch diameter balls. Place 12 balls on waxed paper on Radarange Oven glass tray. Press down each cookie slightly.

4. Bake dozen in Radarange Oven on FULL POWER for 1 minute, 15 seconds to 1 minute, 30 seconds, or until cookies are set but still slightly moist around edges. Allow cookies to cool slightly before removing from waxed paper. Repeat with remaining cookies.

Coconut Oatmeal Cookies

Yield: 3 dozen

1/3 cup butter or margarine
1 cup dark brown sugar, firmly packed

1 egg
1/2 teaspoon vanilla
1/2 teaspoon almond extract

1-1/2 cups all-purpose flour
1 cup quick-cooking, rolled oats
3/4 cup coconut, shredded
3/4 teaspoon baking soda
3/4 teaspoon baking powder

1. Cream butter and brown sugar in large mixing bowl.

2. Add egg, vanilla and almond extract. Beat well.

3. Combine remaining ingredients. Blend into creamed mixture. Shape dough into 3/4-inch diameter balls. Place 12 balls on waxed paper on Radarange Oven glass tray.

4. Bake dozen in Radarange Oven on FULL POWER for 1 minute, 15 seconds to 1 minute, 45 seconds, or until firm but slightly moist. Allow cookies to cool slightly before removing from waxed paper. Repeat with remaining cookies.

Ginger Cream Cookies

Yield: 4 to 5 dozen

3/4 cup butter or margarine
1 cup sugar
1 egg
1/4 cup molasses

3 cups all-purpose flour
2-1/2 teaspoons baking soda
1-1/4 teaspoons cinnamon
1-1/4 teaspoons ginger
1-1/4 teaspoons ground cloves
Sugar

1. Cream butter and sugar in large mixing bowl. Beat in egg and molasses.

2. Blend together flour, soda and spices. Add to liquid ingredients. Mix well. Chill. Shape dough into 3/4-inch diameter balls. Roll in sugar, as desired. Place 12 balls on waxed paper on Radarange Oven glass tray.

3. Bake dozen in Radarange Oven on FULL POWER for 1-1/2 to 2 minutes, or until firm but slightly moist. Allow cookies to cool slightly before removing from waxed paper. Repeat with remaining cookies.

Lemon Drops

Yield: 5-1/2 to 6 dozen

1/2 cup butter or margarine
1-1/2 teaspoons lemon peel, grated
1-1/2 tablespoons lemon juice
1 cup brown sugar, firmly packed
1 egg

2-1/2 cups all-purpose flour
1/2 teaspoon salt
1/2 teaspoon baking soda

Non-pareils (decorative candies)

1. Cream together butter, lemon peel and lemon juice in large mixing bowl. Beat in brown sugar and egg.

2. Combine flour, salt and baking soda. Blend into creamed mixture. Mix well.

3. Shape dough into 1-inch diameter rolls. Chill dough, if necessary, for easier handling. Roll in non-pareils, as desired. Refrigerate for at least 3 hours.

4. Cut rolls in 1/4-inch slices. Place 12 slices on waxed paper on Radarange Oven glass tray.

5. Bake dozen in Radarange Oven on FULL POWER for 1 minute, 15 seconds to 1 minute, 45 seconds, or until cookies are set but still slightly moist around edges. Allow cookies to cool slightly before removing from waxed paper. Repeat with remaining dough.

Granola Chewies

Yield: 3 dozen cookies

1/2 cup butter or margarine
2/3 cup dark brown sugar, firmly packed
1/3 cup honey

1-1/2 cups quick-cooking or old-fashioned, rolled oats
1 cup dried apricots, finely chopped
1/2 cup coconut, shredded
1/2 cup almonds, chopped
1/2 cup wheat germ

1. Place butter in 2-quart glass utility dish. Heat in Radarange Oven on FULL POWER for 1 minute, or until melted. Stir in brown sugar and honey, stirring until smooth.

2. Gradually stir in oats, apricots, coconut, almonds, and wheat germ. Stir until all ingredients are well-mixed. Spread mixture evenly in utility dish.

3. Bake in Radarange Oven on Cookmatic Level 6 (ROAST) for 12 minutes, or until firm but slightly moist. Stir halfway through cooking time. Allow mixture to cool slightly, and then shape into 1-inch diameter balls. Store in tightly-covered container.

Chewy Peanut Butter Bars

Yield: 1 to 1-1/2 dozen bars

1/3 cup butter or margarine
1/2 cup peanut butter
1 cup sugar
1/4 cup dark brown sugar, firmly packed
2 eggs
1 teaspoon vanilla

1 cup all-purpose flour
1 teaspoon baking powder
1/4 teaspoon salt
1 (3-1/2 oz.) can coconut, flaked (about 1-1/2 cups)

1. Cream together butter, peanut butter and sugars until light and fluffy in large mixing bowl. Add eggs and vanilla. Beat well.

2. Mix in flour, baking powder and salt, stirring until thoroughly blended. Stir in coconut.* Spread evenly in greased, 2-quart utility dish.

3. Bake in Radarange Oven on FULL POWER for 6 to 7 minutes, or until top springs back when lightly pressed with finger.** Cool. Cut into squares.

MICRO-TIPS:

*Reserve 1/4 cup coconut to sprinkle over bars as a topping before baking, if desired.

**You may want to turn dish halfway through cooking time.

Cinnamon Bars

Yield: 2-1/2 to 3 dozen

1/2 cup butter or margarine
1/2 cup brown sugar, firmly packed
1 egg yolk
1-1/2 teaspoons cinnamon
Dash salt
1 cup all-purpose flour

1 egg white
1/4 cup confectioners' sugar
1/4 cup pecans, chopped

1. Cream together butter, brown sugar, egg yolk, cinnamon and salt in large mixing bowl. Stir in flour. Spread dough in 2-quart utility dish.

2. Beat egg white until foamy. Stir in confectioners' sugar. Spread this mixture over batter. Sprinkle with pecans.

3. Bake in Radarange Oven on FULL POWER for 4 to 6 minutes, or until toothpick inserted in center comes out clean.* Cool slightly. Cut into squares.

*MICRO-TIP: You may want to turn dish halfway through cooking time.

Fudge Brownies

Yield: 1 dozen brownies

2 (1 oz. each) squares semi-sweet chocolate
1/2 cup butter or margarine

1/2 cup milk

1 cup sugar
2 eggs, slightly-beaten
1 teaspoon vanilla
2/3 cup all-purpose flour
1/2 teaspoon baking powder
Dash salt
3/4 cup walnuts, chopped (optional)

1. Combine chocolate and butter in 8 x 8 x 2-inch dish. Heat in Radarange Oven on Cookmatic Level 6 (ROAST) for 3 minutes, or until mixture is melted. Stir occasionally during melting.

2. Blend in milk. Cool.

3. Stir in sugar, eggs and vanilla with fork until well-blended. Combine flour, baking powder and salt. Stir into chocolate mixture. Stir in nuts.

4. Bake in Radarange Oven on FULL POWER for 5 to 7 minutes, or until top springs back when lightly pressed with finger. May look slightly moist on top when done. Cool. Cut into bars.

   MICRO-TIP: These moist, cake-type brownies may be sprinkled with confectioners' sugar or spread with your favorite chocolate icing, if desired.

Quick 'N' Easy Brownies

Yield: 1 dozen brownies

2 (1 oz. each) squares unsweetened chocolate
1/3 cup butter or margarine

1 cup sugar
2 eggs
1/2 teaspoon vanilla
3/4 cup all-purpose flour
1/2 teaspoon baking powder
1/2 teaspoon salt
1/2 cup nuts, chopped

1. Place chocolate and butter in 1-1/2 to 2-quart casserole. Heat in Radarange Oven on Cookmatic Level 6 (ROAST) for 2 to 2-1/2 minutes, or until mixture is melted. Stir 2 to 3 times during melting.

2. Stir in sugar, eggs and vanilla. Beat well. Combine flour, baking powder and salt. Blend well. Stir into chocolate mixture. Stir in nuts. Spread evenly in greased, 8 x 8 x 2-inch dish, or 8-inch round dish.

3. Bake in Radarange Oven on FULL POWER for 3-1/2 to 4-1/2 minutes, or until top springs back when lightly pressed with finger. Cool. Cut into bars.

Marbled Butterscotch Bars

Yield: 2-1/2 to 3 dozen

1/2 cup butter or margarine
3/4 cup brown sugar, firmly packed
1 egg
1 teaspoon vanilla

1 cup all-purpose flour
1/2 teaspoon baking powder
1/8 teaspoon baking soda
1/8 teaspoon salt
1/2 cup semi-sweet chocolate morsels, melted

1. Cream butter and brown sugar in large mixing bowl. Beat in egg and vanilla.

2. Stir together flour, baking powder, soda and salt. Beat into creamed mixture. Spread batter in 2-quart utility dish. Swirl melted chocolate over top with knife.

3. Bake in Radarange Oven on FULL POWER for 4-1/2 to 5-1/2 minutes, or until top springs back when lightly pressed with finger. Cool. Cut into squares.

Cherry Bars

Yield: 1 dozen bars

1/2 cup butter or margarine
1/2 cup dark brown sugar, firmly
   packed

2 eggs
1-1/2 cups all-purpose flour
3/4 teaspoon baking powder
1/8 teaspoon almond extract

1 (21 oz.) can cherry pie filling
Cinnamon

1. Cream butter and brown sugar in large mixing bowl.

2. Blend in eggs. Add flour, baking powder and almond extract. Spread 1/2 mixture in 8 x 8 x 2-inch dish.

3. Bake in Radarange Oven on FULL POWER for 2 to 2-1/2 minutes, or until top springs back when lightly pressed with finger.

4. Spread cherries evenly over top. Drop remaining dough over cherries by tablespoons. Sprinkle with cinnamon, as desired.

5. Bake in Radarange Oven on FULL POWER for 6 to 8 minutes, or until top of dough springs back when lightly pressed with finger.* Cool. Cut into bars.

MICRO-TIPS:

• Any flavor fruit pie filling may be substituted.

* You may want to turn dish halfway through cooking time.

Banana Bars

Yield: 1 dozen bars

1/4 cup butter or margarine
3/4 cup dark brown sugar, firmly
   packed
1 egg, slightly-beaten

1/2 cup dairy sour cream
1/2 cup bananas, mashed
1/2 teaspoon vanilla

1 cup all-purpose flour
1/2 teaspoon salt
1/2 teaspoon baking soda

1. Cream butter and sugar in large mixing bowl. Blend in egg.

2. Add sour cream, bananas and vanilla. Stir well.

3. Combine flour, salt and baking soda. Blend into banana mixture. Spread in greased, 8 x 8 x 2-inch dish.

4. Bake in Radarange Oven on FULL POWER for 5 to 6 minutes, or until top springs back when lightly pressed with finger. Cool. Cut into bars.

MICRO-TIP: Frost with a confectioners' sugar frosting.

Applesauce Coconut Bars

Yield: 1 dozen bars

1-1/2 cups applesauce
1/4 cup dark brown sugar, firmly
   packed
2 tablespoons all-purpose flour
1 tablespoon lemon juice

1/2 cup butter or margarine
1/2 cup dark brown sugar, firmly
   packed
1/2 cup all-purpose flour
1 cup quick-cooking, rolled oats

1/2 teaspoon cinnamon
1/2 cup coconut, shredded

1. Combine applesauce, 1/4 cup dark brown sugar, 2 tablespoons flour and lemon juice in 1-quart casserole. Cook in Radarange Oven on FULL POWER for 2-1/2 to 3 minutes, or until thick and bubbly. Cool.

2. Cream butter and brown sugar. Blend in flour and oats. Press mixture against bottom of 8 x 8 x 2-inch dish. Bake in Radarange Oven on FULL POWER for 2-1/2 minutes. Let cool 5 minutes.

3. Spread cooled applesauce mixture over bottom layer. Mix cinnamon and coconut. Sprinkle over applesauce. Bake in Radarange Oven on FULL POWER for 5 to 6 minutes, or until filling is bubbly and begins to pull away from sides of dish. Chill. Cut into bars.

Date Bars

Yield: 1 dozen bars

1/3 cup butter or margarine
1 cup dark brown sugar, firmly packed
2 eggs
1 teaspoon orange peel, grated
1 teaspoon vanilla

1 cup all-purpose flour
1/2 teaspoon baking powder
1/4 teaspoon salt
1 (8 oz.) pkg. pitted dates, coarsely chopped
1/2 cup walnuts, chopped

Confectioners' sugar

1. Cream butter and brown sugar in large mixing bowl. Beat in eggs, orange peel and vanilla.

2. Mix together flour, baking powder and salt. Stir into liquid ingredients. Stir in dates and nuts. Spread evenly in 8 x 8 x 2-inch dish.

3. Bake in Radarange Oven on FULL POWER for 6 to 7 minutes, or until toothpick inserted in center comes out clean.* Sprinkle with confectioners' sugar, as desired. Chill. Cut into bars.

   *MICRO-TIP: You may want to turn dish halfway through cooking time.

Applesauce Squares

Yield: 1 to 1-1/2 dozen squares

1/2 cup butter or margarine, softened
1 cup dark brown sugar, firmly packed
1/2 cup applesauce
1 egg
1 teaspoon lemon peel, grated

1-1/2 cups all-purpose flour
1 teaspoon cinnamon
1/2 teaspoon ground cloves
1/2 teaspoon baking soda
3/4 cup raisins or
   3/4 cup walnuts, chopped

ICING (Optional)

1/2 cup brown sugar, firmly packed
1/4 cup butter or margarine
2 tablespoons milk

1/2 cup confectioners' sugar

1. Cream butter and brown sugar in large mixing bowl. Beat in applesauce, egg and lemon peel.

2. Combine flour, spices and baking soda. Stir into creamed mixture. Stir in raisins. Spread evenly in ungreased, 8 x 8 x 2-inch dish.

3. Bake in Radarange Oven on FULL POWER for 5 to 6 minutes, or until top springs back when lightly pressed with finger. Cool. Cut into bars.

4. For icing, combine brown sugar, butter and milk in 1-quart casserole. Cook in Radarange Oven on FULL POWER for 1 to 1-1/2 minutes, or until mixture boils. Boil 1 minute.

5. Blend in confectioners' sugar. Cool slightly. Spread on cool bars.

Scotch Toffee Bars

Yield: 12 bars

1/3 cup butter or margarine, melted
2 cups quick-cooking, rolled oats
1/2 cup brown sugar, firmly packed
1/4 cup dark corn syrup
1-1/2 teaspoons vanilla
1/2 teaspoon salt

1 (6 oz.) pkg. chocolate morsels

1/4 cup nuts, chopped

1. Combine butter, oats, brown sugar, corn syrup, vanilla and salt in 2-quart utility dish. Press firmly against bottom of dish.

2. Bake in Radarange Oven on FULL POWER for 2 to 3 minutes, or until bubbling all over.* Smooth surface. Top with chocolate morsels.

3. Heat in Radarange Oven on Cookmatic Level 6 (ROAST) for 1 minute, or until chocolate morsels are melted. Spread chocolate evenly over bottom crust. Sprinkle with nuts. Chill. Cut into bars. Store in airtight container in refrigerator.

   *MICRO-TIP: You may want to turn dish halfway through cooking time.

Lemon Bars

Yield: 1 dozen

1/2 cup butter or margarine

1 cup all-purpose flour
1/4 cup confectioners' sugar

1 cup sugar
2 eggs
3 tablespoons lemon juice
2 tablespoons all-purpose flour
3 to 4 tablespoons confectioners' sugar

1. Place butter in 2-cup glass measure or small dish. Heat in Radarange Oven on FULL POWER for 1 minute, or until melted.

2. Blend together melted butter, 1 cup flour and 1/4 cup confectioners' sugar. Spread in 8 x 8 x 2-inch dish. Cook in Radarange Oven on FULL POWER for 2 to 2-1/2 minutes, or until slightly firm to touch.

3. Beat together sugar, eggs, lemon juice and flour. Pour over hot bottom layer. Bake in Radarange Oven on Cookmatic Level 7 (BAKE) for 3 to 4 minutes, or until center is firm. Sprinkle generously with confectioners' sugar. Cool. Cut into bars.

Shortbread

Yield: 1, 8 x 8 x 2-inch dish

1 cup butter or margarine
1/2 cup dark brown sugar, firmly packed
1/4 teaspoon vanilla

2-1/2 cups all-purpose flour

1. Cream butter, sugar and vanilla in large mixing bowl, until light and fluffy.

2. Gradually add flour, beating until smooth. Pat mixture into ungreased, 8 x 8 x 2-inch dish. Prick with tines of fork evenly over surface to eliminate air bubbles.

3. Bake in Radarange Oven on FULL POWER for 3 to 3-1/2 minutes, or until evenly raised and set. Cut into bars while warm.

Double-Decker Crunchies

Yield: 1 to 1-1/2 dozen squares

1 (6 oz.) pkg. semi-sweet chocolate morsels
1/2 cup confectioners' sugar, sifted
2 tablespoons butter or margarine
2 tablespoons milk
4 cups toasted rice cereal

1 (6 oz.) pkg. butterscotch morsels
1/2 cup crunchy-style peanut butter

1. Place chocolate morsels, confectioners' sugar, butter and milk in 3-quart casserole. Heat in Radarange Oven on Cookmatic Level 6 (ROAST) for 2 to 3 minutes, or until chocolate morsels are melted. Stir in cereal. Coat well.

2. Place butterscotch morsels and peanut butter in 1-quart casserole. Heat in Radarange Oven on Cookmatic Level 6 (ROAST) for 2-1/2 to 3 minutes, or until butterscotch morsels are melted.

3. Spread half of chocolate mixture in greased, 8 x 8 x 2-inch dish. Spread butterscotch mixture over chocolate layer. Top with remaining chocolate mixture. Chill slightly. Cut into bars.

Pumpkin Squares

Yield: 1 dozen bars

2 eggs, slightly-beaten
1 cup pumpkin, canned
1/2 cup vegetable oil

1 cup all-purpose flour
1 cup dark brown sugar, firmly packed
1/2 cup walnuts (optional)
1-1/2 teaspoons cinnamon
1 teaspoon baking powder
1/2 teaspoon baking soda
1/2 teaspoon ground cloves
1/4 teaspoon salt

ICING (Optional)

1-1/2 cups confectioners' sugar
3 teaspoons milk or light cream
4 teaspoons frozen orange juice concentrate, undiluted

1. Combine and blend eggs, pumpkin, and oil in large mixing bowl.

2. Combine remaining ingredients and blend into pumpkin mixture. Pour batter into greased, 2-quart utility dish.

3. Bake in Radarange Oven on FULL POWER for 6 to 7 minutes, or until top springs back when lightly pressed with finger.* Cool. Cut into bars.

4. For icing, blend together all ingredients until smooth. Drizzle icing over bars before serving.

*MICRO-TIP: You may want to turn dish halfway through cooking time.

Marshmallow Treats

Yield: 1-1/2 dozen,
2 x 2-inch squares

1/4 cup butter or margarine

4 cups miniature marshmallows

5 cups toasted, rice cereal

1. Place butter in 2-quart utility dish. Heat in Radarange Oven on FULL POWER for 45 to 60 seconds, or until melted.

2. Stir in marshmallows, coating with butter. Cook in Radarange Oven on FULL POWER for 2 to 2-1/2 minutes, or until marshmallows are melted. Stir halfway through cooking time.

3. Stir in cereal. Mix until well-coated. Pat evenly into dish. Let stand until cool and set. Cut into squares.

   MICRO-TIP: If large marshmallows are used, slightly more time may be needed for melting.

Triple Treats

Yield: 1-1/2 dozen bars

1/2 cup butter or margarine
1/2 cup dark brown sugar, firmly packed
1 egg
1/2 teaspoon vanilla
1 cup all-purpose flour

1-1/4 cups confectioners' sugar
2 tablespoons evaporated milk
1 tablespoon butter or margarine, softened
1/2 teaspoon vanilla
1/4 teaspoon almond extract

2/3 cup confectioners' sugar
1/2 cup butter or margarine, softened
1/2 cup semi-sweet chocolate morsels
1 egg
1/4 cup almonds, slivered, or
1/4 cup walnuts, chopped

1. Cream butter and brown sugar in large mixing bowl. Add egg, vanilla and flour. Beat until fluffy. Spread evenly in ungreased, 8 x 8 x 2-inch dish. Bake in Radarange Oven on FULL POWER for 3 to 4 minutes, or until firm to touch.*

2. Beat together 1-1/4 cups confectioners' sugar, evaporated milk, 1 tablespoon butter, vanilla and almond extract, until creamy. Spread on cooled bottom layer. Allow to stand and become firm.

3. Cream confectioners' sugar and butter in small bowl. Place chocolate morsels in 1-cup glass measure or small dish. Heat in Radarange Oven on Cookmatic Level 6 (ROAST) for 2-1/2 minutes, or until melted. Stir well. Add to creamed mixture with egg. Beat until fluffy. Spread on white layer. Sprinkle with nuts. Refrigerate. Cut into bars before serving.

   *MICRO-TIP: You may want to turn dish halfway through cooking time.

Five Layer Bars

Yield: 1 dozen bars

1/3 cup butter or margarine

1 cup graham cracker crumbs

3/4 cup milk chocolate morsels
3/4 cup coconut, shredded
2/3 cup walnuts, chopped
2/3 cup sweetened condensed milk

1. Place butter in 8 x 8 x 2-inch dish. Heat in Radarange Oven on FULL POWER for 45 seconds to 1 minute, or until melted.

2. Blend in cracker crumbs. Press evenly against bottom of dish. Cook in Radarange Oven on FULL POWER for 1 to 1-1/2 minutes.

3. Sprinkle on chocolate morsels, coconut and nuts in layers in listed order. Pour condensed milk over all. Bake in Radarange Oven on FULL POWER for 3 to 4 minutes, or until bubbling all over surface. Cool. Cut into bars.

Candies are easily prepared in the Radarange Oven. In fact, some of the Radarange Oven candies, such as Quickie Fudge and Peanut Clusters, are so easily made, that children will want to prepare them.

Candies can be made ahead and stored in airtight containers. Or, you can quickly prepare candies for a spur-of-the-moment party or snack.

Read the general hints for cooking candies before making candies in the Radarange Oven.

General Hints for Cooking Candies

1. Candy becomes very hot during cooking. Select a cooking utensil which will withstand hot temperatures. Select a utensil which is large enough to hold the candy during cooking to avoid boil-overs. Use the recommended utensil in the recipe. Generally candy is cooked uncovered for easy stirring.
2. Candies are prepared using a variety of settings. Some candies are quickly cooked on FULL POWER, while others require a lower Cookmatic Level or setting, due to "delicate" or "special" ingredients.
3. You may wish to use a candy thermometer when preparing candies. Do not leave the candy thermometer in the candy while the microwave oven is in operation. The Automatic Temperature Control should not be used for candy making, since the temperature range of the control ends at 190°F.

4. In this cookbook, candies are described as being completely done when the following stages are reached:

   Soft Ball: The candy syrup, when dropped into very cold water, forms a soft ball which flattens on removal from water.

   Firm Ball: The candy syrup, when dropped into very cold water, forms a firm ball which does not flatten on removal from water.

   Hard Ball: The candy syrup, when dropped into very cold water, forms a hard ball which is hard enough to hold its shape, yet elastic.

   Soft Crack: The candy syrup, when dropped into very cold water, separates into threads which are hard but not brittle.

   Hard Crack: The candy syrup, when dropped into very cold water, separates into threads which are hard and brittle.
5. Since candies do become quite hot during cooking, be careful when removing them from the Radarange Oven. You may wish to keep hot pads handy.
6. When preparing your own favorite candy recipes, select a recipe in this chapter to use as a guide. Then, use the same setting, and approximately the same amount of cooking time. Record the amount of Radarange Oven time on your recipe for later use.

Coconut Almond Balls

Yield: 5 dozen

3/4 cup mashed potatoes
1 lb. confectioners' sugar
4 cups coconut, flaked
1 teaspoon almond extract

5 tablespoons water
2 tablespoons corn syrup
2 tablespoons butter or margarine, softened
1 (15.4 oz.) pkg. chocolate fudge frosting mix
Toasted almonds (optional)

1. Combine potatoes, confectioners' sugar, coconut and almond extract in large mixing bowl. Mix well. Drop by teaspoons onto waxed paper. For easier shaping, chill for 1/2 hour, and then roll into balls. Chill balls for 45 to 60 minutes, or until very firm.
2. Place water, corn syrup and butter in 1-1/2-quart casserole. Cook in Radarange Oven on FULL POWER for 1 to 2 minutes, or until heated through. Stir in frosting mix. Cook in Radarange Oven on Cookmatic Level 6 (ROAST) for 3 minutes, or until smooth and creamy.* Dip balls in chocolate, and place on waxed paper. Top each ball with almond, if desired.

MICRO-TIPS:

• If chocolate mixture hardens, return to Radarange Oven on Cookmatic Level 6 (ROAST), until softened.

*Additional water may be added, if necessary.

Clockwise starting from top left: Peanut Brittle (page 355), Quickie Fudge (page 356), Turtles (page 354), Divinity (page 358), and Peanut Clusters (page 355)

Turtles

Yield: 2 to 2-1/2 dozen

1 (14 oz.) pkg. caramels
2 tablespoons evaporated milk
1 tablespoon butter or margarine

1 (5 oz.) pkg. pecan halves

1 (6 oz.) pkg. semi-sweet
chocolate morsels
1, 1-inch square paraffin

1. Place caramels, milk and butter in 1-quart glass measure or casserole. Heat in Radarange Oven on Cookmatic Level 8 (MEDIUM HIGH) for 3 to 4 minutes, or until caramels are melted.

2. Arrange pecan halves in groups of 3 on buttered baking sheet. Spoon about 1 tablespoon warm caramel mixture over each group of pecans. Refrigerate, uncovered, for 30 minutes.

3. Place chocolate morsels and paraffin in 2-cup glass measure. Heat in Radarange Oven on Cookmatic Level 6 (ROAST) for 3 to 4 minutes, or until chocolate morsels and paraffin are melted. Stir halfway through cooking time. Spoon enough chocolate mixture over each caramel to cover. Allow to cool. Remove from baking sheet.

MICRO-TIP: May be stored in single layer in tightly covered container in refrigerator for as long as 3 weeks.

Chocolate Crispies

Yield: 1-1/2 to 2 dozen

2 ozs. semi-sweet chocolate

1/2 cup sugar
3 tablespoons light corn syrup
1 tablespoon water

2 cups crisp rice cereal

1. Place chocolate in 2-quart casserole. Heat in Radarange Oven on Cookmatic Level 6 (ROAST) for 3 to 3-1/2 minutes, or until melted.

2. Stir in sugar, corn syrup and water. Cook in Radarange Oven on Cookmatic Level 6 (ROAST) for 2 minutes, or until sauce is heated.

3. Add cereal. Stir until cereal is well-coated. Drop by tablespoons onto waxed paper. Allow to cool until set.

Candy Cookies

Yield: 3-1/2 to 4 dozen

2 cups sugar
1/2 cup milk
1/2 cup butter or margarine, melted
3 tablespoons cocoa
1 tablespoon vanilla

3 cups quick-cooking, rolled oats
1 cup coconut, shredded
1 cup nuts, chopped

1. Combine sugar, milk, butter and cocoa in 1-quart glass measure or casserole. Heat in Radarange Oven on Cookmatic Level 8 (MEDIUM HIGH) for 3 to 4 minutes, or until mixture boils. Boil 1 minute. Add vanilla.

2. Pour sauce over oats, coconut and nuts in large mixing bowl. Mix well. Drop by teaspoons onto waxed paper. Allow to cool until set.

Chocolate-Gumdrop Squares

Yield: 24 squares

1 (12 oz.) pkg. semi-sweet
chocolate morsels

2 cups miniature marshmallows,
halved
2/3 cup small gumdrops
1/2 cup walnuts, chopped

1. Place chocolate morsels in 1-quart casserole. Heat in Radarange Oven on Cookmatic Level 6 (ROAST) for 3 to 3-1/2 minutes, or until melted. Stir halfway through cooking time.

2. Spread three-fourths of chocolate on waxed paper in 9 x 6-inch rectangle. Top with marshmallows, gumdrops and nuts. Drizzle remaining chocolate over top. Chill. Cut into squares.

MICRO-TIP: This is a candy that children will like to prepare.

Chinese Clusters

Yield: 3-1/2 to 4 dozen

1 (6 oz.) pkg. chocolate morsels
1 (6 oz.) pkg. butterscotch morsels

1 (3 oz.) can chow mein noodles
1 (6-1/2 oz.) can cocktail peanuts

1. Place chocolate and butterscotch morsels in 1-1/2 to 2-quart casserole. Heat in Radarange Oven on Cookmatic Level 6 (ROAST) for 3 to 3-1/2 minutes, or until melted. Stir until smooth.

2. Stir in chow mein noodles and peanuts. Drop by teaspoons onto waxed paper. Let set until firm.

Peanut Clusters

Yield: 3-1/2 to 4 dozen

1 (6 oz.) pkg. chocolate morsels
1 (12 oz.) pkg. butterscotch morsels

1 (12 oz.) pkg. salted, Spanish peanuts

1. Combine chocolate and butterscotch morsels in 2-quart casserole. Heat in Radarange Oven on Cookmatic Level 6 (ROAST) for 5 to 6 minutes, or until melted. Stir once during melting.

2. Stir in peanuts. Drop by teaspoons onto waxed paper. Let set until firm. Store in airtight container.

MICRO-TIP: If mixture hardens before dropped on waxed paper, return to Radarange Oven on Cookmatic Level 6 (ROAST) for 1 to 2 minutes, or until softened.

Caramel Peanut Puffs

Yield: 30 pieces

1 (14 oz.) pkg. caramels
3 tablespoons water

30 large marshmallows
1-1/2 cups salted, Spanish peanuts, chopped

1. Place caramels and water in 1-quart glass measure or casserole. Heat in Radarange Oven on Cookmatic Level 8 (MEDIUM HIGH) for 3 to 4 minutes, or until melted. Stir halfway through melting.

2. Dip marshmallows into caramel syrup using toothpicks, and roll to coat completely. Roll in peanuts. Place on waxed paper. Let dry at room temperature.

MICRO-TIP: If syrup gets thick, stir in 1/2 teaspoon water and reheat in Radarange Oven on Cookmatic Level 8 (MEDIUM HIGH) for 30 seconds, or until softened.

Peanut Brittle

Yield: about 2 lbs.

2 cups sugar
1 cup light corn syrup
1/3 cup water

1 (16 oz.) pkg. salted, Spanish peanuts

1 tablespoon butter or margarine
1 tablespoon baking soda

1. Grease 2, 15-1/2 x 12-inch baking sheets. Keep warm.

2. Place sugar, corn syrup and water in 3-quart casserole. Cook in Radarange Oven on FULL POWER for 8 to 10 minutes, or until soft ball stage is reached. * Stir occasionally during cooking time.

3. Stir in peanuts. Cook in Radarange Oven on Cookmatic Level 8 (MEDIUM HIGH) for 10 to 12 minutes, or until hard crack stage is reached. **

4. Stir in butter and baking soda. Pour half of candy onto each sheet, spreading to 1/4-inch thickness. Cool. Break into pieces.

MICRO-TIPS:
 *The soft ball stage is described on page 352.
 **The hard crack stage is described on page 352.

Quickie Fudge

Yield: 4 to 5 dozen pieces

1 lb. confectioners' sugar
1/2 cup cocoa
1/4 cup milk
1/2 cup butter or margarine

1 teaspoon vanilla
1/2 cup nuts, chopped

1. Blend together confectioners' sugar and cocoa in 8 x 8 x 2-inch dish. Pour in milk. Place butter on top. Heat in Radarange Oven on FULL POWER for 2 minutes, or until butter is melted. Stir well to mix ingredients.

2. Add vanilla and nuts. Stir until blended. Place in freezer for 20 minutes, or in refrigerator for 1 hour. Chill. Cut into 1-inch squares. Store in airtight container.

Marshmallow Cream Fudge

Yield: 5 to 6 dozen pieces

1/2 cup butter or margarine

2 cups sugar
1 (5.3 oz.) can evaporated milk (2/3 cup)

1 (12 oz.) pkg. semi-sweet chocolate morsels*
1 (7 oz.) jar marshmallow cream
1 teaspoon vanilla
1 cup nuts, chopped (optional)

1. Place butter in 9 x 9 x 2-inch dish. Heat in Radarange Oven on FULL POWER for 1 minute, or until melted.

2. Blend in sugar and evaporated milk. Mix well.

3. Cook in Radarange Oven on Cookmatic Level 8 (MEDIUM HIGH) for 8 to 10 minutes, or until soft ball stage is reached.** Stir mixture frequently during cooking time.

4. Blend in chocolate morsels, marshmallow cream, vanilla and nuts. Stir until smooth. Chill until firm. Cut into 1-inch squares. Store in airtight container.

MICRO-TIPS:

*Two cups milk chocolate morsels may be substituted for 1 (12 oz.) pkg. semi-sweet chocolate morsels.

**The soft ball stage is described on page 352.

Magic Fudge

Yield: 4 to 5 dozen pieces

1 (6 oz.) pkg. semi-sweet chocolate morsels

1/2 cup sweetened, condensed milk
1/2 teaspoon vanilla
Dash salt
1/4 cup nuts, chopped

1. Place chocolate morsels in 1-quart glass measure or casserole. Heat in Radarange Oven on Cookmatic Level 6 (ROAST) for 2-1/2 to 3 minutes, or until melted. Stir once during melting. Stir until smooth.

2. Blend in milk, vanilla, and salt. Add nuts. Turn mixture into greased, 8 x 8 x 2-inch dish. Chill until firm. Cut into 1-inch squares. Store in airtight container.

Peanut-Butterscotch Mash

Yield: 2 lbs.

2 cups sugar
1-1/2 cups miniature marshmallows, or 32 large marshmallows
1 (5.3 oz.) can evaporated milk (2/3 cup)

1 (12 oz.) pkg. butterscotch morsels
1 teaspoon vanilla

1 (12 oz.) pkg. chocolate morsels
2/3 cup peanut butter, chunky-style
1 cup raw peanuts, chopped

1. Combine sugar, marshmallows and milk in 1-1/2-quart casserole. Cook in Radarange Oven on Cookmatic Level 8 (MEDIUM HIGH) for 3 to 4 minutes, or until marshmallows are melted. Stir once or twice during cooking time.

2. Stir in butterscotch morsels and vanilla. Stir until melted and well-blended. Spread in greased, 2-quart utility dish. Cool slightly.

3. Combine chocolate morsels and peanut butter in 1-quart glass measure or casserole. Heat in Radarange Oven on Cookmatic Level 8 (MEDIUM HIGH) for 2 to 2-1/2 minutes, or until melted. Stir halfway through cooking time. Blend in nuts. Spread over butterscotch layer. Cut before too hard.

MICRO-TIP: For Cherry Chip Mash, use 10 to 12 ounces of cherry morsels instead of butterscotch morsels.

Old-Fashioned Taffy

Yield: 1 lb.

2 cups sugar
1/4 cup vinegar
1/4 cup water
1 teaspoon vanilla

1. Combine sugar, vinegar, and water in 1-1/2-quart casserole. Cook in Radarange Oven on FULL POWER for 8 to 10 minutes, or until soft crack stage is reached.* Add vanilla.

2. Divide mixture into 3 equal amounts and pour onto three well-greased dinner plates. Allow to cool until taffy feels warm to hand, but not hot.

3. Grease hands well. Pull taffy until it turns shiny white color and is quite stiff to handle. Twist as rope, and snip strand into bite-size pieces.

MICRO-TIPS:

•If batches become too hard to pull, heat in Radarange Oven on FULL POWER for 30 seconds to 1 minute, or until softened. Allow to cool, and pull the same as above.

*The soft crack stage is described on page 352.

Almond Bark

Yield: 1 pound

3/4 lb. white or dark chocolate*

2/3 cup roasted almonds **

1. Place chocolate in 2-cup glass measure or mixing bowl. Heat in Radarange Oven on Cookmatic Level 6 (ROAST) for 3 to 3-1/2 minutes, or until melted.

2. Stir in almonds. Pour immediately onto waxed paper or aluminum foil. Spread thinly. Cool for approximately 1 hour, and then break into pieces for serving.

MICRO-TIPS:

*1 (12 oz.) pkg. semi-sweet chocolate morsels may be substituted for 3/4 lb. chocolate, if desired.

**Pecans may be substituted for almonds.

Divinity

Yield: 6 to 7 dozen pieces

4 cups sugar
1 cup light corn syrup
3/4 cup water
1/4 teaspoon salt

3 egg whites

1 teaspoon vanilla
1/2 cup nuts, chopped (optional)

1. Mix together sugar, corn syrup, water and salt in 1-1/2-quart casserole. Cook in Radarange Oven on FULL POWER for 20 to 22 minutes, or until hard ball stage is reached.* Stir once or twice during cooking.

2. While syrup cooks, beat egg whites until stiff peaks form in large mixing bowl. Gradually pour hot syrup over egg whites while beating at high speed until mixture is thickened and candy starts to lose its gloss. Beating may require about 12 minutes.

3. Add vanilla and nuts to beaten mixture. Drop by teaspoons onto waxed paper.

MICRO-TIPS:

• Candy may be tinted with food coloring for special occasions.

*The hard ball stage is described on page 352.

Cathedral Window Candy

Yield: 40 to 50 slices

1/2 cup butter or margarine
1 (12 oz.) pkg. semi-sweet chocolate morsels

1 (10 oz.) pkg. colored miniature marshmallows
1 cup nuts, chopped

2 to 2-1/2 cups coconut, shredded

1. Place butter in 3-quart casserole. Heat in Radarange Oven on FULL POWER for 1 minute, or until melted. Add chocolate morsels. Heat in Radarange Oven on Cookmatic Level 6 (ROAST) for 3 to 3-1/2 minutes, or until chocolate is melted.

2. Cool chocolate enough so that marshmallows won't melt when stirred in. Add marshmallows and nuts. Allow to stand until stiff enough to form into rolls.

3. Spread coconut on 2, 1-1/2 feet each, sheets of waxed paper. Divide marshmallow mixture in half. Form in long rolls on coconut. Coat all sides of rolls evenly with coconut. Store in refrigerator until firm. Cut in 1/4 to 1/2-inch slices.

MICRO-TIP: If the chocolate mixture hardens too much to roll out, heat in Radarange Oven on Cookmatic Level 6 (ROAST) for 1 to 1-1/2 minutes, or until softened.

Vanilla Caramels

Yield: 2-1/2 lbs.

1 cup butter or margarine

2 cups sugar
2 cups dark corn syrup
2 cups light cream

1. Place butter in 3-quart casserole. Heat in Radarange Oven on FULL POWER for 1 to 1-1/2 minutes, or until melted.

2. Blend in sugar, corn syrup and 1 cup light cream. Heat in Radarange Oven on FULL POWER for 20 to 25 minutes, or until firm ball stage is reached.* Stir occasionally during cooking time to avoid boil-overs.

3. Gradually blend in remaining light cream. Cook in Radarange Oven on FULL POWER for 10 to 15 minutes, or until firm ball stage is reached.*

4. Pour mixture into greased, 2-quart utility dish. Cool for 3 hours, or until firm. Turn out on cutting board. Cut into squares. Wrap squares individually in small pieces of waxed paper, if desired.

*MICRO-TIP: The firm ball stage is described on page 352.

Chocolate Sandwiches

Yield: 4 dozen

1/4 cup butter or margarine, melted
1/4 cup cocoa
1/2 cup confectioners' sugar
1 egg
1 teaspoon vanilla
1-1/2 cups graham cracker crumbs
1/2 cup walnuts, chopped
1/2 cup coconut, shredded

1. Combine butter, cocoa, 1/2 cup confectioners' sugar, egg and vanilla in 2-quart utility dish. Stir in cracker crumbs, nuts and coconut. Press mixture firmly against bottom of dish. Chill.

1/4 cup butter or margarine, melted
2 tablespoons milk
1 teaspoon vanilla
2 teaspoons dry vanilla pudding mix (not instant)

2. Combine butter, milk, vanilla and pudding mix in 1-cup glass measure. Cook in Radarange Oven on FULL POWER for 45 to 60 seconds, or until mixture boils and is thickened.

2 cups confectioners' sugar

3. Beat above mixture into confectioners' sugar, until smooth. Spread over first layer.

1 (6 oz.) pkg. semi-sweet chocolate morsels
1/4 cup walnuts, chopped

4. Place chocolate morsels in 1-cup glass measure. Heat in Radarange Oven on Cookmatic Level 6 (ROAST) for 2-1/2 to 3 minutes, or until melted. Spread over vanilla layer. Sprinkle nuts over top. Chill. Cut into small squares.

Chocolate Creams

Yield: 2 dozen

2 tablespoons extra-strong coffee
4 (1 oz. each) squares semi-sweet chocolate, melted

1. Stir coffee into melted chocolate. Set aside.

1/4 cup light cream, scalded
2 egg yolks, slightly-beaten

2. Blend hot cream into egg yolks, stirring constantly. Cook in Radarange Oven on Cookmatic Level 8 (MEDIUM HIGH) for 30 seconds. Stir with wire whip.

1/2 cup butter or margarine
1 teaspoon vanilla
1/2 cup confectioners' sugar
1/2 cup salted peanuts, chopped
Coconut, shredded

3. Cream butter, vanilla and confectioners' sugar. Add chocolate and egg mixtures, gradually. Mix well. Stir in peanuts. Refrigerate until stiffened. Spoon by heaping teaspoons into bon-bon cups. Sprinkle with coconut, as desired. Refrigerate.

Christmas Wreaths

Yield: 2-1/2 dozen

1/2 cup butter or margarine
30 large marshmallows

1. Place butter and marshmallows in 3-quart casserole. Heat in Radarange Oven on FULL POWER for 2 to 2-1/2 minutes, or until melted. Stir until smooth.

1 teaspoon vanilla
Few drops green food coloring
3 cups cornflakes cereal
Red cinnamon hots candy

2. Stir in vanilla and food coloring. Blend in cornflakes. Drop by teaspoons onto waxed paper. Shape into wreaths. After shaping into wreaths, add 3 or 4 red cinnamon hots candies, as desired, to each wreath for a look of holly.

The Radarange Oven is well-known as a great cooking device, but it can also be used for a wide variety of other uses. Some of these uses involve food, such as toasting nuts or rehydrating dried fruit. Try making your own dried bread crumbs, croutons, and yogurt, quickly and economically, in the Radarange Oven.

Do you have a baby in the house? Quickly heat your child's food in the Radarange Oven. Better still, make your own homemade baby food and heat it quickly to the temperature desired, in the Radarange Oven.

The Radarange Oven is also a time-saver when it is used for non-food related tasks, such as drying flowers. Make your own Radarange Oven-dried flower arrange-ments for gifts. Also, when the holiday season arrives, your Christmas tree can be extra-special by decorating it with your very own hand-made Christmas ornaments. Dough ornaments are quickly and easily made in the Radarange Oven, and can be designed for other holidays, as well.

You can see that the Radarange Oven will save you time and energy in many "extra" ways. Enjoy using your creative talents with your Radarange Microwave Oven. **Note:** Do not leave the microwave oven unattended when drying **anything.** Foods or other items being dried can become too dry and can ignite. Press the STOP switch and open the oven door only after the ignition ceases.

Cinnamon Toasted Pecans

Yield: 1 cup nuts

1 tablespoon butter or margarine

1 (3 to 4 oz.) pkg. pecan halves (about 1 cup)

1/4 cup sugar
1/2 teaspoon cinnamon
1/4 teaspoon nutmeg (optional)

1. Place butter in small dish or glass measure. Heat in Radarange Oven on FULL POWER for 20 seconds, or until melted.
2. Place pecan halves in plastic bag. Pour melted butter over nuts and toss in bag.
3. Mix together sugar, cinnamon and nutmeg. Pour over pecans in bag. Shake to coat evenly. Spread pecans on paper plate.
4. Cook in Radarange Oven on Cookmatic Level 8 (MEDIUM HIGH) for 1 to 1-1/2 minutes, or until hot.

Toasted Almonds

Yield: 1 cup nuts

1 cup almonds (or other nuts)

Place almonds on paper plate. Cook in Radarange Oven on Cookmatic Level 8 (MEDIUM HIGH) for 1-1/2 to 2 minutes, or until hot.

Spicy Walnuts

Yield: 1 cup nuts

1 tablespoon butter or margarine, melted
1 teaspoon soy sauce
1/2 teaspoon paprika
1/4 teaspoon ginger
1/8 teaspoon garlic salt
1 cup walnut halves

1. Combine all ingredients, stirring to coat each nut with other ingredients. Spread walnuts in single layer in 2-quart utility dish.
2. Cook in Radarange Oven on Cookmatic Level 8 (MEDIUM HIGH) for 1-1/2 to 2-1/2 minutes, or until nuts are light brown. Stir twice during cooking time.

Dried Flowers (page 365)

Blanched Almonds

Yield: 1 cup nuts

1 cup unsalted almonds*
1 cup hot water

1. Place almonds in 1-quart glass casserole. Pour water over nuts.

2. Cook in Radarange Oven, covered, on FULL POWER for 1-1/2 to 2 minutes, or until skins are easily removed. Drain. Remove skins and allow nuts to dry on paper towels.

   MICRO-TIPS:

   • After almonds are dry, store in airtight container for future use.

   * Other nuts, such as filberts, may also be blanched using this method.

Dried Bread Crumbs

Yield: 1/2 cup crumbs

2 slices of bread

1. Place bread slices on plastic rack. Heat in Radarange Oven on FULL POWER for 1 to 1-1/2 minutes, or until dry. Cool.

2. Break each slice into several pieces. Grate in blender, or crush into crumbs with rolling pin. Store in airtight container.

Croutons

Yield: 1-1/2 cups

2 cups bread cubes, with crusts removed
2 tablespoons butter or margarine, melted
1/2 teaspoon paprika
1/2 teaspoon onion salt

1. Mix together all ingredients in 2-quart utility dish, stirring to coat bread cubes with other ingredients.

2. Heat in Radarange Oven on FULL POWER for 2 to 2-1/2 minutes, or until croutons are dry. Stir halfway through heating. Croutons will become crisper as they cool.

   MICRO-TIPS:

   • Serve on salads or casseroles.

   • If croutons become soggy, reheat in Radarange Oven on FULL POWER for 1 minute, or until crisp.

   • For cheese-flavor croutons, substitute 1/2 teaspoon of cheese flavor salt for the onion salt.

DRIED FRUIT REHYDRATING CHART

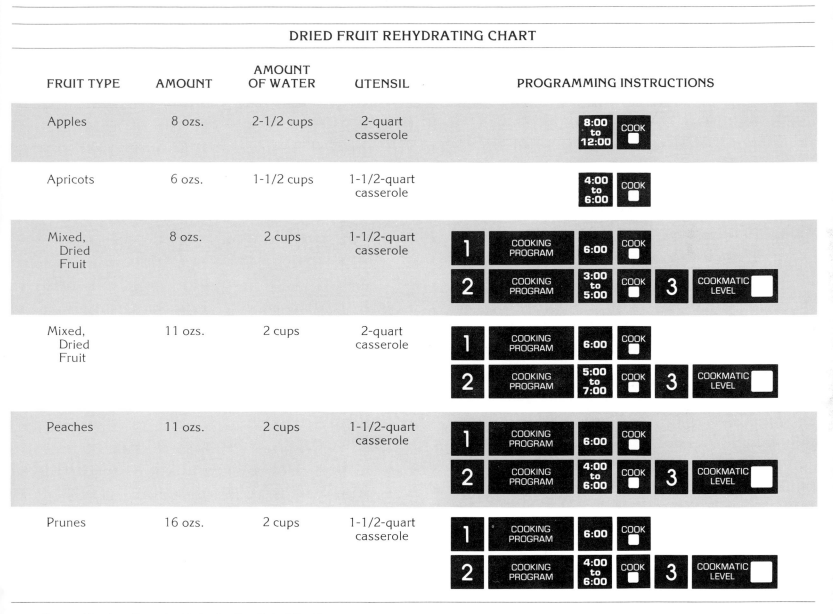

FRUIT TYPE	AMOUNT	AMOUNT OF WATER	UTENSIL	PROGRAMMING INSTRUCTIONS
Apples	8 ozs.	2-1/2 cups	2-quart casserole	**8:00 to 12:00** — COOK ☐
Apricots	6 ozs.	1-1/2 cups	1-1/2-quart casserole	**4:00 to 6:00** — COOK ☐
Mixed, Dried Fruit	8 ozs.	2 cups	1-1/2-quart casserole	**1** COOKING PROGRAM — **6:00** — COOK ☐ / **2** COOKING PROGRAM — **3:00 to 5:00** — COOK ☐ — **3** COOKMATIC LEVEL ☐
Mixed, Dried Fruit	11 ozs.	2 cups	2-quart casserole	**1** COOKING PROGRAM — **6:00** — COOK ☐ / **2** COOKING PROGRAM — **5:00 to 7:00** — COOK ☐ — **3** COOKMATIC LEVEL ☐
Peaches	11 ozs.	2 cups	1-1/2-quart casserole	**1** COOKING PROGRAM — **6:00** — COOK ☐ / **2** COOKING PROGRAM — **4:00 to 6:00** — COOK ☐ — **3** COOKMATIC LEVEL ☐
Prunes	16 ozs.	2 cups	1-1/2-quart casserole	**1** COOKING PROGRAM — **6:00** — COOK ☐ / **2** COOKING PROGRAM — **4:00 to 6:00** — COOK ☐ — **3** COOKMATIC LEVEL ☐

General Instructions for Rehydrating Dried Fruit

1. Place dried fruit and water in utensil recommended on the chart. Cover with a glass lid.

2. Cook in the Radarange Oven, covered, according to the instructions on the chart, or until the fruit is plump and tender, as desired. Stir 1 or 2 times during cooking, to separate fruit pieces.

Yogurt
Yield: 2 cups

2 cups 2% milk
1/3 cup non-fat-dry milk powder

2 tablespoons plain yogurt (no additives added)

1. Combine milk and non-fat-dry milk in 4-cup glass measure. Heat in Radarange Oven on Cookmatic Level 8 (MEDIUM HIGH) for 6 to 7 minutes, or until mixture boils. Cool to 110° F.*

2. Stir in yogurt with wire whip, until smooth. Cover with plastic wrap. Insert temperature probe through plastic wrap into mixture. Program the Radarange Oven

Use Temperature-Control to maintain 110°F for about 1-1/2 to 2 hours, or until mixture reaches consistency of thick cream or thin custard. Refrigerate. If yogurt seems lumpy after refrigerating, beat slightly with wire whip.

MICRO-TIPS:

*Even while the Radarange Oven is not in operation, use the Temperature-Control to determine when the temperature has reached 110°F.

•Serve the yogurt with fruit, or as a salad dressing.

•This yogurt is thinner than commercially-made yogurt. Try your own recipe, if desired. Also, use 2 tablespoons of your own yogurt as a "starter" for the next batch.

Dough Ornaments
Yield: 7 to 9 ornaments

3 cups all-purpose flour
1 cup salt
1-1/4 cups water
Food coloring (optional)
Instant tea (optional)

1. Combine all ingredients. Food coloring for added color, or instant tea for browning may be added to the water, as desired. Knead dough for 5 to 7 minutes, or until smooth.

2. Roll portion of dough to 1/8 to 1/4-inch thick on waxed paper sheet cut to fit Radarange Oven glass tray. Cut out 7 to 9 designs with cookie cutter. Remove excess dough and save to use later. Decorate and then pierce surface of each ornament evenly all over with toothpick or straight pin to eliminate air bubbles. Make small hole at top of each ornament for hanging. Slide waxed paper onto Radarange Oven glass tray.

3. Cook in Radarange Oven on FULL POWER for 2 to 3 minutes, or until ornaments are dry and firm. Remove from waxed paper before completely cool.

MICRO-TIPS:

•Roll out long strands of dough, and use them to make added details, such as bows and facial features.

•Ornaments may be decorated with colored crystal sugar or nonpareils. When cooled, you may varnish or paint each ornament to seal out moisture.

DRYING FLOWERS IN THE RADARANGE OVEN

Drying flowers in the Radarange Oven is another wonderful use of this labor-saving appliance. As in any craft, it is important to follow the directions carefully and accurately.

Brightly colored flowers dry best. Flowers, such as roses, carnations, violets and zinnias work well with this process. For flower drying, you will need silica gel, which is available in most hobby shops, and, of course, fresh flowers.

For best results, flowers should be only partially opened. Avoid using flowers with thick centers. Use the chart as a guide for drying other flowers.

FLOWER DRYING CHART

FLOWER TYPE	HEATING TIME ON FULL POWER	MINIMUM AMOUNT OF STANDING TIME***
*Carnation	2-1/2 to 3 min.	5 to 10 min.
Daffodil	1-1/2 to 2 min.	5 to 10 min.
Pansy — 1st drying	45 sec.	5 min.
2nd drying	1 to 1-1/2 min.	10 min.
Rose	1-1/2 min.	2 to 5 min.
Sunflower	1-3/4 min.	1-1/2 days**
Violet	1-1/2 to 2 min.	5 to 10 min.
Zinnia	2 to 2-1/2 min.	5 to 10 min.

*For best results dry three carnations at one time.
**Sunflowers should stand covered with a plastic bag during standing time.
****You may wish to increase the standing time for some flowers.

General Instructions for Drying Flowers

1. Partially fill a large glass or jar with silica gel. Place a flower stem-down into the silica gel. Slowly fill the remaining portion of the jar with gel. Be careful to place the silica gel between all petals of each flower. Use a toothpick to separate the petals. Cover the flower completely with silica gel.

2. Place the jar in the Radarange Oven. Place 1 cup of water in the rear left corner of the Radarange Oven. Heat in Radarange Oven on FULL POWER for 1 to 3 minutes, depending upon the general size of the flower. Longer heating times are required for larger flowers. Check the chart for specific times.

3. Use a separate jar for each flower. Silica gel may be reused only after it is completely cooled. Remove the flower from the jar when it is cooled. See the chart for the recommended amount of standing time.

4. After the standing time, slowly pour the silica gel from the jar. Carefully remove the flower. Gently brush any excess grains of gel from the petals or stem. Allow the silica gel to cool before reusing.

5. Floral wire may be used to support the stems. Artificial coloring may be added to the flowers when the flowers are completely dry, if desired. Leaves should be dried separately, and then added to the stems.

BABY FOOD HEATING CHART*

JAR SIZE	HEATING TIME ON COOKMATIC LEVEL 9 (HIGH)
1/2 (4-1/2 to 4-3/4 oz.) jar	10 to 15 sec.
1 (4-1/2 to 4-3/4 oz.) jar	15 to 30 sec.

*The heating times on this chart include main dishes, vegetables, fruits, or fruit desserts. Use this chart as a guide for heating your own homemade baby foods.

General Instructions for Heating Baby Food

1. Place the baby food in a custard cup or on a serving plate. Baby food should not be heated in jars. Avoid using jars or bottles having restricted openings in a microwave oven.
2. Heat in the Radarange Oven on Cookmatic Level 9 (HIGH), according to the time on the chart, or until warmed to desired temperature.
3. A plate of baby foods, including half of the contents of each of 3 jars (such as a main dish, vegetable and dessert) may be heated. Heat in the Radarange Oven on Cookmatic Level 9 (HIGH) for 45 seconds to 1 minute, 15 seconds, or until warmed to desired temperature.

S

EVERYDAY FOODS HEATING AND REHEATING CHART

FOOD	AMOUNT	HEATING TIME	COOKMATIC LEVEL or SETTING	SPECIAL INSTRUCTIONS
Bread (defrosting)	1 loaf (1-1/2 lbs.)	6 to 7 min.	DEFROST	Leave in plastic wrapper. Remove metal twist. Loosen end.
Bread (reheating)	1 loaf (1-1/2 lbs.)	45 sec. to 1-1/4 min.	Cookmatic Level 5 (SLO COOK)	Leave in plastic wrapper. Remove metal twist. Loosen end.
Brownies (2-inch squares)	2 to 3	20 to 30 sec.	FULL POWER	Wrap with napkin or plastic wrap.
Butter (melting)	1 tablespoon or less	20 sec.	FULL POWER	—
	2 to 3 tablespoons	20 to 30 sec.	FULL POWER	—
	1/4 cup	30 to 40 sec.	FULL POWER	—
	1/2 cup	40 to 60 sec.	FULL POWER	—
(softening)	1/4 cup	30 to 45 sec.	Cookmatic Level 3 (SIMMER)	—
	1/2 cup	1 to 1-1/2 min.	Cookmatic Level 3 (SIMMER)	—
Cheese (softening)	1 (5 oz.) jar	2 to 3 min.	Cookmatic Level 3 (SIMMER)	—
Chicken, cooked (2 pieces)	6-1/2 to 7 ozs.	1 to 2 min.	FULL POWER	Cover with plastic wrap.
Chocolate, morsels (melting)	6 ozs.	2-1/2 to 3 min.	Cookmatic Level 6 (ROAST)	—
	12 ozs.	3 to 3-1/2 min.	Cookmatic Level 6 (ROAST)	—
squares (melting)	1 oz.	2 to 3 min.	Cookmatic Level 6 (ROAST)	—
Coffee or Tea	1 cup	1 to 1-1/2 min.	FULL POWER	—
Coffee Cake (2-inch squares)	1 to 2	15 to 20 sec.	FULL POWER	Wrap with napkin or plastic wrap.
Cookies (defrosting)	2 to 3	15 to 30 sec. (10 sec. per cookie)	FULL POWER	Wrap with napkin or plastic wrap.
Cream Cheese (softening)	3 ozs.	1 to 2 min.	Cookmatic Level 3 (SIMMER)	—
	8 ozs.	2 to 3 min.	Cookmatic Level 3 (SIMMER)	—